references to *anda⸗ma* in texts which she considered to be c. 1400 and later, some of which we would date earlier. See now HW[2] 102 *andan* IV 1 c. Most exx. known to us are MH rather than OH. Although full treatment will be under *anda⸗ma*, we give here representative exx. of OH and MH *anda⸗ma* (adv.): KBo 17.2 i 4 (OH/OS), KBo 16.24 ii 7, KUB 36.114 right col. 18, KBo 16.50:9, KUB 31.103:7, 27 (all MH/MS), KUB 26.19 ii 16, KBo 16.46 obv. 13, KBo 13.58 iii 13, 26, KUB 31.112:4, KUB 13.9 iii 19 (all MH/NS), KUB 13.4 ii 25, 52, 73, iii 35, 44, 55, iv 12, 25, 34, 56, KUB 13.3 ii 20, iii 3 (all pre-NH/NS).

b′ *appa⸗ma* which is clause initial, frequently paragraph initial, is not the preverb, but a transitional adverb, relating paragraphs in a temporal sequence. Selected exx. are: KBo 20.61 iii 44, KUB 32.87 + KBo 23.72 rev. 29 (both OH/MS), KBo 15.10 iii 62, 65, 67 (MH/MS), KBo 10.37 iv (16) (OH/NS), KUB 12.11 iv 23, 27 (MH/NS), KBo 24.50 rev. 10 (NH).

c′ *appanda⸗ma* clause initial adverb, frequently paragraph initial: selected exx. are: EGIR-*an-ta-ma* KBo 12.96 i 8 (MH/NS), EGIR-*an-da-ma* KBo 10.2 i 16, (9), 33 (OH/NS), KBo 11.10 ii 17 (pre-NH/NS), KBo 9.119A i 4 (MH/NS), KUB 29.7 rev. 27, 63 (MH/MS), KBo 2.5 iv 23 (Murš. II), EGIR-*ŠU-ma* KBo 10.23 v 11, 14, KBo 10.24 i 1, 6, iii 15 (OH/NS), EGIR-*ŠÚ-ma* IBoT 3.148 ii 16, 22, iii 64 (MH?/NS); and see further refs. in HW[2] 154-56.

d′ *maḫḫan⸗ma* see refs. under *maḫḫan*.

e′ *para⸗ma* as adv. at head of paragraphs see e.g., KBo 20.123 iv 5, 8, 11, 13, etc.

f. position of *-ma* in the clause — **1′** attached to the first word in its clause: passim, see exx. in b 1′. If sentence enclitics are to be appended to the word on which *-ma* depends, *-ma* usually precedes them, e.g., *⸗ma⸗war⸗an⸗zan* KBo 14.12 iv 12, but not always see Houwink ten Cate, FsOtten 133 and n. 77, and above under *liššiyala*. See Kammenhuber, FsLaroche 187f., 192f.

2′ exceptions — **a′** delayed to the second word in its clause — **1″** discussion: Ungnad (ZA 36 [1925] 103-06) first observed that in most cases ("im allgemeinen") in clauses beginning with conditional *mān* ("if"), *takku* "if", relative *kui-* "who, which", and *našma* "or (if)" the enclitic particles *-ma* and *-(y)a* are attached to the second accented word rather than to the first. He did not know of the existence of OH temporal *mān* ("when"), and therefore could not realize that the delayed *-ma* also could be found with *mān* "when". He also added *kuššan* "whenever" (law 28, copy C), which following a suggestion by Götze (apud Chrest. 226) we have read *ku-iš*!-*ša-an* (*kuiš⸗an*). In 1925 Ungnad could not have known either that the exx. for this delayed *-ma* were almost all old. No exx. of *mān⸗ma* (undelayed *-ma*) in OS or MS are known to us. Some NH compositions which are formulated in a language inherited from OH or MH prototypes (treaties, festivals or rituals) preserved the delayed *-ma* construction alongside the *mān⸗ma* NH innovation. The fact that no exx. of *mān⸗ma* have been found in OS or MS, while the same construction is clearly predominating in NH, suggests that the distinction is primarily a diachronic one. — **2″** in clauses introduced by *takku* — **a″** open conditions with present-future tense — **1‴** OS: *takku natta⸗m*[(*a kuitki tezz*)*i*] KUB 43.25:7 (myth, OS?), with dupl. KUB 33.60 rev. 6; [*takk*]*u natta⸗ma taranzi* KBo 17.1 iv 12 (OS); *takku* GIŠTUKUL-*li⸗ma mimmai* KBo 19.1 ii 20 (laws, OS); *takku⸗at⸗an parna⸗ma kuēlka peššizzi* KBo 6.2 ii 35 (laws, OS); *takku* A.ŠÀ.ḪI.A *kulei⸗ma arki* KBo 6.2 ii 47 (laws, OS); [*ta*]*kku udniya⸗ma wemizzi* ibid. iii 59; *takku natta⸗ma šarnikzi* KBo 6.2 iv "58" (laws, OS); — **2‴** OH/NS: [*takk*]*u laḫḫa⸗ma pēḫutet*⸢*teni*⸣ KUB 1.16 ii 45, ed. HAB ii 45; *takkuwaššan kī ḫazzizi . . . takku⸗waššan natta⸗ma ḫa*[*zzizi*] KBo 3.60 ii 14-15 (legend, OH/NS), ed. Güterbock, ZA 44:106f.; *takku natta⸗ma kapueši* KBo 3.28 (BoTU 10γ):13 (OH/NS); *takku* DUMU.LUGAL*⸗ma waštai* KBo 3.1 ii 55 (Tel. pr., OH/NS), cf. ibid. iv 54; *takku* SAL-*za⸗ma* KBo 6.4 i 10 (laws, NH par. series); *takku tezzi⸗ma* KBo 6.3 iii 75 (laws, OH/NS); [*takku m*]*immai⸗ma* KBo 6.3 iv 47 (laws, OH/NS); *takku dannattan⸗ma* KBo 6.11 i 10 (laws, OH/NS), dupl. [*takk*]*u* [*t*]*an⸗nanda⸗ma* KBo 19.9:7 (OH/NS); *takku* ÌR*⸗ma* KBo 6.13 i 12 (laws, OH/NS); *takku* É-*ri⸗ma ēpzi* KBo 6.26 iv 7 (laws, OH/NS); *takku ḫal⸗liyan⸗ma* SA$_5$ *uwanzi*[. . .] . . . *takku ḫalli⸗yaš⸗ma* GE$_6$ x[. . .] KUB 34.22 iv 3, 5 (omens, pre-NH/NS); *takku arunaz⸗ma . . . takku* ÍD-*az⸗ma* KUB 43.60 i 12, 14 (myth, OH/NS); — **3‴** MH/NS: *takkuwaš karštari⸗ma* KUB 13.4

iii 31 (instr., pre-NH/NS); *takku papri*[*šteni*]*⸗ma* ibid. iv 33; *takku šānatteni⸗ma* KUB 13.3 iii 18 (instr., pre-NH/NS); *takku ELLAM⸗ma kuiški daiyazi* KUB 13.9 ii 16 (instr., MH/MS); — **b″** contrary to fact conditions with potential *man* and past tense: *takku⸗man⸗a*<*š*>*ta UL⸗ma šan*[*ḫun* GAM-*an šarā⸗m*]*a*(*n*)*⸗mu lālit ēpten* "Had I not sought (tears) from (her), you would have [sl]andered me with the tongue" KUB 1.16 + KUB 40.65 iii 7-9 (edict, OH/NS); see also sub *lala-*; cf. [*takku⸗manaš*]*ta* GUD.ḪI.A*⸗ma mekki peḫḫun* ibid. iii 11, which assures the restoration of *šan*[*ḫun*] (preterite); — **3″** clauses introduced by temporal *mān* "when" — **a″** with preterite tense: *mān* ^{URU}*Ḫattuša⸗ma uwawen* "But when we came to Ḫ." KBo 8.42 obv. 5 (OS); *mān āppa⸗ma* ^{URU}*Nēša* [*uwan*(*un*)] KBo 3.22:76 (OS) w. dupl. KUB 36.98b rev. 5 (NS) (Anitta Text), ed. StBoT 18:14f.; *mān appezziyan⸗ma* ÌR.MEŠ DUMU.MEŠ LUGAL *maršeššer* (var. *maršer*) "But later when the subjects (and) the princes became false" KBo 3.1 i 20 (Tel.pr., OH/NS), with dupl. KUB 11.1 i 20; *mān⸗aš šallešta⸗ma* "When he (new subject: the son of the Stormgod) grew up" KBo 3.7 iii 6 (Illuyanka, OH/NS); — **b″** with historical present: *mā*[*n⸗a*]*š⸗apa laḫḫaz⸗ma* EGIR-*pa uizzi* "But when he returned from a campaign" KBo 3.1 i 17 (Tel.pr. OH/NS); — **c″** with present-future: *mān lukkatta⸗ma* KBo 17.1 ii 30 (rit., OH/OS); *mān luggatta⸗ma* KBo 17.3 iv 21 (OH/OS); *mānaš lazziatta⸗ma* KBo 6.2 i 18 (laws, OH/OS); — **4″** clauses introduced by conditional *mān* "if": *mān AWAT* LUGAL*⸗ma UL paḫḫašnutteni* KUB 1.16 iii 36 (OH/NS); *mān* DUMU.LUGAL*⸗ma* . . . NU.GÁL KBo 3.1 ii 38 (Tel.pr., OH/NS); *mānmukan arḫa⸗ma kuiški išparzazi* KBo 16.47:10-11 (treaty, MH/MS); *mān* ^{LÚ}*pitteantan⸗ma kuiški munnaizzi* KUB 8.81 ii 13-14 (treaty, MH/MS); *mānwakan BĒL⸗ma šer UL šarnikzi* ibid. iii 6; *mānzakan gamaršuwanza⸗ma kuin tamašzi* IBoT 1.36 i 43 (Mešedi instr., MH/MS), cf. i 48, ii 63, iii 35, 47, iv 20, 22, 23, etc.; *mānaš uizzi⸗ma* KUB 23.77:80 (treaty, MH/MS), cf. KUB 13.27 rev.! 26 and KUB 26.40:101 + KUB 13.27 rev.! 30, which are fragments of the same tablet; *mān ŠA* É.NA$_4$*⸗ma ḫinqanaš waštul kuiški waštai* KUB 13.8:11f. (instr., MH/NS), cf. line 16; *mān wetummar⸗ma kuitki* KUB 13.20 i 20 (instr., MH/NS), cf. i 26; *mān* ^{LÚ}KÚR*⸗ma kuwapi walḫzi* KUB 13.2 i 15f. (Bel Madg., MH/NS), cf. i 20, iii 21, 23; *mānkan* KUR-*ya⸗ma ištarna* 1 URU-*LUM wašd*[*ai*] KUB 23.68 obv. 25 (treaty, MH/NS), cf. obv. 27, 28; also in NH texts imitating the style and syntax of their generic forebears (treaties, rituals, etc.): *mān zik⸗ma* ^{m}*Ḫuqqanaš* ^{d}UTU-*ŠI-pat paḫḫašti* KBo 5.3 ii 10 (Ḫuqq.); cf. iv 31 (§44); *mānan ḫannešni⸗ma* [*k*]*uwapi ittiša*⌜*nu*⌝*anzi* (emend to *ti*!-*it*!-*ta*!-⌜*nu*⌝-*an-zi*?) KUB 19.26 i 12 (decree, Šupp. I); cf. further exx. in Dupp. §§14, 15, 16, Targ. §§7, 8, 9, Kup. §§24, 26, Alakš. §16, *mānaš ḫarkannaš⸗ma* KBo 4.10 obv. 10 (Ulmi-tešub treaty); *mān* KA.IZI*⸗ma* KUB 13.4 iii 48 (instr. pre-NH/NS), cf. iii 76, 78, iv 43, KUB 13.5 ii 11, but the later *mānma* . . . also occurs in KUB 13.4 iii 74, iv (7); — **5″** clauses introduced by *našma* "or (if)": *našma ANA* KUR ^{LÚ}KÚR*⸗ma* KBo 5.3 ii 16 (Ḫuqq.); cf. ibid. ii 29, iv 21; *našmaš artari⸗ma* KBo 14.86 i 8 (rit., OH/NS); *našmanza* ALAM*⸗ma iyazi* KUB 7.5 iv 16 (rit. of Paškuwatti, MH/NS); "or else": *našmawakan katta⸗ma īt* IBoT 1.36 i 50 (Mešedi instr., MH/MS); — **6″** clauses introduced by relative *kui-*: *kuišan āppa⸗ma uwatezzi* KBo 6.2 i "53" (law §23, OS); *kuišza* ^{LÚ}*ASĪRUM⸗ma ḫappar*[*iy*]*azi* KBo 6.4 iv 38-39 (late parallel series of laws, NH); *kuiš arḫa tar⸗nummaš⸗ma* ERÍN.MEŠ-*az* KUB 13.20 i 11 (instr., MH/NS), cf. ibid. i 24; *kuiškan ḫannai⸗ma* KUB 21.17 iii 39 (NH): probably also *ku-iš*!-*ša*[-*a*]*n pittenuz*[(*i⸗ma*)] KBo 6.5 ii 11 (law §28, OH/NS) with dupl. KBo 6.3 ii 6, following emendations suggested by Götze apud Chrest. 226; — **7″** While *mān* . . . *⸗ma* continues to be used in NH, although sparsely and especially in treaties, festivals, or rituals where the genre has an OH or MH tradition, the newer form *mān⸗ma* (clause initial) seems to appear for the first time in NH: *mān⸗ma⸗k*[*an* DUMU-*KA*] ŠEŠ-*KA QADU* ERÍN.MEŠ-*KA* ANŠU. KUR.RA.MEŠ-*KA ANA* LUGAL KUR ^{URU}*Ḫ*[*att*]*i warri parā UL nāit*[*ti*] KBo 5.9 ii 22f. (Dupp., Murš. II) ed. SV 1:16f.; [*m*]*ān⸗ma⸗ši⸗at⸗kan* :*ušaiḫa* KUB 14.3 iii 60 (Taw., Ḫatt. III?), ed. AU 14f.; [*m*]*ān⸗ma⸗wa UL* ibid. iii 67; *mān⸗ma kē AWATE*^{MEŠ} *paḫḫašti* KUB 21.1 iv 37-38 (Alakš., Muw.), ed. SV 2:82f.; *mān⸗ma⸗aš ANA* ^{d}UTU-*ŠI kurur* KUB 23.1 iv 10-11 (Šaušgamuwa treaty, Tudḫ. IV), ed. StBoT 16, 14f., cf. ibid. iv 6; *mān⸗*[*m*]*a⸗at ANA* ŠEŠ-*YA UL* ⌜ZI⌝-*za* KUB 21.38 obv. 65

(letter, Puduḫepa), ed. Helck, JCS 17:92; often in NH the *-ma* occurs twice in the same clause: *mān⸗ma⸗wa ša*[*nḫ*]*eškiši⸗*[*m*]*a* KUB 26.79 i 5 (AM 98f.); *mān⸗ma⸗wa⸗za ammuk⸗ma* DI-*ešnaza šarazziš* KBo 6.29 ii 6-7 (decree, Ḫatt. III), ed. Ḫatt. 48f. Until instances of this double *-ma* construction are identified in OS or MS, one must assume that those in pre-NH/NS (e.g., *mān⸗ma⸗aš karštari⸗ma* KUB 13.4 iii 73) are NH modernizations.

b′ delayed beyond the second word in its clause: In the construction employed with double questions, discussed above in a 1′ b″ 4″, the *-ma* is often delayed beyond the second word in its clause, being appended to that element in the second question which is central to the opposition to the first alternative.

c′ *-ma* on the first accented word of the clause and *mān* later in the clause: *anda⸗ma⸗z⸗kan mān* ^{LÚ}KÚR-*aš kuwāpi uwalḫūwanzi dāi* KBo 16.50: 9-10 (MH/MS); *anda⸗ma mān ḫalkin aniyatteni* KUB 13.4 iv 12 (pre-NH/NS), cf. 56; and cf. *-ma* e 2′ a′; *ŠA* ^{f}*Danuḫepa⸗ma ḫargaš ANA* ^{d}UTU ^{URU}TÚL-*na mān* ZI-*anza ēšta* KUB 14.7 i 20-21 (Ḫatt. III).

The essential function of *-ma* (from OH/OS) is to mark a correlation, either between single words or phrases within adjacent clauses (usage a), or between entire clauses (b). The anaphoric use (d) is merely a specialization of this function, in which the repetition of the key word is highlighted by transposition to the head of the clause and marked by *-ma*. The paragraph-introducing, continuative use (e) is an extension of the series-marking use seen in a 1′ a′ KUB 24.8 iv 13-18. It is clear from its use relating two main clauses (b 1′-4′), two dependent clauses (b 5′), a dependent clause with a following main clause (b 6′), and the members of a series of paragraphs (e) that *-ma* does not function to mark either subordination or coordination, but merely a correlation between words, clauses or paragraphs regardless of their dependent or independent status.

Hrozný, SH (1917) 102 n. 4 ("*-ma* führt wohl gewöhnlich die Erzählung weiter, bedeutet somit etwa 'dann, ferner', gelegentlich auch wohl 'aber' u. ä. Vielleicht darf es mit griech. μέν, μά (dieses im Thess. = att. δέ) zusammengestellt werden."); Sommer, Heth. 1 (1920) 4 n. 1 ("*-ma* . . . nach meiner Prüfung an allen deutbaren Stellen 'aber' heisst"): Ungnad, ZDMG 74 (1920) 417 and ZA 36 (1925) 103-06 (on syntax of *-ma*); Friedrich, KlF 1 (1930) 293 with n. 3 ("Andererseits entspricht das heth. *-ma* unserem 'aber' zwar in den meisten, jedoch keineswegs in allen Fällen") and HE §318f.; Starke, StBoT 23 (1977) 31 n. 32 ("hat, soweit ich sehe, keine adversative Bedeutung ('aber') [but see our b 1′]. Vielmehr drückt der *⸗ma*-Satz eine zur Haupthandlung parallel verlaufende, meist untergeordnete Nebenhandlung aus."), 74 (contrasting *-a* and *-ma*: "Dagegen hat *⸗ma* ausschliesslich subordinierende, erläuternde Funktion . . . [diese Funktion] lässt sich . . . leicht in jedem beliebigen Text nachprüfen", a claim which our survey did not substantiate, see b 6′); ad usage a 1′ b′ 1″ see Ehelolf, OLZ 1926:769 note 8 (complementary pairs); ad usage a 1′ b′ 4″ see Sommer, AU 77f. (double questions).

-ma- see *-mi-*.

ma- v.; to disappear(?), vanish(?); from OH/MS.†

imp. sg. 3 *ma-du* KUB 30.10 rev. 6 (OH/MS).
iter. imp. sg. 3 *ma-aš-ki-id-du* KUB 12.43:4, KBo 24.110 iv 5 (both MS).

[o o o o o o o o] *katta namma ešaru nat āp*[*pa* o o *ka*]*rdišši ma-du* "Would that [the god's anger(?)] might yet subside, and that it (*-at*, subject same as the preceding?) might disappear(?) in his heart again" KUB 30.10 rev. 6 (Kantuzzili prayer, OH/MS), cf. ANET 400 and StBoT 5:29-31 w. note 29, (*katta eš-* takes *paḫḫur* "fire" as its subject, hence our tr. "subside" here); *nu māu šišdu* GEŠTIN-*aš* x[. . .] *nat māu šišdu* § [. . . *k*]*allar ma-aš-ki-id-du* "Let it (the land?) be fruitful and prosper! Wine [. . .]; let it be fruitful and prosper! Let the unfavorable thing (*kallar*) disappear(?)! (. . . And let the king and queen be in good health!)" KUB 12.43:2-5 (incant., MS); *nuwa ma-aš-ki-id-du* "Let it disappear(?)!" in quoted speech in KBo 24:110 iv 5 (rit., frag., OH?/MS).

The proposed translation is based on the fact that the speaker wishes that unpleasant or evil things (anger(?), *kallar-*) should do this. We therefore separate this word from the verb *maškiške-* "to give presents".

[*mā*] (HW 132) in *māwa* is treated under *mān*.

maḫḫan **1.** like (postpos.), **2.** as, just as (subordinating conj. of comparison), **3.** how (in indirect statement or question), **4.** how (interrogative), **5.** when, as soon as (temporal subordinating conj.), **6.** GIM-*an* GIM-*an*, GIM-*an imma* GIM-*an* in whatever manner, however (conj.); wr. syll. and GIM-*an*; from OS.

1. like (postpos.) in single word comparison, from OH/MS
  a. following a substantive
    1′ wr. syll.
      a′ MS
      b′ NS
    2′ wr. GIM-*an* (all NS)
      a′ in hist. texts
      b′ in an oath of loyalty
      c′ in mythological narratives
      d′ in descriptions of humans and deities in literary texts
      e′ in rituals
      f′ in omens
  b. following *kuit* (*kuit maḫḫan* "like what") in dependent clauses
    1′ in letters
      a′ MH/MS
      b′ NH
        1″ in dependent clauses with verb "to be" implied
        2″ in dependent clause with *ištamaš-* "to hear"
    2′ in instructions texts
2. as, just as (subordinating conj. of comparison), from OH/MS
  a. resumed by a correlative adv. in the main clause (from OH/MS)
    1′ with the correlative adv. *apeniššan* (log. *QĀTAMMA*)
      a′ *maḫḫan* clause preceding the main clause
        1″ OH in later copies
        2″ MH and NH
      b′ *maḫḫan* clause following the main clause
    2′ with the correlative adv. *kiššan*
  b. without correlative adverb
    1′ *maḫḫan* clause preceding the main clause
    2′ *maḫḫan* clause following the main clause
3. how, that (conj., in indirect statement or question), from MH/MS
  a. *maḫḫan* clause following the main clause
  b. *maḫḫan* clause preceding the main clause
  c. as the predicate in the second of two coordinate *mān* ("if") clauses expressing alternatives
4. how (interrogative adv.), from OH/MS
5. when, as soon as (temporal subordinating conj.), from MH/MS
  a. with pret.
    1′ introducing time expressions
    2′ introducing actions
      a′ MS
      b′ NS
        1″ in hist. texts
        2″ in a prayer
        3″ in mythological narratives
  b. with present-future
    1′ historical pres.
    2′ present or future
      a′ introducing time expressions, NS
        1″ times of year
        2″ times of day
      b′ introducing actions
        1″ MS
        2″ NS
          a″ OH/NS
          b″ MH/NS
          c″ NH
  c. GIM-*an* . . . *kuwapi*
6. GIM-*an* GIM-*an*, GIM-*an imma*, GI[M-*an imm*]*a* GIM-*an* "in whatever manner, however" (conj.), NH.

ma-a-aḫ-ḫa-an (with no enclitics) KBo 9.73 obv. 9 (OS), KUB 30.10 rev. 5, KUB 36.75 iii 14, 19 (OH/MS), KBo 7.28:(42) (OH/MS), KUB 33.34 rev.? 4 (OH/NS), *ma-a-aḫ*<*-ḫa*>*-an* KUB 13.12 obv. 9 (OH/NS), *ma-a-aḫ-ḫa-an* (with attached enclitics) KUB 23.72 rev. 65, KUB 17.21 iv 16, IBoT 1.36 i 22, 64, ii 23, 27, KBo 16.47:6, Maşat 75/10:3 (all MH/MS), cf. Carruba, StBoT 2:31f.

ma-aḫ-ḫa-a-an KUB 51.19 obv. 9, note however the scribal error in the preceeding line.

ma-aḫ-ḫa-an KUB 33.7 iii 4, KUB 33.68 ii 1, 7, 9, 13, 14 (all OH/MS), KUB 14.1 obv. 6 and passim, KUB 36.114 rt. col. 21, often in Maşat letters ed. Alp, Belleten 44 (1980) 38-53 (but *ma-a-aḫ-ḫa-an* in Maşat 75/10:3) (all MH/MS), most exx. in NS, including KBo 5.3 i 22, KUB 14.12 obv. 12, KUB 26.19 ii 19, KUB 26.43 obv. 63, rev. 9, KBo 6.3 iii 22, 50 (OH/NS, replacing *ma-a-aḫ-ḫa-an-da* in OS archetype).

GIM-*an* (all exx. NS) KBo 3.4 ii 15, KBo 4.14 iii 22, 32, KBo 5.6 ii 5, KUB 6.45 i 8, iv 45, 47, KUB 23.1 i 28, 40, etc., GIM KUB 26.85 ii 15(?).

OS only *ma-a-aḫ-ḫa-an*, MS *ma-a-aḫ-ḫa-an*, *ma-aḫ-ḫa-an*, NS *ma-a-aḫ-ḫa-an* (only in copies of OH or MH compositions), *ma-aḫ-ḫa-an*, *ma-aḫ-ḫa-a-an* (once!), GIM-*an*, and possibly GIM (only in KUB 26.85 ii 15 in broken context). THeth 9:170 claims *ma-a-aḫ-ḫa-an* for compositions of Ḫatt. III or later, but produces no exx.

On the possibility that GIM-*an* represents *mān* cf. s.v. *mān*.

Mng. 1 may occur in the Hittite version of Signalement lyrique, lines 36, 38, 44, 57, 62 and 64 as GIM-*an*, if that logogram in that text represents *maḫḫan*, not *mān*. If so, the Hittite translator has used postpos. *maḫḫan* "like" to render what in the Sumerian and Akkadian versions is metaphor ("She is a . . ."). For discussion cf. *mān* 1 c 3′ c′.

Mng. 2 a 1′ a′ 2″ (Akk.) *ki-i* . . . *intatḫaṣu* KUB 3.14 obv. 17-18 = (Hitt.) *ma-aḫ-ḫa-an* [(*zaḫḫiš*)*kit*] "As he used to fight . . . " KUB 21.49 obv. 14-15 restored from dupl.

KUB 3.119 obv. 17 (Dupp. treaty), ed. SV 1:8f., cf. [*qa*]*tamma* in line 19 of Akk. vers., apodosis of Hitt. vers. broken; **mng. 4** (Akk.) [*rēmam*] . . . ⌜*ki-i*⌝ *ileq*[*qe*] KUB 1.16 (=BoTU 8) i 19 = (Hitt.) *m*[*aḫḫanaš*] (or *m*[*ānaš*]) . . . *genzu ḫ*[*arzi*] "How can he have pity . . . ?" ibid. ii 18-19 (edict of Hatt. I, OH/NS), ed. HAB 4f., 48f.; **mng. 5 a 2′ b′ 1″** (Akk.) *iš-tu* URU*Ullum ittūram* KBo 10.1 obv. 20 = (Hitt.) [*ma-*]*aḫ-ḫa-an-ma* KUR URU*Ulmaza* EGIR-*pa uwanun* "But when I returned from Ulma" KBo 10.2 i 41 (ann. Ḫatt. I, OH/NS).

(Sum.) [o].DU.GAM = ("Akk.") *mu ma mi* = (Hitt.) *ma-a-an* / [o].LÚ = *ḫu ḫa ḫi* = *ku-it* / [o].DÙ.A.BI = *lu la li* = ⌜GIM⌝-*an* KBo 26.20 ii 39-41 (Erimḫuš Bogh.A) □ obviously the Hitt. is not a translation of the Sum. or "Akk.".

ma-aḫ-ḫa-an KBo 14.42:14, (15) = GIM-*an* in dupl. KUB 19.22:5, 6 (DŠ), ed. Houwink ten Cate, JNES 25:28; *ma-aḫ-ḫa-an* KBo 16.1 iii 15 = GIM-*an* in dupl. KBo 3.4 ii 15, ed. AM 46.

1. like (postpos.) in single word comparison, from OH/MS; Hoffner apud DeVries, Diss. (1967) 82ff., cf. *mān* mng. 1 — **a.** following a substantive — **1′** wr. syll. — **a′** MS: *dudduwaranzakan* LÚ-*aš ma-a-aḫ-ḫa-an pitteuwar peššiyanun* "Like a lame man I have given up running" KUB 36.75 iii 14-15 (prayer, OH/MS), cf. van Brock, RHA XXII/75:142 ("comme un homme brisé"), Josephson, Part. 223; cf. *wātar ma-a-aḫ-ḫa-an* ibid. 19; GIŠ-*ru ma-a-aḫ-ḫa-an* ibid. 21; *nuwarat ḫāšu*[*wai*]*aš*SAR *iwar* ⌜*miy*⌝*ān ēšdu* . . . *kinunat kāš*[*a mi?-*]⌜*e*⌝*-eš-ta* ⌜*n*⌝*at* DINGIR-*LUM* LÚŠE.KIN.KUD-*aš ma-a-aḫ-ḫa-an miyān iyatnuwan ḫāšuwāi*SAR [. . .]x *waršta nammat anda puššāit idāluya uttar* . . . *ḫašuwāi*SAR *ma-a-aḫ-ḫa-an anda puššaiddu nat ḫaššan* [*iya*]*ddu* "Let it (the evil) be luxuriant (lit. growing or grown) like a *ḫ*.-plant! . . . Now behold it has become luxuriant, and the deity like a reaper has reaped it, the luxuriant, *iyatnuwant- ḫ*.-plant [. . .]. Furthermore he has ground it up. Let him grind up the evil word too . . . like a *ḫ*.-plant, and let him make it into soap!" KUB 29.7 rev. 18-23 + KBo 21.41 rev. 27-30 (Šamuha rit., MH/MS), ed. Goetze, JCS 1.316-18, Lebrun, Samuha 123, 130, tr. ANET 346.

b′ NS: *natzakan šāšaš ma-aḫ-ḫa-an kunkiškantari* "They (the royal family) set themselves in order(?) like the *š*.-animal (sg.)" KUB 29.1 iii 43-44 (rit., NS), cf. StBoT 5: 102; cf. also ÁMUŠEN.ḪI.A GIM-*an* ibid. iii 50; *nu* GIŠBAN.ḪI.A *weker* KUŠ*IŠPATU* AN.ZA.GÀR *ma-aḫ-ḫa-an unuwāir nat ANA* m*Gurparanzaḫu piran katta tīēr* "They requested bows. They decorated a quiver like a tower and put it down before G." KUB 36.67 ii 18-20 (Gurparanzaḫu story, NS), ed. Güterbock, ZA 44:86f.; □ The traces on the right edge belong to line 17 rather than 18; *nuwaruš arḫa dannaruš* DUGUTÚL.ḪI.A *ma-aḫ-ḫa-an duwarniškiši* "You (the king) will break them (the enemy) like empty vessels" KBo 15.52 v 16-17 (*ḫišuwaš* fest., NS); *nu* DINGIR.MEŠ *ḫūmanteš ANA* d*Ullukummi* NA4ŠU.U-*zi* GUD!.ḪI.A *ma-aḫ-ḫa-an uwayauwanzi tīer* "All the gods began to bellow like cattle at Ullukummi, the Basalt(?)" KUB 33.106 iv 19-20 (Ullik. III A, NH), ed. Güterbock, JCS 6:30f.; *ma*[*lt*]*an*[*išaš*] *ma-aḫ-ḫa-an karp*[*išk*]*attari* NA4ŠU.U-*ziš* "The Basalt(?) lifts itself (grows rapidly?) like a *m*." KBo 26.65 i 18-19 (Ullik. III A i 18-19), ed. JCS 6:18f. (as KUB 33.106 without joins); cf. the same phrase in KUB 33.92 iii 16 (=Ullik. I A iv 31), KUB 33.106 (=Ullik. III A) iii 14-15, 36-38, where the writing GIM-*an* could cover either *mān* or *maḫḫan*. Cf. *mān* mng. 1 c 3′.

2′. wr. GIM-*an* (all NS), cf. *mān* mng. 1 c 3′ — **a′** in hist. texts: *nankan INA* URU*Šamuḫa* ŠAḪ GIM-*a*[*n*] *:ḫūmma* EGIR-*pa ištappaš* "(Šauška) shut him (Urḫitešub) up in Šamuḫa like a pig in a pen" KBo 3.6 iii 56-57 (Ḫatt. iv 25-26), ed. Ḫatt. 32f., StBoT 24:24f.; *apūnmakan* d*IŠTAR* URU*Šamuḫa* GAŠAN-*IA* KU6-*un* GIM-*an :ḫūpalaza* EGIR-*pa ištapta* "Šauška of Šamuḫa, my lady, shut him (Urḫitešub) up like a fish (caught) with a net" KBo 6.29 ii 33-34 (Ḫatt. III), ed. Ḫatt. 50f.; *nukan* URU*Neriqqaš* URU-*aš* NA4*akuš* GIM-*an* [*aruni?*] *anda ēšta* . . . *nukan* URU*Neriqqan* URU-*an* NA4*akun* GI[M]-*a*[*n*] *ḫalluwaz witaz šarā udaḫḫu*[*n*] "The city of N. was like a seashell in the [sea(?)] . . . I (Ḫattušili) brought the city of N. up like a seashell out of deep water" KUB 21.19 + 1303/u iii 14-17 (prayer of Ḫatt. III and Pud.), ed. Haas, KN 7 n. 5, Sürenhagen, AOF 8:94f., cf. Hoffner, BiOr 35 (1978) 245.

b′ in an oath of loyalty: *numu* EN-*IA* [U]R?.TUR GIM-*an* . . . *šallanut* "My lord raised me like a puppy(?)" KUB 26.32 i 7-8 (oath of scribe to Šupp. II), ed. Laroche, RA 47:74f., cf. Sommer, HAB 73 w. n. 2.

c′ in mythological narrative: [f]D*Aranzaḫaš* ÁMUŠEN-*aš* GIM-*an tarnaš* "The Tigris River took flight like an eagle (and went to Akkad)" KUB 17.9 i 14 (Gurparanzaḫu legend, NS), cf. i 35.

d′ in hymns: *kuin uwateši nan* GIŠAN.ZA.GÀR GIM-*an parganuši kuin⸗ma⸗kan*... "You bring one here and make him high like a tower; another one (you...)" KUB 24.7 ii 11-12 (hymn to Ištar, NH), ed. Archi, OA 16 (1977) 307, 309, Wegner, AOAT 36 (manuscript complete 1976, published 1981) 49, cf. also pp. 48ff., Güterbock, JAOS 103 (1983) 158; cf. further in the same hymn: TÚGNÍG.LÁ[M.MEŠ-*m*]*a*?-*aš-za* GIM-*an parkuwaya waššeškiši* ibid. ii 9; *eša⸗rašilašmaš arišand*[*a*-...] GIM-*an duwarniškiši* ibid ii 6f.; perhaps in nominal sentences in the following two examples: ANŠE-*ašmaza* GIM-*an puntarriyališ z*[*ik*] SAL.LUGAL-*aš* d*IŠTAR-iš* "Like an ass you are stubborn, Queen Ištar" ibid. ii 18f.; UR.MAḪ-*maza* G[IM-*an*...] "Like a lion you are [...]" ibid. ii 21; note the only exception to the use of postpos. GIM-*an* in this hymn: [*nuz*]*a* LÚ.MEŠ *ḫuelpi* GA.RAŠSAR *iwar arḫa kari*[*pta*] "You at[e up] men like (*iwar*) a fresh leek" ibid. ii 5, where postpos. *iwar* is not construed as it usually is with a preceding genitive. For GIM-*an*, possibly representing *maḫḫan*, in Signalement lyrique cf. above, bil. section, and *mān* 1 c 3′ c′.

e′ in rituals: *šumanza* GIM-*an* KBo 11.11 i 9; AN.ZA.GÀR GIM-*an* KUB 17.27 ii 30, 33; *išḫa⸗minan* GIM-*an* ibid. 31, 34; UR.MAḪ-*aš* GIM-*an* VBoT 120 ii 5; MUŠ.ŠÀ.TÙR GIM-*an* ibid. 7.

f′ in omens: *takku IZBU* IGI.ḪI.A-*ŠU* UR.MAḪ-*aš* GIM-*a*[*n* ...] "If the eyes of a malformed newborn animal (are) like a lion's" KUB 34.19 i 6, ed. StBoT 9:54ff.

b. following *kuit* (*kuit maḫḫan* "like what" for a similar construction see *kuit ḫanda* "why") in dependent clauses, from MH/MS — **1′** in letters, where the *k. m.* clause is followed by a main clause containing the imperative of the v. *ḫatrai*- or its log. *ŠUPUR* "write, send" — **a′** MH/MS: *nu kuit ma-aḫ-ḫ*[*a-an numu*...] *ḫūman ḫat*[*reški*] (or *ḫat*[*rai*]) "Write [me, ...,] how it is!" Maşat 75/64:23-24, ed. Alp, Belleten 44 (1980) 52f.

b′ NH — **1″** *kuit maḫḫan* in dependent clauses with verb "to be" implied: *MAḪAR* dUTU-*ŠI* SAL.LUGAL *aššul kuit ma-aḫ-ḫa-an* ŠÀ ERÍN.MEŠ *šarikuwayakan U* ŠÀ ERÍN.MEŠ UKU.UŠ *ḫattulannaza kuit ma-aḫ-ḫa-an numu* EN-*YA* EGIR-*pa ŠUPUR* "Write back to me, O my lord, how it is with (lit. what the well-being is like before) Your Majesty and the Queen, and what the state of health(?) is like among the *š*.-troops and the UKU.UŠ soldiers!" KBo 18.54 obv. 3-6; *MAḪAR* dUTU-*ŠI MAḪAR* SAL.LUGAL *aššul kuit* GIM-*an numu ABI* DÙG.GA-*YA* EGIR-*pa ŠUPUR* "Write me, my dear father, how it is with (lit. what the well-being is like before) His Majesty and the Queen" KBo 18.4:8-12; [*MA*]*ḪAR* dUTU-*ŠI* EN-*YA* SILIM-*la kuit* GIM-*an numu* EGIR-*p*[*a ŠUPUR*] Bo 6632:3 (old translit. by HGG); cf. KUB 48.88 obv. 10; on the formula *aššul kuit maḫḫan* cf. Güterbock, KBo 18 p. IV no. 1; *kuit maḫḫan* without expressed *aššul*: *nu kuit ma-aḫ-ḫa-an* [*nu*... *AN*]*A* dUTU-*ŠI* EN-*YA* [... *ḫatram*]*i*(?) KBo 18.30:10-12, cf. KBo 18.44:6, KBo 18.114 obv. 3.

2″ *kuit maḫḫan* in dependent clause with *ištamaš*- "to hear": INIM.MEŠ *ŠA* KUR *Mizriya kuit* GI[M-*an*] *ištamaškiši natmu* DUMU-*YA ḫatreški* "O my son, keep writing me what you are hearing about how the affairs of Egypt are" KUB 26.90 iv 1-3.

2′ in instruction texts: [*š*]*ummaš ANA* LÚ.MEŠ.SAG ŠU-*i* [o-]x-x *kuit* GIM-*an uškatteni* [*nuza*] *memian parā lē kuedanikki* [*mem*]*atteni* "Do not divulge, O eunuchs, a word to anyone of whatever (lit. like what) you see for yourselves privately(?)" KUB 26.8 ii 4-7, ed. Dienstanw. 11; [(*š*)]*ummašma kuit* GIM-*an išdammašten nat ANA* dUTU-*ŠI UL mematteni nat* GAM *NĪŠ* DINGIR-*LIM* GAR-*ru* "Whatever (lit. like what) you have heard for yourselves — (if) you do not report it to His Majesty, let that be put under the oath of the gods!" KUB 26.1 iii 50-52, ed. Dienstanw. 14; "If someone has a long lifespan (lit., 'day of his father and mother')" *nuza kuit* GIM-*an kišari nu apāt kuiški memai* "and someone says with regard to (lit. like) what happens:" (followed by a quote) KUB 26.1 iii 16-17, ed. Dienstanw. 13.

2. as, just as (subordinating conj. of comparison), from OH/MS; cf. *mān* mng. 2 — **a.** resumed by a correlative adv. in the main clause (from OH/MS) — **1′** with the correlative adv. *apeniššan* (log. *QĀTAMMA*) (cf. HW^2 171ff.) — **a′** *maḫḫan* clause preceding the main clause (MS and NS) — **1″** OH in later copies: for *maḫḫan* in post-OS copies, replacing *māḫḫanda* in the OS archetype see the *māḫḫanda, mān⸗ḫanda, mān ḫanda* article; *ma-aḫ-ḫa-an dayazilaš apāšša QĀTAMMA* "He is the same as a thief" KBo 6.3 iii 69 (Law §73, OH/NS), ed. HG 40f.; ^{GIŠ}GEŠTIN.È.A *ma-aḫ-ḫa-an* GEŠTIN-*ŠU* ŠÀ-*it ḫarzi* ^{GIŠ}*SERDUM ma-aḫ-ḫa-an* Ì-*ŠU* ŠÀ-*it ḫarzi* ^{d}IM-*ša ŠA* LUGAL SAL.LUGAL *ŠA* DUMU.MEŠ-*ŠUNU āššu* TI-*tar innarauwatar* MU.ḪI.A GÍD.DA *tušgarattan QĀTAMMA* ŠÀ-*it ḫark* "Just as the raisin holds its wine in (its) heart, (and) just as the olive holds its oil in (its) heart, so too may you, O Stormgod, likewise hold in (your) heart the good, life, vigor(?), long years (and) happiness of the king and queen and of their children" KUB 33.68 ii 13-16 (incantation, OH/MS); ^{GIŠ}*SERDUM-ma⸗z ma-a-aḫ-ḫa-an* Ì-*ŠU* ŠÀ-*it* [*ḫarzi* ^{GIŠ}GEŠTIN-*ma⸗z ma-a-aḫ-ḫa-an*] GEŠTIN-*an* ŠÀ-*it ḫarzi zikka* ^{d}*Telepinu* [. . .] *ištanzanit* ŠÀ-*it QĀTAMMA āššu ḫar*[*k*] KUB 17.10 ii 19-21 (incantation, OH/MS), translit. Myth. 33, tr. ANET 127b, cf. HW^2 172b; cf. KUB 33.74 i 5ff. sub 2 b 1′ below; *nu* MU-*ti mieniyaš armalaš ma-aḫ-ḫa-an nuza ukka QĀTAMMA kišḫat* "I have become like someone who is sick for the course/extent of a year(?)" KUB 30.10 rev. 15-16 (prayer, OH/MS), cf. Josephson, Part. 108; cf. KUB 30.11 rev. 12f. below sub 2 b 1′ for same sentence with *apāš* instead of *QĀTAMMA*.

2″ MH and NH: See ex. from Dupp. in bil. sec. above; *kī* $^{\text{NA}_4}$*pēru ma-a-aḫ-ḫa-an uktūri BĒLU U* DAM-*SU* DUM[U.MEŠ-*Š*]*U QĀ⸗TAMMA uktūreš ašandu* "Just as this boulder is everlasting so let the lord (the king) and his wife and his children be everlasting" KBo 15.10 ii 5-6 (incantation, MH/MS), ed. THeth 1:20f. and StBoT 22:58; *kāšwa* IM-*aš ma-aḫ-ḫa-an wappui* EGIR-*pa UL paizzi kappanimawa ḫarkēšzi UL nu⸗waratza tamai* NUMUN(!)-*an UL kišari iššanaš⸗mawakan kāš* DINGIR!.MEŠ-*aš* ^{NINDA}*ḫarši UL paizzi kēdašawakan ANA* 2 EN.SISKUR.SISKUR *idāluš* EME-*aš* NÍ.TE-*ši QĀTAM⸗M*[*A*] *lē paizzi* "Just as this clay does not go back to the river bank, and the (black) cumin does not become white and does not become another seed, and this dough does not go into the gods' bread, in the same way may the evil tongue not go into the body of these two clients" KUB 15.39 + KUB 12.59 ii 15-20 (incantation in 1 Mašt., MH/NS), with dupl. KBo 2.3 ii 11-15, tr. ANET 351; □ note that in its second occurrence the demonstrative *kāš* follows its noun in order to avoid **kāšmawakan iššanaš*, which could be misunderstood as *kāšma⸗wa⸗kan*; (The previously rebellious troops of Ura and Mutamutaši will march at my side into battle, and) *ma-a-aḫ-ḫa-an-ma-at-mu ANA* ^{d}UTU-*ŠI* [*āšš*]*aueš nuš apeniššan maniyaḫḫiškimi* "In the way that they are [pl]easing to me, My Majesty, in that way I will command them" KBo 16.47 obv. 6-7 (treaty, MH/MS), ed. Otten, IM 17:56f.; *nu ma-aḫ-ḫa-an* ^{LÚ}*kururaš* GUD.ḪI.A UDU.ḪI.A *unniyanzi šumenzanna QĀTAMMA unniyanzi* "Just as they drive the enemy's cattle and sheep, in the same way they will drive yours too" KUB 26.19 ii 19-20 (treaty with the Kaška, MH/NS), tr. Kaškäer 131; *ma-aḫ-ḫa-an-wa-at-ta āššu nuwa QĀTAMMA iya* "Do as it seems good to you" KUB 14.1 obv. 83 (Madd., MH/MS), ed. Madd. 20f.; GIM-*an* LUGAL-*i* ZI-*za nu QĀTAMMA iyazi* "The king does as he pleases" KBo 4.9 i 9-10 (AN.TAḪ.ŠUM fest., OH?/NS); *nat ma-aḫ-ḫa-an karū* (var. *nat karū* GIM-*an*) *wedan ēšta nat* EGIR-*pa QĀTAMMA wedandu* "Let them rebuild it (i.e., the temple) the way it was built before" KUB 13.2 ii 34-35 (Bel Madg., MH/NS), with dupl. KUB 31.90 iii 3-4 (NS), ed. Dienstanw. 46; *ma-aḫ-ḫa-an-kán kī kištanunun idāluyakan ANA* EN.MEŠ-*TIM šer QĀTAMMA kištaru* "As I have quenched these, so may the evil be likewise quenched for the lords (i.e., sacrificers)" KUB 27.67 ii 7-8 (rit. of Ambazzi, MH/NS), tr. ANET 348; *nutta mān tuel ma-aḫ-ḫa-an* SAG.DU-*KA nakkiš nutta≪ma≫ mān* SAG.DU ^{d}UTU-*ŠI QĀ⸗TAMMA UL nakkiš* "If the person of My Majesty is not as dear to you as your own person" KBo 5.3 i 18-20 (Ḫuqq. treaty, Šupp. I), ed. SV 2:108f.; *tuqqaš ma-aḫ-ḫa-an* ^{LÚ}KÚR-*aš ANA* ^{d}UTU-*ŠI-yaš QĀTAMMA-pat* ^{LÚ}KÚR-*aš* "Just as he is your enemy, so too he is an enemy of My

Majesty" KUB 21.5 ii 8 (Alakš., NH), ed. SV 2:58f.; LUGAL KUR *Aššur ANA* ^{d}UTU-*ŠI* GIM!-*an kurur tuqqaš QĀTAMMA kurur ēšdu* "As the king of Assyria is an enemy to My Majesty, so let him also be an enemy to you" KUB 23.1 iv 12-13 (treaty with Šaušgamuwa, NH), ed. StBoT 16:14f.; EZEN *ḫadauri INA* É ^{d}U *ma-aḫ-ḫa-an* [(SI×SÁ-*at*) *I*]*NA* É ^{d}*Ḫašammeliyan QĀTAMMA iya*[(*nzi*)] "They will perform the *ḫ.*-festival in the temple of Ḫašammeli in the same way that it was determined (by oracle to be performed) in the temple of the Stormgod" KUB 22.27 i 26-27 (oracle, NH) with dupl. KBo 24.119 iii 1-4; *nu* GIM-*an ANA* LUGAL [KU]R ^{URU}*Ḫatti* ZI-*anza nan QĀTAMMA iyaddu* "Let the king of Ḫatti treat him as he wishes" KBo 4.10 obv. 10 (treaty with Ulmitešub, Tudḫ. IV); cf. KBo 4.9 i 9f., KUB 26.58 obv. 17f., and HW[2] 174d (III 3); *naš karū* GIM-*an* LU[GAL K]UR *Wiluša ēšta kinunaš QĀTAMM*[*A ēšdu*] KUB 19.55 rev. 42 + KUB 48.90 rev. 10, cf. ibid. 43/11-44/12 (Milawata letter), ed. Hoffner, AfO Beiheft 19.131f.; *nu ABUYA* ^{m}*Tudḫaliyaš* LUGAL.GAL GIM-[*a*]*n ašanza* LUGAL-*uš ēšta nukan QĀTAMMA ašanda* LÚ-*natar*$^{HI.A}$ *andan gulšun* "As my father T., the Great King, was a true king, so I inscribed (his) true exploits on (the statue)" KBo 12.38 ii 11-14 (hist., Šupp. II), ed. Güterbock, JNES 26.76, 78.

b′ *maḫḫan* clause following main clause: *andamakan QĀTAMMA-pat memaḫḫi* É-*rikan anda* [*m*]*a-aḫ-ḫa-an memiškinun* "Meanwhile I speak just the same way I was speaking in the house" KBo 12.96 i 5-6 (rit. for ^{d}LAMMA ^{KUŠ}*kuršaš*, MH/NS), ed. Rosenkranz, OrNS 33:239, 241; □ modifying the vb. *mema-*, *maḫḫan* here expresses content more than manner of speech and thus bears a resemblance to its use below in mng. 3, where its clause usually follows the main clause.

2′ with the correlative adv. *kiššan*: *nu kinun ma-aḫ-ḫa-an* ^{d}UTU-*ŠI* [(*ANA* ^{m}*Alakšandu išḫi*)]*ullaš ṬUPPA* DÙ!-*nun nu ziqqa* ^{m}*Alakšanduš* [DUMU.MEŠ-*KA ḫašša ḫa*(*nz*)]*ašša išḫiulaš ṬUPPA kiššan* (var. *kiš-an*) [(*iya*)] KUB 21.5 ii 14-16 (Alakš., Muw.), with dupl. KBo 19.73 + KUB 21.1 ii 8-10, ed. without KBo 19.73 in SV 2:58f., cf. Melchert, RHA XXXI (1973) 68f.

b. without correlative adv. — **1′** *maḫḫan* clause preceding the main clause: *nuza* 1 ŠAḪ *ma-a-aḫ-ḫa-an* ŠAḪ.TUR.ḪI.A *mekkuš ḫaškizzi kēllaz ŠA* ^{GIŠ}KIRI$_6$.G[EŠTIN] 1-*ašša* ^{GIŠ}*māḫlaš* ŠAḪ-*aš iwar mūriuš mekkuš ḫaškiddu* "Just as one sow bears many piglets, so also let every single (1-*aššša*) (vine) branch of this vineyard, like a sow, bear many grape clusters" KUB 43.23 rev. 19-22 (blessings upon Labarna, OS), ed. Ehelolf, OLZ 1933:5, Otten and Siegelová, AfO 23:36, Archi, FsMeriggi[2] 34; *nu* MU-*ti mēniaš armalaš ma-aḫ-ḫa-an n*[*uza ūgg*]*a apāš kišḫat* "I have become like someone who is sick for the course/extent of a year" KUB 30.11 rev. 12-13 (prayer, pre-NH/MS) cf. above 2 a 1′ a′ 1″; *nu šankuš alil ma-aḫ-ḫa-an parkiyat tuella ŠA* ^{d}U ZI-*KA alil parktaru* "Just as the *š.* flower grew, let your soul too, O Stormgod, grow (like) a flower" KUB 33.68 ii 1-2 (incantation in myth, OH/MS), cf. ibid. ii 7-10, cf. Güterbock, JAOS 88.70; [*nu* ^{GI}]^{Š}GEŠTIN.È.A GIM-*an* GEŠTIN ŠÀ-*it ḫ*[*arzi* ^{GIŠ}*S*]*ERDUM-ma* [GIM-*a*]*n* Ì-*an* ŠÀ-*it ḫarzi z*[*iga* DINGIR-*LUM* LU]GAL-*un* [*and*]*a* ŠÀ-*it aššuli ḫark* "As the raisin holds wine in its heart, as the olive holds oil in its heart, may you too, O god, hold the king in your heart with kindness" KUB 33.74 i 5-7 (missing god myth, OH/NS), translit. Laroche, Myth. 104f.; *nuwakan kāš* KU$_6$ [*m*]*a-a-aḫ-ḫa-an arunaz tuḫḫuštat kinuna tuḫšandu* [*ap*]*edaš* UD-*aš* EME[.ḪI].A *ḫūrtāuš* "Just as this fish has been removed from the sea, let them now remove the tongues (and) curses of those days" 2Mašt. i 38-40 (incantation in rit., MH/MS); *karūliyazya* [*m*]*a-aḫ-ḫa-an* KUR.KUR-*kan anda ḫurkilaš išḫiūl iyan* "however the obligatory procedure for *ḫurkel* has been performed from ancient times in the (various) lands," (let them follow that procedure) KUB 13.2 iii 11-12 (instr. for *BĒL MADGALTI*, MH/NS), ed. Dienstanw. 47, cf. Hoffner in FsGordon (1973) 85 w.n.19; É KUR ^{URU}*Ḫattiza* ŠEŠ-*YA* GIM-*an šakti natza ammuk UL š*[*aggaḫḫi*] "Do I not know the (royal) residence of the land of Ḫatti as well as you, my brother, know it?" KUB 21.38 obv. 10 (letter of Pud.), ed. Helck, JCS 17:88, cf. Houwink ten Cate in FsGüterbock 126; ^{d}*Kumarpišwa* GIM-*an* ^{d}U-*an šallanut* IGI-*andamawa*[*šši* (*k*)]*ān* ^{NA_4}*kunkunuz*<*zi*>*n tarpanallin šalla*[*nut*] "Just as Kumarbi raised up the Stormgod, he raised up against him this Basalt(?) (as) a rival" KUB 33.95 + KUB 36.7b iv 17-19 + KUB 33.93 iv 12-13 (Ullik. I A iv 17-19) with dupl. D = KUB 33.92 iii 4-5, ed. JCS 5:156f.; *ini ŠA* ^{URU}*Išgazzuwa uttar ma-aḫ-ḫa-an memir nu* ^{d}UTU-*ŠI ukila paimi* "As they explained (lit. spoke) that matter of the city Išgazzuwa, I, My Majesty, will go myself; (is that all right?)" KBo 16.97 rev. 7-8 (oracle question, MH/NS?).

2′ *maḫḫan* clause following the main clause: EGIR-*andamaza gimra<š>* SISKUR.SISKUR *ienzi gimraš* GIM-*an* SISKUR.SISKUR *iššanzi* "But afterwards they perform the ritual of the (battle-)field, as they usually perform the ritual of the (battle-)field" KUB 17.28 iv 55-56 (rit. lustration of a defeated army, NS), ed. StBoT 3:151.

3. how, that (conj., in indirect statement or question); from MH/MS. How-clauses are the objects of verbs of seeing, hearing, knowing, inquiring, telling and writing, (Sommer, AU 69; Güterbock, OrNS 20:331) — **a.** *maḫḫan* clause following the main clause: *zik* ^{d}*IŠTAR* ^{URU}*Nenuwa* GAŠAN-*NI UL šakti* KUR ^{URU}*Ḫatti* GIM-*an* (var. *ma-aḫ-ḫa-an*) *dammešḫan* "O Ištar of Nineveh, our lady! Don't you know how the land of Ḫatti is oppressed?" KBo 2.9 i 38-39 (prayer in rit., MH/NS) with dupl. KBo 21.48 obv.? 10 (MS), ed. Archi, OA 16:299f.; *nu ABUYA išḫiulaš namma tuppi wekta annaz ma-aḫ-ḫa-an* LÚ ^{URU}*Kuruštama* DUMU ^{URU}*Ḫatti* ^{d}U-*aš dāš nan* KUR ^{URU}*Mizri pedaš naš* LÚ.MEŠ ^{URU}*Mizri iyat nukan* ^{d}U-*aš* [*ANA*] KUR ^{URU}*Mizri U ANA* KUR ^{URU}*Ḫatti ma-aḫ-ḫa-an* [*išḫ*]*iul ištarnišummi išḫiyat uktūriatkan* [*ma*]*-aḫ-ḫa-an ištarnišummi aššiyanteš* "Then my father asked again for the tablet of the treaty (in which it was told) how, long ago, the Stormgod took the people of Kuruštama, Hittite subjects, and carried them to Egyptian territory and made them Egyptian (subjects), and how the Stormgod concluded a treaty between the countries of Egypt and Ḫatti, and how they (were to be) forever on friendly terms with each other" KBo 14.12 iv 26-32 (DŠ), ed. Güterbock JCS 10:98, cf. also StBoT 23:190f.; [(*ŠA*)*N*(*Û*) *ṬUPP*]*U-ma ŠA* ^{URU}*Kuruštamma* LÚ.MEŠ ^{URU}*Kuruštamma ma-aḫ-ḫa-an* [(^{d}U ^{URU}*Ḫa*)]*tti INA* KUR ^{URU}*Mizri pēdaš nušmaš* ^{d}IM ^{URU}*Ḫatti ma-aḫ-ḫa-an* [(*išḫiū*)]*l ANA* LÚ.MEŠ ^{URU}*Ḫatti menaḫḫanda iyat nammat IŠTU* ^{d}U ^{URU}*Ḫatti li*[*n*]*ganuwanteš* "The second tablet (concerned) Kuruštamma: how the Hittite Stormgod brought people of K. into Egyptian territory, and how the Hittite Stormgod made a treaty with the Hittites concerning them (the people of K.), so that they were put under oath by the Hittite Stormgod" KUB 14.8 obv. 13-16 (2nd Plague Prayer, Murš. II), with dupl. KUB 14.10 ii 2-7, ed. Götze, KlF 1:208f. "wie", tr. ANET 395 and Kühne in NERT 171 (both taking *m.* as temporal); [(*nuz*)]*a kāšma au* ^{d}U NIR.GÁL-*mu BĒLIYA ma-aḫ-ḫa-an piran ḫūiyanza numu idālawi parā UL tarnāi āššawimamu parā tarnan ḫarzi* "See how the mighty Stormgod, my lord, is my helper (lit. the one who goes before me), (how) he doesn't let me come to harm, but always lets me come to good!" KBo 5.8 i 12-14, ed. AM 148f., cf. Sommer, AU 69; *nu šumeš* DINGIR.MEŠ *UL uškattēni* É *ABIYA-kan ma-aḫ-ḫa-an ḫūman INA* É ^{NA_4}*ḫekur* ^{d}LAMMA *INA* É.NA$_4$ DINGIR-*LIM neyat* "O gods, don't you see how she (Tawannanna) has diverted the whole house of my father to the *ḫekur*-house of the Tutelary Deity, to the Stone House of the deity?" KUB 14.4 ii 3-5 (prayer, Murš. II), cf. Güterbock apud Laroche, Ugar. 3:102f., Otten, HTR 133, Neu, StBoT 5:125 and Imparati, SMEA 18:26; "Right away I shall make an accounting (*arkuwar*) of your temples (and) your statue(s)...," DINGIR.MEŠ *ŠA* KUR $^{URU.GIŠ}$PA-*ti* GIM-*an iyanteš* GIM-*an-na-at* (var. *ma-aḫ-ḫa-na-at*) *idalawaḫḫanteš* "how the gods of the Land of Ḫatti are worshipped and how they are mistreated" KUB 6.45 i 21-24 (prayer, Muw.), with dupl. KUB 6.46 i 24-25, tr. ANET 398, Houwink ten Cate, RHA XXV/81:104; DUB.1.KAM *ANA* EZEN *pūruliyašza ma!-aḫ-*⌜*ḫa*⌝*-an* $^{LÚ.MEŠ}$*ḫapīēš unuwašḫuš danzi ḫalkueššarra ma-aḫ-ḫa-an ḫanda*[*nz*]*i* $^{SAL.MEŠ}$*zintūḫīēšša ma-aḫ-ḫa-an* SÌR GAL SÌR-*RU* "One tablet: how the *ḫ.*-men take to themselves (i.e., put on) ornaments for the *p.* festival, how they determine the provisions, and how the *z.* women sing the great song" KUB 8.69 iii 5-9 (cat. entry, NH), ed. Laroche, CTH p. 186; DUB.2.KAM *ŠA* SISKUR.SISKUR ^{URU}*Šamuḫa UL QATI* $^{LÚ.MEŠ}$AZU *ma-a-aḫ*[*-ḫa*]*-an* SISKUR.SISKUR *ienzi* "Second tablet of the ritual of

Šamuḫa, (text) not finished: how the exorcists ($^{LÚ.MEŠ}$AZU) perform the ritual" KUB 29.7 rev. 65 (colophon to rit., MH/MS); on the basis of the clause internal position of *m.* in this and other exx. of colophons and incipits it is more likely that they mean "how" (manner) than "whenever" (temporal); cf. also KUB 14.3 i 33-34 (Taw.), KUB 15.5 iii 4-5, KUB 23.101 ii 5-6 (letter). The how-clause with *maḫḫan* as the object of *šak-* "to know" is similar to the that-clause with *kuit*: DUMU-*YA UL šakti kuitmukan* ŠÀ KUR.KUR.MEŠ *kašza ēšta* "My son, don't you know that there was a famine in the midst of my lands?" Bo 2810 ii 11-12 (letter, NH), copy and ed. Klengel, AOF 1 (1974) 171ff.

b. *maḫḫan* clause preceding the main clause: ^{LÚ}KÚR.M[EŠ]-*ma ma-a-aḫ-ḫa-an* KUR ^{URU}*Ḫatti* [*walḫir?*...] KUR-*e šaruwer natza dāir nat* x x x [o o] *šumāš ANA* DINGIR.MEŠ *memiškiuwanipat nušmašš*[*a*]*n DĪNAM ar-nuškiuwani* "We shall surely (*-pat*) continue to tell you gods how the enemies [attacked(?)] the land of Ḫatti, plundered the land, and took it away, [and ...], and we shall continually bring (our) case before you" KUB 17.21 ii 4-7 (prayer of Arn. I and Ašm., MH/MS), ed. Kaškäer 154f.; "Come, make (your) plea with me, and I shall put you on your way." KASKAL-*ši-ma-wa-ta-kkan* GIM-*an teḫ*[*ḫi*] *nuwarat ANA* ŠEŠ-*YA ḫatrāmi* "But as for how I will put you on your way, that I shall write to my brother" KUB 14.3 ii 64-66 (Taw., NH), ed. AU 10f. (with anaphoric *-ma*, see *-ma* d); *nuza* KUR.KUR.ḪI.A-*aš waštul*$^{ḪI.A}$ *ma-aḫ-ḫa-an* EGIR-*pa lāmi* [*natza k*]*ī* ⌈*arku*⌉*war iyam*[*i*] *nat* ^{d}U EN-*YA ištamašdu* "Let the Stormgod, my Lord, hear how I remove the sins of the countries and (how) I make that into this accounting" KBo 11.1 obv. 12-13 (prayer, Muw.), ed. Houwink ten Cate, RHA XXV/81:106, 115 ("as I ask for remittal"); *ḫan-tezziušmat* LUGAL.MEŠ *ma-aḫ-ḫa-an arḫa pittalāer nat* ^{d}UTU ^{URU}TÚL-*na* GAŠAN-*YA šakti* "O Sungoddess of Arinna, you know how the former kings neglected it (Nerik)" KUB 21.27 i 16-18 (prayer, Pud.), ed. Haas, KN 9 note 1, Sürenhagen, AOF 8:108-111, tr. ANET 393, cf. Hoffner, FsLacheman 191; *nukan* ^{m}*Ḫattušilin* ÌR-*KA ANA* ^{URU}*Neriqqa ma-aḫ-ḫa-an anda* [...] *nat* ^{d}UTU ^{URU}TÚL-*na* GAŠAN-*YA šakti* "O Sungoddess of Arinna, my lady, you know how (Urḫitešub) [...-ed] Ḫattušili, your servant, to Nerik" ibid. i 41-43, ed. Ünal, THeth 3:123 n. 47, Sürenhagen, AOF 8:110f., tr. ANET 393; cf. also KBo 4.10 obv. 38-39 (treaty, NH) and possibly KBo 15.28 rev. 11-12 (letter).

c. as the predicate in the second of two coordinate *mān* ("if") clauses expressing alternatives, cf. also sub *mān* 4 b 2′ b′ and 8 a 2′: *punuššuwenima nāwi mān mem*[*ia*]*š ašanza mān ma-aḫ-ḫa-an* "We haven't yet inquired if the word (i.e., the statement of Ammatalla) is true or how (it is)" KUB 22.70 obv. 31 (oracle, NH); *nan mān arḫa tarnanzi mān ma-aḫ-ḫa-an nu ANA* EN-*YA ḫatrāimi* "I will write to my lord if they will release him, or how (they will act)" Bo 2154 + Bo 1608 obv. 10-12 (letter), from translit. by HGG; "Herewith we have communicated the results of the oracles" *nukan* EGIR-*an tiya mān anda ēp mān ma-aḫ-ḫa-an* "Take care of (the matter): either include (it) or (act) however (you see fit)" KBo 18.140 obv. 5-8 (letter, NH); □ for EGIR-*an tiya-* in this usage cf. Maşat 75/43:13-16, Maşat 75/104:8-12, ed. Alp, Belleten 44 (1980) 47, 49, 50.

4. how (interrog. adv.), from OH/MS; cf. Sommer, HAB 48, Hoffner, JNES 31:29f.; cf. *mān* mng. 3: *ma-a-aḫ-ḫa-an iyaweni* "How shall we proceed?" KUB 17.10 i 29 (missing deity myth, OH/MS), translit. Laroche, Myth. 31, tr. ANET 127, RPO 532, NERT 161; *nuwa ma-aḫ-ḫa-an iyaweni* ABoT 60 obv. 19 (letter, MH/MS), ed. Laroche, RHA XVIII/67:82f.; *nuwa wattaru ma-a-aḫ-ḫa-an iyan kunnanitat wedan arzilitat ḫaniššān* AN.BAR-*at iškiyan* "'How is the fountain made?' It is built with copper; it is plastered with *a.*; it is ...-ed with iron" KBo 21.22:41-43 (blessings for Labarna, OH/MS), ed. Kellerman, Tel Aviv 5:200, 202; *kī ma-aḫ-ḫa-an iy*[*aweni*] "How shall we do this?" KUB 17.1 ii 17 (Keššī story, NH), ed. Friedrich, ZA 49:238f.; *mān akima nanzankan* GIDIM-*an* ⌈Ù⌉-*it uškiuwan dāi našmanzankan* Ù-*hit išpanti išpanti uškiuwan dāi nanšikan* EGIR-*an* GAM GIM-*an karšmi* "But if he dies, and he (another person) begins to see him as a ghost in dreams, or begins to see him nightly in dreams, how shall I cut him (the ghost) off from him?" § (followed by a list of materials for the rit.) KUB 39.61 i 4-7 (rit., NS); (The *ḫalugaš* went to DINGIR.MAḪ and asked:) *ma-aḫ-ḫa-*

an-wa (var. GIM-*an-wa*) *iyaweni* [(*mānwa iyawen*)]*i* "When we act, how shall we act?" KBo 22.128 iii! 7-8 + KBo 22.145 iii 7 + KUB 43.52 iii 1-2 + 350/z iii 1 (NS), with dupl. KUB 7.1 iii 9-10 (NS), translit. Otten-Rüster, ZA 67:58; for another ex. cf. KUB 1.16 i/ii 18-19 in bil. sec.

5. when, as soon as (temporal subordinating conj.), from MH/MS — **a.** with pret. — **1′** introducing time expressions: *ma-aḫ-ḫa-an-ma ḫamešḫanza kišat* "But when it became spring," KUB 14.15 i 23, ed. AM 36f.; cf. KBo 3.4 ii 50, ed. AM 60; KBo 4.4 iii 57, ed. AM 130; iv 42, ed. AM 138; iv 56, ed. AM 140; *ma-aḫ-ḫa-an-ma nekuttat* "As soon as it became evening" KBo 5.8 iii 19, ed. AM 156f.; *ma-aḫ-ḫa-an-ma-kán* (var. [G]IM-*an-ma-kán*) ᵈUTU-*uš ūpta* "But when the sun rose" KBo 5.8 iii 23 with dupl. KBo 16.8 iii 27, ed. AM 158f.; *ma-aḫ-ḫa-an-ma uēr* MU.HI.A-*uš* EGIR-*anda pāir* "But as the years passed" KBo 4.2 iii 45 (Murš. speech loss, NH), ed. MSpr. 4f., line 6; GIM-*an* GE_6-*anza kišat* "as soon as it was night" KUB 40.83 obv. 9 (protocol, NH), ed. StBoT 4:64f.

2′ introducing actions — **a′** MS: *ma-aḫ-ḫa-an-ma-an-za-kán* GAL.GEŠTIN *awan arḫa tarnaš* "But when the Chief of the Wine (a high ranking military officer) let him escape" KUB 14.1 rev. 26 (MH/MS), ed. Madd. 26f., cf. ibid. obv. 6, 45-(46).

b′ NS — **1″** in hist. texts: [*nukan*] *ma-aḫ-ḫa-an ABUYA* ŠÀ KUR-*TI āraš* "And when my father came into the midst of the land" KBo 14.3 iii 12 (DŠ frag. 14); *ma-aḫ-ḫa-an-ma-za* EZEN. MU.KAM-*TI karpta* "But when he (Šupp. I) had celebrated the year festival, (he went into the country of . . .)" KBo 14.11 i 13 (DŠ frag. 28), ed. Güterbock, JCS 10:91; *nuza* GIM-*an* ERÍN.MEŠ *SUTE*ᴹᴱŠ *tarḫta* "And when he had defeated the tribal troops" KBo 5.6 ii 5 (DŠ frag. 28), ed. JCS 10:92; LÚ.MEŠ ᵁᴿᵁ*Ḫurri*⸗*makan ma-aḫ-ḫa-an* ᴸᵁSANGA EGIR-*anda awer* "But when the Hurrians saw that 'the Priest' (Telepinu) was gone, (they attacked)" ibid. ii 15; *ma-aḫ-ḫa-an-ma-aš* EGIR-*pa uit* "But when he (Šupp. I) came back" KBo 12.33 ii 4 (hist., Arn. II); *ma-aḫ-ḫa-an-ma* KUR.KUR.MEŠ ᴸᵁKÚR ᵐ*Arnuwandan* ŠEŠ-*YA irman ištamaššir* "But when the enemy lands heard that Arnuwanda, my brother, was ill" KBo 3.4 i 6-7 (ten-year ann.), ed. AM 14f.; *ma-aḫ-ḫa-an-ma-za* ᵐ*Arnuandaš* ŠEŠ-*YA* DINGIR-*LIM-iš kišat* "But when Arnuwanda, my brother, became a god (i.e., died)" ibid. i 8; *ma-aḫ-ḫa-an-ma-za-kán* ᵈUTU-*ŠI ANA* ᴳᴵŠGU.ZA *ABIYA ēšḫat* "But when My Majesty had sat down on the throne of my father" ibid. 19; cf. with *kuwapi* instead of *maḫḫan*: *nuzakan ANA* ᴳᴵŠGU.ZA *ABIYA kuwapi ēšḫat nuza kē araḫzenaš* KUR.KUR.MEŠ ᴸᵁKÚR *INA* MU.10.KAM *tarḫḫun natkan kuenun* "When I had sat down on the throne of my father, I defeated these surrounding enemy lands in ten years and laid them low" ibid. 28-29; (Piḫḫuniya didn't rule in the Kaškean manner;) *ḫūdāk ma-aḫ-ḫa-an INA* ᵁᴿᵁ*Gašga UL ŠA* 1-*EN tapariyaš ēšta ašima* ᵐ*Piḫḫuniyaš ŠA* LUGAL-*UTTI iwar taparta* "Suddenly—when among the Kaška there was no rule by one person,—that P. ruled as a king" KBo 3.4 iii 74-75, ed. AM 88; [*ma-a*]*ḫ-ḫa-an-ma-an-za-an-kán* (var. GIM-*an*-) EGIR-*pa ūḫḫun* "But when I saw him (the enemy) behind (me)" KUB 14.16 ii 15 w. dupls. KUB 19.40:7 and KBo 12.37:3 (det. ann.), ed. AM 42f.; *ma-aḫ-ḫa-an-ma INA* ᵁᴿᵁ*Tarkuma ārḫḫun nu* ᵁᴿᵁ*Tarkuman arḫa warnunun* "But when I reached T., I burned T. down" KBo 4.4 iii 43-44 (det. ann.), AM 128f.; *nukan ma-aḫ-ḫa-an ANA* KASKAL ᵁᴿᵁ*Taggašta tiyanun* "When I had set out on the road to T." KBo 5.8 i 14-15 (det. ann.), ed. AM 148f.; *ma-aḫ-ḫa-an-ma ištantanun . . . ma-aḫ-ḫa-an-ma* (var. GIM-*an-ma*) *ŠA* KUR ᵁᴿᵁ*Taggašta* ERÍN.MEŠ *NARĀRĒ arḫa parāšeššir* "But when I had waited, . . . and when the auxiliary troops of T. had deployed themselves," (I received a sign from the bird(s) to proceed into the land of T.) KBo 5.8 i 18, 21-22 with dupl. KUB 19.36:16 (det. ann.), ed. AM 148f.; *našta ma-aḫ-ḫa-an* ᵁᴿᵁ*Timmuḫalan ANA* ᵈIM (var. ᵈU) *šipandaḫ*⸗*ḫun* "But when I had dedicated the city of T. to the Stormgod" KUB 19.37 ii 35 with dupl. KBo 16.16 ii 8, ed. AM 170f.; *nu ma-aḫ-ḫa-an aušta* [*anda*]*kan kuit ḫatkešnuwanteš* "And when (Aitakkama's oldest son) saw that they were besieged" (and that their grain was running short, he killed his father) KBo 4.4 ii 4-5, ed. AM 112f.; (Because I had not celebrated the great festival of *purulliya* in the *ḫešti*-house for the goddess Lelwani, I came up to Ḫattuša and celebrated it) *nukan* *ma-aḫ-ḫa-an INA* É *ḫešti* GAL-*in* EZEN-*an aššanunun* § *nuza ANA* KARAŠ.ḪI.A *uwātar INA* URU*Arduna iyanun* "And when I had provided for/arranged the great festival in the *ḫešti*-house, I reviewed (my) troops in Arduna" KBo 2.5 iii 46-48, ed. AM 190f. □ Götze understood the *m.* clause as a main clause because of the paragraph line and translated "und richtete zunächst ... ein grosses Fest aus". That the *m.* clauses followed by a paragraph line are truly subordinate clauses followed by main clauses beyond the line was convincingly argued by Ose, Sup. (1944) 25, 52; [*n*]*u tuk ma-aḫ-ḫa-an-ma* dUTU-*ŠI IŠTU AWAT ABI*[*K*]*A* EGIR-*an šaḫḫun nutta ANA AŠAR ABIKA titta*[*nu*]*nun* "But when I, My Majesty, sought you out because of the word of your father, and I installed you in the place of your father" KBo 5.9 i 19-20 (Dupp. treaty), ed. SV 1. 10ff. □ The position of temporal *maḫḫanma* after *nu tuk* is probably due to the desire of the speaker to place emphasis on the direct object *tuk* "you"; for *nu ... -ma* outside of double questions cf. *-ma* a 1′ b′ 4″ final paragraph; *numukan* GIM-*an* UN.MEŠ-*annaza* (var. UN.MEŠ-*annanza*) *ŠA* d*IŠTAR* GAŠAN-*YA kaniššūwar ŠA* ŠEŠ-*YA-ya* [(*aš*)]*šulan awer* "And when men saw my lady Šaušga's recognition of me and the favor of my brother (to me)" KUB 1.1 i 30-32 with dupl. KBo 3.6 i 26 (Ḫatt. i 30-32); cf. [*m*]*a-aḫ-ḫa-an-ma uit IŠTU* ⌜É⌝.LUGAL *ḫanneššar kuitki* EGIR-*pa ḫuittiyattat* KUB 19.67 i 1-2 (Ḫatt. iii 14-15), ed. NBr. 16f. and StBoT 24:18f., 72; [(*nušši kurur*)]*iyaḫḫun kururiyaḫḫunmašši* GIM-*an* "I made war on him. But when I made war on him, (I didn't do it as an impure act)" KUB 1.6 iii 12 with rest. from dupl. KUB 1.4:32 (Ḫatt. iii 66); note that here, contrary to expectation, *m.* follows its verb which is placed at the head of its clause with an anaphoric *-ma*, cf. sub *-ma* d; GIM-*an-ma-za-kán ŠA* DINGIR-*LIM aššulan uškiškiuwan teḫḫun* "As soon as I began to see the deity's favor, (with the deity's help things went better and better for me)" KBo 6.29 i 9-10 (Ḫatt. III), ed. Ḫatt. 44f.; (Both the lands to whom I wrote for help and those to whom I didn't write supported me,) *apāšma* GIM-*an ištamašta* "But when *he* (Urḫitešub) heard, (he fled to Šamuḫa)" KBo 6.29 ii 18 (Ḫatt. III), ed. Ḫatt. 48f.; *nu kāša ma-aḫ-ḫa-an epurešgauen* "Every time we tried to storm (the fortress, we didn't succeed in taking it)" KBo 18.54 rev. 12-13 (letter to king, NH), ed. Pecchioli Daddi, Mesopotamia 13-14:204, 207, cf. Neu, StBoT 5:44f.; [m*Piyam*]*aradušmamu* GIM-*an luriyaḫta* "When P. had defamed me," (and had set up Atpa in authority over me) KUB 19.5 obv. 7-8 (letter, NH), ed. Forrer, Forsch. I/1:90; m*Atpāšma* GIM-*an* INIM m*P*[*iy*]*amaradu IŠME* "But when A. heard P.'s word" ibid. 23; *kinunma* GIM-*an ŠA* EN-*YA ḫargan išdamaššer* "But now, when they heard of the death of my lord" KUB 19.23 rev. 15 (letter, NH); LÚ.MEŠ URU*Ḫatti* GIM-*an* dUTU-*ŠI* EN-*YA dammela* KAR-*at* "When His Majesty, my lord, found that the people of Ḫatti belonged to someone else" KUB 26.32 i 5-6 (oath of a scribe to Šupp. II), ed. Laroche, RA 47:74; cf. Güterbock, RHA XXII/74:105; [GI]M-*an-ma-kán ḫadanteya arḫa arḫun* "But when I disembarked (from the ships) on the dry land(?)" KBo 12.38 iii 10 (conquest of Cyprus), ed. Güterbock, JNES 26:76ff.; for further exx. of temporal *maḫḫan*/GIM-*an* with pret. in hist. texts cf. the indices in AM 298f., SV 2:197, Ḫatt. 122, 125, NBr 84, and AU 411, 415, and cf. bil. sec.

2″ in a prayer: *ma-aḫ-ḫa-an-ma-za* m*Mūwattalli*[*š ...*] DINGIR-*LIM-iš kišat* KUB 21.27 i 38-39 (prayer of Pud.).

3″ in mythological narratives: *nu* GIM-*an* d*Irširr*[*uš* IN]IM.MEŠ-*ar ištamaššir* "And when the I.-goddesses heard the words" KUB 33.95 iv 6 + KUB 33.93 iv 1 (Ullik. I A iv 6′), ed. JCS 5:156; cf. KBo 26.58 iv 41 (Ullik. I A iv 41), ed. ibid. 158; *nu* GIM-*an* MUŠ*Ḫedammušša* [*warš*(*ulan* KAŠ *ištaḫta*)] "Now when Ḫ. had smelled the odor (of) the beer" KBo 19.111:5 with dupl. KUB 33.84:6 (Ḫedammu), ed. StBoT 14:58f.; GIM-*an-ma-at* [UR(U*Ninuwa erir*)] "But when they reached Nineveh" ABoT 48:10 with dupl. KBo 19.108 left col. 9 (Appu), ed. StBoT 14:16f.; *ma-aḫ-ḫa-an-ma* dÉ.A-*aš* dL[AMMA?-*aš uddār*] *išta*[*m*]*ašta* "But when Ea had heard [the words of] dL[AMMA?]" KUB 36.5 i 7-8 (kingship of dLAMMA), translit. Myth 150; *nu ma-aḫ-ḫa-an* d*Ḫepadduš* d*Tašmišun aušta* "And when Ḫ. saw T." KUB 33.106 ii 7 (Ullik. III A), ed. JCS 6.20f.; *nu ma-aḫ-ḫa-an* d*Tašmišuš memian memiyauwanzi zinnit* "Now when T. had finished speaking" ibid. 10-11.

b. with present-future, cf. AU 255 n. 4 —

1′ hist. pres. "as, when": *nu ABUYA ma-aḫ-ḫa-an nannai* "And as my father was driving" KUB 19.18 i 24 (DŠ frag. 15), ed. JCS 10:76; *nukan ma-aḫ-ḫa-an* [^{m}*Arnuwa*]*ndaš* ^{m}*Zitašša* KUR-*e kattanda aranzi* "And when A. and Z. came down into the country" KBo 5.6 ii 31-32 (DŠ frag. 28), ed. JCS 10:93; [*nu ABUYA m*]*a-aḫ-ḫa-an* [*ištam*]*ašzi* "When [my father h]eard" ibid. ii 39-40; cf. ibid. iii 5-6; LÚ ^{URU}*Aššurmazakan ma-aḫ-ḫa-an pāriyan ištamašzi* "But when the Assyrian overheard(?)" KUB 14.16 i 18, ed. AM 28f.; ^{LÚ}KÚR KUR ^{ÍD}*Kummišmaḫašma* [*ma-a*]*ḫ-ḫa-an ištamašzi* "But when the enemy from the Kummišmaḫa-River Land heard" KBo 5.8 i 40-41, ed. AM 150f.

2′ present or future "when, as soon as" — a′ introducing time expressions (a representative selection is given untranslated, with only one well-preserved ref. cited for each, all exx. NS — 1″ times of year: GIM-*an zēnaš kišari* KUB 38.32 obv. 8; [GIM-*a*]*n-ma zeni* DÙ-*ri* KBo 2.13 obv. 25; GIM-*an-ma ḫamešḫanza* DÙ!-*ri* KBo 2.7 rev. 4; *ma-aḫ-ḫa-an-ma* Ú.BURU$_{7}$-*anza kišari* KUB 30.39 obv. 7; GIM-*an-ma ḫamišḫi* DÙ-*ri* KUB 25.23 i 8; GIM-*an-ma TEŠI* DÙ-*ri* KBo 2.7 obv. 9; *ma-aḫ-ḫa-an-*[*k*]*án* BURU$_{14}$-*anza kišari* KUB 31.84 iii 65; GIM-*an-ma ŠA* AN.TAḪ.ŠUM *meḫur tiyazi* KUB 18.12 i 3; GIM-*an-ma-wa* EZEN MU.KAM *kišari* KBo 14.21 i 30; *nu ma-aḫ-ḫa-an* ITU[.4.KAM *tiya*(*zzi*)] KUB 44.59 rev. 5 w. dupl. KBo 17.65 obv. 35; GIM-*an-ma ANA* ITU.KAM UD.13.KAM *tiyazi* KBo 2.4 i 23.

2″ times of day: *ma-aḫ-ḫa-an-ma* GE$_{6}$-*anza lukzi* MUL.UD.ZAL.LI-*kan uizzi lukzi nawi* KUB 9.15 ii 16-18; *ma-aḫ-ḫa-an-ma lukkatta naš* . . . KUB 1.13 ii 12; *ma-aḫ-ḫa-an-na lukkatta nankan* . . . KBo 4.2 i 38; *ma-aḫ-ḫa-an-ma* ^{d}UTU-*uš uizzi* KUB 1.11 i 6; *ma-aḫ-ḫa-an-ma-kán* $^{[d]}$UTU-*uš ūpzi* KUB 46.57 i 7-8; *ma-aḫ-ḫa-an-ma* UD-*az takšan tīēzzi* KBo 3.5 iii 14-15; *ma-aḫ-ḫa-an-ma* UD-*az waḫnuzi* KUB 29.40 ii 11; *ma-aḫ-ḫa-an-ma* UD-*az* 2 *AMMATI weḫzi* KBo 3.5 iv 18; *ma-aḫ-ḫa-an-ma* [U]D-*MU* EGIR-*pa* 2 *AMMATI waḫzi* KUB 1.13 i 48-49; *nukan ma-aḫ-ḫa-an ANA* UD-*MI* 5 *gipeššar* 8 *wakšur āšzi* KUB 30.31 i 45-46; *ma-aḫ-ḫa-an-ma-kán ANA* UD-*MI* 2 $^{1}/_{2}$ *kipeššar* 5 *wakšur paizzi* KUB 30.31 i 6-7; *ma-aḫ-ḫa-an-ma* ^{d}UTU AN![-*E l*]*aḫurnuzzieš appanzi* KBo 14.142 ii 17; *ma-aḫ-ḫa-an-ma mištiliya meḫur tīēzzi* KBo 5.2 iv 27-28; *ma-aḫ-ḫa-an-ma* GE$_{6}$-*anza kīša* KUB 13.4 iii 46; [*m*]*a-aḫ-ḫa-an-ma nekuz meḫur kišari* KUB 1.13 iii 64; GIM-*an-ma nekuza mēḫuni kišari* KBo 2.13 obv. 19; *nu ma-aḫ-ḫa-an nekuzi* VBoT 24 i 10; *ma-aḫ-ḫa-an-*⌜*ma*⌝ *apedani* UD-*ti nekuz meḫur* MUL-*aš watkuzzi* KUB 29.4 ii 28-29; *ma-aḫ-ḫa-an-ma ištarniya ḫāli* [*t*]*īēzzi* KUB 29.52 iv 2-3; *ma-aḫ-ḫa-an-ma* EN.NU.UN MURUB$_{4}$ *kiš*[*ar*]*i* KUB 1.11 + KUB 29.57 i 1; GIM-*an-ma āppazzi*(sic) *ḫāli tīyazi* KUB 42.98 i 22.

b′ introducing actions — 1″ MS: *ma-a-aḫ-ḫa-an-ma-at* EGIR-*pa aranzi* "As soon as they (i.e., the Kaška people) get back" KUB 17.21 iv 16 (prayer of Arn. I and Ašm., MH/MS), ed. Kaškäer 160f.; *ma-a-aḫ-ḫa-an-ta kāš tuppianza anda wemiyazzi nu MAḪAR* ^{d}UTU-*ŠI liliwaḫḫuwanzi unni* "As soon as this tablet reaches you, drive quickly to His Majesty" Maşat 75/10:3-7 (letter, MH/MS), ed. Alp, Belleten 44 (1980) 39f.; cf. *ma-aḫ-ḫa-an-ša-ma-aš kāš tuppianza anda wemizzi* Maşat 75/11:4-5 (letter, MH/MS), ed. ibid. 40f.; *numu ma-aḫ-ḫa-an memian* EGIR-*pa udanzi* "As soon as they bring word back to me" Maşat 75/113:22-23, ed. Alp, FsLaroche 30f.; *ma-a-aḫ-ḫa-an-ma* ^{GIŠ}*ḫulugannin waḫnuwanzi* "but as soon as they turn the chariot" IBoT 1.36 iv 12 (*MEŠEDI* instr., MH/MS), ed. Jakob-Rost, MIO 11:198f., cf. ibid. i 22, 23, 64, ii 23, 27, 29; *ma-a-aḫ-ḫa-an-ma-kán* LUGAL-*uš* ^{GIŠ}*ḫuluganaz katta tīēzzi* ibid. 18, cf. 24; *nu ma-a-aḫ-ḫa-an* DINGIR.MEŠ *irḫāizzi* KBo 15.33 ii 28 (rit., MH/MS), cf. ibid. 39.

2″ NS — a″ OH/NS: *ma-aḫ-ḫa-an-ma kē ḫūitār šarazzi* ^{É}*kašgaštipaz* KÁ.GAL-*az katta ari* KBo 10.24 i 10-13 (KI.LAM fest.); *ma-aḫ-ḫa-an-ma-aš-kán* KÁ-*aš and*[*a ari*] LUGAL-*uš* EGIR-*pa aruwāizz*[*i*] KBo 10.28 iii 5-6 (KI.LAM fest.).

b″ MH/NS: *andamakan* ^{LÚ}NIMGIR *kuiš* ^{URU}*Ḫattuši šer ma-aḫ-ḫa-an* LÚ.MEŠ EN.NU.UN *auri ḫalzāi* KBo 13.58 iii 13-14 (instr. for *ḪAZANNU*), ed. Otten, BagM 3:94-95 with n. 17; cf. ii 21-22; *ma-aḫ-ḫa-an* [*tuzz*]*iš* ERÍN.MEŠ ANŠE.KUR.RA.ḪI.A *anda ari* KUB 13.20 i 6 (instr. of Tudḫ.); *ma-aḫ-ḫa-an-ma* ^{LÚ}KÚR *aki našmakan*

KIN-*az aššanuddāri* ibid. i 22; *nu ma-aḫ-ḫa-a*[*n*] $^{LÚ.MEŠ}$NÍ.ZU *ŠA* ^{LÚ}KÚR *ūrkin uwanzi nu memian ḫudāk udanzi* KUB 13.2 i 5-6 (*BĒL MADGALTI* instr.), ed. von Schuler, Dienstanw. 41; *ma-aḫ-ḫa-an-ma* NAM.RA.ḪI.A *pianz*[*i*] KUB 31.84 iii 68 (ibid.), ed. ibid. 50; *ma-aḫ-ḫa-an-ma ḫalinduwa taranzi* KBo 5.11 iv 9, cf. 18, 23 (instr. for the gateman).

c″ NH: *zig*⸗*an* GIM-*an ištamašti* "as soon as you hear him" KBo 5.3 ii 34 (Šupp. I treaty w. Ḫuqq.), ed. SV 2:116f.; *ma-aḫ-ḫa-an-na* DAM-*KA tatti* "when you shall take your wife" KBo 5.9 i 24 (Dupp.), ed. SV 1:12f.; [(*nutt*)]*a* GIM-*an* [^{d}UT(U-*ŠI* EGIR-*pa ḫ*)]*atrāmi* "when I, My Majesty, write back to you" KUB 21.5 iii 37 (Alakš.) rest. from dupl. KBo 19.73a + KUB 21.1 iii 22, ed. SV 2:70f.; *nu kī* GIM-*an ṬUPPU udanzi* "when they bring this tablet" KBo 18.24 i 13 (letter to Šalmaneser I), ed. Otten, AfO 22:112 with n. 8.

c. GIM-*an* . . . *kuwapi* (only Ḫatt. III), cf. *mān* . . . *kuwapi*(*kki*) sub *mān* 9 d 2′: GIM-*an-ma uit* Š[(EŠ-*Y*)]*A kuwapi INA* KUR *Mizrīpait* "At the time my brother went into Egyptian territory (to battle)" KUB 1.1 ii 69 (Ḫatt. ii 69), with virtually no difference in meaning but without GIM-*an* cf. *nu uit ABUYA kuwapi INA* KUR ^{URU}*Mizri p*[*ait*] KUB 14.13 i 47 (Murš. II prayer); GIM-*an-ma ABUYA kuwapi* BA.ÚŠ "At the time my father died," (my brother Muwatalli sat down on the throne of his father, and I was governing lands before him) KBo 6.29 i 22 (shorter history of Ḫatt. III), ed. Ḫatt. 46f.; Götze (Ḫatt. 86, comment on ii 69): "*kuwapi* ist, nach KBo VI 29. I 22 . . . zu urteilen, in der Stellung nach GIM-*an* (= *maḫḫan*) 'als' fast bedeutungslos." Probably not [GIM-*an-ma*] *ḫamešḫi kuwapi ḫēun karpzi* KUB 35.139 obv. 6 as in DLL 171, but [*A-NA*] *ḫamešḫi kuwapi* . . . ; cf. *ANA zeni ḫamešḫiya kuwa*[*pi* . . .] *appanzi* KUB 25.30 i 10.

6. GIM-*an* GIM-*an*, GIM-*an imma*, GI[M-*an imm*]*a* GIM-*an* "in whatever manner, however" (late NH), cf. Laroche, RA 47:73 ("quoquo modo"): *ammukma kēdai* KASKAL-*ši* GIM-*an* GIM-*an nakkēškit* GIM-*an-za* GIM-*an kišḫaḫat taparriyan*[*m*]*a UL kuedaniki pedi wašdanunun* "However difficult it was for me on this mission, whatever happened to me (lit., for me on this road however many times it became difficult, however I became), in no place did I find fault with the command" KUB 40.1 rev.! 18-20 (letter, NH); *mānmu* [EN-*Y*]*A* GIM-*an* GIM-*an peḫuteš*⸗*kiz*[*zi*] GIM-*an-mu* [GI(M-*an*)] DUGUD-*zi* (var. DUGUD-*eš*[*zi*]) "However my lord may carry me off (lit. If my lord should carry me off in any manner), however difficult it becomes for me, (I will not desert or defect from my lord)" KUB 26.32 iii 3-4 + KUB 23.44 rev.! 12-13 (oath of a scribe, Šupp. II), ed. Laroche, RA 47:72f. iii 16-17, restorations and variant from the dupl. or parallel KBo 14.113:2-3; *mānma* GI[M-*an im-*]⸢*ma*⸣ GIM-*an* "But if (it should happen) in any way whatsoever, (I will protect only the offspring of my lord Šupp.)" KUB 31.106:10 + KUB 23.44 rev.! 6 (oath of a scribe, Šupp. II), ed. Laroche, RA 47:72f. ("Quoi qu'il arrive?"); □ [. . .]x *ma-a-an im-ma* [*ma-a-an*? . . . *kēd*]*ani uddāni šer ḫ*[*u*- . . . .] KUB 35.92 + KBo 9.146 rev. 16-17 (rit. for Išḫara, NS) and [*ma-a-an*?] *im-ma ma-a-an* [. . .] *tarḫta* KUB 31.71 ii 20-21 (deposition?, NH), might indicate that the construction is to be read **mān mān* and **mān imma mān*, but the latter two passages are so badly broken as to allow no certainty for the suggested restorations. And since there is no secure example of syll. writing *ma-a-an* for the GIM-*an* in this construction, we prefer to read *maḫḫan maḫḫan*. *našmat* GIM-*an ašān imma* :*maršašša mēḫur* "Or whatever sort of treacherous time it may be" KBo 4.14 ii 58-59 (Šupp. II), ed. Stefanini, AANL 20:42f., 63; cf. adj. *marša*-.

The position of *māḫḫanda* q.v. and *m.* in their clauses requires comment.

māḫḫanda, which occurs in OH with the same mng. as *maḫḫan* 2, is clause initial nine out of ten times. The exception is *mānḫanda* in KBo 25.112 ii 14 (OS).

In mng. 1 *maḫḫan* always follows the compared word and does not determine its case.

In mngs. 2, 3, and 4 the subject of the clause usually either precedes *maḫḫan* or is expressed by an enclitic pron. appended to *m.* Rarely only a part of the phrase constituting the subject may precede *m.* (e.g., *tuel maḫḫan* SAG.DU-*KA*, *gimraš* GIM-*an* SISKUR.SISKUR).

In mng. 5 (temporal usage) *m.* is usually (80-90%) clause initial. It can be preceded by *nu* and its enclitics, *kāša* "lo!", temporal expressions such as *karu, kinun, lukkatta, INA* UD.x.KAM, *nekuz meḫur, ḫudak*, by the optative-potential particle *ma-an*, or by words transposed to the head of the clause to call attention to them, often because they are emphatic, have an anaphoric function, or introduce a new subject. Cf. Götze, Ḫatt. 122 s.v. GIM-*an*.

In mng. 6 the subject, if one is expressed, always precedes GIM-*an* GIM-*an*.

There is no use of *maḫḫan* or GIM-*an* in main clauses with the meaning "first of all" (German "zunächst"), as Götze claimed (AM 246). For refutation of Götze's arguments see Ose, Sup. 25 n. 2, 52, and see discussion of KBo 2.5 iii 46ff. above sub 5 a 2′ b′ 1″.

Hrozný, MDOG 56 (1915) 35 (temporal "als"), idem, SH (1917) 185 ("als, nachdem, sobald, wenn; wie"). Cf. bibliography at the beginning of the major sections.

māḫḫanda, mānḫanda, mān ḫanda subordinating conj.; just as; OH; written syll. (OS, MS) and (?) GIM-*anda* (OH/NS).†

ma-a-aḫ-ḫa-an-da KBo 6.2 iii 19, KBo 19.1 iii 45, KBo 17.1 iii (1), KBo 17.22 iii 8, KBo 25.122 ii 4 (all OS), [*m*]*a-a-aḫ-ḫa-an-ta* KUB 33.59 iv 7 (OH/MS), *ma-a-an-ḫa-an-da* KBo 25.112 ii 14 (coll.), KBo 22.1:22, KUB 28.75 ii 24 (all OS), *ma-a-an ḫa-an-da* (two words) KBo 16.45 obv. 7 (MS), GIM-*an-da* KUB 31.74 ii 17 (OH/NS), this last may be an example of *māḫḫanda* or of *māḫḫan* + -*da* "you", the context is broken.

a. with correlative *apeniššan*/*QĀTAMMA* in the following clause: *ANA* [*ḫal*]*pūti* (var. GIŠ*ḫalpūti*) *ma-a-an-ḫa-an-d*[*a*] *māldi kēa QĀTAMMA* "As he chants before(?) the *ḫ*., so also (he chants) these things in the same way" KBo 25.112 ii 14-15 (invocations to Ḫattian deities, OS), w.par. KUB 28.75 ii 24, translit. Neu, StBoT 25 p. 191 and 194, resp.; cf. StBoT 2:34; *ma-a-aḫ-ḫa-an-da* (var. *ma-aḫ-ḫa-an*) *areš*[(*meš*)] *šumešša apeniš-šan īšte*[(*n*)] (var. *ēšten*) "Do (var. be) just as your comrades (with regard to *šaḫḫan* and *luzzi*)" KBo 6.2 + KBo 22.62 iii 19-20 (Law §55, OS) with dupl. KBo 6.3 iii 22-23 (early NS) and KBo 6.6 i 29 (NS), ed. Friedrich, HG 36f., cf. StBoT 23:143f. and Oettinger Stammbildung 508 n. 32, □ *i-iš-te-e-ni* may be found in KBo 22.1:27 (OS), *i-iš-te-ni-i* ibid. 33; in Law §55 the omission of the verb in the *māḫḫanda* clause is unexpected; only *eš-* "to be" is regularly omitted in nominal sentences; cf. *maḫḫan* 2, especially KUB 30.10 rev. 15-16, KBo 15.10 ii 5-6, KBo 16.47 i 6-7; no ex. shows omission of a verb other than *eš-* in this type of comparative *maḫḫan* / *māḫḫanda* clause; *ma-a-aḫ-ḫa-an-da* x[. . .] *watkutta nu Labar-našša* LUGAL-*w*[*aš* . . .] *ḫaššeš ḫanzā*[*šš*]*eš QĀTAMMA wa*[*tkuwandu*?] "Just as the [. . .] springs away, in the same way [let] the children and grandchildren of Labarna the king spring away" KBo 25.122 ii 4-6 (blessings on Labarna, OS), ed. StBoT 2:33, StBoT 5:194f., cf. StBoT 25:204; cf. *ma-a-aḫ-ḫa-an-da* KBo 6.2 + KBo 19.1 iii 45-46 (Law § 65, OS), with NS var. *ma-aḫ-ḫa-an*.

b. without a correlative: [*ma-a-a*]*n-ḫa-an-da* (var. *ma-a-an*) dUTU-*uš* dIM-*aš nēpiš tē*[(*kan-na*) . . .] *uktūri* (var. [. . .]-*re-eš*) LUGAL-*uš* SAL.LUGAL-*ašša* DUMU.MEŠ-*ša* (var. DUMU.MEŠ-*ešša*) *uktūreš aš*[(*a*)]*nd*[*u*] (var. -*tu*) "Just as the Sungod, the Stormgod, heaven and earth . . . are everlasting, let the king, the queen and the princes be everlasting" KBo 17.1 iii 1-2 with dupl. KBo 17.3 ii 15-iii 2 (rit., OS), ed. StBoT 8:30f.; *mānšamaš ABI parnašma tarnai nušmaš ma-a-an-ḫa-an-da ḫatreškizzi nattašamaš* LÚ.MEŠDUGUD-*aš tuppi ḫazzian ḫarzi* "When my father lets you (pl.) go to your house, just as he customarily writes to you, has he not inscribed a tablet for you dignitaries?" (followed by a quote from the tablet) KBo 22.1:21-23 (instr., OS), slightly different tr. Archi, FsLaroche 47 ("comme il a l'habitude de prescrire").

c. in broken context and written as two words: *nu ma-a-an ḫa-an-da* DUMU.SAL.MEŠ [. . .] *U* f*Ḫaniyatta kēa* DUMU.SAL.MEŠ x[. . .] KBo 16.45 obv. 7-8 (MS), cf. *kēa QATAMMA* in KBo 25.112 ii 14-15 cited above.

māḫḫanda is all but once KBo 25.112 ii 14 and par.) clause initial. See the discussion at the end of the *maḫḫan* article.

Hrozný, SH (1917) 185 ("wenn" u. ä.); Carruba, StBoT 2 (1966) 32-34; Otten and Souček, AfO 21 (1966) 5f.; StBoT 8 (1969) 98; Hoffner, JNES 31 (1972) 30; Starke, StBoT 23 (1977) 192.

Cf. *mān*, *maḫḫan*.

maḫirraši- Hurr.; belonging to the market place; NH.†

1 NINDA⌜.SIG⌝ ^d^*Iršappiniš damkarrašši* KI.MIN (=*paršiya*) 1 NINDA. ⌜SIG⌝ DINGIR. MEŠ *ma-ḫi-i-ir-ra-ši-na* (over eras.) KI.MIN "He breaks one thin bread (for) Iršappa of commerce; he breaks one thin bread (for) the gods belonging to the market place" KUB 27.1 ii 23-24 (cult of Ištar), ed. Lebrun, Samuha 78 (misread).

The Hurrian word is borrowed from Akk. *maḫīru* "market place".

Laroche, RA 48 (1954) 220, GLH 165.

maḫit (Hurr. epithet of the goddess ^d^NIN. GAL); MH.†

... 3 MUŠEN.GAL *ANA* ^d^NIN.GAL *ma-ḫi-it tūḫulziya šipanti* KUB 45.47 ii 9-12 (fest., MH/MS?), cf. Otten, MDOG 83:55f. n. 7, Imparati, FsLaroche 169-76. Cf. ^d^Maḫitti (iv 17) and ^d^Maḫittēna (pl.) (iii 8) in the same text. For the Hurr. word see GLH 165 sub *maḫitti-*.

(GIŠ)maḫla- n. com.; branch of a grapevine; from OS to MH/NS.

sg. nom. *ma-aḫ-la-aš* KUB 24.9 iii 25, KUB 24.11 iii 16 (both MH/NS), ^GIŠ^*ma-a-aḫ-la-aš* KUB 43.23 rev. 21 (OS); **acc.** ^GIŠ^*ma-aḫ-la-an* KBo 6.12 i 1, KBo 6.11 i 12, 15, KUB 29.1 iv 13, HT 38 obv. 9 (all OH/NS); **loc.** ^GIŠ^*ma-aḫ-li* KBo 6.12 i 3 (OH/NS), ^GIŠ^*ma-a-aḫ-li* KBo 21.22:46 (OH/MS).

pl. acc. ^GIŠ^*ma-aḫ-lu-uš* KUB 29.1 iv 15, 16 (OH/NS); **broken** ^GIŠ^*ma-a-aḫ*[-...] KUB 43.23 rev. 5 (OS); OS and MS regularly write the first syllable plene.

a. produces grape clusters: *nuza* 1 ŠAḪ *māḫḫan* ŠAḪ.TUR.ḪI.A *mekkuš ḫaškizzi kēllaz ŠA* ^GIŠ^KIRI₆.G[EŠTIN] 1-*ašša* ^GIŠ^*ma-a-aḫ-la-aš* ŠAḪ-*aš iwar mūriuš mekkuš ḫaškiddu* "Just as one sow bears many piglets, let every single (1-*ašš⸗a*) (vine) branch of this vineyard, like the sow, bear many grape clusters" KUB 43.23 rev. 19-22 (blessings upon Labarna, OS), ed. Ehelolf, OLZ 1933:5 ('jede einzelne Rebe'); cf. also Otten and Siegelová, AfO 23:36 and Archi, FsMeriggi² 34.

b. contrasted with the roots of a grapevine: *nu* ^GIŠ^GEŠTIN-*aš* ^GIŠ^*ma-aḫ-la-an tianzi* KI.MIN (= *nu kiššan memiyanzi*) ^GIŠ^GEŠTIN-*wa maḫḫan katta šūrkuš* (D8: *šurk*[*in*]) *šarāmawa* ^GIŠ^*ma-aḫ-lu-uš* (D9: ^GIŠ^*ma-aḫ-la-an*) *šīyaizzi* LUGAL-*ša* SAL.LUGAL-*ša* (D10: [LUGAL-*u*]*šša* SAL. LUGAL-*aš*) *katta šurkuš kattama* ^GIŠ^*ma-aḫ-lu-uš šiyandu* "They place a branch of a grapevine, and speak as follows: 'Just as the grapevine sends down roots (var. a root) and sends up branches (var. a branch), let the king and queen also send down roots and send up (text erroneously: send down) branches'" KUB 29.1 iv 13-16 (rit. for foundation of a palace, NS) with dupls. D=HT 38 obv. 7-9, ed. Schwartz, OrNS 16:38f. ("vine branch"), 45 (citing parallels to this figure of speech in ancient West Semitic texts), Kellerman, Diss. 19, 31.

c. trained or made to grow along a supporting surface: [... *š*]*aliki* ^GIŠ^*ma-a-aḫ-li napa iškiši⸗tti āppa lāk* "Approach the branch (of the grapevine) and train (it) on your back" KBo 21.22 rev. 46 (incant., OH/MS), ed. Kellerman, Tel Aviv 5 (1978) 200, 202; cf. sub *lak-* 3, *laknu-* 4.

d. fresh or newly grown (*ḫuelpi-*) vine branch: KUB 24.11 iii 6 with dupls. KUB 24.9 iii 25, KBo 21.8 iii 6, ed. Jakob-Rost, THeth 2:46f. ("eine junge Rebe"), tr. Sommer apud Ehelolf, OLZ 1933:6 ("Erstlingsrebe").

e. laws concerning theft of a *m.*: [(*takku* ^GIŠ^GEŠTIN)-*an našma*] ^GIŠ^*ma-aḫ-la-an našma* ^GIŠ^*karpinan* [*našma* SUM.SIKIL.SAR *kui*]*ški tāyezzi karū* [*ANA* 1 ^GIŠ^GEŠTIN x GÍ]N.GÍN KÙ.BABBAR *ANA* 1 ^GIŠ^*ma-aḫ-li* 1 GÍN.GÍN KÙ.BABBAR ... [*peškir*] ... *kinuna takku arauwannieš* [(6 GÍN.G)ÍN KÙ.BABBAR *p*]*āi takku* ÌR-*ša* 3 GÍN.GÍN KÙ.BABBAR *pāi* "If someone steals a vine, or a vine branch, or a *k.*, or garlic, formerly [they used to give x she]kel of silver [for each (lit. one) vine,] (and) one shekel of silver for each (lit. one) vine branch ...Now, if (the thief) is a free man, he gives six shekels of silver, but if he is a slave, he gives three shekels of silver" KBo 6.12 (c) i 1-7 (Law § 101, OH/NS) with dupl. KUB 29.21:1-2 (NS), line 1 restored from KBo 6.13 colophon; □ Presumably the thief would be stealing a vine (^GIŠ^GEŠTIN) in the narrow sense of a two or three year old vine (German: "Reifling"), as older stocks are virtually impossible to transplant. Such a young stock would be worth about the same as a mature branch (see Ehelolf, OLZ 1933:6); note that it is the same fine for the theft of a GIŠGEŠTIN as for a *maḫla-*; *takku taggaliyandaza* GIŠKIRI6.GEŠTIN GIŠ*ma-aḫ-la-an kuiški tāiyazi takku* 1 *ME* GIŠ!-*ṢÚ* (var. o3 9: 1 *ME* GIŠ.ḪI.A, KBo 19.9:9: [. . .] *ME*ḪI.A GIŠ.ḪI.A) [(6)] GÍN KÙ.BABBAR *pāi parnaššēa šuwāizzi* [(*takk*)]*u UL-ma tag-galiyanda nu* GIŠ*ma*(over eras.)-*aḫ-la-an tāi*[*yazi*] (var. [*d*]*āiezzi*) 3 GÍN KÙ.BABBAR *pāi* "If someone steals a vine branch from a . . .-ed vineyard, if there are 100 plants (lit. trees), he gives six shekels of silver, . . . but if they are not . . . -ed, and he steals a vine branch, he gives three shekels of silver" KBo 6.11 i 12-15 (Law § 108, OH/NS) with dupls. KBo 19.9:9-12 and KUB 29.23 (o3):8-11.

Hittite texts have preserved terms for the grapevine, i.e., the entire plant (GIŠGEŠTIN, which is occasionally a young, still transplantable "Reifling" and at other times a mature "Weinstock"), for the vine branch (GIŠ*maḫla-*), the grape cluster (*muri-*) and the roots (*šurki-*). Cf. also *akuka-* (a part of the vine?).

Ehelolf, OLZ 1933:5f.; Hoffner, AlHeth (1974) 39ff., 113.

UZU**maḫrai-** see UZU*muḫ*(*ḫa*)*rai-*.

NINDA**maḫḫue/i(l)la-** n. com.; (a kind of bread or pastry); NH.†

sg. nom. [NINDA*ma-a*]*ḫ-ḫu-i-la-aš* KUB 35.70 iii 5; **sg. acc.** NINDA*ma-aḫ-ḫu-e-el-la-an* KBo 13.62 obv. 9.

[o o]x-*ya-ma-mu kuit kī :tapašaš uttar ḫatrāit* f*Aruḫipaš-at-mu ḫatrāiš namma* NINDA*ma-aḫ-ḫu-e-el-la-an* GIŠ*INBU-ya ezzazzi* "This matter of a fever(?) (about) which you wrote to me, A. (also) wrote to me (about) it. Furthermore (I hear that) (s)he is eating *m.*-bread and fruit." (I am very distressed about this.) KBo 13.62 obv. 7-9 (letter, NH); NINDA*m.* of ½ *UPNI* is also in a list of breads KUB 35.70 iii 5.

The partial phonetic similarity of NINDA*maḫ-ḫuella-* and NINDA*muḫḫila-* is no proof that they are the same word.

Laroche, apud van Brock, RHA XX/71 (1962) 166; Hoffner, AlHeth (1973) 172.

maḫḫuitta v.; (mng. unkn.); MH/NS.†

[. . .]-*pa ma-*⌈*aḫ-ḫu-it-ta*⌉ *ku-i-ša-*[o] KUB 48.75:5 (Soldiers' Oath), ed. Oettinger, StBoT 22:16f., who reads [. . .]x-*pa ma-ni-* x x x x *ku-i-ša*. Collation showed word space after *-pa*. The preceding word is probably either [EGIR]-*pa* or [*a-ap*]-*pa*. The interpretation of *maḫḫuitta* as pret. 3 sg. of a verb is based upon the assumption that the following *kuiša*[-o] begins a new clause or sentence, as interpreted by Oettinger in his translation "und wer." For the dating of this and other copies of the Soldiers' Oath, cf. StBoT 22:95ff.

maḫurai- n. com.; (mng. unkn.); OS.†

[*šēr*]*a*!*ššan* 1 *ma-ḫu-ra-i*[*n* . . .] ABoT 35 obv. 9, translit. StBoT 25:122. Possibly the same as UZU*muḫ*(*ḫu*)*rai-*, q.v.

maḫḫūri- n.; (a foodstuff); from MH?.†

EGIR-*andama ma-aḫ-ḫu-u-ri da*[-. . .] *šeraš-šan* LÀL *tarnai na*[*t* . . .] "Afterwards [(s)he/they(?) . . .] *m.*, and on top (s)he adds honey and [. . .]" KUB 32.95 rev. 4-5 (rit., MS?); [. . .]x NINDA.KU7 UZUNÍG.GIG-*y*[*a* . . . -]⌈*e*⌉-*ez-zi ma-aḫ-ḫu-u-ri*[(-) . . . -]⌈x⌉-*ez-zi* KBo 24.73 obv. 6-7 (rit., MS?). An additional reference in Hurr. context is ABoT 39 iii 8 + KBo 20.129 iii 27 given in GLH 165, if it is the same word.

If *maḫḫūri* in KUB 32.95 rev. 5 is the direct obj., the word is an *i*-stem neut. If it is loc., we cannot be certain of either the stem (*r*-stem, *a*-stem?) or the gender. In KBo 24.73 NINDA. KU7 and UZUNÍG.GIG seem to be objects of the first verb, and *maḫḫūri*[(-) . . .] and [. . .] of the second verb.

maḫḫurišša; (mng. unkn.).†

āškimakan [. . . (-)]*anda naš ma-aḫ-ḫu-*⌈*ri-iš-ša*⌉ [. . .] in broken context KUB 36.2b ii 17-19, translit. Myth. 147 (myth of the kingship of dLAMMA).

Possibly related to *maḫḫūri-* n.

mai-, miya-, miešš- v.; **1.** to grow, **2.** to grow up, reach ripeness, or maturity, **3.** (of baby) to arrive at term, be born, **4.** to increase, be plentiful, abundant(?), **5.** to thrive, prosper; from OS.

act. pres. sg. 3 *ma-a-i* KUB 17.10 i 14 (OH/MS), KBo 3.7 i 7 (OH/NS), KUB 17.28 ii 47 (MH/NS), KUB 8.27 left edge 2a (pre-NH/NS), *mi-i-*⌜*e*⌝*-eš-zi* KUB 36.55 obv. 36; **pl. 3** *ma-a-i-an*[*-zi*] KUB 34.11:11 (pre-NH/NS); *mi-eš-ša*[*-an-zi*] KUB 16.76:11 (NH).

pret. sg. 1 *mi-ia-ḫu-un* 2464/c obv. 12 (StBoT 5:117 n. 2); **sg. 3** *mi-e-eš-ta* KUB 33.106 iii 14, 36, KUB 44.4 rev. 6 (both NH), [*mi?-*]⌜*e*⌝*-eš-ta* KBo 21.41 rev. 29 (MS).

imp. sg. 3 *ma-a-ú* KBo 25.112 ii 7, (8) (OS), KBo 7.28 obv. 15, 41 (OH/MS), KUB 12.43:2, 3 (MS), KBo 3.7 i 5 (OH/NS), KUB 8.3 obv. 14 (pre-NH/NS), KUB 14.12 rev. 14 (Murš. II), *mi-e-eš-du* KBo 22.116 obv. (18), 21, 22 (NS), KUB 24.1 iv 15 (Murš. II); **pl. 2** *ma-iš-te-en* KBo 8.35 ii 15 (MH/MS); **pl. 3** *mi-e-eš-ša-du* KUB 24.2 rev. 16 (Murš. II).

mid. pres. sg. 3 *mi-ia-ri* KBo 17.63:8 (pre-NH/MS?), KBo 2.35 rt. col. 8, KUB 8.35 obv. 2-10 passim (all pre-NH/NS), KBo 13.2 obv. 9 (NH), KUB 33.120 iii 11 (NS), *mi-i-ia-a-ri* KUB 43.55 ii 13 (pre-NH/NS), KBo 11.8:4 (NS), *mi-i-ia-ri* KUB 44.59 rev. 4 (NS).

mid. pret. sg. 1 *mi-eš-ḫa-ti* KUB 30.10 obv. 11 (MH/MS); **sg. 3** *mi-ia-ti* KBo 17.22 ii 4 (OS), KBo 12.3 iv 3 (OH/NS), KBo 17.65 rev. 39, 43 (MS?), KBo 17.63:4 (MH?/NS), KBo 13.49:(3) (NS).

mid. imp. sg. 3 *mi-i-ia-ru* KBo 3.38 obv. 6 (OH/NS), KUB 17.28 iii 1 (MS?/NS), *mi-ia-ru* KBo 22.116 obv. 17 (NS).

iter. act. pres. sg. 3 *mi-i-e-eš-ki-iz-zi* KUB 12.44 ii 27 (NH); **imp. sg. 3** *ma-i-iš-ki-i*[*d-du?*] KUB 24.6 obv. 4 (pre-NH/MS), *mi-ia-aš-k*[*i-id?-du?*] KUB 39.41 rev. 10 (NH).

iter. mid. imp. sg. 3? *mi-i-e-eš-ki-it-ta-r*[*u?*] KUB 43.23 rev. 9 (OS).

iter. sup. *mi-iš-ki-u-an* KUB 12.44 ii 28 (NH).

part. cf. ⁽ᴸᵁ́⁾*mayant-* and *miyant-*.

verbal subst. perhaps *mi-ia-u-wa*, see *miyawa* article.

scribal error *me-ia-u-wa-an-zi* KUB 39.68 left col. 3 is to be read *me-*<*mi-*>*ia-u-wa-an-zi*.

(Sum.) [...]=(Akk.) [o *-k*]*a?-a-ru*=(Hitt.) TUR*-aš kuwapi mi-ia-ri nu aiš a*[*rḫ*]*a ēpzi* "When a child is born, she (the mother or an attendant) holds (its) mouth open(?)" KBo 13.2 obv. 9 (vocab.), tr. differently HW² 48a.

It is possible that the Hittite which underlay the Akk. expression *lišrī lirpiš* "let (the land of Mittanni) become rich and wide" in KBo 1.1 rev. 73, a treaty with Šattiwaza drafted in Akk. by Hittites, was *māu šešdu* (Götze, KlF 1:241), but this is not certain.

1. to grow (act.) — **a.** the stone monster Ullikummi: *A-nikan kuiš* ᴺᴬ⁴ŠU.U*-ziš anda mi-e-eš-ta UL-an šakti* "Do you not know about the Basalt which grew in the water?" KUB 33.106 iii 35-36 (Ullik., NH), ed. Güterbock, JCS 6:26f.; cf. ibid. iii 14.

b. grain: *nuza* DUMU.NITA DUMU.SAL *lē ḫaši nušši ḫalkiš lē ma-a-i* "Let him not beget a son (or) a daughter; let his grain not grow" KUB 17.28 ii 46-47 (incant., MH/NS); cf. *numu ḫalkiš ma-a-ú* "Let my grain grow" ibid. iii 2-3; *ḫalkiš* ZÍZ*-tar UL ma-a-i nuza namma* GUD.ḪI.A UDU.ḪI.A DUMU.LÚ.U₁₉.LU.MEŠ *UL armaḫḫanzi* "(Because the deity has gone,) barley (and) wheat do not grow; cattle, sheep (and) people no longer become pregnant" KUB 17.10 i 14-15 (missing deity, OH/MS), tr. ANET 126 ("So grain and spelt thrive no longer"), RTAT 182 ("Da hörten Korn und Spelt zu wachsen auf").

c. other plants: [*ḫ*]*eun wekešgaweni* [...] ... GÚ.ŠEŠ.ŠEŠ *mi-e-eš-du* [...] GEŠTIN*-yawa mi-e-eš-du* "We will keep asking for rain ... let the bitter vetch grow ... let the grapevine grow" KBo 22.116 obv. 19-22 (NS); GIDIM *kuwapi* EGIR ᴳᴵᡃᴬᴾᴵ[ᴺ .... *nu taranzi*] *kēzzawaza IŠTU* ᴳ[ᴵŠ?]APIN ...] *nuwaratši mi-ia-aš-k*[*i-id-du?*] "When [they ...] the deceased (or: When the deceased [... -s]) behind the plo[w, they say:] 'With this p[low(?) let him ....,] and let it grow for him" KUB 39.41 rev. 8-10 (compilation of recitations prescribed for certain days in the funerary rit., NH)□for other iter. forms in these recitations cf. i 2 and rev. 15.

d. plants, animals and humans, the entire community of growing and reproducing beings, often referred to by the word *utne* "land": [...*ḫ*]*alkiyaš* ᴳᴵŠGEŠTIN*-aš* ᴳᴵŠ*šēšanaš* GUD.ḪI.A*-aš* UDU.ḪI.A*-aš* ÙZ.ḪI.A*-a*[*š* (ŠAḪ!*-aš* ANŠE.GÌR)].NUN.NA.ḪI.A*-aš* ANŠE(var. ANŠE!.KUR.RA)*-aš gimraš ḫūitnit* [(DUMU.LÚ.U₁₉.LU*-ašša Š*)]*A* EGIR. UD*-MI miyātar piški nu mi-e-eš-ša-du* (var. lacks *-ša-*) [... *š*]*iššawaš* (var. *šēššauwaš*) *ḫūwaduš* (var. IM.ḪI.A*-uš*) *iyantar*[*u* (*nu INA* KUR ᵁᴿ)]ᵁKÙ.BABBAR*-TI ma-a-ú šišdu* (var. *šešdu*) *nu panku*[(*š apāt*)] *ēšdu ḫalzāi* "Grant future growth of cereal crops, vines, fruit(-trees?), cattle, sheep, goats, pigs, mules, asses (var. horses) — together with wild animals of the steppe — and of humans, and let them (var. it) grow.... And may the winds of proliferation(?) pass over, and may there be growth and proliferation(?) in the land of Ḫatti. And the congregation cries: So be it!" KUB 24.2 rev. 14-19 (prayer of Murš. II) with dupl. KUB 24.1 iv 12-18, ed.

Gurney, AAA 27:34f., cf. HW^2 168a; we follow Gurney AAA 27:115 in assuming that both KUB 24:1 and KUB 24.2 have *šeššawaš* through an error for the correct *še-iš-du-wa-a*[*š*] of KUB 24.3 iii 39 (AAA 27:36).

e. uncleanness/evil: cf. *maḫḫan* 1 a 1′ a′.

2. to grow up, reach ripeness or maturity, bear fruit — **a.** grapevines in a vineyard: *mān* ^{GIŠ}KIRI$_6$.GEŠTIN *kuiš UL mi-i-e-eš-ki-iz-zi* [. . . *k*]*iššan aniyami naš mi-iš-ki-u-an dāi* "If some vineyard never bears fruit, I will perform the following ritual, and it will begin to bear fruit" KUB 12.44 ii 27-28 (rit., NH), cf. Dressler, Plur. 202 n. 101, 204; [*mā*]*n kēdani* MU-*ti ḫalkiuš mi-eš-ša*[*-an-zi*] "If the cereal crops will ripen in this year" KUB 16.76:11 (oracles, NH).

b. humans (cf. ^{LÚ}*mayant-*): *kuita imma mi-eš-ḫa-ti* "even when I grew up" KUB 30.10 obv. 11 (prayer, MH/MS), cf. *kuitmuza* AMA-*YA ḫašta* "since my mother gave birth to me" obv. 6; but Neu, StBoT 5:117 and Kühne, RTAT 189 propose: "Und je mehr ich heranwuchs" ("And the more I grew"); possibly also [*m*]*ānw*[*a*] *mi-ia-*⌈*ri*⌉*-ma* "But when he grows up" KUB 33.120 iii 11 (Kingship in Heaven, NH).

3. (of a baby) to arrive at term, to be born (mid.): *mān INA* ITU.5.KAM TUR-*aš mi-ia-ri* "If a child is born in the fifth month" KUB 8.35 obv. 3 (birth month omens) and passim in this text, ed. Beckman, Diss. 13ff.; *nu mān* DUMU.NI[TA *k*]*uwapi mi-ia-ri* "Whenever a *boy* is born" KBo 17.62 iv 13 + KBo 17.63 rev. 8 (birth rit., pre-NH/MS?), ed. Beckman, Diss. 38, 40; [*m*]*ān antuḫšaš kuwapi mi-i-ia-a-ri* (var. *mi-ia-ri*) "If/when anywhere a person is born" KUB 43.55 ii 13 (rit., pre-NH/NS) dupl. Bo 2872 ii 3, ed. Otten and Siegelová, AfO 23:38 n. 21, for *mān . . . kuwapi* cf. *mān* 10 b; *nu* DUMU.NITA *mi-ia-ti* "And a son was born" KBo 12.3 iv 3 (story of Anumḫerwa and Zalpa, OH/NS); another ex. above in lex. section

4. to increase, be plentiful, abundant(?) (act., from OS): *nuwa* ^{d}U-*aš* NINDA.KUR$_4$.RA *ma-a-ú* "Let the bread of the Stormgod increase (or: be plentiful)" KUB 25.23 iv 59 (cult inv., Tudḫ. IV), ed. Carter, Diss. 162, 173; A.ŠÀ A.GÀR *taḫātauššaš ma-a-ú* [. . .] ^{NINDA}*ḫarša⸗šmaš* ^{URU}*Kākuma⸗ḫima ma-*⌈*a*⌉*-*[*ú*] "Let the field and fallow of *t.* grow/increase(?). Let the bread be plentiful for them (in?) K." KBo 25.112 ii 7-9 (invocations to Hattian deities, OS), translit. StBoT 25:191; [*na*]*mma⸗nnaš* KUR ^{URU}*Ḫatti* G[UD-*it* UDU-*it* . . .] / [*ḫal*]*kit* GEŠTIN-*it ma-i-iš-ki-i*[*d-du*] "Let our land of Ḫatti increase in (lit. with) cattle, sheep, . . . , grain, (and) wine" KUB 24.6 obv. 3-4.

5. to thrive, prosper (of lands, cities, people): *utnē ma-a-i* "the land will prosper" KUB 8.27 left edge 2a (omen); *utniwa ma-a-ú šešdu* "let the land thrive and prosper" or "in the land let it thrive and prosper" KBo 3.7 i 5 (Illuyanka, OH/NS); cf. *nu mān ma-a-i šešzi* ibid. i 6-7; *nu INA* KUR ^{URU}*Ḫatti ma-a-ú šešdu* "in the land of Ḫ. let it thrive and prosper" KUB 24.1 iv 17 (prayer, Murš. II), ed. Gurney, AAA 27:34f; cf. KBo 7.28:15, 41, KUB 12.43:2, 3; KUB 14.12 rev. 14, VBoT 121 obv. 6; *našta QATI* LUGAL (var. *n*[*a*](sic) *QATI* LUGAL-*i*) *ma-iš-te-en šišten* (var. *ma-a-ú ši-iš*<*-te*>*-en*) "thrive and prosper in the hand of the king!" KBo 8.35 ii 15 (treaty, MH/MS), with dupl. KUB 23.78b:11 + KUB 26.6 ii 12; [*p*]*aiddu mi-i-ia-ru* ^{URU}*Zalpūwaš* [*nu*? EG]IR.U[D-*MI* . . .] "Henceforth let Z. prosper, and in the fu]tur[e . . .]" KBo 3.38 obv. 6 (Zalpa tale, OH/NS), ed. StBoT 17:8f.

The verb *mai-* essentially describes growth. When the process is viewed in its final stages, as it is in the intransitive participles $^{\text{(LÚ)}}$*mayant-* and *miyant-*, it may require the English translation "mature", "ripe", "fruit-bearing".

The stems *mai-* and *miya-* are attested already in OS. *mai-* is used exclusively in the act; *miya-* is used in the mid. (including mid. iter.). The stem *miešš-* is first unambiguously attested in NS, and can be confused with its homograph *miešš-* "to be soft, mild, gentle". The form *ma-iš-te-en* KBo 8.35 ii 15 (MS) offers no evidence for a stem *maiš-*, but is like *pašti* "you give" (*pai-*) and *naišteni* "you (pl.) turn/send" (*nai-*).

Sommer in Zimmern, Streitbergfestgabe (1924) 438; Friedrich, ZA 36 (1925) 53f., ZA 37 (1927) 200f.; Götze, KlF 1 (1930) 240f.; Gurney, AAA 27 (1940) 114f.; Neu, StBoT 5 (1968) 117.

Cf. *maya-*, $^{\text{(LÚ)}}$*mayant-*, *mayantaḫḫ-*, $^{\text{(LÚ)}}$*mayantatar*, *mayantili*, *mayantešš-*, *miyant-*, *miyatar*, *miyawa*, **mieššar*.

maya- n.; adulthood(?); NH.†

sg. gen.(?) *ma-ia-aš* KUB 26.61:5, KUB 31.63 ii 3.

mŠ*una*-DINGIR-*LIM* m*Ultedukkiš* 1 DUMU-*ŠU* mŠ*una*-DINGIR-*LIM* Š*UMŠU* [mŠ]*una*-DINGIR-*LIM* ŠU.NIGÍN 4 LÚ *ma-ia-aš* ŠU.N[(IGÍN 6?)] SAG.DU mAMAR.MUŠEN-*iš* LÚ*urayanniš pešta* (var. *uppešta*) "Š., U., his one son named Š., Š.: total 4 adults (men of adulthood), (grand) total 6 persons A., the *urayanniš*, gave (var. sent)" KUB 31.61 + KUB 26.31 ii 7-9 and dupls. (Vow of Pud.), ed. StBoT 1:22ff.; dupl. M (KUB 31.63 + KUB 26.63 recopied StBoT 1 pl. IV) ii 3′ seems to have written [mŠ*unailiš* ŠU.NIGÍN 4 SAG.D]U.MEŠ SAL *ma-ia-aš* ŠU.NIGÍN 6(?) SAG.DU; the tr. of 4 LÚ-*ma-ia-aš* as "das sind aber 4 Männer" (StBoT 1:24f.) assumes enclitics *=ma=ya=aš*, which can hardly be correct. Either LÚ/SAL*mayaš* "adult" is a nom. sg. noun after the numeral, or one should read LÚ/SAL *mayaš* "Man/woman of adulthood".

Cf. *mai-*, (LÚ)*mayant-*.

(LÚ)**mayant-** n. com. and adj.; **1.** (noun) young man, man in the prime of life, grownup, **2.** (adj.) grown-up, mature, youthful, vigorous; from OH; written syll. and LÚGURUŠ.

sg. nom. *ma-ia-an-za* KUB 30.10 rev. 7 (OH/MS), KUB 31.127 i 10 (OH/NS), LÚGURUŠ-*an-za* KUB 24.8 i 42 (pre-NH/NS), KUB 3.94 i 19! (NH), KBo 3.4 i 12, KBo 16.1 i 19 (both Murš. II); **sg. acc.** *ma-ia-an-ta-an* KBo 17.88 iii 10, 24 (pre-NH/NS), LÚGURUŠ-*an* KUB 24.7 ii 4; **gen.?** *ma-ia-an-ta-aš* KBo 22.201 iii 6; **dat.** *ma-ia-an-ti* KBo 17.88 iii 7 (pre-NH/NS).

pl. acc. LÚ.MEŠ*ma-ia-an-du-uš* KBo 3.40:4 (OH/NS), without det. KBo 20.42 i 41 (MH/MS), LÚ.MEŠGURUŠ-*uš* KBo 13.78 rev. 2 (OH/NS); **gen. or d.-l.** LÚ.MEŠGURUŠ-*aš* KUB 24.7 ii 23.

[...] = [...] = (Hitt.) LÚGURUŠ!-*an-za* KUB 3.94 i 19 (vocab.); LÚ.MEŠGURUŠ-*uš* KBo 13.78 rev. 2 corr. in dupl. to LÚ.MEŠ*ma-ia-an-du-uš* KBo 3.40:4 (StBoT 14:22).

1. (noun) young man — **a.** LÚGURUŠ-*ant-* "young man, man in the prime of life, grownup": DUMU-Š*U-mawaššizakan kuiš ANA* GIŠGU.ZA *ABIŠU ešat nuwa apašša karū* LÚGURUŠ-*an-za ēšta* "His son, who sat down on his father's throne, he too was formerly a man in the prime of life" (but he became sick and died) KBo 3.4 i 11-12 with dupl. KBo 16.1 i 18-19, ed. AM 16ff.; contrast ibid. 14: *kinunmawazakan kuiš ANA* GIŠGU.ZA *ABIŠU ešat nuwaraš* TUR-*laš* "But now the one who has sat down on his father's throne is a child", cf. StBoT 14:22 n. 13.

b. LÚ.MEŠGURUŠ "young men" in association with SAL.MEŠKI.SIKIL "young women, girls": Š*UŠI* [LÚ].M[EŠ]GURUŠ-*makan* URU*Duddulaz* [...] "sixty young men [...] from Tuttul" KBo 26.82:5 (myth of Ḫedammu), ed. StBoT 14:70f., cf. ibid. 6; Š*UŠI* SAL.MEŠKI.SIKIL-*m*[*ak*]*an* URU*Duddulaz* [...] "sixty young women [...] from Tuttul" ibid. 7; URU-*LU*[*M ḫ*]*ūmanza* LÚ.MEŠ.ŠU.GI SAL.<MEŠ>.Š[U.GI] LÚ.MEŠGURUŠ SAL.MEŠKI.SIKIL *ḫūma*[*nza*] *anda ari* "The entire town — old men, old women, young men and young women — all (of it) arrives" 15/r v 11-14 (cult inv.). The age class of the two sexes here is intended to be the same, but we cannot demonstrate that SAL.MEŠKI.SIKIL was also read **mayanteš*, cf. below in discussion.

c. in athletic competition: NA4 LÚ.MEŠ GURUŠ *karpa*<*n*>*zi* "young men lift a stone (or: stones?)" KBo 2.8 iii 28 (cult inv., NH), cf. Carter, Diss. 193; Š*UŠI* [LUG]AL.MEŠ 70 LÚGURUŠ ≪*ši*≫ *šiyauwanzi tarḫta* "He defeated sixty kings (and) seventy young men at archery" KUB 36.67 ii 23 (Gurparanzaḫ), ed. Güterbock, ZA 44:84ff., the extra *ši* was probably erased, coll. HGG, cf. [Š*U*]Š*I* LUGAL.MEŠ 70 *šargaueš* "sixty kings, seventy heroes" ibid. ii 14. Possibly we should read LÚ.MEŠ KALAG "strong men" and consider this a logogram for *šargaweš*, cf. ZA 44:60, 84, 86.

d. in real and mock warfare: *mān ANA* EN.KARAŠ *gimri ḫatukišzi našma*≪*aš*≫*kan* ŠÀ MÈ LÚKÚR ZAG-*naḫḫiškizzi anzelwama* (sic) LÚGURUŠ.ḪI.A *UL* ZAG-*naḫḫānzi* "If it becomes threatening(?) in the field for the leader (lit. 'lord') of the army, or (if) the enemy keeps winning in battle, and our young men do not win" KUB 7.58 i 18-22 (rit.), opening lines of a new composition on a Sammeltafel; *nu* LÚ.MEŠGURUŠ *takšan arḫa šarranzi naš lamniyanzi* "They divide the young men into two groups and name them" KUB 17.35 iii 9 (cult inv.), ed. Ehelolf, SPAW 1925:270, Carter, Diss. 129, 143, cf. *lamniya-* 1 b.

e. in other situations: dUTU-*uškan nepišaza katta š[akuwayat] našza* LÚGURUŠ-*an-za kiš[at]* "The Sungod looked down from the sky and became a young man" KUB 24.8 i 41-42 (story of Appu, NS), ed. StBoT 14:6f.; cf. KUB 24.7 ii 54 (story of the cow); ŠÀ Ù-*TI-kan* GIM-*an* SAL. LUGAL *INA* URU*Iyamma* É*tarnui* EGIR-*an* LÚ.MEŠGURUŠ *kuiešqa ḫatkiššanuškir* "When in a dream some young men were molesting the queen in Iyamma behind the *t.*-building, (the queen vowed in the dream one *t.*-building made of gold to Šarruma of Urikina)" KUB 15.1 ii 6-8 (vow, NH), cf. Güterbock apud Oppenheim, Dreams 227, cf. ibid. ii 38-40; [... L]Ú.MEŠGURUŠ EGIR-*ŠUNU* SÌR-*RU* "Young men sing after them" KBo 13.175 obv. 1 (fest.); *nu* LÚGUDÚ LÚ.MEŠGURUŠ *šarā karpanzi* "Young men lift up the G.-priest (and carry him into the temple)" VAT 7448 iii 6 (StBoT 15:31); *kuinmaza* LÚ-*an* LÚGURUŠ-*an-pát ḫarnikta* (one man you..., another you...), "another man you destroyed when only(-*pat*) a youth" KUB 24.7 ii 4, ed. Güterbock, JAOS 103: 158 ("even in his prime"), Archi, OA 16:306f., 309, ("un uomo vigoroso") and leaving *-pat* untranslated; [(*uga*)] LÚ.MEŠ*ma-ia-an-du-uš* (var. LÚ.MEŠGURUŠ-*uš*) *punuškimi* "I ask the young men" KBo 3.40 (BoTU 14α):4 with dupl. KBo 13.78 rev. 2 (both OH/NS).

2. (adj.) grown-up, mature; youthful, vigorous — **a.** grown-up, mature (male): dUTU-*uš šuwaru ma-ia-an-za* DUMU dN[IN].GAL "O Ištanu, fully grown-up son of Ningal" KUB 31.127 i 10-11 (prayer, OH/NS), ed. Güterbock, JAOS 78:239, cf. KUB 30.10 rev. 7 (prayer of Kantuzzili, OH/MS); □ the reference to Ištanu's beard in the following line suggests that it is his having reached manhood which is intended, not his youth.

b. youthful, vigorous, (w. *āppa*) rejuvenated — **1′** of the king (and queen?): *āššušaš ḫalugaš wemiškiddu ma-ia-an-ta-an* dUTU-*šummin* f*Tawanannan* AN.BAR-*aš* GIŠDAG-*ti* "Let it (-*aš*), (namely) the 'good message' find our vigorous Sungod (i.e. the king) (and) the *Tawananna* on a throne dais of iron" KBo 17.88 + KBo 24.116 iii 23-25 (monthly fest.); cf. *ma-ia-an-ti-ma* dUTU-*šum*[(*mi*)...] MU.ḪI.A *upp*[*i*]*š*⁄⁄*k*[*an*]*du* "Let them send... years to our vigorous 'Sungod'" KBo 17.88 iii 7-8; *ma-ia-an-ta-aš* dUTU-*šummaš* KBo 22.201 iii 6-7 (genitive); *kar(a)ppiya ziga warkantaš* GU₄.MAḪ.ḪI.A-*aš* UDU.NITÁ.MEŠ-*aš* EGIR-*pa*! *ma-ia-an-ta-aš* dUTU-*šummi* SAL*tawanannai auriyalaš piddāi* "Arise, you! Run as the sentinel to the fat bulls (and) rams (and) to the rejuvenated ones, (namely,) 'Our Sungod' (and) the *Tawannanna*," KBo 17.88 + KBo 24.116 iii 19-21. □ Elsewhere *m.* always refers to a male, but it refers to both king and the Tawananna here. It cannot refer back to the bulls and rams, since they are hardly "rejuvenated" (EGIR-*pa*). In all other occurrences of this formula the *m.* is singular, referring only to the king. Cf. Archi, FsMeriggi² 42 ("fiorente").

2′ of the knee ("youthful, supple, strong, vigorous"?): *šer arḫatkan* (var. [*šer*] *arḫama*⁄⁄*ššiššan*) *mūdaiddu* 12 UZUÚR.ḪI.A-*ŠU* (var. omits -*ŠU*) *ma-ia-an-ti-ia* (so also in dupl.) *ginušši* "Let it (the piglet) also uproot them (-*at*; the evils) all over his (i.e., the patient's) twelve body-parts and (his) vigorous knee" (lit. "on (his) vigorous knee") KUB 9.4 iii 32-34 (Old Woman rit., NS) with parallel or dupl. Bo 3436 rev. 4-6 (translit. HGG); In view of the reading *ma-ia-an-ti-ia* in the par./dupl. Bo 3436 rev. 5 it is risky to emend with Goetze, Tunn. 69 to *i!-ia-an-ti-ia*, in spite of the support of KUB 9.34 iii 34 and KBo 17.54 + KBo 20.73 i 20. Eichner in Heth.u.Idg. 48ff. restored [*ma-i*]*a-an-da-an ginuššin* in HT 6 obv. 27 + KBo 9.125 i 12 and translated "dem kraftvollen Kniegelenk". Cf. also Eichner, MSS 31 (1972) 59 n. 24.

It is not clear whether *mayant-* refers exclusively to males (cf. above 2 b 1′). All occurrences of the words *mayandaḫḫ-*, *mayandatar*, *mayantili*, and *mayantešš-*, whenever the sex of the living being referred to can be determined, relate to males. Other than KBo 17.88 + KBo 24.116 iii 19ff. cited in 2 b 1′, the only evidence for a female described by a word in this word family would be SAL *ma-ia-aš* "woman of adulthood" (cf. *maya-*), which is itself a somewhat problematic interpretation. Women of the same age as the LÚ.MEŠGURUŠ are designated SAL.MEŠKI.SIKIL not *SAL.MEŠ GURUŠ, and there is no proof that the syllabic equivalent of SAL.MEŠKI.SIKIL was **mayanteš*.

Sommer, HAB (1938) 150f; Siegelová, StBoT 14(1971):22.

Cf. *mai-*, *maya-*, *mayantaḫḫ-*, (LÚ)*mayantatar*, *mayantili*, *mayantešš-*.

mayantaḫḫ- v.; to rejuvenate, instill youthful vigor (mostly with *dān* or *āppa*); from OH; wr. syll. and LÚGURUŠ-*aḫḫ-*.†

pres. pl. 3 [L]ÚGURUŠ-*aḫ-ḫa-an-*⌜*zi*⌝ Bo 3670 (Istanbul), obv. rt. col. 7 (NS); **pret. pl. 3** *ma-ia-an-da-aḫ-ḫi-ir* KUB 29.1 iii 7 (OH/NS); **imp. sg. 2** *ma-ia-an-ta-aḫ* KUB 41.23 ii 11 (OH/NS) and dupl. KUB 43.63 obv. (8), 14 (NS).

iter. imp. sg. 2 *ma-ia-an-ta-aḫ-ḫe-eš-ki* Bo 2489 + Bo 4008 ii 37 (StBoT 5:111).

broken LÚGURUŠ-*a*[*ḫ-* . . .] KUB 31.22:4.

dUTU-*ušza* dIM-*ašša* LUGAL-*un* EGIR-*pa kappūēr nan dān ma-ia-an-da-aḫ-ḫi-ir* MU.KAM.ḪI.A-*šaššan kutriš UL iēr* "The Sungod and the Stormgod have taken the king to heart again. They have rejuvenated him. They have made no limit(?) to his years (lit. Of his years a limit(?) they have not made)" KUB 29.1 iii 6-8 (rit., OH/NS), ed. Kellerman, Diss. 16, 29 ("l'ont rajeuni une deuxième fois"), cf. Friedrich, JCS 1:284f. ("und machten ihn wieder zum kräftigen Manne"), ANET 358 ("renewed his strength"); *ešrišše*t *newaḫ* [(*nan* EGIR-*pa*)] *ma-ia-an-ta-aḫ* "Renew his (the king's) frame and make him young again" KUB 43.63 obv. 13-14 (incant., OH/NS) with dupl. KUB 43.61 i 6; cf. KUB 41.23 ii 11 (incant. frag.); *nuš ma-ia-an-ta-aḫ-ḫe-eš-ki ukturiyaḫḫeški* "rejuvenate them (the king and queen) and make them eternal" Bo 2489 + Bo 4008 ii 37-38 (StBoT 5:111) (prayer in fest., OH?/NS).

The adverb *dān* and the preverb EGIR-*pa* indicate that the person has been restored to a condition he had been in before ("made him young again"). They do not indicate that the act of rejuvenation is taking place a second time ("rejuvenated him again").

Sommer, HAB (1938) 151; Otten apud HW 2. Erg. 17.

Cf. *mai-*, (LÚ)*mayant-*.

(LÚ)**mayantatar, mayatatar** n. neut.; young adulthood, youth, youthful vigor; from OH; wr. syll. and LÚGURUŠ-*tar*.†

sg. nom.-acc. LÚ*ma-ia-an-da-tar* KUB 1.16 iii (29) (OH/NS), KBo 20.42 i 35 (MH/MS), LÚ*ma-ia-an-ta-tar* Bo 3234 iii 8 (HAB 151 n. 2), *ma-ia-an*⌜*-da-tar*⌝ KBo 15.10 ii 35 (MH/MS), *ma-ia-ta-tar* KUB 29.1 ii 37 (OH/NS), *ma-ia-an-t*[*a*?*-a-t*]*ar* KBo 10.37 iii 15 (OH/NS), [. . . *ma-ia-a*]*n-*⌜*ta*⌝*-tar* KBo 13.121:11 (OH/NS), LÚGURUŠ-*tar* KBo 6.34 iv 9 (MH/NS), KUB 23.92 rev. 9 (Tudḫ. IV); **loc.** [*ma*?*-i*]*a-an-da-an-ni* KBo 25.2 ii 9 (OS).

mān LÚ*ma-ia-a*[*n-d*]*a-ta*[*r kardit*]*ti* "When young adulthood is in your heart" KUB 1.16 iii 29-30 (edict, OH/NS), ed HAB 12f., contrast [*mānma* L]ÚŠU.GI-*tarra kardi*tti "But [when] old age is in your heart" ibid. iii 31; *miḫuntataršekan dāš ma-ia-ta-tar-ma-aš-ši* EGIR-*pa paiš* "(S)he took old age from him (i.e., the king) and gave back to him (his) youth" KUB 29.1 ii 36-37 (rit., OH/NS), ed. Kellerman, Diss. 14, 28 ("la maturité"), tr. ANET 358 ("vigor"); *našta apella* TI-*taršet* LÚGURUŠ-*tar-še-et lulušše*t *INA* EGIR.UD-*MI QADU* DAM.MEŠ-*ŠU* DUMU.MEŠ-*ŠU QĀTAMMA kištaru* "Let that one's life, his youth, (and) his *lulu* — together with his wives and his sons — be likewise extinguished forever!" KBo 6.34 iv 9-11 (soldier's oath, MH/NS, ed. StBoT 22:14f., cf. KBo 10.37 iii 15 (dupl. KBo 13.121:11), and KBo 15.10 + KBo 20.42 i 35, ii 35, iii 36 (rit., MH/MS), ed. THeth 1:18f., 24f., 40f.; [. . .]x LÚGURUŠ-*tar* GIM-*an* EGIR-*pa memi*[(*r*)] "As they attributed [to him] youthful vigor" KUB 23.92 rev. 9 with dupl. KUB 23.103 rev. 10, ed. Otten, AfO 19:42; [. . . *ma*?*-i*]*a-an-da-an-ni-iš-ši aki* "He will die in his young manhood (i.e., in his prime)" KBo 25.2 ii 9 (apodosis to birth omen, OS).

Sommer, HAB (1938) 150; Siegelová, StBoT 14 (1971) 22.

Cf. *mai-*, (LÚ)*mayant-*.

mayantili (mng. unknown).†

i-ia(-)*u-wa-at-ta-u-wa-ar a-aš-šu* / GEŠTU (or: *wa*)*-ar* LUGAL-*it-ta* / *ma-ia-an-ti-li* § LUGAL-*it-ta ma-ia-an-*⌜*ti-li*⌝ / d*Pí-ir-wa-aš-*⌜*wa*⌝ (broken) Bo 1391 obv. 8-12, copy Otten, JKF 2(1952/53):65.

Formally the word resembles an adverb in *-ili* from *mayant-* "young adult, youth", but the context allows no decision. This passage may not be in Hittite.

Cf. *mai-*, (LÚ)*mayant-*.

mayantešš-, mayatešš- v.; to become a young man, (with *appa*:) become young again; from OH; wr. syll. and LÚGURUŠ-*antešš-*.†

pres. sg. 3 ^{LÚ}GURUŠ-*an-te-eš-zi* KUB 14.12 obv. 9 (NH); **pret. pl. 3** *ma-ia-te-eš-še-er* KUB 24.8 iii 17 (NH); **imp. sg. 2** *ma-ia-an-te-eš* KBo 21.22:55 (OH/MS); **broken** *ma-a-ia-an-te-i*[*š*-. . .] KBo 19.103:1 (NS) (or perhaps a form of *mayant-* q.v.).

[DUMU.MEŠ ^{m}*Appu šall*]*išer nat ma-ia-te-eš-še-er* [*nat* LÚ-*ni me*]*ḫuni erer* "[The sons of A. gr]ew up. They became young men. They reached [the ti]me [of manhood]" KUB 24.8 iii 17-18 (Appu story, NS), ed. StBoT 14:10f., restored following ibid. iv 1-2; cf. *ma-a-ia-an-te-i*[*š*-. . .] KBo 19.103:1; [. . . *naš*] ^{LÚ}GURUŠ-*an-te-eš-zi UL-maš* ^{LÚ}*miyaḫ*[*ḫuntešzi*] "He will reach young manhood, but he will not reach old age" KUB 14.12 obv. 8-9 (PP 3, Murš. II), ed. Götze, KlF 1:236f., 240, cf. StBoT 14:22; *nuwa āppa ma-ia-an-te-eš* "Become young again!" KBo 21.22:55 (incant., OH/MS), translit. Kellerman, Tel Aviv 5:200.

Sommer, HAB (1938) 150f.; Siegelová, StBoT 14 (1971) 22 n. 13.

Cf. *mai-*, $^{\text{(LÚ)}}$*mayant-*.

mayatatar see *mayantatar*.

mayatešš- see *mayantešš-*.

[$^{\text{TU}_7}$*māiša*(?)] Most probably to be read *kam-ma-a-i-ša* KBo 20.129 i 33.

^{SÍG}**maišta-** n. com.; fiber, flock or strand of wool; MH/MS.†

sg. acc. ^{SÍG}*ma-iš-ta-an* KBo 16.47:8, KUB 23.72 rev. (8).

[*m*]*ān* ^{SÍG}*ma-iš-ta-an-na mašiwantan waštanzi* "Even if (*mān* . . . -*a*) they (the people of Ura and Mutamutašši) are remiss in respect to so much as a fiber of wool," (You and I will make war on them) KBo 16.47:8-9 (treaty, MH/MS), ed. Otten, IM 17:56f.; *āppa* ^{SÍG}*ma-iš-t*[*a-a*]*n* [*m*]*ašiwantan UL ap*[*panzi*] "They will not withhold so much as a fiber of wool" KUB 23.72 rev. 8 (Mita text, MH/MS), ed. Hoffner, JCS 28.61; cf. [*āppa* ^{SÍG}*maiš-t*]*an mašiwantan lē apteni* "Do not [with]hold so much as a fiber of wool" ibid. + 1684/u obv. 42, restore ibid. rev. 15 similarly; *āppa ep-* "withhold" in the Mita passages is contrasted with *arnutten* (obv. 41) and [*parā p*]*išten* (obv. 43).

The word is used in the treaties as a nugatory item, in the same way as *ezzan taru* "chaff (and) wood" is used in later texts.

Hoffner, JCS 28 (1976) 61f.; idem, Finkelstein Mem. 109.

Cf. *maštaimi-*, ^{SÍG}*kišri-*.

magalti- (Hurr. offering term); MH/NS.†

Only in the EZEN *ḫišuwaš*: *nu* 4 NINDA. KUR$_4$.RA KU$_7$ . . . *ma-a-gal-ti-ia šipanti* "He offers *m.* four sweet cakes (and other breads)" KBo 15.37 i 13-17; *nu PANI abalkiti kuit* SISKUR *ANA* ^{d}ZA.BA$_4$.BA$_4$ *ḫandān natši ma-kal-ti-ia šipandanzi* "The sacrifice which is made ready for Z. before the *a.* they offer to him *m.*" KUB 30.40 i 26-28, ed. HW^2 164.

Cf. ^{NINDA}*makalti-*, *magalzi-*, *magantiḫi-*.

^{NINDA}**makalti-**, ^{NINDA}**makanti-** n. com.; (a foodstuff made from flour); from MH (EZEN *ḫišuwaš*); wr. syll. always with det.

^{NINDA}*ma-kal-ti-iš* KUB 17.20 iii 12, KBo 13.193:9, Bo 2432:9, 12, ^{NINDA}*ma*<*-kal*>*-ti-iš* KUB 17.20 iii 6, [^{NINDA}*ma-k*]*al-ti-iš* ibid. 4, Bo 2432:14, ^{NINDA}*ma-kal-ti-uš* IBoT 3.83:8, 9, KBo 14.142 i 59, ^{NINDA}*ma-kán-de-eš* KBo 22.246 ii 24, ^{NINDA}*ma-kán-te-eš* KUB 10.92 ii 5, ^{NINDA}*ma-kán-ti-iš* KBo 22.246 ii 8, ^{NINDA}*ma-kán-ti-uš* KBo 14.142 i 44, 45, ii 8.

Frequent in lists of foodstuffs offered in the cult of Hurrian deities. Once 1-*NU-TUM* ^{NINDA}*ma-kal-ti-uš* "one set of *m.*'s" 38/r iv 4. The alternation of *l* and *n* suggests that the word is not Hittite (cf. Kronasser, EHS 58ff), while its frequent occurrence in texts relating to the Hurr. cult points to a Hurr. source. Cf. Hurr. *magaltiya*, *magalziya*, and *magantiḫiya*. The word does not occur in unilingual Hurr. texts studied to date. No *mākaltu*(*m*) designating food is known from Akkadian. Akk. ^{DUG}*mākaltu* (a bowl) occurs as an Akkadogram in Hitt. texts (e.g., KUB 32.113:6). ^{NINDA}*makalti-* might denote the cereal-porridge (NINDA) which one eats from a bowl (^{DUG}*MĀKALTU*). Both 1-*NUTUM* and *TAPAL* can be used with foodstuffs. In some cases it is probable that "servings" of food (not discrete loaves) are in view. Cf. *etri*, ^{NINDA}*šaramma*, *šuppa*, ^{NINDA}*wagāta*, ^{NINDA}*zannita*, *ARZANNU*, ŠÀ.GAL.ḪI.A.

Hoffner, AlHeth (1973) 170.

magalzi- n.; (Hurrian offering term); NH.†

EGIR-*ŠU-ma* 1 MUŠEN.GAL *dāi nan ANA āp[i kattan?*...]x *ma-ga-al-zi-ia šipanti* "Afterwards he takes one duck and offers it [down] in the pit [to ...] (and) to *magalziya*" KBo 17.94 iii 35-36 (Kizzuwatna rit., NH); cf. Haas and Wilhelm, AOATS 3 (1974) 89 s.v.

Cf. NINDA*makalti-*, *magalti-*, *magantiḫi-*.

NINDA**makanti** see NINDA*makalti.*

magantiḫi- (Hurr. offering term); NH.†

In lists of bird offerings: [2? MUŠEN] ⸢*a*⸣*šapšiya ma-ga-an-ti-ḫi-ia* KUB 47.89 iii 9; 2 MUŠEN *ašapšiya ma-gán-t[i-ḫi-ia]* KBo 11.7 obv. 7.

Haas & Wilhelm, AOATS 3 (1974) 89; GLH 164.

Cf. NINDA*makalti-/makanti-*, *magalti-*, *magalzi-*.

magareš n. (nom. pl.); (objects made at least partly of copper); MS.†

In a list: [... MA.N]A? KÙ.BABBAR *ma-ga-a-re-eš-ši-eš* [(break of uncertain length) ... M]A.NA(coll.) URUDU-*ŠUNU* [...] "[a ... of x min]as silver, its *m.*'s [... are x m]inas, their (the *m.*'s) copper [is ...]" KUB 34.89 rev. 3-5.

The *m.*'s seem to be attachments to the object of silver mentioned in the preceding break. The *m.*'s themselves are partly of copper, since the texts says "their (referring back to the *magāreš*, nom. pl.) copper [is ...]". Although the badly broken context makes certainty impossible, one is reminded of the GIŠGIGIR KÙ.BABBAR given to Ḫatt. I by the King of Tišna KBo 10.2 iii 25. That the wheels of such a "silver chariot" might be trimmed in copper or have copper rims fits with the known Akk. word *magarru* "wheel (of chariot, wagon, etc.)" CAD M/1 32. GIŠ!GIGIR! *anda appān QADU* GIŠ*MU-KAR-RU* 40(coll.) GIŠBAN "a chariot with all appurtenances, together with wheels(?) (and) 40 bows" KBo 18.170a rev. 6, ed. THeth 10:110f.; for *anda appanda* GIŠMAR.GÍD.DA cf. Law §122 and Goetze, MSpr. 44 "mit allem Zubehör". This interpretation would assume that Akk. *magarru* was borrowed as **magarri-* into Hitt. as a specialized word for "chariot wheel" alongside *ḫurki-* "wheel (in general)". The city name URU*Ma-kar-wa-an-da* KUB 31.44 i 7 cited by Laroche may not after all contain this word. Even if the interpretation "wheels" proves wrong, there is nothing in KUB 34.89 rev. 3-5 to suggest plants. Thus it would be difficult to explain URU*Makarwanda* on the basis of the objects mentioned in KUB 34.89.

Laroche, RHA XIX/69 (1961) 60 (une matière ou une plante); RGTC 6:255.

makkī (mng. unkn.); OH/NS.†

[...]x *ma-ak-ki-i a-ap-pa*[(-)...] KBo 3.46 ii 4 translit. BoTU 17A "iii" 4 (hist., OH/NS), ed. Kempinski and Košak, Tel Aviv 9:89, 92, 93.

makkešš- v.; **1.** to be or become numerous, **2.** to be or become too many, excessive; from OH.†

act. pres. sg. 3 *ma-ak-ke-eš-zi* IBoT 1.36 i 13 (MH/MS), *ma-ak-ke-e-eš-zi* KUB 23.68 rev. 4 (MH/NS); **pret. sg. 3** *ma-ak-ke-e-eš-ta* KUB 30.10 rev. 17 (OH/MS), *ma-ak-*⸢*ke-eš-ta*⸣ KUB 30.11 rev. 13 (OH/MS), KBo 3.1 ii 48 (OH/NS), KUB 14.14 obv. 31 (Murš. II), *ma-ak-ki-iš-ta* KUB 21.48 obv. 4, KUB 31.127 iii (3) (both OH/NS), *ma-ak-kiš-ta* A 11176 obv. 8 (NS); **pl. 3** *ma-ak-ki-iš-še-er* KBo 13.49:5 (NS).

imp. pl. 3 *ma-ak-ke-eš-ša-an-du* KUB 29.1 iv 2 (second half of rit. is possibly post-OH/NS).

iter. mid. imp. sg. 3 *ma-ak-ki-iš-kat-ta-ru* Bo 2489 + Bo 4008 ii 41 (StBoT 5:111).

part. nom. sg. com. *ma-ak-kiš-ša-an-za* KBo 16.8 ii 23 (Murš. II); **nom. sg. neut.** *ma-ak-ki-iš-ša-an* KBo 5.8 iv 14 (Murš. II).

1. to be or become numerous (of offspring), populous (of a land): *nuš mayantaḫḫeški ukturiyaḫḫeški nu labarnaš* LUGAL-*waš an*-*tuš*[*š*]*it*(coll.) *parā parā ma-ak-ki-iš-kat-ta-ru* "Rejuvenate them and make (them) eternal! Let the ... of the Labarna, the king, become more and more numerous" Bo 2489 + Bo 4008 ii 37-41, ed. StBoT 5:111; *nu* DUMU.NITA.MEŠ DUMU.SAL.MEŠ *ḫaššeš ḫanzeššeš ma-ak-ke-eš-ša-an-du* "Let (the king's) sons, daughters, children (and) grandchildren be numerous!" KUB 29.1 iv 1-2 (rit. for erection of palace, NS; i 1 - iii 12 is OH/NS; iii 13 - iv 29 is somewhat younger, perhaps still pre-NH), ed. Kellerman, Diss. 18,31; *kuwapima* KUR-*e ma-ak-ke-*

e-eš-zi "But when the land becomes populous" KUB 23.68 rev. 4 (treaty with Išmerika, MH/NS), ed. Kempinski and Košak, WO 5:196f. and comment on p. 211.

2. to be or become too many, too numerous: *karūwa ēšḫar* URU*Ḫattuši ma-ak-ke-eš-ta* "In former times (cases of) bloodshed were too numerous in Ḫattuša" KBo 3.1 ii 48 (Tel. pr., OH/NS), ed. Chrest. 190f., cf. *ēšḫar pangariyattati* ibid. ii 31, 33; (The Sun-goddess of the Earth is asked:) *išḫarwa kuit ma-ak-kiš-ta išḫaḫrumawa* [*kuit pa*]*ngariyatati* "Why have (cases of) bloodshed become too numerous? [Why] have tears become general?" A 11176 obv. 8-9 (rit., NS); (Twelve guards take their places and stand holding spears. If, however, twelve guards are not available,) GIŠŠUKUR.ḪI.A-*ma ma-ak-ke-eš-zi* "(so that) there are too many spears, (they carry away the extra spears)" IBoT 1.36 i 13 (instr. for *MEŠEDI*, MH/MS), ed. Jacob-Rost, MIO 11:174f.; "I have become like one who is sick for the course/extent of a year," *kinunamuššan inan pittuliyašša ma-ak-ke-e-eš-ta* "and now (my) illness and fear have become too much for me (to bear), (so that I am telling it to you)" KUB 30.10 rev. 15-17 (prayer of Kantuzili, OH/MS), cf. KUB 36.79a iii 18-20 + KUB 31.127 iii 1-3, KUB 30.11 rev. 12-13; *numukan šā*[*ru*] *kuit* NAM.RA GUD UDU *mekki ma-ak-ki-iš-ša-an ēšta* "And because the booty in deportees, cattle (and) sheep had become far too numerous for me, (I did not go out again with the army)" KBo 5.8 iv 13-14, ed. AM 160ff., cf. Watkins in Heth.u.Idg. 273; LÚKÚR URU*Gaš⸗gašmaššikan ma-ak-kiš-ša-an-za ē*[*šta*] "The Kaška enemy became too numerous for him" KBo 16.14 ii 8 + KBo 16.8 ii 23 (annals of Murš. II), ed. without KBo 16.14 (2764/c) by Otten, MIO 3:167f.

Götze, Hatt. (1925) 69 ("zu viel sein"); Otten, OLZ 1943:113 ("zu viel sein"), MIO 3 (1955) 167f. ("zu mächtig sein").

Cf. *maknu-*, *mekki-*.

makit(a)- n.; (mng. unknown); OS.†

[*nuššan*] 8-*inzu nepiši ēš*[*š*]*i nuzakan* 2-*iš* 8-*taš kiš*[*tunaš*] / [. . . -*š*]*i nu⸗kkan* 2-*iš* 8-*taš ma-ki-ta-aš akkuškēši* "As an Octad you remain seated in the sky; you [. . .] twice in/on/for eight *k*. and you drink twice in/on/for eight *m*. KUB 31.143 ii 15-16 with restorations from ii 8-9 (invocations to Ḫattic deities, OH/OS), ed. Laroche, JCS 1:202 with discussion on pp. 205-06. Note the agreement in number, gender and case between 8-*taš* and *makitaš*. Laroche translated "Twice thou drinkest the eight . . . -s" and regarded both *kištunaš* and *makitaš* as acc. pl. Com. acc. pl. in -*aš* in OH/OS seems unlikely. Perhaps rather loc. pl.? Elsewhere in Hitt., where one drinks from vessels, the word for the vessel is either accusative or instrumental, never locative.

Laroche, JCS 1 (1947) 202ff.; Friedrich, HW 133 ("ein Trinkgefäss?").

mākkizzi(ya)- see É*makzi*(*ya*)-.

maklant- adj.; thin, emaciated; from OH.†

sg. acc. *ma-ak-la-an-ta-an* KUB 13.4 iv 65 (pre-NH/NS), *ma-ak-la-an-da-an* ibid. iv 75, KUB 13.5 ii 19, KUB 13.17 iv (25), 33.

pl. nom. *ma-ak-la-an-te-eš* KBo 3.34 ii 14 (OH/NS), KUB 12.43:10 (MS), *ma-ak-la-an-te-eš* KBo 13.2 rev. 7 (NH).

Sum. [nam- o (o) -mu] = Akk. [o o]-*ti* "my [. . .]" = Hitt. *ma-ak-la-an-te-eš* KBo 13.2 rev. 7 (Izi?, NH). The photo shows the second sign in the Hitt. word might have a single horizontal, not a double as in KBo 13.2; the preserved Hittite words, when "translated" back into Sum., yield a sequence similar to MSL 13 pp. 47 and 221, all entries beginning with nam-.

URU*Kuzurūi* (var. 19: URU*Kuzzurūi*) *kaqqapuš* (var. 19: *kakkapuš*) *marakta* URU!*Ankuwa kaq⸗qapiš* (var. 20: *kakapuš*) *ma-ak-la-an-te-eš* "In the city K. he butchered *k*.-animals; (but) in A. the *k*.-animals (were) emaciated" KBo 3.34 ii 12-14 (anecdotes, OH/NS) with dupl. KBo 3.36 (NS); (If you priests remove a fattened ox or sheep from the animals brought to the temple as offerings,) [(*šumaš⸗ma⸗z kui*)]*n ma-ak-la-an-da-an markan ḫarteni nankan anda tarnatteni* "and you substitute an emaciated one which you have butchered for yourselves" KUB 13.5 ii 19 (instr. for temple officials, pre-NH/NS) with dupl. KUB 13.6 ii 2, ed. Chrest. 152f.; (If on the way an oxherd or shepherd tries to deceive by making an exchange of a fattened ox or fattened sheep, or he kills it,) *nan arḫa adanzi pede⸗šši⸗ma ma-ak-la-an-ta*(var. -*da*)-*an tarnanzi* "and they eat it up and put in its place an emaciated one" KUB 13.4 iv 64-65 (ibid.) with dupl. iv 24-25; cf. also KUB 13.4 iv 75 with dupl. KUB 13.17 iv 33, ed. Chrest. 166f.; [. . . *well*]*uwa pāir* *ma-ak-la-an-te-eš tameššanteš* [GUD.UDU. ḪI.A? . . . -]*ānteš* SAL.MEŠ*karšant*[*ēš . . .*] *pāir ma-ak-l*[*a-an-te-eš . . .* -]*kanzi* GUD-*uš* UDU-*uš* [. . .] KUB 12.43:10-12 (incant., MH or OH/NS).

The word describes animals which are abnormally thin due either to a lack of food or to an emaciating disease. More than simply the lack of special fattening seems implied in several passages. Their inferior status, as compared to healthy cattle, is clear from the prohibition against exchanging them with those fattened for temple sacrifice. From KUB 13.4 iv 28 it is clear that the man who claimed that "It died from *maklatar*" thought this was an acceptable excuse for not returning livestock belonging to the temple. See *maklatar*.

Götze, NBr (1930) 67.

Cf. *maklatar*.

maklatar n. neut.; emaciation; NS.†

(If you who work the plow oxen belonging to the threshing floor of the temple sell a plow ox, or kill and eat it, and thus steal it from the gods, saying,) *ma-ak-la-an-na-az-wa-ra-aš* BA.ÚŠ "It died from emaciation (caused by a disease?)" KUB 13.4 iv 28, ed. Chrest. 164-65 ("from thinness").

Sturtevant, JAOS 54 (1934) 392.

Cf. *maklant-*.

maknu- v.; to make abundant, to increase (something), to accumulate (something); from OH/NS.†

pret. sg. *ma-ak-nu-nu-*[*u*]*n* KUB 31.17:5 (OH/NS); **iter. pres. sg. 1** *ma-a-ak-nu-uš-ki-mi* KUB 41.20 obv. 6 (NH?); **imp. sg. 2** *ma-ak-nu-uš-ki* KUB 31.64 iv 8 (OH/NS); **pl. 3** ⸢*ma-ak*⸣*-nu-uš-kán-*[*du*] KUB 31.100 obv.? 12 (pre-NH/MS).

Beginning a new paragraph following a list of 34 towns which contained storehouses ("seal houses"): *nuššan ḫalkiuš* EGIR-*an ma-ak-nu-nu-*[*u*]*n* "I accumulated crops back there (in the afore-mentioned storehouses)" KBo 3.67 + KUB 31.17:5 (Tel. edict §39, OH/NS), for the plur. *ḫalkiuš* as "crops" see AlHeth. 62; *nat ŠA* EGIR-UD-*MI wetummar ēš*[*tu . . .*] *ḫūtekkiškandu* EGIR-*andam*[*a . . .*] ⸢*ma-ak*⸣*-nu-uš-kán-*[*du*] "Let it be a permanent building (lit. a building of the future). Let them keep . . .-ing [it], and afterwards let them increase (or accumulate) [. . .]" KUB 31.100 obv.? 10-12 (instr., pre-NH/MS); [. . .] KUR-*eya*⸗*z* GUD UDU *pidda* [*. . . -u*]*š*? *ma-a-ak-nu-uš-ki-mi* "[. . .] "In the land I will keep accumulating (or increasing) cattle, sheep, *pidda* [. . .]" KUB 41.20 obv. 5-6 (rit., NS); [. . . .]x-*anduš* URU.DIDLI.ḪI.A-*KA* / [. . . . *nē*]*uwaḫ*⸗*ḫiški* / [. . . . A.ŠÀ?.ḪI.]⸢A⸣-*KA wešaušša* / [. . . .]x *aniyatta ma-ak-nu-uš-ki* KUB 31.64 iv 5-8 (hist., OH/NS?); because of the large lacunae at the beginnings of the lines, it is not clear if line 5 belongs to the same clause as line 6, or line 7 to the same clause as line 8.

The translation "make abundant" is based on the assumption that *maknu-* is a factitive verb in *-nu-* from the adj. base **mak-*/*mek-* "much, abundant", cf. *mek-*, *mekki-*.

Sommer, OLZ 1941:60 ("anhäufen, vermehren"; derivative from *mekki-*).

Cf. *makkešš-*, *mekki-*.

makkuya- or **makkuyan-** n.; churn; pre-NH/NS.†

sg. acc. *ma-ak-ku-ia-an* KUB 39.45 obv. 10, KUB 39.35 iv 8, 10; **unclear** *ma-ak*⸢*-ku-ia*⸣*-aš-ša-an* ibid. iv 5, cf. below.

INA UD.9.KAM GA *š*[*appa*]*nzi ma-ak-ku-ia-an* [*unuwanzi*(?)] *šappuwaš* GIŠ-*ru* [o *AŠR*] *A IŠTU* KÙ.BABBAR *ḫališ*[*šiyan*] 1 GIŠ*intaluzi*[*š ŠA*] 1 MA.NA . . . "On the ninth day they churn milk. [They decorate(?)] the churn. The dasher (lit. 'wood of beating') is inlaid with silver in [x] places. One butter scoop(?) [of] one mina (weight) . . . " KUB 39.45 obv. 10-12; *šappanzi* and *unuwanzi* in line 10 were restored by Laroche, BiOr 21:320 from KUB 39.6 obv. 9-10; cf. Otten, WO 2:478f.; Güterbock, RHA XXV/81:141; *maḫḫanmašši* ⸢*I*⸣ *NA* 3 KASKAL-*NI ANA* DUG K[A.DÙ . . .] / *akūwanna pianzi nu* LÚSAGI.[A . . .] / *šipanti ma-ak-*⸢*ku-ia*⸣*-aš-ša-an kuiš anda* [. . .] / [GAL.]⸢GIR₄⸣ *waḫnuzi nanšan dāgan* [*duwarniazzi*(?)] / [*nu kalg*]*ali*⸗*naizzi nu* SAL.MEŠ*tapdaraš w*[*eškiwan dai*] § [o o-*ká*]*n* SAL.MEŠ*tapdaraš ma-ak-ku-*⸢*ia*⸣*-an* A-*i*[*t*? *šunnai*] / [GIDIM-*aš*(?) *k*]*uiš ḫaššannaššiš nuza*

G[A . . .] / [*apaš d*]*āi nu* ⸢*ma-ak*⸣*-ku-ia-an apāš* [*ḫarzi*] / [*nuza* ^{GIŠ}*i*]*ndaluzzin* KÙ.BABBAR *apāš* [*dāi*] "But when for the third time they give him [*PĪḪU*-beer] to drink in(?) a cup, the cupbearer libates [the buttermilk] which is in the churn. [Then] he turns the clay [cup] and [breaks(?)] it on the ground [and gr]oans. The wailing women begin to l[ament]. The wailing women [fill] the churn with water. He who is a member of the family [of the deceased(?) ta]kes for himself the [milk]. He [holds] the churn, and he [takes(?)] the silver butter-scoop" KUB 39.35 iv 3-11 (funerary rit.). The interpretation of lines 5-6 is quite uncertain. It is not clear if a verb stood in the lacuna at the end of line 5. If so, *anda* might be a preverb for the verb which stood in the break. If that verb was transitive *makkuyaššan* would be sg. acc. *makkuya(n)šan*. If, however, the verb was *ešzi* or the sentence was nominal, *anda* might be an adv., and *makkuyaššan* a loc. The stem can be *makkuyan-* only if *makkuyaššan* stands for *makkuya(n)šan*. In this context, the putative **makkuyan* would be either sg. acc. or endingless loc. For [*duwarniazzi*(?)] cf. ^{LÚ}SAGI.A-*aššan išqāru*[*ḫ* (*dagān*)] *duwarniyazzi namm*[*a kalgal*(*inaizzi*)] KUB 39.40 ii 12-13 with dupl. KUB 30.24 ii 32-33 (part of the same tablet as KUB 39.35).

^{É}**makzi(ya)-, mākkizzi(ya)-,** ^{É}**mazki(ya)-** n.; (a building); OH.†

sg. gen. *ma-a-ak-ki-iz-zi-ia-aš* KBo 20.8 obv.? 8 (OH/OS), ^{É}*ma-ak-zi-aš* KUB 34.71 i 6 (OH?/NS), [^{É}*ma-a*]*k-zi-ia-aš* KBo 25.17:5 (OS), [*ma-a*]*k-zi-aš* KBo 13.227 i 3 (OH/NS); **all./loc.** ^{É}*ma-ak-zi-ia* KUB 34.71 i 4, KBo 22.186 ii 8 (both OH?/NS), KBo 25.17:(3) (OS), [^{É}*ma-a*]*z-ki-ia* Bo 88 i 2 (translit. HGG); **abl.** ^{É}*ma-a-ak-zi-ia-az* KBo 17.15 rev! 19 (OS), ^{É}*ma-az-ki-ia-az* Bo 88 i 11 (translit. HGG); **broken endings** *ma-a*[*-ak-ki-iz-* . . .] KBo 20.8 obv.? 10, ^{É}*ma-*⸢*ak*⸣*-* [*zi-* . . .] HHT 73 (Bo 5478) iv 5 (StBoT 25 p. 108) (OH/OS), ^{É}*ma-ak-z*[*i-*. . .] KBo 7.40 obv.? 8 (OH/NS), KBo 25.80:5.

[*mān*(?)] *šīwaz* 8 *wakšur āšzi* LUGAL-*ušša* ^{É}*ma-a-ak-zi-ia-az uizz*[*i* . . .] ^{GIŠ}*ḫulukanniya eša* "[When(?)] the day remains (at?) 8 *w.* (a time expression) (or:when 8 *w.*-s of the day remain), the king come[s] out of the *m.* [. . .] he sits down in the light carriage" KBo 17.15 rev! 19-20 (fest. for infernal deities, OH/OS), ed. Haas, UF 8:82f., translit. StBoT 25 p. 74; LUGAL SAL.LUGAL ^{É}*ma-ak-zi-ia pānzi* "The king and queen go into the *m.*, (the assembly does not sit down, the foreign dignitaries do not sit down, and the men of Tiššaruliya sing outside the windows)" KBo 22.186 ii 8-14 (fest., OH?/NS); *ma-a-ak-ki-iz-zi-ia-aš šūḫḫ*[*i* . . .] / *arkīuaz pauwānzi m*[*emianzi*?] "[they] s[ay] to go to the roof of the *m.*-building [. . .] by way of the *a.*-structure" KBo 20.8 obv.? 6-9 (fest., OH/OS); cf. *t⸗e ma-a*[*-ak-ki-iz-zi-* . . .] ibid. 10; cf. [*a*]*rkiuaz* [. . .] / [*ma-a*]*k-zi-aš š*[*uḫḫi* . . .] / [*k*]*ē* $^{\text{LÚ.MEŠ}}$ALA[N.ZU$_{x}$ . . .] KBo 13.227 i 2-4 (fest., OH/NS) with no space in break for det. according to copy; "On the morrow [. . .]. The king [comes] out of the bathhouse, and sits down in the light carriage" ^{É}*ma-ak-zi-ia tu*[*nnakkišni*? . . . *waššanzi* . . .] ^{É}*ḫeštī* UGU-*aš* x[. . .] ^{É}*ma-ak-zi-aš-ma-kán a-a*[*š-ki* . . .] LUGAL-*uš kuin* ERÍN.MEŠ *NAPTAN*[*IM* . . .] KUB 34.71 i 4-7 (fest., OH?/NS); The restorations are based on the similar passage [*ḫantezziy*]*a šīwat mā*[*n luk⸗katta* . . .] / [. . . ^{KUŠ}NÍG.BÀ]R-*ašta ūššianzi* LUGAL[- . . . *-i*(*z-zi*) . . .] / [. . . ^{É}*m*(*a-a*)]*k-zi-ia tunnakki*[*šni*/*a* . . . *-zi*) . . .] / [. . . (x *IN*)]*A* ^{É}*ḫištī INA* É. DINGIR-*L*[*IM* . . .] / [. . . (x-*anzi* ^{É}*ma-a*)]*k-zi-ia-aš āški* KASKAL-*š*[*i* . . .] KBo 25.17 i 1-5 (OS), translit. StBoT 25 pp. 49f., with dupl. KBo 25.18 i 1-7; cf. also [. . . LUG]AL ^{É}*ma-ak-z*[*i-* . . .] KBo 25.80:5; LUGA[L-*uš* ^{É}*m*(*a-a*)]*k-z*[(*i-i*)]*a-aš āš*[*ki t*(*iyazi*)] "The king goes to the entrance of the *m.*-building" KUB 2.3 iv 9-10 w. dupl. Bo 2505 iv 1-2 (KI.LAM fest.), ed. Singer, Diss. 371; cf. Bo 1205 iv (4) (Istanbul); and cf. KUB 2.3 iv 4; [*nuza*? ^{É}*ma-a*]*z-ki-ia ārri* "He washes in the *m.*" Bo 88 i 2 (rit.), translit. HGG, cited by Singer, Diss. 106 n. 1, but cf. [*nuza*(?) ^{GIŠ}]ZA.LAM.GAR-*aš ārri* "He washes in the tent" ibid. i 5; After a § line: (The king takes up his regalia (*aniyatta*), dresses, and) ^{É}*ma-az-ki-ia-az uizzi* "comes out of the *m.*" ibid. i 11.

From these albeit broken passages we learn that the *m.*-building has a gate/ entrance (*aška-*), a roof (*šuḫḫa-*), windows (^{GIŠ}AB.ḪI.A), and an inner chamber (*tunnakkiššar*), and that it is frequently mentioned in conjunction with the ^{É}*ḫešta*. In KBo 22.186 ii 8ff. the assembly and the foreign dignitaries do not sit while the royal couple washes and/or dresses there.

Laroche, OLZ 1955: 226 no. 40; Singer, Diss. (1978) 106 n. 1.

mal n. neut.; (a quality desirable for men in combat, such as boldness, ferocity, skill); from MH/NS.†

sg. nom.-acc. *ma-al* KUB 33.113 i 22 (NS), Bo 6472:15 (JCS 6:39), ⌈*ma-a-al*⌉ KUB 33.113 i 25, KUB 36.1 iii 12 (both NS), KUB 26.29 obv. 24 (MH/NS), KBo 12.68:8, KUB 22.40 iii 28, KUB 49.14 iii 5, *ma-a-al-l(a)* KBo 2.9 i 26 (MH/NS).

a. in an enumeration of attributes and implements appropriate to men in combat, followed by an enumeration of domestic implements and garments appropriate to females: *našta ANA* LÚ.MEŠ *arḫa* LÚ-*natar tarḫuilatar ḫaddulatar ma-a-al-la* GIŠTUKUL.ḪI.A GIŠBAN.ḪI.A GIŠKAK.Ú.TAG.GA.ḪI.A GÍR *dā* "Take away from the (enemy) men manhood, courage, vigor and *mal*, maces, bows, arrows (and) dagger(s), (and bring them to Ḫattuša)!" KBo 2.9 i 25-27 (prayer to Ištar, MH/NS), ed. Sommer, ZA 33:98f., Carruba, OA 16:299f., Haas-Wilhelm, AOAT 3.67; implements and garments of females in KBo 2.9 i 28f.

Oettinger's interpretation (Stammbildung 278 w. n. 38), taking up Sommer's (ZA 33 (1921) 98 n. 2), taking *ma-a-al-la* as imp. sg. 2 of the verb *malla(i)*- is improbable. There would be no conjunction beginning the GIŠTUKUL.ḪI.A ... *dā* clause. The verb *malla(i)*- is nowhere else written with long *a* in the first syllable. In fact, the structure of lines 25-27 is the same as lines 31-32: *našta ANA* LÚ.MEŠ *arḫa* ... *dā nat INA* URU*Ḫatti uda ANA* SAL.MEŠ-*makan arḫa* ... *dā natkan ANA* KUR URU*Ḫatti ištarna uda*. Since GIŠTUKUL.ḪI.A begins a list of objects, the "and" after *mal* is understandable as connecting it with the preceding physical conditions.

b. something which is "known" or "recognized" (obj. of vb. *šak*-): (Ištar says to Teššub with reference to the stone monster:) *ma-al-wa-za tepuya UL* [*šak*]*ki* UR.SAG-*tarmašši* 10-*pa piyan* [o]x [o o o?]-*ia*?-*wašmaš kuin* TUR-*an ḫaššanzi* / [*nuwaza a-pé-*]⌈*e-el*⌉[-*la*?] *ma-a-al UL šakti* "He knows not for himself even a little *mal*, but courage has been given to him tenfold. The child whom the ...-s beget for themselves, you do not know the *mal* of it [either]" KUB 33.113 i 22-24 + KUB 36.12 i 35-37 (Ullik., NS), ed. JCS 6:12f.; *nu* SAL.LUGAL-*ma kuit ma-a-al IDI* KUB 49.14 iii 5 (oracle question, NH).

c. restored to a man through a rite: *kinun* m*Nanenzin* KASKAL-*aḫḫanzi* [o] x *ŠA* m*Tarupšaniya ma-a-al* EGIR-*pa* DÙ-*anzi* [dZ]*awalliyaš aniur* KIN-*anzi* "Now they will put (the deceased) N. on the road (i.e. exorcise his spirit?), and they will restore the *mal* of Tarupšaniya by performing (lit., and will perform) the ritual of Zawalli" KUB 22.40 iii 27-29 (oracle question, NH); Tarupšaniya here might be another deceased person, or he might be a living client whose *mal* is being restored by pacifying the deceased Nanenzi. On the nature of Zawalli rituals cf. Archi, AOF 6:81ff., who, however, does not treat the entire passage. In addition to the PN Tarupiššani/Tarupišni/Tarupšani, there is also a DN Taruppašani, (Laroche, OLZ 1956:421, NH p. 292).

d. in obscure contexts: "Šeriš said to the Stormgod: 'My lord, why do you curse them? ... Ea will hear you! ... " [o (x-*ki šalli ma-a-a*)]*l* KUR-*e mašiwan ma-a-la*(!?)-*an-ták*?-*kán* [...] "'[...] (is?) great; the *mal* (is?) as big as the land. Powerful(?) for you [is ...]'", or perhaps: "'The great *mal* (is?) as big as the land ... '" KUB 33.120 iii 35 with dup. KUB 36.1 right col. 12 (Kingship in Heaven, NS);□in *ma-a-la*?-*an-ták*?-*kán* the third sign resembles *du* (copy confirmed by photo), the fifth could be *ták* or *e* (photo), but the proposed AN-*E* (JCS 6:39) is excluded by the position of -*kán* and the lack of space for word division; for the form see sub *mālant*- "powerful(?)"; in KUB 36.1 the word before *šalli* can only be three signs long; [... -*m*]*a*-⌈*at*⌉ *šuppaeš* [... (*uterma*)]*t ḫāraniš*MUŠEN *pittiyaleš* [... *katteran*? *ḫ*(*a*)]-*a-an* IM-*aškan waršta šarazziyan* [(*ḫa-a-an ma*)]-⌈*a-al*⌉-*az-kán* (dupl. *ma-al-az-kán*) *waršta nu ištarniyan* [*ḫān* G(IŠ*š*)]*amamakan waršta* KUB 33.62 ii 2-6 with dupl. Bo 6472:13-16 (JCS 6:39) (incant. of Stormgod of Kuliwišna); for *ḫān*, imp. of *ḫān*- "to dip/draw (water)", cf. *ḫēnir* in the similar passage KUB 33.34 obv.(?) 6-8; the restoration *katteran* is suggested by the following *šarazziyan* and *ištarniyan* ("lower", "upper", "middle"); cf. KUB 49.98 ii(?) 8.

mal in KBo 2.9 i 25-27 (usage a) is a quality possessed by fighting men and by virtue of which they pose a threat. To "know" this quality for oneself (usage b) may be a way of saying that one possesses it (i.e., to know something for oneself is to experience it). But the expression may also have the force of recognizing the quality in another (e.g., in an opponent). The passage cited in c demonstrates that this quality could be lost, and that it could be restored through a ritual. Only in KUB 33.62 (usage d) does it alternate in the same construction with IM-*aš* and ^{GIŠ}*šamama*, words denoting concrete objects.

Güterbock, JCS 6 (1952) 39f. (tentative proposal "much; abundance").

Cf. *māla*, :*mālī*, *mālant*-.

māla (mng. unknown); MH?†

With the verb *šipant-* in birth rituals: [. . . *I*]*NA* ITU.7.KAM *armaḫḫuaš ma-a-la šipanti* "In the seventh month he offers *mala* of (i.e. for) the pregnancy" KBo 17.65 obv. 6; *nuza ma-a-la-pát šipanti* "He offers the same *mala*" ibid. obv. 8; *našta ḫaš*[*ša*]*ntaš ma-a-la a*[*p*]*ēdani* UD.7.KAM *anda* [*šipanti*] "Then he offers *mala* of (i.e. for) the newborn on that seventh day" ibid. rev. 38-39 and ibid. obv. 27-28 with dupl. KUB 44.39 obv. 13; [. . . *maḫḫ*]*an ma-a-la ŠA* ^{d}*Aprittaya* [*šipanti*] "When he offers *mala* of (i.e. for) the deity Aprittaya" KBo 17.65 rev. 6, all ed. Beckman, Diss. 163ff.

A connection with the Hurrian offering term *mālī* considered possible by Beckman (Diss. 190f.) and seemingly favored by the Hurr. terms following in obv. 8-9 (*namma uziya zurki*[*ya*] *šipan*[*ti*]) and following rev. 6 in rev. 9, is unlikely because of the different ending (*-a* versus *-i*) and *mala*'s construction with Hitt. genitives. Identification with the noun *māl*, deemed "likely" by Beckman (Diss. 191), can be neither proven nor disproven.

Cf. *mal*, *mālī*.

malla/i-, malliya/i- v.; to mill, grind; from OH.

pres. sg. 3 *m*[*a-al-l*]*a-a-i* KBo 15.35 + KBo 15.33 i 11(OH/MS), *ma-al-li* KUB 7.1 ii 1 (pre-NH/NS), *ma-al-la-i* KUB 25.23 iv 52 (NH), *ma-al-li-iz-zi* KUB 41.8 ii 38 (MH/NS), Bo 6870 ii 11 (translit. HGG), KBo 14.133 iii (2), *ma-al-li-ia-az-z*[*i*] KBo 14.75 i 8 (NH), *ma-al-*⌈*la-zi*⌉ VAT 7502 obv. 12 (Oettinger, Stammbildung 277); **pl. 3** *ma-al-la-an-zi* IBoT 1.29 rev. 19 (OH/MS or NS?), KBo 6.34 ii 21 (MH/NS), KUB 33.103 ii 8 (NS), KBo 2.7 obv. 10, 24 (NH), *ma-la-an-zi* KBo 26.182 i 6 (NH), *ma-al-la-zi* KUB 17.35 i 4 (NH).

pret. sg. 1 *ma-al-la*!*-nu-un* HT 35 rev. 7; **sg.3** *ma-al-li-e-et* Bo 6870 obv.? ii 3, 20 (Oettinger, Stammbildung, 277). **imp. pl. 3** *ma-al-la-an-du* KBo 6.34 ii 27 (MH/NS). **iter. pres. pl. 3** *ma-al-liš-kán-zi* KUB 5.6 ii 27 (NH). **part. sg. neut. nom.-acc.** *ma-al-la-an* KUB 24.14 i 10 and passim in NH cult inventories and sim. texts, *ma-la-an* KUB 46.39 iii 15, KBo 13.231 obv. 7, 12, rev. 9; **gen.** *ma-al-la-an-ta-aš* KUB 45.58 iv 6, [*ma-a*]*l-la-an-da-š*(*a-aš-ša-an*) KUB 44.49 obv.! 5; **abl.** *ma-la-an-da-za* KUB 46.42 iv 3; **inf.?** *ma-al-lu-wa-an-zi* KUB 18.3 left col. 25, KBo 26.220:4; **verbal subst.** [*m*]*a-al-lu-wa-ar* KUB 24.7 i 33.

a. objects — **1′** various cereals: NUMUN.ḪI.A *ḫūmanda* MUNU$_8$ BAPPIR *nat* EGIR-*pa paršza ma-al-la-an-zi* "(One takes) all kinds of grains, malt, (and) beer-bread, and they mill it 'backwards'" KUB 43.59 + KUB 9.39 i 4-5 (rit. of Šeḫuzzi, NS), cf. below under d; *nu* NUMUN.ḪI.A *ḫūman* (var. MU.KAM(sic) *dapian*) [(*dāi*)] *nat IŠTU* (dupl. omits) NA$_4$.ARA$_5$ *ma-al-li-iz-zi* KBo 10.45 iii 2-3 (rit. for infernal deities, MH/NS) with dupl. KUB 41.8 ii 37-38, ed. Otten, ZA 54.126f., 152.

2′ wheat (ZÍZ): ZÍZ *ma-al-la-an-zi ḫarranzi* KBo 2.7 obv. 10 (cult inv., NH), ed. Carter, Diss. 90, 96; cf. also ibid. obv. 24, rev. 6, 18; KUB 38.32 rev. 26; KBo 13.246 i 10.

3′ barley (*ḫalki-*): [. . .] *ḫalkin ma-al-la-an-zi* [. . .] IBoT 3.100:2; perhaps: [. . . *ḫalk*]*in*⸗*war*⸗*at ma-al-l*[*a-an-zi* . . .] KBo 14.133 iii 3, ed. AlHeth 144.

4′ *šeppit*: 1-*EN šeppit*(-)x x x[. . . (*nat ma-al-li šal*)]*kzi* KUB 43.52 ii 8-9 rest. from dupl. KUB 7.1 ii 1 (rit. of Wattiti, pre-NH/NS).

5′ *kar-aš*: *nu* 1 *UPNU kar-aš ma-al-la-an nat šalgami* KUB 24.14 i 10 (rit., NH).

6′ flour (ZÍD.DA) (unspecified): [*kā*]*ša kūn* ZÍD.DA *kāš* SAL-*za ma-al-li-e-et* "This woman has [ju]st milled this flour" Bo 6870 ii 3 (ritual), translit. HGG, cf. ibid. ii 20.

7′ (cereal) contents of storage jars (^{DUG}*ḫarši-* and ^{DUG}*ḫaršiyalli-*): "When it becomes spring (and) it thunders, they break open the storage jars" *nat ma-al-la-i ḫarrai* "and he mills and grinds it (i.e., the contents)" KUB 25.23 iv 51-52 (cult inv., Tudḫ. IV); ^{DUG}*ḫarši ma-al-la-an-zi ḫarranzi* KUB 17.35 ii 15, VBoT 26:11, KBo 26.182 i 6, cf. KBo 25.183 rt. col. 7; GIM-*anma ḫamišhi tetḫai* *nukan* ^{DUG}*ḫaršiyalli ginuwanzi nat* LÚ.MEŠ ^{URU}*Urišta ḫarranzi ma-al-la-an-zi* KUB 25.23 i 38-39.

8′ 'beer bread' and bones: *kī₌wa* BAPPIR GIM-*an IŠTU* NA₄.ARA₅ *ma-al-la-an-zi . . . nu ḫaštai₌ši≪ti≫t QĀTAMMA ma-al-la-an-du* "Just as they grind up this 'beer bread' with the millstone . . ." (May these oaths seize the perjurer,) "and may they grind up his(!) bones in the same way!" KBo 6.34 ii 21, 26-27 (Soldier's Oath, MH/NS), ed. Friedrich, ZA 35 (1924) 161ff.(?) and StBoT 22:10-11; cf. also a 1′.

b. subjects — **1′** females: □The normal sex distribution is for the males to plow, sow and reap, and the females to mill (cf. KBo 10.2 iii 16-17 w. dupl. KUB 23.20:2-3 and Akk. vers. KBo 10.1 rev. 11-12; discussion Hoffner, AlHeth 132f.); [o o o] *uizzi* ^{d}U-*aš* ^{URU}*Kummiyaš* UR.SAG-*uš* (var. -*iš*) LUGAL-*uš* ^{GIŠ}APIN-*an* [*apaši*]*la ēpzi nu uizzi₌ma* ^{d}*IŠTAR*(var. ^{d}GAŠAN)-*iš* ^{d}*Ḫebadušša* [NA₄.A]RA₅ *apāšila ma-al-la-an-zi* "It will happen that the Storm-god, K.'s valiant king, will seize the plow [him]self, or it will happen that *IŠTAR* and Ḫebat will themselves mill (with the) [mil]l-stone" KUB 33.103 ii 6-8 with dupl. KUB 33.100 + KUB 36.16 iii 14-16 (Ḫedammu, NS), ed. StBoT 14:46f.; *nu* ^{SAL}*BELTI* É-*TIM INA* É NA₄.ARA₅ [(*paizzi*) *naš*? *IN*]*A* NA₄.ARA₅ *m*[*a-al-l*]*a-a-i* KBo 15.35 + KBo 15.33 i 10-11 (rit., MH/MS) with dupl. KUB 41.10 obv. 14; [. . .] SAL-*za ma-al-l*[*i-iz-zi* . . .] KBo 14.133 iii 2, ed. AlHeth 144; cf. KUB 5.6 ii 26-27 (oracle question, NH), ed. AU 278f.; cf. sub SAL.MEŠ NA₄.ARA₅.

2′ males: *ta* NA₄.ARA₅ DUMU.LUGAL 1 *tazelliš* ^{LÚ}ŠÀ.[TAM] ^{LÚ}ŠU.I ${}^{LÚ.MEŠ}$*mi*!-*na-al-li-e-eš ma-al-la-an-zi* IBoT 1.29 rev. 18-19 (EZEN *ḫaššumaš*, OH/MS?); *nat* LÚ.MEŠ ^{URU}*Urišta ḫar₌ranzi ma-al-la-an-zi* KUB 25.23 i 39 (cult inv., Tudḫ. IV), cf. ibid. i 9.

c. participle "milled (grain)" usually in the combination *taršan mallan* "roasted?/dried? (and) milled" (cf. AlHeth. 139-43): *tar-ša-an ma-al-la-an* KUB 38.12 i 26, ii 10, iv 6, KUB 42.100 i 6, 13, 14, iii 20, iv 27, KUB 12.4 i 11, KBo 22.246 iii 19; *tar-ša-an ma-la-an* KBo 13.231 obv.? 7, 12, KUB 46.39 iii 15; [*tar-š*]*a-an-da-za ma-la-an-da-za* KUB 46.42 iv 3; cf. *ḫātan ma-al-la-an* "dried (and) milled" KBo 16.78 i 8; [1 NINDA.LÀ]L GÚ.GAL.GAL *ma-al-la-an-ta-aš* (dupl. [*ma-a*]*l-la-an-da-ša-aš-ša-an*) "[1 hone]y [bread] of milled bean" (followed by 4 other types of NINDA.LÀL) KUB 45.58 iv 6 (EZEN *ḫišuwaš*, MH/NS), dupl. KUB 44.49 obv! 5.

d. *appa par*(*š*)*za malla-* to mill "backwards": cf. KUB 43.59 + KUB 9.39 i 4-5 above under a 1′; [*and*]*ama* NA₄.ARA₅ *udanzi nan* x[...]/[*nu*] EN.SISKUR NA₄.ARA₅ *šar*!-*li-in* EGIR-*pa parza* [*mallai*(?) ...]/[ḪU]L-*uš* UN-*aš* UḪ₄-*aš kuie* INIM.MEŠ [*memiškit*(?) *nuwarat* EGI]R-*pa parza ma-al-la*!(text *ku*)-*nu-un* HT 35 rev. 4-7 (rit., NS), cf. Goetze, Tunn. 93□the KUB 43.59 + KUB 9.39 passage (cited sub a 1′) combined with the presence of NA₄.ARA₅ in the HT 35 context make the emendation -*la*!- virtually certain.

Sommer, ZA 33 (1921) 98 n. 2.

malai- v.; to approve, to approve of; all exx. NS.

pres. sg. 2 *ma-la-a-ši* KUB 14.3 iii 62, KUB 21.38 obv. 9, AT 125:8 (all NH), *ma-la-ši* KUB 21.38 rev. 4 (NH), *ma-la*!-*ši* KBo 18.48 rev. 18 (NH), *ma-a-la-a-ši* KUB 40.1 rev! 21 (NH); **sg. 3** *ma-a-la-i* KUB 17.16 i 9 (NH), *ma-l*[*a*]-*a-i* KBo 2.4 l.e.2 (NH); **pl. 3** *ma-a-la-an-zi* KUB 41.54 iii 14 (NH).

pret. sg. 3 *ma-la-a-iš* KBo 22.6 iv 26 (NS), *ma-la-a-it* KBo 19.111:3, KUB 33.119:19 (both NS).

imp. pl. 3? [. . . *m*]*a-a-la-an-d*[*u*? . . .] KBo 14.110:5 (NH).

part. sg. nom. com. *ma-la-a-an-za* KUB 21.38 obv. 26, KUB 22.37 obv. 7, 12 (all NH); **nom.-acc. neut.** *ma-la-a-an* KUB 5.1 i 8, 11 etc., KUB 22.70 obv. 50, rev. 5 etc. (all NH), *ma-la-an* KUB 22.70 rev. 53, 62, KBo 24.118 i 16, ii 15 (all NH), *ma-la-*<*an*> KBo 24.118 i 6 (NH), *ma-a-la-an* KBo 23.118 ii 8, KUB 22.46: 2 (both NH).

inf. *ma-*⌜*a*⌝*-la-wa-an-zi* KUB 40.1 rev.! 25 (NH).

iter. pres. sing. 3 *ma-le-eš-ki-zi* KUB 5.6 iii 8 (NH).

For :*ma-li-ši* KBo 4.14 ii 78 (coll.) see *mali-* v.

a. finite forms of *malai-*, with obligatory -*za* — **1′** contrasted with -*za markiya-* "to disapprove": *natza UL markiyaši ma-la-a-ši-ya-at-za* "You will not disapprove of it. You will approve of it" KUB 21.38 obv. 9 (letter of Puduḫepa), ed. Helck, JCS 17:88., Stefanini, Pud. 14f.; ŠEŠ-*YA-matza UL markiši ma-la-ši-at-za* "My brother, you will not disapprove of it. You will approve of it." ibid. rev. 4; *markiškiwanziyamuza ma-a-la-*

wa-an-zi RI-*za lē ḫa-ap-x-an-zi* KUB 40.1 rev! 25 (letter of a commander to the king), cf. Kühne, ZA 62:237f.; cf. KBo 2.4 left edge 2-3.

2′ without associated antonym *markiya-*: *nuwaza mān* EN-*YA apē* MUŠEN.ḪI.A *ma-la-a-ši nuwamu* EN-*YA* [EG]IR-*pa ḫatrāu* "If, my lord, you approve of those birds, let my lord write back to me" AT 125:7-9 (letter, NH), ed. Rost, MIO 4:340f.; [(LUGAL-*g*)*in*]*aš* $^{LÚ.MEŠ}$UR.SAG-*aš uddār IŠME taz ma-la-a-iš* "Sargon heard the words of the warriors and he agreed" KBo 22.6 iv 26 (epic of Sargon, NS) with dupl. KBo 12.1 iv 8-9 (NS), ed. Güterbock, MDOG 101:21, 23; *taparriyanma apunpat* DIB-*un* ^{d}UTU-*ŠI-za* ⌜EN-*YA*⌝ *kuin ma-a-la-a-ši* "I held fast the command— that very one, which you approve, Your Majesty, my lord" KUB 40.1 rev.! 21 (letter, NH).

b. in the *malan ḫar*(*k*)- construction, almost always with *-za* or the equivalent dat. pron. (*-mu*, *-ta*, *-šmaš*, etc.): *manmašmaš* DINGIR.MEŠ ^{URU}KÙ.BABBAR-*an* URU-*an ŠA* ^{d}U ^{URU}*Ḫalap ANA* ^{d}UTU-*ŠI* SAL.LUGAL ŠE$_{12}$-*uanzi* ⌜*da*⌝*piaz tak*<*š*>*an ma-la-a-an ḫarteni* "If you gods have jointly(?) approved Ḫattuša... in all respects for His Majesty and the queen to winter in" KUB 18.12 obv. 4-5 (oracle question, NH), ed. Ünal, RHA XXXI 43f.; [...]x KASKAL-*an ḫūmandaz takšan ma-la-a-an ḫ*[*ar*⸗*teni*] KUB 16.47:11 (oracle question, NH); *ANA* ^{d}UTU-*ŠI laḫḫiyatar* DINGIR-*LUM kēdani* MU-*ti* ZAG ^{KUR}*Durmitta ma-la-a-an ḫarti* "Have you, O god, approved the border (i.e., territory) of the land of Durmitta for a campaign for His Majesty this year?" KBo 22.264 i 1-2 (oracle question, NH), cf. ibid. i 14-16; *mānmaza* DINGIR.MEŠ *ŠA* ^{fd}*IŠTAR-atti* SISKUR *mantalliya ITTI* ^{d}UTU-*ŠI* BAL-*uwanzi ma-la-a-an ḫarteni* "If you, O gods, have approved the *m.*-ritual of Šaušgatti to be offered together with His Majesty" KBo 2.6 iii 32-33 (oracle, NH); DINGIR-*LIM-za QĀTAMMA ma-la-a-an ḫarti* "Have you, O god, likewise approved?" KUB 22.70 rev. 5, 47, cf. 53 (oracle question, NH), ed. THeth 6:82ff.

c. participial form *malant-* outside of the *malan ḫar*(*k*)- construction, not requiring *-za*—**1′** without preverb: TA DINGIR-*LIM kuit ma-la-a-an* "Since (it) was approved by the god" KUB 5.1 ii 14 (oracle, NH); [*I*]*Š*[*T*]*U* DINGIR-*LIM apāš ma-la-a-an-za* "Is he approved by the god?" KUB 22.37 obv. 7 (oracle, NH), cf. ibid. 12; for KBo 15.1 i 35-36 and KUB 33.120 iii 35 see the article *mālant-* adj.

2′ with preverb *anda*: *ammuqqa*⸗*aš*⸗*kan UL anda ma-la-a-an-za* "Was she (the daughter) / it (the matter) not approved by me?" KUB 21.38 obv. 26 (letter of Pud.).

The particle *-z*(*a*) is obligatory with the finite forms of *malai-* (usage a), optional with *malan ḫar*(*k*)- (usage b), and does not occur in usage c. The criteria for its use are syntactical; its presence does not require a different translation.

Forrer, Forsch. 1/2 (1929) 179 ("billigen"); Sommer, AU (1932) 161f. ("akzeptieren, genehmigen, billigen"); Friedrich, OLZ 1936:308; HW (1952) 133 ("billigen, gutheissen, einverstanden sein").

Cf. *malaimi*, *:mali-* n., *:mali-* Luw. vb., (:)*maliyašḫa-*.

:malāimi- Luw. Pass. Part.; (mng. unknown); NH.†

In a deposition: [...] ⌜*kuit*⌝ *:ma-la-a-i-mi-in* [o o *ku*]*wapi kuin pešta* "With regard to the ...-ed [...] which you (or: he) once gave" KUB 40.80 obv. 19.

The context of the above example is too badly broken to offer a basis for translating *:malāimi-*. Since, however, there is a Luw. verb *:mali-* q.v., this might be that verb's participle. For the vocalization of the stem cf. the Luw. verb *dup*(*a*)*i-* with pres. sg. 3 *du-ú-pí-ti* and part. *dupaimmiš*, *dupai*(*m*)*min* (DLL 99), and cf. Oettinger, Stammbildung 562f; Starke, KZ 93:251.

malak- see *malk-*.

malali (mng. unkn.); pre-NH/NS.†

(In a rit. the Old Woman takes various kinds of foliage (^{GIŠ}*laḫḫurnuzzi*) and offers bread upon it) *nu kiššan memai ma-la-li* x[...] *kēdani* UD.KAM-*ti iyanun* "and she speaks thus: *malali* [...] I have made (or: done) on this day" KBo 4.2 iii 35-36, ed. Kronasser, Die Sprache 8:95

with comments on context on p. 98, but no comment on *malali*.

mālant- adj.; powerful(?), vigorous(?); NH.†

sg. acc. com. *ma-a-la-an-ta-an* KBo 15.1 i 36; **nom.-acc. neut.** *ma-a-la*!-*an*(-*ták*?-*kán*) KUB 33.120 iii 35.

[*n*(*uwaraš m*)]*ān* DINGIR-*LIM* LÚ *nuwatta* GU_4.MAḪ *unuwa*(*ndan ašuša*)*n*]*tan ma-a-la-an-ta-an AD*[*DIN*] "If he is a male deity, I have given you an adorned, *ašušant*-, powerful(?) bull" KBo 15.1 i 35-36 (rit. of Puliša), w. dupl. KBo 21.9:3-4, ed. StBoT 3:114f. and 125, where Kümmel disassociates this form from *malai*- "approve" and proposes the tr. "kraftstrotzend"; [o(x-*ki šalli mā*)]*l* KUR-*e mašiwan ma-a-la*(!?)-*an-ták*?-*kán* [...] KUB 33.120 iii 35, for tr. and discussion see under *māl* d; the occurrence together of *māl* and *mālant*- may support Kümmel's interpretation.

Since *māl* is a quality possessed by fighting men, an adj. based on *māl* ("provided with *māl*") might be appropriate to describe a bull. Cf. HE 1 §48b2. Because most of KBo 15.1 i 40 is broken away, we cannot tell if the female UDU.ÁŠ. SAL.GÀR was *mālant*-.

Cf. *māl*.

ma-a-la-at-x[...] (mng. unknown); OH/NS.†

In bil. Akk.-Hitt. edict of Ḫatt. I: Akk. vers.: *ša kīdānum* [*nakrēya* ... *a*-?*b*]*u*?-*ri-iš ukīl* "[I ...-ed my] external [enemies(?) ... and] I held/kept [my land(?)] in [p]eace(?)" = Hitt. vers.: [*araḫzenuš*] LÚ.MEŠ[K]ÚR-*uš*-*muš ma-a-la-at*-x [...-*u*]*n n*[*u* ... *hark*]*un* "I [...-]ed my external enemies *m*., and I held / kept [...]" KUB 1.16 (BoTU 8) i 27-28, ii 27-28, traces following BoTU 8, ed. HAB 4f. with comments on p. 60 with n. 3; HAB restored more than the above and considered only two possible meanings for *m*.: a mode of fighting or a type of weapon. Of the latter possibility he excluded the commonly occurring GIŠTUKUL in favor of Ehelolf's proposal that GIŠTUKUL = *ḫatanti*-. He tentatively favored an equation with the Sumerogram GÍR "dagger" and restored Akk. *ina paṭri* in Akk. vers. at i 28. But this passage is much more unclear than the editors admitted.

:malḫa(š)šallaḫit- n. neut.; performance of a sacrifice or ritual, (lit. "offering relatedness", Luw. abstract from adj. in -*alli*- from *malḫašša*-= SISKUR.SISKUR "sacrifice, ritual"); NH.†

sg.d.-l. :*ma-al-ḫa-aš-šal-la-ḫi-ti* KUB 5.6 ii 44, :*ma-al-ḫa-šal-la-ḫi-ti* ibid. 67.

"They made further oracle inquiries about them (i.e., the deities of Zitḫara) ... the following was also determined by the diviner" *ANA* dUTU-*ŠI-waratkan* :*ma-al-ḫa-aš-šal-la-ḫi-ti areškantari* "They (the deities) will be questioned by oracles (to determine if) the performance of sacrifice (is incumbent) upon (lit. *ANA* "to, for") His Majesty" KUB 5.6 ii 42-44 (oracle question, NH), ed. Sommer, AU 280f., cf. StBoT 5:13; "Since sickness is still pressing His Majesty, if Zawalli of Ankuwa too is responsible for (?) this sickness of His Majesty" *naškan ANA* dUTU-*ŠI* :*ma-al-ḫa-šal-la-ḫi-ti areškattari* "shall he (Zawalli) be questioned by oracle (to determine if) the performance of a sacrifice (is incumbent) upon His Majesty? (Then let the extispicy be unfavorable. Result: unfavorable. They brought the god Z. of A. and made sacrifice for him.)" ibid. 65-69, ed. Archi, AOF 6:88f. (tr. following DLL). Cf. perhaps ÍD-*i ma-al-ḫa*[-...] KUB 43.60 iii 8.

Laroche DLL (1959) 66 ("à l'aide de la magie").

malli- v. see *malla*/*i*-.

:mālī n. (d.-l., Luw.); thought, idea, suggestion; NH.†

(If someone approaches you for something good, be good to him.) *mānmatakk*[*an*] :*kupyatima šer naššu Š*[*A* m]*Šuppiluliuma* ḪUL-*ui* :*ma-a-li-i ŠA* DINGIR[.MEŠ] :*zam*-*muratti U ŠA* KUR URU*Ḫatti* ḪUL-*l*[*awann*]*i šer kuiški* EGIR-*p*[*a*] *a*[*nda uizzi*] (continuation broken) "But if someone approaches you for the sake of a plot, either for an evil thought (or: suggestion) concerning Šuppiluliuma, an insult to the gods, or (lit.: and) the detriment of Ḫattiland, (do not listen to him!)" KBo 12.30:12-15 (treaty or instr., Šupp. II), ed. Otten apud Schirmer, WVDOG 81:52f. (:*mālī* left untranslated).

Cf. :*mali*- v.

:mali- Luw. v.; to think, contemplate; NH.†

pres. sg. 1 *:ma!-li-wi₅* KBo 4.14 iv 34, **sg. 2** *:ma-li-ši* ibid. ii 78.

(If any land turns away from me, or if any lords defect from me, and you join them, claiming they forced you,—don't do it!) § *našmat zik :ma*(coll.)*-li-ši aši⸗man⸗kan* ZAG[*-aš* GAM*-an*?] *niyari našma⸗<m> an⸗wa⸗kan uniuš* EN.MEŠ *:alla*[*llā*] *pānzi ūqqa⸗man⸗wa pēḫu⸗danzi nat lē šanḫti* ÚŠ*-an⸗ta* ZAG*-aš ēš*[*du*] "Or (if) *you* contemplate it: 'That province might turn (i.e., change its allegiance), or those lords might defect and take me away with them'—Don't try it! Let death be your boundary!" KBo 4.14 ii 78-81 (treaty of Šupp. II), ed. Stefanini, AANL 20:43f., comments on p. 65 ("prendere in considerazione . . . queste (ipotesi): '. . . potrebbe . . .' "); *ūkmawa<r>an* [. . . *-a*]*t UL :ma!-li-wi₅* "But *I* will not contemplate it" ibid. iv 33-34 in broken context; collation showed *:ku-*, but one should probably emend to *:ma-*.

In the paragraph KBo 4.14 ii 73-76 a rebellious province and rebellious lords force the vassal to join their faction. Despite the excuse that "They forced me" the vassal is held accountable for his complicity. In the following paragraph KBo 4.14 ii 77-81 he is held accountable for even entertaining fears regarding the danger to him if certain lands or lords should rebel and carry him off. The interpretation of the crucial verb *:mališi* depends upon the interpretation of the *⸗man* clauses. If they are examples of the speaker optative (cf. *man* usage a1') to be translated "Would that . . . " or "I wish that . . . ", it is conceivable that the vassal is himself planning rebellion, or even proposing it to others. If, however, the *⸗man* clauses are potential and to be translated " . . . might . . . " (Stefanini's "potrebbe"), then the vassal can only be entertaining thoughts about threats posed to his safety and contemplating action along the lines of least danger (i.e., desertion if it becomes necessary). Favoring the latter interpretation is the phrase "Let death be your limit (ZAG*-aš*)", which concludes this pericope. This phrase occurs elsewhere in this text only in those situations where the vassal is tempted to abandon the Hittite king through outside threat or invasion (ii 23, 29, 61). It seems to have been similar in force to LUGAL*-i* GAM*-an āk* "Give your life for the king!" (ii 65) and is inappropriate to a situation in which the vassal is conceived as fomenting a rebellion.

In spite of the phonetic similarity to *malai-* "to approve" and the possibility of translating these passages as "If you approve it (i.e., the rebellion or foreign invasion)", we must keep this verb apart from *malai-* because of the marker wedge and the absence of *-za*, which is obligatory for the finite forms of *malai-* (cf. *malai-* usage a).

According to Starke (KZ 93:251 n. 18-19) two participles of this verb are attested: an older one *ma!-li-im-ma-aš-ši(-wa)* in the broken Luw. context KUB 35.79 iv 9, and a younger one *:malāimi-* in KUB 40.80 obv. 19. The latter, being in a Hittite context, occupies its own lemma above in this dictionary.

Starke, KZ 93 (1979) 251 ("billigen").

Cf. *:mali-* n., *:malāimi-*.

ma-le-e-x[. . .] (mng. and form unknown); NS.†

[*m*]*ānkan* ŠÀ UD.KAM.ḪI.A *ma*(coll.)*-le-e-*x[. . .] "If/when in the midst of the days . . ." KUB 39.52 ii 12 (instructions, NS).

malliya/i- see *malla/i-*.

:ma-li-ia-an?-za? (Luw. acc. or dat.-loc. pl.? mng. unknown); NH.†

[. . . *ANA*(?) EZ]EN(?).SA[G(?).U]Š *:ma-*⌈*li-ia-an?-za?*⌉ *ḫalziḫḫi* KUB 18.46 rev. 7 (oracle question, NH). HW 332 read this word *:maliyari*(?).

Laroche, DLL 66 (no translation).

(:)maliyašḫa- n. com.; approval; NH.†

sg. nom.? [*:ma-l*]*i-ia-aš-ḫa-aš* KUB 6.39 rev.? 9; **abl.** *ma-li-ia-aš-ḫa-az* KUB 9.15 ii 12 (2x), *:ma-li-ia-aš-ḫa-az* KUB 49.92 iv 4, *:ma-li-ia-aš-ḫa-az*?(coll.) KUB 6.39 rev.? 8.

nu šallayaz [*k*]*uiš piran uiyanza nu ANA* LÚ.MEŠ URU*-LIM ma-li-ia-aš-ḫa-az memāu* *nankan ma-li-ia-aš-ḫa-az* KASKAL-*ši tiyandu* "Let one who was sent ahead from the great (place) (i.e. capital) speak to the men of the city with (their) approval, and let them set him on the road with (their) approval. (... Let him not quarrel at all. Let him not hit or curse anyone.)" KUB 9.15 ii 10-13 (instr.) □ The context shows that the messenger was not permitted to coerce the townspeople. Cf. also in broken context in oracles: KUB 6.39 rev.? 8, 9, KUB 49.92 iv 4.

Friedrich, HW 133, 1.Erg.13 ("Einverständnis(?), Entgegenkommen(?)").

Cf. *malai-*.

malikk- v.; (mng. unknown); OH or MH/MS.†

"You, O my god, who gave the sickness to me, pity me!" [... *i-n*]*a*?-*ni piran tariaḫḫun ma-li-ik-*⌜*ku*⌝*-un nuza namma UL* ⌜*tar*⌝*ḫmi* "I have toiled and ... -ed in the face of [illn]ess, but still I do not succeed" KUB 30.10 rev. 3-4 (Kantuzzili prayer), the parallel in KUB 31.127+ beginning of col. iii is broken.

m. is probably similar in meaning to *dariya-*, i.e., exertion, toil, and weariness.

[EZEN "*ma*"-*le-el-la*] KUB 27.15 iv 25 is to be read EZEN *Ku-le-el-la.* For this scribe's *ma* cf. i 3, 8, 12, iv 5, 8. For EZEN [URU]*Ku-le-el-la* cf. KUB 12.4 i 4.

mališku-, milišku- adj.; **1.** weak, **2.** light, unimportant(?); from OH.†

sg. nom. com. *mi-li-iš-ku-uš* KBo 1.42 i 14 (NH); **neut.** *ma-li-iš-ku* KUB 23.72 rev. 53 (MH/MS), KUB 33.66 iii 13 (OH/MS?); **abl.** *ma-li-iš-ku-wa-az* KBo 3.13 rev. 13 (OH/NS).

pl. nom. com. *ma-li-iš-ku-e-eš* KUB 29.55 ii 6 (NS).

(Sum.) ⌜á⌝-nu-g[ál] = (Akk.) *qal-lu* = (Hitt.) *mi-li-iš-ku-uš* "light", "unimportant" KBo 1.42 i 14, ed. MSL 13:133, line 24. Cf. á-gál = *ka*[*b-tù*] = *da-aš-šu-uš* "heavy", "important" ibid. i 9. Sum. á-gál and á-nu-gál can mean "strong" and "weak", but Akk. *kabtu* and *qallu* cannot be so translated.

1. weak (opp. of *daššu-* "strong") — **a.** in OH: [...]-*edaz ma-li-iš-ku-wa-az gi-nu-*⌜*wa*?-*az*?⌝ "from [the]se(?) weak knees" KBo 3.13 rev. 13 (Naram-Sin, OH/NS), ed. Güterbock, ZA 44:72; (The eight junior gods say to the Stormgod:) *dālawa* KI.⌜KAL?⌝-*liwa uddanā*[*š* ...] *ma-li-iš-ku* KUB 33.66 iii 12-13 (myth, OH/MS), translit. Laroche, Myth. 71.

b. in MH and NH: "How the springs and roads are, everything [you shall] de[scribe(?)] ..." *nu ma-li-iš-ku* [*uttar lē tašn*]*uttani taššuma uttar lē mališkunuttan*[*i* ... *š*]*ākuwaššar memišten* "Do not make a weak thing strong; do not make a strong thing weak. [...] Say what is accurate." KUB 23.72 rev. 53-54 (Mita text, MH/MS), tr. Gurney, AAA 28:38, 44; *ma-li-iš-ku-e-eš k*[*uiēš* ANŠE.KUR.RA.ḪI.A *nušmaš INA*] ⌜2⌝ KASKAL-*NI* ḪA.LA.ḪI.A *pia*[*nzi*] "They give rations for the second time to the horses which are weak" KUB 29.55 ii 6-7 (hipp., NS), ed. Kammenhuber, Hipp.Heth. 154f.; cf. ibid. ii 36, 46, iii 19. Contrasted with *daššaweš* "strong" in ibid. ii 40 (restored in ii 13, 25, and 52) and with *daššuš* "strong" restored in iii 22. Cf. Hipp.Heth. 154 n. 22.

2. light, unimportant(?) (opp. of *daššu-* "heavy"): Cf. KBo 1.42 i 14 in lex. sect., where *m.* translates Akk. *qallu* "light, unimportant".

Since the antonym *daššu-* has the meanings "heavy", "important" and "strong", and Akk. *qallu*, which *m.* translates in KBo 1.42 i 14, can mean "light (in weight)" or "unimportant" (but not "weak"), we consider it possible that *m.* meant "light (in weight)" or "unimportant". As in the case of *daššu-* heaviness was associated with importance and strength, so in the case of the antonym *m.* lightness was associated with insignificance and weakness.

Hrozny, BoSt 1 (1917) 8; Güterbock, ZA 44 (1938) 76.

maleškuešš- v.; to become weak, to become less serious; NH.†

In an oracle question: "His Majesty will do this:" *BĒLŪ*[[H]I.A]-*za kuēš* [d]UTU-*ŠI* ZI-*ni* GAM-*an IDI naškan arḫa ḫalzāi* URU-*anmakan parā nāi apezza ma-le-eš-ku-eš-zi* SIG₅-*ru* "The lords whom His Majesty has in his mind he will call away, but the city he will send forth(?). Will (the bad situation) thereby become less serious? Let (the oracle) be favorable." KBo 13.76 obv. 12-14 □ The addition between the lines follows an unpublished handcopy by Güterbock. SIG$_5$-*ru* implies that the question asked if something good will happen, i.e. if a bad situation will become weak or less serious by the king's actions. *daššu-*, the antonym of the adj. *mališku-*, is used of a strong or severe struggle in KUB 33.96 iv 10 + KUB 36.7a iv 47 (Ullik.I A iv 47).

mališkunu- v.; to make weak, weaken; from MH.†

"How the springs and roads are, everything [you shall] de[scribe(?)] . . ." *nu mališku [uttar lē tašn]uttani taššuma uttar lē ma-li-iš-ku-nu-ut-ta-n[i memian(?) š]ākuwaššar memišten* "Do not make a weak thing strong; do not make a strong thing weak. Say what is accurate." KUB 23.72 rev. 53-54 (Mita text, MH/MS), tr. Gurney AAA 28: 38, 44; *nu* K[UR.KUR].ḪI.A ^{LÚ}KÚR *daššanuškitten* KUR.KUR ^{URU}*Ḫatti-ma ma-li-iš-ku-nu-ut-ten* "You have strengthened the lands of the enemy, but you have weakened the lands of Ḫatti" KUB 21.42 ii 7-8 (instr. for the LÚ.SAG, NH), ed. von Schuler, Dienstanw. 25.

Güterbock, ZA 44 (1938) 76.

mallitalli- Luw. n. com.; container for honey(?); NH.†

Luw. pl. nom. *ma-al-li-ta-al-le-en-zi* KUB 12.1 iv 31.

"One silver sun disk inlaid(?) with go[ld]" 2 *ma-al-li-ta-al-le-en-zi* ŠÀ.BA 1 *ḫunta*[- o o]x KÙ.GI NA$_4$ 1 *ḫapal<ki>yaš* 2 ^{GIŠ}BAR.KÍN KÙ .GI "two containers for honey(?), of which one (is) a *ḫ.* of gold (and) stone, (and) one (is) of iron (having?) two layers(?)/surfaces(?) of gold" KUB 12.1 iv 31-32 (inv.), ed. Košak, Linguistica 18:102, 106, cf. Laroche, RHA XV/60:10.

Luw. derivative in *-alli-* (DLL 139) from Luw. n. *mallit-* "honey".

Laroche, DLL 66; van Brock, RHA XX/71:110.

:mallitiwalla- Luw. n. com.; (a kind of bread or cake containing honey(?)); NH.†

sg. nom. *:ma-al-li-ti-wa-al-la-aš* KUB 42.91 ii 2.

7 *:ma-al-li-ti-wa-al-la-aš kuišša* KA×UD "seven (loaves of) *m.*-bread, each (made like) a tooth" KUB 42.91 ii 2; cf. 5 NINDA.LÀL *kuišša* KA×UD-*aš iyanza* KUB 38.25 i 20, cf. Hoffner, AlHeth 198f. s.v. NINDA KA×UD.

It is possible that this is the Luw. word for NINDA.LÀL, the Hitt. reading of which is still unknown. The word appears to contain the Luw. *mallit-* "honey" (DLL 66), but no derivational suffix *-iwalla-* is known yet for Luw. References for NINDA.LÀL will be treated among the logograms, as long as its Hitt. reading has not been found.

Hoffner, AlHeth 171 (*mallitiwalla-*), 202 (NINDA.LÀL).

Cf. NINDA.LÀL.

maliddu- see *miliddu-*.

malk-, malkiya- v.; 1. to spin, 2. (with *appa parza*) to unravel; from OH.†

pres. sg. 3. *ma-la-ak-zi* KUB 7.1 ii 14 (pre-NH/NS), *ma-al-ki-i-iz-zi* Bo 2709 ii 7 (Oettinger, Stammbildung 346), *ma-al-ki-iz-zi* KBo 22.110 obv. 4; **pl. 3.** *ma-al-ki-ia-an-zi* KUB 29.1 ii 8 (OH/NS); **pret. sg. 3.** *ma-al-ki-ia-at* KUB 17.27 ii 29 (MH?/NS).

verb. subst. *ma-⸢a-al⸣-ku-u-wa-[ar]* KBo 26.12 v? 22 (NH), *ma-al-ki-ia-wa-ar* KBo 1.42 iv 45, (49), KBo 26.10 iv (6), *[ma-a]l-ki-ia-u-wa-ar* KBo 26.11 rev. 4.

(Sum.) da-rí-an-šub!(text ŠI) = (Akk.) *pa-tá-lu*! (text NU) = (Hitt.) *ma-al-⸢ki⸣-ia-wa-ar* KBo 1.42 iv 45, (Sum.) še-be-da = (Akk.) *pa-ta-lu*!(text: NU) (= Hitt.) *ma-al-ki-[ia-wa-ar]* ibid. 49 (Izi Bogh., NH), ed. MSL 13 142:272, 276, cf. Hoffner, JAOS 87 (1967) 301f. for discussion of this section; (Akk.) *ki-it-x-zu* = (Hitt.) *ma-⸢a-al⸣-ku-u-wa-[ar]* KBo 26.12 rev. 21-22 (Diri, NH).

1. to spin; (The eagle replies to Ḫalmašuit:) "(One) holds a distaff, (others) hold full spindles" *nu* LUGAL-*waš* MU.KAM.ḪI.A-*uš ma-al-ki-ia-an-zi* "They are spinning the years of the king" KUB 29.1 ii 5-8 (myth in rit., OH/NS), ed. Kellerman, Diss. 13, 27; "Whatever spells the sorcerer spoke" *taruppiyat kue ma-al-ki-ia-at kue* "whatever he twined (and) whatever he spun" KUB 17.27 ii 28-29 (rit., MH?/NS), cf. tr. ANET 347 ("wove"); cf. [. . . S]ÍG.ZA.GÌN *ma-al-k[i?-* . . .] KUB 17.1 ii 25 (Keššì story).

2. (with *appa parza*) to unravel: "She takes (lengths of) black wool, yellow wool, red wool (and) blue wool" *nat* EGIR-*pa parza ma-la-ak-zi nammat parā ḫandān anda tar⸢nai⸣* "She unravels them and then lays them together (stretched) out straight" KUB 7.1 ii 13-15 (rit., pre-NH/NS), ed. Kronasser, Die Sprache 7: 149, 151, our tr. follows Hoffner, in Finkelstein Mem. (1977) 108; the broken and ambiguous context of HT 35 rev. 5-7 makes it possible to attribute *ma-al*-KU(read *ki*! or *la*!)-*nu-un* to either *malk-* or *malla-*. The presence of NA$_4$.ARA$_5$ favors *malla-*, as does KUB 43.59 + KUB 9.39 i 4-5, see *malla/i-* a1′, d.

Goetze, Tunn. (1938), 93-4 ("entangle, tie up, enforce inactivity"); HW 134 ("verwickeln(?), zusammenflechten(?)"); Stefanini, JNES 28 (1969) 46-7; Neu, StBoT 18 (1974) 93f.; Oettinger, Stammbildung (1979) 346.

malkeššar n. neut.; spun wool(?); from OH?/NS.†

[GAL DU]B.SAR.MEŠ.GIŠ-*kan* UGULA $^{\text{LÚ.MEŠ}}$E.DÉ.A-*ya* [*m*]*a*?-*al-ke-eš-šar anda pēdanzi* GUNNI-*ankan piran danzi* § . . . *ta* ^{GIŠ}BANŠUR-*az gankiškizzi* LUGAL SAL.LUGAL SÍG.BABBAR SÍG.SA$_5$ *karzanaz daškanzi ta tarup*⸗*panzi tuš pittuluš ē*[*š*]*šanzi* "The chief 'wood-scribe' and the chief smith carry in spun wool(?) and take the hearth in front. . . . He (the chief table man) hangs (the *malkeššar*) from the table. The king and queen take white and red wool from the *k*. and join (them). And they make them (-*uš*) into loops" IBoT 2.94 vi? 4-6, 10-15 (fest., OH?/NS) □ note the use of -*šk*- forms in lines 8-10, probably indicating the plurality of objects (cf. *t*⸗*uš pittuluš*), on vi? 11-15 cf. Szabó, THeth 1:98f.; [UGULA $^{\text{L]Ú.MEŠ}}$AGRIG(?) *ŠA* É $^{\text{NA}_4}$KI[ŠIB . . .] / *kar-za ḫarkanzi* . . . *taš paizzi* x[. . .] / *ma-al-ke-eš-šar ḫarzi* Bo 996 + Bo 999:9-10, 13 (Istanbul) (fest. frag., NS). Note the occurrence of *karza*(*na*)- in both passages.

The unpublished Istanbul fragment Bo 996 + Bo 999:13 assures the reading [*m*]*a*- in IBoT 2.94 vi? 5. As a deverbal -*eššar* noun like *ḫulaleššar*, *kureššar*, *ḫatreššar*, *ḫatteššar*, *malteššar*, cf. Friedrich, HE §44c, *malkeššar* should mean "that which has been spun (*malk-*/ *malkiya-*)". The wool mentioned in the immediately following context supports this translation.

Cf. *malk-*.

mald-, malda- v.; **1.** (intrans.) to recite, make recitations, **2.** (trans. or intrans.) to make a vow, to vow (something) (usually with particle -*za* after OH), **3.** (mng. unkn., trans. v. with a deity as obj.); from OH; written syll. and with Akkadogram *KARĀBU*.

pres. sg. 1 *ma-al-da-aḫ-ḫi* Bo 3308 iii 7 (StBoT 18: 40 n. 19, 45) (NH), *ma-al-ta-aḫ-ḫi* 348/v:6 (ibid.) (NS); **sg. 3** *ma-a-al-di* KBo 25.112 ii 15 (OS), KBo 25.121 i 9, 10 (OS), KUB 28.75 iii 24 (OS), KBo 20.71:11 (OH/MS?), KUB 28.77 i 3 (OH/NS), KBo 8.133:7, 11 (OH/NS), KUB 48.12 rt. (7), 13 (OH/NS), KBo 21.69 iv 12 (MS), *ma-a-al-ti* KBo 21.80 i 17 (OH/MS), KBo 19.132 rev.? 12 (MH/NS), KUB 30.42 iv 10 (NH), *ma-al-di* KBo 20.19:9 (OS), KBo 21.84 iv 1 (OH/MS?), KUB 25.17 vi 8 (OH?/NS), KBo 11.30 rev. 13 (OH/NS), KBo 11.45 iii (9), 15, 18 (OH/NS), KBo 24.113 i? 6, KUB 1.14 ii 14 (NS), KUB 48.9 ii 15 (NS), IBoT 1.30 obv. 1 (NS), *ma-al-ti* KBo 20.10 i 12, ii 9 (OS), KUB 25.36 i 17, v (10), 17, 23, 29 (MS?), KUB 41.23 ii 9 (OH/NS), KBo 9.115 obv. 2 (MH/NS), KUB 17.28 iii 7 (MH/NS), KUB 25.37 iii 8 (NS), KUB 28.95 ii? 2 (NS), KUB 41.44 vi 8 (OH/NS), *ma-al-ta-i* KBo 2.2 ii 40 (NH), *ma-al-*⸢*ta*⸣(or: ⸢*da*⸣)-*i* KBo 24.126 rev. 3 (NH), *ma*!(copy GIŠ)-*al-da-i* ibid. 9, *ma*(over eras.?)-*al-da*!-⸢*i*⸣ ibid. 15, *ma-al-te* (coll.) IBoT 2.44:5.

pret. sg. 1 *ma-a-al-taḫ-ḫu-un* KBo 3.22:59 (OS), *ma-al-da-aḫ-ḫu-un* KUB 26.71 i 7 (OH/NS), KUB 15.17 i 3 (Pud.), Bo 5956:(3) (StBoT 18:45) (NH); **sg. 3** *ma-al-ta-aš* KUB 5.6 i 32 (NH), 432/e left col. 3, 5, 6, 8 (StBoT 18:45 n. 35), for possible *ma-al-t*[*i-iš*?] KBo 9.115:2 (MS) cf. below sub mng. 3.

imp. sg. 2 *ma-al-di* KUB 15.3 i 18 (NH).

iter. pres. sg. 1 *ma-al-za-ki-mi* KUB 14.4 ii 18 (Murš. II); **pret. sg. 1** *ma-al-za-ki-nu-un* KBo 23.111:13 (NS), ⸢*ma-al*⸣-*za-ki-nu-un* KUB 14.10 i 25 (coll.), [*m*]*a*-⸢*al*⸣-*za-aš-ki-nu-un* KUB 14.10 i 25 (coll.) w. dupl. KUB 14.11 i 18 (coll.).

part. sg. neut. *ma-al-ta-an* KBo 15.33 iii 16 (MH/MS), KUB 15.11 ii 13 (NH); **inf.** *ma-al-tu-u-an-zi* KUB 15.28 iii 8 (NH); **verbal subst. nom.** *ma-al-du-wa-ar* KUB 5.6 i 31 (NH), KUB 25.36 i (12), (25), v (11), 20, 24, 32 (MS?).

broken *ma-a-al*[- . . .] KUB 26.29 obv. 24 (MH/NS) (this might be the noun *māl* q.v.); *ma-al-du-u-w*[*a*- . . .] KBo 13.247 obv. 14 (NS).

Akkadogram pret. sg. 1 *AK-RU-UB* KBo 15.33 iii 21 (MH/MS), KUB 48.123 i 5 (NH); **sg. 3** *IK-RU-UB* KUB 15.1 i 4, 20 and passim, KUB 15.23:18, KUB 15.3 i 5, KUB 10.11 i 9 (all NH).

1. (intransitive) to recite, make recitations (w. adv. *kiššan*, *ḫattili*, *duddumili*, etc.) — **a.** with recitation in Hittite: ⸢LUGAL⸣-*uš kuwapi* DINGIR.MEŠ-*aš aruwāizzi* ^{LÚ}GUDU$_4$ *kišan ma-al-di* (var. *me-ma-i*) "When the king prostrates himself before the gods, the ^{LÚ}GUDU$_4$-priest recites (var. says) the following: (Let the *Labarna*, the king, be dear to the gods. . . . He (the Stormgod) made the *Labarna*, the king, his governor. He gave him the whole land of Ḫattuša. Let the *Labarna* keep governing the whole land with his hand. May the Stormgod destroy the one who infringes upon the person or the borders of the *Labarna*, [the king])" IBoT 1.30:1-8 (NS), parallel KUB 48.13 rev 9-16, ed. Goetze, JCS 1.90-91, Haas, KN 97-8 w. n. 4, cf. tr. by Goetze, Kleinasien 88 and Güterbock, JAOS Suppl. 17:16; "He puts one loaf of (broken) bread on the ground" *nu ma-al-ti* ᵈUTU-*i*<-*wa*> *kuiš piran arta nuwakan* ᵈUTU-*i parranda* SIG₅-*in memiški* "and recites (addressing the table mentioned in line ii 51): (You) who stand in front of the Sungod, keep interceding graciously with the Sungod!" KUB 17.28 iii 7-9 (rit., MH/NS), cf. KUB 41.23 ii 9 (followed by a string of imperatives), KUB 48.13 obv. 11 (followed by an imperative in 16, cf. below sub 1d), and KUB 25.37 iii 8 (text of the following recitation is fragmentary).

b. with recitation in Ḫattic: [*nu k*]*iššan ma-a-al-di* "and (the ᴸᵁ́GUDU₄) recites the following" (there follows the usual statement of the deity's name among mortals and his name among gods.) KUB 28.77 i 2-3 (invoc. of Ḫattic deities, OH/NS); cf. in the same composition after the statement of the deities' names *QĀTAMMA ma-a-al-di* KUB 28.75 iii 24, iv (12) (OS), note also *QĀTAMMA memai* ibid. iii 10, 14, 28 and only *QĀTAMMA* ibid. 18; "The ᴸᵁ́ALAN.ZUₓ (reciter?) dips wine from the *kalti*-vessel" *nu kiššan ma-al-di* "and recites the following" (there follow two lines of Ḫattic) KUB 48.9 ii 14-15 (KI.LAM fest., OH/NS), cf. Singer, Diss. 144; "Next (two) *zilipuriyatalla*-men come and strike themselves (*walḫ*-) six times. One cuts himself (-*za ḫatta*-) on his hand; the other cuts himself on his foot" [UGULA ᴸ]ᵁ́.ᴹᴱŠ*zilipuriyatallaš* [*ḫ*]*attili kiššan ma-al-di* "The [chief] *z*.-man recites as follows in Ḫattic" (the following passage is in Ḫattic) KUB 1.14 ii 8-14 (fest., NS), cf. Neu. StBoT 5:52.

c. recitation not quoted: "The king goes and prostrates himself to ᵈZABABA. The ᴸᵁ́GUDU₄-priest steps behind him" *ta ma-al-ti ḫattīli mān* ᴸᵁ́GUDU₄ *ma-al-du-wa-ar zinnizzi* "and makes a recitation in Ḫattic. When the ᴸᵁ́GUDU₄-priest finishes the recitation," KUB 25.36 v 22-25 (fest., OH?/MS), cf. ibid. i, v passim; (One 'long tablet': When the singer breaks leavened bread) *ta kiššan ma-a-al-ti ḫattili* "He makes a recitation in Ḫattic as follows" KUB 30.42 iv 8-10 (shelf list, NH), ed. Laroche, CTH pp. 163-4; "(The chief palace attendant) ushers in the Man of the Stormgod (who) consecrates the king. He scatters water three times" *ta ma-al-ti* "and recites" KBo 20.10 ii 7-9 (fest., OS), cf. ibid. i 10-12; [(*na*)*n* ᴸᵁ́A(ZU *dāi nu* DI)]NGIR.MEŠ-*aš* [(*m*)]*a-a-al-ti* [(*nan duwarni*)]*zzi* "The diviner takes it (the vessel), and recites to the gods, and breaks it" KBo 19.132 rev? 12-13 (rit., MH/NS), with dupl. KUB 9.28 iii 25-26 (NS); ᴸᵁ́ALAN.ZUₓ *ma-al-di* "The reciter(?) recites" KUB 25.17 vi 8 (fest., OH??/NS); (They give a *ḫuppar*-vessel of wine to the reciters(?) (ALAN.ZUₓ) [(*ta*)] GEŠTIN *ma-al-ti* (var. *ma-al-di*) "He recites (pertaining to) the wine (and the ALAN.ZUₓ takes for himself the vessel of wine)" KUB 41.44 vi 6-10 (*nuntariyašḫaš* fest., OH/NS), with dupl. KBo 11.30 rev. 12-14 (NS).

d. with adv. *duddumili* "silently(?), quietly(?)": [. . .]x *ma-al-di duddumili* [*kiššan*?] "[The . . .] recites quietly(?) [as follows:] (followed by a paragraph line and two lines of Ḫattic) KUB 48.13 obv. 11-12 (fest., NS), cited as Bo 3138 Ehelolf, KlF 399, as Bo 3130 by Laroche, Prière hittite 9. If the meaning of *duddumili* is "silently", one could think the reciter merely mouths or whispers the words (Laroche, ibid. "sourdement, à voix basse"). In any case, it seems clear that the whispered words are intended either for the god(s) or for the reciter himself, not to be heard by human bystanders. The passage demonstrates at least that *mald*- does not always denote a solemn public proclaimation (cf. bibliography).

2. (trans. or intrans.) to make a vow, to vow (something) (usually with the particle -*za* or the enclitic dat. -*ši* in a reflexive use after OH): (I built temples and endowed them with the booty I brought back from campaigns) § *nu ma-a-al-taḫ-ḫu-un* (var. *ma-al-da-aḫ-ḫu-un*) *nu* [(*ḫūwar*)*n*- . . .] "I made a vow and [I went] hun[ting]" (there follows a list of the animals caught and brought to Neša) KBo 3.22:59 (Anitta, OS), with dupl. KUB 26.71 i 7, ed. StBoT 18:14f., for restoration cf. Hoffner, BASOR 226:78; *nuzan mān* ^LÚ^EN É-*TIM kuitki ANA* DINGIR-*LIM ma-al-ta-an ḫarzi* "If the owner of the house has vowed something to the god, (be it some implement or an ox (or) sheep)" KBo 15.33 iii 16-17 (rit. for Stormgod of Kuliwišna, MH/MS); "He himself (the owner of the house) speaks before the god" *kāšawaza kī kiya kēdani uddanī šer AK-RU-UB* "I vowed this and this for the sake of this matter (now I have brought it to the god)" ibid. iii 20-22; ^d^UTU-*ŠI-yaššikan šer ma!-al-da-i* "also, His Majesty will make a vow for the sake of it" KBo 24.126 rev. 9 (oracle, NH), cf. ibid. 3, 15 which use *-za* and do not have *-ši*; *ANA* ^d^*Lelwani-za-kan* GAŠAN-*YA AŠ*[(*ŠU*)]*M BALAṬ* SAG.DU ^d^UTU-*ŠI šer ma-al-da-aḫ-ḫu-un* "I made a vow to Lelwani, my lady, for the sake of the life of the person (SAG.DU) of His Majesty" KUB 15.17 + KUB 31.61 i 2-3 (vow of Pud., NH), with dupl. KUB 15.16 i 2-3, ed. StBoT 1:16f.; *ANA* DINGIR-*LIM ma-al-du-wa-ar ŠA* ^d^UTU-*ŠI* SI×SÁ-*at nu* 1 GUD.ŠE 6 UDU-*ia* SI×SÁ-*at nuzakan karū ma-al-ta-aš* "It was determined by oracle that His Majesty should make a vow to the deity. It (the vow) was determined to be one fattened ox and six sheep. He has already made the vow. (When he gets well, they will give them)" KUB 5.6 i 31-33 (oracle, NH); "A dream of the queen: 'Someone keeps saying to me in a dream'" *ANA* ^d^NIN.GAL-*wazakan kišan ma-al-di* "Make a vow to Nikkal as follows" KUB 15.3 i 17-18 (queen's dreams, NH), tr. Güterbock apud Oppenheim, Dreams 255; *nuzakan* SAL.LUGAL *ŠÀ* Ù-*TI ANA* ^d^*Ḫebat* ^URU^*Uda kiššan IK-RU-UB* "The queen made the following vow to Ḫebat of Uda in a dream" KUB 15.1 i 3-4 (queen's dreams, NH), cf. ibid. i 20, ii 2, 10 and passim; *kūnmanzan* NINDA.KUR$_4$.RA [GAL] LUGAL.GAL ^m^*Šuppilul*[*iumaš*] *ANA* ^d^IM *ANA* KASKAL ^URU^*A*[*r-...*] *šer IK-RU-UB* "The great king, Šuppiluliuma, vowed this [large] loaf of bread to the Stormgod for the sake of the campaign to the city of A[r-...]" KUB 10.11 i 6-9 (fest., NH). *nuza ḫingani šer* / *ANA* DINGIR.MEŠ *ḫūmandāš ārkūwar* / [*ēš*]*šaḫḫun IK*[*RIBI*^ḪI.A^-*ašmašk*]*an* / [*m*]*a-*⌈*al*⌉*za-aš-ki-nu-un* (coll.) (var. [*ma-a*]*l-za-aš-ki-nu-un*, coll.) "I repeatedly made a self-justification to all the gods with respect to the plague. I repeatedly made vows (lit., vowed vows; cognate acc.) to them." KUB 14.10 i 22-25 (PP 2) w. dupl. KUB 14.11 i 16-18; for *š* cf. *išpanzaški-* from *išpant-/šipant-*.

3. (mng. unknown; transitive v. with a deity as obj.), pre-NH†: ^m^*Palliyaš* LUGAL ^URU^*Kum-manni kuwapi* ^d^U *Kummann*[*i*] *šarā tittanut nan kiššan ma-al-t*[*i-iš*?] (var. *ma-al-ta*[*-aš*?]) "When Palliya, king of Kummanni, erected (the statue of) the Stormgod of K., he ... -ed him (or "it") as follows" (the text which follows is a purification ritual) KBo 9.115 i 1-2 (NS), with dupl. KUB 7.20 obv. 1-3 (NS); "when (*kuwapi*) he erected (pret.)" in the preceding dependent clause leads one to expect a pret. in the main clause; the description of actions commences with the pret. *dāš* (i 4) and only changes to the pres., the usual tense in rit. descriptions, seven lines later (i 11). **maltiš* pret. sg. 3 would be a formation like *akkiš*, *šakkiš*, *wakkiš*, *penniš* (all *ḫi*-conjugation). If the pres. tense were likely, one could restore *ma-al-t*[*i*] and *ma-al-ta*[*-i*] cf. StBoT 18:45. Laroche (Prière hittite 11) translated "il l'a proclamé/voué ainsi", although what follows is neither a proclamation nor a vow, but a ritual performed for the deity. Also against the tr. "vowed" is the absence of *-za*. Note also that in the colophon KUB 7.20 rev. 4 what immediately follows *nan kišan* is not *mald-*, as in the opening lines of the ritual, but a word beginning with *i*[*š-* or another sign of similar shape; perhaps read *i*[*ššai*]?

Since the text is a purification ritual which includes offerings, and since according to the colophon the king re-erected the god (*dān šarā* [*tittanut*] KUB 7.20 rev. 3), it is conceivable that the ritual was meant to fulfill a vow to replace the previous statue. A tentative rendering might be: "He provided him (the deity) with offerings/a ritual in fulfillment of a vow." For some connection of the root *mald-* with offerings cf. *maltalli-*, *malteššanala-*, *malteššar*.

One seeks an area of meaning common to the usages distinguished above. Laroche sought such a meaning in a solemn, public declaration or pronouncement. But vows made to a deity are not necessarily announced to be heard by a human audience. The occasional use of *dud-dumili*, "quietly, silently, secretly" with this verb (cf. usage d) indicates that the recitation could be done privately. The recitations (mng. 1) quoted in Hittite following *kiššan maldi* often contain imperative verbs and are therefore requests. A vow (mng. 2) is a promise in return for a requested benefit, a kind of contractual request.

Forrer, ZDMG 76 (1922) 191 ("geloben"); Laroche, Prière hittite (1964) 8-13 (without -*z* "proclamer publiquement, affirmer solennellement," with -*z* "s'engager par une déclaration solennelle"); Sürenhagen, AOF 8 (1981) 143f.

Cf. *maltalli-, malteššanala-, malteššar, mammalt-*.

malda- see *mald-*.

maltalli- adj.; obliged to make a *malteššar*(?); NH.†

sg. nom. com. *ma-al-ta-al-liš* KBo 8.68 i? 6, (8), (9); **acc.** *ma-al-ta-al-li-in* ibid. 12; **d.-l.** *ma-al-ta-al-li* ibid. (5), 13, 14, (18); **unclear** *ma-al-ta-li* 34/p:1, [... *ma-a*]*l-ta-li-ia-aš* 34/p:3 (both Alp, TTKYayin VI/23:362) here or under SISKUR*mantalli-*, SISKUR*maltalli-*?

The text KBo 8.68 is a Kizzuwatnean ritual. The context which concerns the *m.* person is badly broken and difficult to restore or interpret. It appears that the *m.* person has not made the required *malteššar*: *mān ma-al-ta-al-liš* UN-*aš* [*malteššar*(?) *Ú-UL*] *kuitki iyat* (i? 6-7). The ritual's purpose seems to be the purification of certain rooms or buildings (É.MEŠ, i? 2 and 10), as well as the purification of the *m.* man himself through a statuette(?) of wax which is placed at his feet (i? 12-14). The bread and the libation cup are placed upside down (i? 15-17). *m.* is an adj. in -*alli-*, always used attributively with the noun UN-*a*- (= *antuḫša*-) "person". *m.* seems to be derived from the verb *mald-* "to recite, vow; treat (a deity) with a ritual". It hardly denotes a "reciting person" as the title of a functionary, since no other functionary is designated by an adj. + *antuḫša-*. Since *malteššar* can designate an offering, and the verb *mald-* once describes the treating of a god with a purification ritual (cf. *mald-* mng. 3), it seems likely that the *m.* person is one obliged to make such an offering; cf. 34/p:1-3 cited under SISKUR*mantalli-* b 3'.

Cf. *mald-*, (:)(SISKUR)*mantalli-*/SISKUR*maltalli-*, *malteš(ša)nala-*, *malteššar*.

[SISKUR]**maltalli-** see (:)SISKUR*mantalli-*.

(:)maltani- n. (com.); (meaning unknown); NH.†

sg. nom. :*ma-al-ta-ni-eš* KUB 33.106 iii 36, :*ma-al-da-ni-š(a-aš)* KUB 33.92 iii 16, ⌜*ma*⌝[*-al-t*]*a-*⌜*ni*⌝[*- ...*] KBo 26.65 i 18.

naš :*ma-al-ta-ni-eš* GIM-*an šarā karpiškattari* "He (Ullikummi) lifts himself up (i.e., grows rapidly?) like a *m.*" KUB 33.106 iii 36-37 (Ullik., NH), ed. Güterbock, JCS 6:26-27, cf. Neu, StBoT 5:81, 82 n. 16. The same simile occurs in KUB 33.92 iii 16 and KBo 26.65 i 18-19 and is restored in KUB 33.106 iii 14-15, all from Ullik., RTAT 174 tr. KUB 33.106 iii 14f. "Wie ein ... (Ringmauer? Schirm? Pilz?) ragt(?) er empor".

It is not clear whether the simile intends the rapidity of rise/ascent/growth ("mushroom(?)", etc.) or the height attained ("tower", etc.). although for the latter one might have expected "he is as tall/big (*šalli-*) or high (*parku-*) as a *m.*"

Goetze, ANET 123 ("tower"); Laroche, DLL (s.v. *maldaniš-*, no tr.); Hoffner, EHGl 60 (sub "mushroom(?)").

malteš(ša)nala- adj.; recipient of *malteššar* (chants, vows, votive offerings); MH/NS.†

sg. com. acc. *ma-al-ti-eš-na-la-*⌜*an*⌝ KUB 7.8 iii 13, *ma-al-ti-eš-ša-na-la-an* KUB 7.5 i 22 (same tablet as KUB 7.8 + KUB 9.27).

"He will give you (=ᵈUliliyašši) a house; he will give you a male and a female slave; he will give you cattle and sheep," *nudduššan ma-al-ti-eš-ša-na-la-an iyazi* "He will make you a recipient of *malteššar* (votive offerings?)" KUB 7.5 i 20-22 (rit. of Paškuwatti to cure impotence); "He will make you his personal deity" *nuduza ma-al-ti-eš-na-la-*⌜*an*⌝ *iyazi* "He will make you the recipient of his own (-*za*) *malteššar*" KUB 7.8 iii 13-14 (same tablet as KUB 7.5).

Adj. in -*ala-* from oblique stem of *malteššar*.

Sturtevant, Gl. (1936) ("invoked by *malteššar*"); Goetze, ANET (1969) 350 ("He will make vows to thee").

Cf. *mald-*.

malteššar n. neut. and com.; **1.** recitation, prayer(?), hymn(?), **2.** vow, votive offering, **3.** ritual; written syll. and (only in mng. 2) *IKRIBU*; from OH.

sg. nom.-acc. *ma-al-te-eš-šar-r*(*a*) KUB 27.1 i 11, 26 (NH), *ma-al-de-eš-šar* KUB 27.1 i 31, [*m*]*a-al-te-eš*$_{17}$ *-šar* KUB 9.19:4 (NS); **gen.?** *ma-al-de-eš-na-aš* KUB 22.70 obv. 22 (NH), *ma-al-te-eš-n*[*a*(coll.)*-aš*] KUB 44.12 ii 8 (NS).

pl. acc. *ma-*⸢*al*⸣-[*te-eš*]-⸢*šar*⸣ KUB 28.80 iv 8 (NS); **gen.** *ma-al-te-eš-na-aš* ibid. iv 1; **d.-l.** *ma-al-te-eš-na-aš* ibid. 10, KUB 31.143 ii 17, (23), 27, (31!), 35 (OS), VBoT 124 ii! 9 (OS), *ma-al-te-eš-na*<*-aš*> KUB 8.41 obv. ii 13 (OS); **abl.** ⸢*ma*⸣*-al-te-eš-na-az-z*(*i-ia*) KUB 5.24 ii 2 (NH).

sg. or pl. *ma-al-di-šar*? 116/r:4.

Akkadogram: sg. nom. [*IK*]*-RI-BU* StBoT 1:34 iv 10 (Pud.); **acc.?** *IK-RI-BU* KBo 2.2 iii 33 (NH); **abl. or inst.** (with TA) *IK-RI-BI* KUB 46.40 obv. 3 ; **pl. nom.-acc. with neut. concord** *IK-RI-BI*$^{\text{ḪI.A}}$ StBoT 1:34 iv 15 (Pud.); **pl. nom. with com. concord** *IK-RI-BI*$^{\text{ḪI.A}}$ KBo 2.2 iv 7; **pl. acc. with com. concord** *IK-RI-BI*$^{\text{ḪI.A}}$ KUB 22.38 i 2, KUB 22.65 iii 13, KUB 6.13:15 (NH); **d.-l.** (with *ANA*) *IK-RI-BI*$^{\text{ḪI.A}}$ ibid. iii 11, 15, KUB 6.22 iii 13.

1. recitation, prayer(?), hymn(?) (from OH): *ṬUPPI ma-al-te-eš-na-aš* ⸢*ŠA* EZEN⸣ ^{URU}*Nerik KAYAMĀNIM . . . nukan kī ma-*⸢*al*⸣*-*[*te-eš*]*-*⸢*šar*⸣ *apēdaš dāēr . . . karuiliaš ma-al-te-eš-na-aš natta ḫan*[*d*]*ā*[*n*] "Tablet of recitations of the regular festival of Nerik . . . They took these recitations from those (refugee priests) . . . (This tablet) does not correspond to the former recitations" KUB 28.80 iv 1-11 (Ḫattic speeches, NS); [*kīmašt*]*a* ^{d}*Inaraš ma-al-te-eš-na-aš ḫandān* "[This (recitation)] corresponds to the recitations of Inara" KUB 31.143 ii 17 (OS); [*kīmašta*] ^{d}IM*-aš ma-al-te-eš-na-aš* [*ḫandān*] VBoT 124 obv.! ii 9 (OS), the parallel has *kēašta ANA A-WA-AT* ^{d}[IM *ḫantān*] KUB 8.41 ii 9, ed. Laroche, JCS 1:187ff.; cf. KUB 30.68 rev. 4-9 (shelf list), translit. CTH p. 173, and cf. s.v. *mammalt-*.

2. vow; votive offering (all NS, mostly NH): [(*k*)]*ēmakan IK-RI-BI*$^{\text{ḪI.A}}$ *ŠA* ^{d}*L*[*elwani . . .*] "These objects vowed to L[elwani . . .] (three small gold cups, five persons, [. . .] thirty gold month emblems and thirty silver ones)" KUB 31.54:15 with dupl. KUB 31.52 iv 3, ed. StBoT 1:34 iv 15-17; cf. *ŠA* MU.2.KAM *ma-al-te-*[*eš-šar . . .*] KUB 31.51 obv. 6, ed. StBoT 1.18 i 11; 2 GILIM KÙ.GI*-makan kue ma-al-de-eš-na-aš* SAL.LUGAL *ANA* DINGIR*-LIM ēššešta* "The two gold headbands which the queen had made for the deity (in fulfillment) of a vow" KUB 22.70 obv. 22 (oracle, NH), ed. THeth 6:60f.; *mānza* ^{d}UTU ^{URU}TÚL*-na zikpat* DUMU*-annaš ANA IK-RI-BI*$^{\text{ḪI.A}}$ *šer kar*<*timmiya*>*uwanza nammama* KI.MIN "If you alone, Sungoddess of Arinna are angry because of vows (made to obtain) offspring, and in addition no other deity is joined with you, (let the exta be favorable . . . Unfavorable.)" KBo 2.2 iii 13-17 (oracle question, NH), cf. ibid. 10-12, 30-31; *nu IK-RI-BI*$^{\text{ḪI.A}}$*-ma kuiēš šarninkuēš nat šarninkanzi* "They will make compensation for the (unfulfilled) vows which are to be compensated for" ibid. iv 7-8; [o] x *ku*⸢*it* DINGIR⸣ GAL ⸢TUKU.TUKU⸣*-uanza nu ANA* DINGIR*-LIM* ⸢*kuit me*⸣*qqauš IK-RI-BI*$^{\text{ḪI.A}}$ *meman ḫarmi* "Since [. . .] the great god is angry, since I have spoken many vows, (let it be set aside)" KUB 22.38 i 1-3 (oracle, NH), ed. Laroche, RA 52:150f.; cf. *ANA* DINGIR*-LIM IK-RI-BI*$^{\text{ḪI.A}}$ *meman ḫarz*[*i*] KUB 15.20 ii 9; *nuza apēdaš gimraš šer* SISKUR *ambaššin keldianna ma-al-te-eš-šar-ra ariyanzi* "They will investigate by oracle the *a.*- and *k.*-ritual and the vow(s) (made) for the sake of those campaigns" KUB 27.1 i 10-11 (fest., NH), ed. Lebrun, Samuha 75, 86, cf. ibid. i 26, 31, 33; *mān*⸢*na*⸣ (coll.) *ma-al-te-eš-n*[*a*(coll.)*-aš . . .*] *ēšzi nankan šipan*[*ti*] *mānma UL ēšz*[*i*] *nukan UL kuitki* [*šipanti*] "If there is [a . . .] of a vow (i.e., a . . . which has been promised), he offers it; but if there is not, he offers nothing" KUB 44.12 ii 8-11, NS).

3. ritual (in fulfilment of a vow?): [(*nam*=*ma*)]*šmaššan ma-al-te-eš-na-aš* (var. [S]ISKUR.SISKUR.ḪI.A*-aš*) *parkuyannaš uddanī* [(*naḫ*=*š*)]*arattan kiššan UL kuiški tiyan ḫarta* "Further, no one had such respect for you in the matter of the purity(?) of rituals" 398/u + 1945/u i 5-6 (prayer of Arn. and Ašm., MH/NS) with older dupl. KUB 17.21 i 19-20 (MS), ed. Kaškäer 152f. and Lebrun, Hymnes 134, 143, tr. ANET 399 (translated SISKUR.SISKUR.ḪI.A*-aš parkuyannaš* "cleanliness connected with your sacrifices"); In a text describing an itinerary (of the king?): [^{URU}*Ta*]*pparuta*[*z*]=*ma*=*aš* ^{URU}*Anniyatta paizzi nu* LÚ.MEŠ.ŠU.GI [MÁ]Š.[G]AL DUG K[A].DÙ NAG 12 NINDA.KUR$_4$.

RA *pianzi* [*m*]*a-al-te*[*-eš*]*-šar-ši-it* *QĀTAMMA* "But from T. he proceeds to A. And the elders (of A.) give a goat, a jug of *PĪḪU*-beer for drinking (and) twelve loaves of bread. And the *m.*-ritual/offering is just the same." KBo 22.242 + 1003/z ii 5-7 (NH), restored also in iii 5, 9. Since the gift of the elders has been described in full, it cannot be meant by the *malteššar*. Yet what is provided for the king on his visit is probably not a recitation, but either an offering or a ritual of some kind.

The variant *maltešnaš* for SISKUR.SISKUR.ḪI.A-*aš* in the prayer of Arn. and Ašm. (cf. HW 3.Erg. 23) cannot be used to prove that *m.* is the normal reading of SISKUR.SISKUR. This logogram is used in Hittite for both "offering" and "ritual". The definition of SISKUR.SISKUR as "magisches Ritual" (HW² 85) is much too narrow. Beside the alternation of SISKUR.SISKUR with *malteššar* there is also an alternation with *mu-ke*[*-eš-šar*] KUB 30.51 obv. 11 and dupl. KBo 14.68 obv. 8 (Otten, MDOG 93:77 n. 5). Additionally, LÚ*mukišnaš* EN-*aš* KBo 14.86 i 7, LÚ*mukišnaš*(*-pat*) *išḫāš* KBo 12.19 ii 12 (Kuliwišna rits.) is likely to be a reading of EN.SISKUR (cf. Otten, MDOG 93.77 n. 5). SISKUR-*eššar* in RS 25.421 iv 54 (Laroche, Ugar. 5:774f., 779) could be either *mugeššar* (thus Laroche) or *malteššar*; since it is "lovely to behold", it cannot be "recitation", but must be either "ritual" or "offering". On the basis of the meanings of *mald-* and *mugai-* (q.v., cf. Laroche, Prière hittite) *mugeššar* could be a ritual (including offerings and words) aimed at invoking the gods, *malteššar*, a ritual performed in fulfilment of a vow. In the prayer of Arn. and Ašm., the phrase *maltešnaš parkuyannaš uddani* of the newer version may be understood as "in the matter of the purity of recitations" or "in the matter of the purity of the offerings/rituals performed in fulfilment of vows". The second translation is closer to the SISKUR.SISKUR.ḪI.A-*aš parku*-*yannaš uddani* of the older version and more accurately captures the meaning of *maltešnaš* in this context. Note that the context which precedes deals with temples, precious objects, and statues; that which immediately follows deals with "rituals (SISKUR.SISKUR) and festivals (EZEN)". Cf. comments on *mald-*, *maltalli-* and *malteššanala-*.

Kammenhuber, MIO 2.108f. with n.15; Laroche, Prière hittite 8-13.

Cf. *mald-*, SISKUR.

maltešnala- see *malteš*(*ša*)*nala-*.

malwara- Luw. n.; (mng. unknown); NS.†

Luw. pl. nom. *ma-al-wa-ra-an-zi* KUB 35.145 obv. 2; **acc.** *ma-al-wa-ra-an-za* ibid. 15, var. [*malwaranz*]*i* KUB 17.15 ii 9.

With other Luwian pl. nouns in Hittite context: [*našt*(*a anda taḫḫa*)]*ranzi ma-al-wa-ra-an-zi ura*[*nta*] "Therein *t.* (and) *m.* are burn[ing]" KUB 35.145 obv. 2 with dupl. KUB 35.143:10; *našta anda* [(*taḫḫaran*)*za*] *ma-al-wa-ra-an-za* KI.MIN (var. [*malwaranz*]*i kištanunun*) "Therein I extinguished *t.* (and) *m.*" KUB 35.145 obv. 14-15 with dupl. KUB 17.15:8-9.

DLL 67 (without tr.).

malwiš n.; (mng. unkn.); NH.†

In an inventory: 1-*EN* GIŠPISAN 20 *URAKI* KÙ.GI 10(-)*m*[*a*(-) . . .] 10 *URAKI* KÙ.BABBAR 4(-)*ma*(-)*al-ú-i-iš* x[. . .] "one chest (containing) 20 bars of gold, 10 [. . .], 10 bars of silver, 4 . . . [. . .]" lines 1-2 of a fragment of a Hittite inv. text from an unpublished hand copy by A. Goetze at Yale University; the copy bears the notation in Goetze's hand "Col. Univ. Lib.", but a search of cuneiform fragments in Columbia University Library in New York City revealed no Hittite fragments. The original cannot therefore be checked to determine the spacing of 4(-)*ma*(-)*al-ú-i-iš*. Goetze's copy will be published in a volume of Yale Hittite fragments by Beckman and Hoffner. If the *ma* in line 2 is the conjunction ("but four . . ."), the word in question here would be a hapax, *alwiš*. If the word is *malwiš*, it may also occur in line 1: 10 *m*[*a*- . . .]; possibly also *ma-al-*⌈*ú-i*⌉*-i*[*a*- . . . KUB 49.54 obv. 3 (oracle, NH).

māluli- see *mīluli-*.

:malušteya- n. [com.]; (an animal); NS.†

In a fragment of a myth in the Kumarbi cycle: *numukan kuiš wāki* . . . *:ma-lu-uš-te-ia-aš-ma-mu wākit* "Who is biting me? . . . A/The *m.* bit me" KUB 36.25 iv 11, ed. Otten, MGK 32f., cf. Laroche,

Myth. 188; □ in the immediately preceding lines dogs, pigs, and the *ḫalmešnas*-animal have been mentioned.

Laroche, DLL 67.

malzaki- see *mald-*, *malda-*.

malzaški- see *mald-*, *malda-*.

mammalt- v.; to recite (chants); OH.†

iter. mid. pres. pl. 3 *ma-am-ma-al-zi-kán-ta* KUB 30.68 rev. 9 (OH/NS); **broken** *ma-am-ma-al*[-. . .] KBo 8.45:7 (OH/NS).

[DUB.x x *ma*]*ltešnaš* (PNs) . . . *mān* DUMU-*aš* *ANA* DINGIR.MEŠ [URU]*Za*[*lp*]*uwa* [. . . -*z*]*i* *ki*⸗*ma* *ma-am-ma-al-zi-kán-ta* "[Tablet . . . of the ch]ants of (PNs, several identified as singers) . . . When the prince [goe]s to [worship] the gods of Z., they (the named singers) recite these (chants)" KUB 30.68 rev. 6-9 (entry in a NH catalogue describing an OH collection of chants), ed. CTH pp. 173-4; contra Laroche *kima mammalzikanta* is not the title of the song ("l'intitulé du chant").

This is a reduplicated form of the stem *mald-*, showing *a*-vocalism in the initial syllable; cf. van Brock, RHA XXII/75 (1964) 125, type *lalukk*(*a*)*i*-.

Cf. *mald-*.

mamman see *man* b 2′ b′.

:mamanna- Luw. v.; to look upon, regard (as one's own), accept; NH.†

(The sacrificer, a Tudḫaliya, has given substitutes [*tarpalliuš*] and valuable gifts to the Sungoddess of the Netherworld and the Infernal deities.) *nukan zik* KI-*aš* [d]UTU-*uš* GAM-*rašša*(sic) DINGIR.MEŠ *kēdāš tarpalliuš*(sic) *arkammi*⸗*ya* *:ma-ma-an-na-ten* *ŠA* [m]*Tudḫaliya*⸗*ma*⸗*mu* *ŠA* [LÚ]GURUŠ *ḫaštariyatar* . . . *šarā tarnešten* "You, O Sungoddess of the Netherworld and (you) O infernal deities, look upon (i.e., accept) these substitutes and the tribute, but send up the *ḫ*. . . . of me, Tudḫaliya, as a youth" KUB 24.12 ii 28-33 (purification rit.), ed. van Brock, RHA XVII/65:122(differently), cf. Starke apud Hawkins, Kadmos 19:146; . . . *kēdāš tarpalliuš arkammi*[⸗*ya*] *:ma-ma-an-na-ten* <*ANA*> EN.SISKUR⸗*ma*⸗*wa*⸗*mu* ALAM [LÚ]GURUŠ(text [d]KAL) . . . *ḫaššaz* EGIR-*pa pešten* "Look upon (accept) these substitutes and upon the tribute, but from the fireplace give back to me, the sacrificer, the form of a youth" ibid. iii 4-7.

In Hierogl. Luw. the verb LITUUS-*na*- seems to mean "see", "behold", "regard" (Hawkins and Starke, Kadmos 19:123ff.). The Hierogl. Luw. verb LITUUS.LITUUS-*na-i* in its one occurrence (ibid. 136), "He who fears this god, he too shall *behold* his benefit here," may be freely paraphrased "he too shall *receive* his benefit here" (cf. below). According to Starke (ibid. 142ff.), LITUUS-*na*- represents cuneiform Luw. *manā*- "sehen, erleben", and LITUUS.LITUUS-*na*- cuneiform Luw. *ma*(*m*)*manna*- "schauen", although the second is not a reduplicated form of the first (ibid. 147, contra 137). To the Luw. text [d]UTU-*waz* [d]*Kamrušepai daueyan ma-am-ma*[-*an-na-at-ta*] *zāniwa kuwati* "The Sungod . . . -ed toward Kamrušepa: 'How is this?'" (KUB 35.107 iii 8-9) he adduces parallels from the Hittite version of this same text, showing . . . *aušta ini*⸗*ma*⸗*wa kuit* "looked . . . , (saying:) 'What is that?'" KBo 12.89 iii 10 (ibid. 146). Starke also cites the Hittite passage KUB 24.12 ii 28-30 and iii 4-5 as examples of *:mamanna*- "schauen".

In the prayer-incantations to the infernal deities with regard to the substitutes (*tarpalli*-), two consecutive imperatives are used: "X these substitutes, but Y the sacrificer." In all the other exx. X and Y are virtual antonyms: *da*- "take" vs. (*arḫa*) *tarna*- "release", *nuwa kūš akkandu ammuk*⸗*ma*⸗*w*[*a l*]*ē akmi* "Let these die, but let me not die" (cf. StBoT 3:8 line 16, p. 10 line 34f., p. 12 line 7, 16f.). In KUB 24.12 the contrast is just as clear (-*ma* and shift from substitutes as object to sacrificer). The verb *:mamanna*- with the d.-l. should express the opposite of *šarā tarna*- "let go (back) up" and EGIR-*pa pai*- "give back". Starke may be right in connecting it with Hierogl. Luw. LITUUS.LITUUS-*na*-, disassociating it etymologically from Luw. *manā*-, yet retaining a meaning like "look" or "regard". It seems likely that both LITUUS.LITUUS-*na*- in Sultanhan stela line 5 (cited Kadmos 19:136) and *:mamanna*- in KUB 24.12, though literally "look upon", conveyed the idea of "receive" or "retain". The 2 pl. imperative ending on :*ma-ma-an-na*-TEN can be read as either Hitt. *-ten* or Luw. *-tan*, since TEN has both values in NS.

Laroche, DLL 67 ("dire"); van Brock, RHA XXII/75:137 ("dire"); Hawkins and Starke, Kadmos 19 (1980) 123-148.

^{GIŠ}**mammarr(a/i)-** n.; (a woody plant, tree or bush); OH/NS.†

(The bee reports that she has searched for but not found the missing deity. She says that he is going to Ḫattuša.) [. . . -]*ti šešzi naš katta*[*n* . . . *še*]*šzi naš kattan AN*[*A* . . . *k*]*attan* ^{GIŠ}*ma-am-mar-r*[*i* . . . *k*]*attan dankui t*[*akni*? . . .] KUB 33.13 ii 27-30 (missing god myth fragm.), translit. Myth. 99.

For the disassociation of this word from *marmarra-* see discussion there.

[*ma-mar-nu-wa-an-zi*] in KUB 35.146 ii 15 according to coll. is to be read *ku-mar-nu-wa-an-zi*.

mammaš in the phrase *āliš mammaš* (mng. unknown); MH/NS.†

nu kišan memai a-a-li-iš ma-am-ma-aš ^{d}A.NUN.NA.KE$_4$ *kēdanišmaš* (var. *kēdanimaš*) *uddanī ḫalziḫḫun* "And he speaks thus: '*āliš mammaš*. (You) infernal deities! On this occasion I have invoked you: (Decide the case of this house!)'" KUB 41.8 iii 6-7 (rit.) with dupl. KBo 10.45 iii 15-16, ed. Otten, ZA 54:128f.

While Otten (ibid. 153) thinks this phrase may be in Luwian, Kammenhuber (HW^2 s.v. *a-a-li-*^{3}) claims that it is a Hurrian epithet of the Anunnaki. For Luwian *ali-* cf. Rosenkranz, JCS 2 (1948) 249 n. 3 ("white"), Meriggi, WZKM 53 (1957) 203f., 213 w. n. 54, 215, DLL 25, and Rosenkranz, OrNS 33 (1964) 246.

$^{\text{NA}_4}$**mamḫuišt[a(-)** n.; (a stone or an object of stone).

1 ^{GIŠ}*tuppaš* NA$_4$ x[. . .] $^{\text{NA}_4}$*ma-am-ḫu-iš-t*[*a*(-) . . .] KUB 42.18 ii (coll.) 7-8 (inv., NH). The reading $^{\text{NA}_4}$*ma-am-ḫu-iš-ga*[(-) . . .] is also possible.

man, -man (rarely also **mān**); (particle denoting the optative, the unreal and the potential); from OH.

a. optative
- **1′** expressing a wish of the speaker
  - **a′** positive
    - **1″** OH
    - **2″** MH and NH
  - **b′** negated with *lē* and pres.
    - **1″** in OH
    - **2″** in NH
- **2′** expressing a wish of the subject of the verb
  - **a′** pres.
  - **b′** pret.
    - **1″** followed by no statement to indicate that the wish or intent was frustrated
    - **2″** followed by a statement indicating what frustrated the wish or intent

b. the unreal ("irrealis")
- **1′** in the main clause without conditional protasis
- **2′** in both protasis and apodosis of contrary to fact conditional sentences
  - **a′** *takku=man* . . . *=man*
  - **b′** *māmman*/*mamman* (= *mān* + *-man*) . . . *man*, or *man mān* . . . *=man*, or *mānman* . . . *man*
  - **c′** particle *man*, sometimes written plene (*ma-a-an*, *ma-a-na-* etc.) in both protasis and apodosis, and without conj. "if" (*takku* or *mān*) in the protasis

c. potential, with pres.-fut. tense expressing a possible outcome
- **1′** expressing a possibility
- **2′** in questions.

ma-an KBo 3.46 obv. 13 (OH/NS), KUB 23.53:3 (OH/NS), KBo 6.2 ii 55, 57 (OS), ABoT 65 rev. 6 (MH/MS), KBo 4.4 iii 22, iv 42, KBo 5.8 iv 12 (all Murš. II), KUB 1.9:6 (var. *ma-a-an*, KUB 1.4 iii 43), KBo 3.6 iii 65 (all Ḫatt. III), *ma-an-* . . . KUB 14.1 obv. 4, 5 (MH/MS), VBoT 2:2 (MH), KUB 19.24 rev. 23 (MH), KBo 5.6 iii 13, KBo 5.8 iii 16, KBo 2.5 i 5 (all Murš. II), KUB 1.9:5 (var. *ma-a-an-* . . . KUB 1.4 iii 42) (Ḫatt. III), *ma-n*(*a-* . . .) KUB 36.79 ii 49, KUB 26.71 iv 17 (both OH/NS), KUB 33.106 ii 9 (NH), *ma-n*(*u-* . . .) KBo 3.55 rev. 10 (OH/NS), *ma-a-an* KUB 14.3 ii 16 (also 11, 12?), KUB 24.8 ii 18, KBo 3.6 iii 64, *-ma-an* KUB 30.10 obv. 22 (OH or MH/MS), KUB 14.1 obv. 12 (MH/MS), KUB 1.16 iii 65 (OH/NS), KBo 16.17 iii 6, KBo 3.3 iii 6, KUB 14.17 ii 6, KUB 6.44 iv 13 (all Murš. II), KUB 31.66 iii 5, 7, 19, KUB 31.68:41 (all NH), *-ma-n*(*a-* . . .) KUB 1.16 iii 7 (OH/NS), *-ma-a-n*(*a-* . . .) KUB 14.3 i (45,) 46, *ma-a-n*([*e* . . .]) KBo 6.2 ii 54 (OS), *ma-a-n*(*u-* . . .) KBo 3.1 ii 11 (OH/NS), *ma-a-n*(*a-*. . .) KUB 14.1 rev 27 (MH/MS), KBo 2.5 i 5, KUB 14.17 ii 8, KBo 3.3 iii 9, 22, 23, KBo 3.4 iii 11 (all Murš. II), KUB 31.101:16, (18).

(Sum.) ⌜e⌝-bi-še = (Akk.) *lu-m*[*a-an*] "now; if only . . .!" = (Hitt.) *ma-an-ma-an-*[. . .] "if . . . had . . ." or perhaps "if only . . .!" KBo 1.50 obv. 11 + KUB 3.99 ii 21 (Erimḫuš Boğ., NH).

a. optative: — **1′** expressing a wish of the speaker: — **a′** positive: **1″** OH: (Because certain officials want to take the estates of princes, they say:) *a-ši-ma-an-wa* URU-*aš ammel k*[(*išari*)] "I wish that city were mine" KUB 11.6 ii 11 restored from dupl. KBo 3.1 ii 64 (Tel.pr., OH/NS), ed. Chrest. 190f.

2″ MH and NH: (The king of Arzawa reports to the pharaoh:) "Kalbaya has said this to me . . . " *ma-an-wa-an-*⌈*na-aš*⌉ [*i*]*šḫanittarātar iyaweni* "We should establish (lit. make) a blood relationship between ourselves" VBoT 2:2-3 (letter, MH), ed. L. Rost, MIO 4:328ff., already tr. as optative by Hrozný, JA 218 (1931) 313; (The young Assyrian king says:) *iyami⸗ma-an-pát-wa kuitki ma-a-an-wa-mu araḫzenuš* LÚ[GAL.MEŠ . . . (*a*)*pi*(*ya⸗ya⸗ma-an-wa-mu uwanzi*)] *ma-an-wa-za* (var. *ma-a-an-wa-za*) *ŠUM-an kuitki iyami* "If only I could do something! If the neighboring kings would [start war] with me and then they would come against me; if only I could make some name for myself." KUB 23.103 rev. 13-14 with dupl. KUB 23.92 rev. 12-13 (royal letter to Assyria, NH), ed. Otten, AfO 19:42-43, cf. already Güterbock, OrNS 12 (1943) 154; (Tatti told the queen:) "UR.MAḪ-*ziti* said to me:" *ma-an-wa* ᵈUTU-*ŠI* TI-*ešzi* "I hope His Majesty recovers (lit. 'lives')" (For then he will give . . . to Šauška of Šamuḫa) KUB 15.30 iii 5 (dreams and vows, NH), since there is no *ma-an* in the "For . . . " clause, we prefer not to translate: "Were His Majesty to recover, he would give . . . ".

b′ negated with *lē* and pres. tense — **1″** in OH: see KUB 1.16 iv 65-66 cited in *lē* bilingual section.

2″ in NH: to the ex. in *lē* usage b add only: [. . .] *le-e-ma-an-ta* DINGIR.MEŠ *pí*[-. . .] KBo 19.121:2-3.

2′ expressing a wish of the subject of the verb (subject optative) — **a′** pres. tense: *ma-na-an-kán* (var. *ma-a-na-an-kán*) ᵐ*Āškaliyaš kuienzi šan ANA* É EN.NU.UN *daiš* "A. wanted (hist. pres.) to kill him (Išpudašinara), so (A.?) put (I.?) in prison" KBo 3.34 (= BoTU 12A) ii 17 (anecdotes, OH/NS), with dupl. KBo 3.36 obv. 22 (NS).

b′ pret. tense — **1″** followed by no statement to indicate that the wish or intent was frustrated: (The grandees of the City of Athulišša had decided upon rebellion. I captured them, and their people denounced them, saying:) BAL-*ma-an-wa iēr ma-a-an-wa-ra-at INA* [ᵁᴿᵁ*Gašga*] EGIR-*pa pāīr* "They wanted to rebel. They wanted to return to [Gašga]." (They were proven guilty, and I relocated them.) KBo 14.19 ii 18-19 (Murš. II annals), ed. Houwink ten Cate, JNES 25:174, 182; *nuššan ANA* ᵐ*Madduwatta kuit šer zaḫ*[*ḫ*]*ir* [*ma-a*]*n-kán šēr ANA* ᵐ*Madduwatta kuenir* "Because they had fought (lit. struck) on behalf of Madduwatta, they wanted to kill (certain persons) on behalf of M." (followed by § line and *a*[*-ap-pa-*]*ma-kán*) KUB 14.1 obv. 59 (Madd., MH/MS), ed. Götze, Madd. 14f.; possibly also in: [...] *ma-an warkan ulinī anda imienun* KBo 3.46 (BoTU 17A) obv. 13 (OH/NS).

2″ followed by a statement indicating what frustrated the wish or intent: all exx. adduced under b 1′.

b. the unreal ("irrealis") — **1′** in the main clause without conditional protasis: *ma-a-nu-uš-kán* ᵐ*Ḫuzziyaš kuenta nu uttar išduwāti* "Ḫ. would have killed them, but the matter became known" KBo 3.1 ii 11 (Tel.pr., OH/NS), ed. Chrest. 186-87, 197; possibly: *ma-na-an ḫarnikta* [. . .] KUB 26.71 iv 17-18 (OH/NS); *ma-a-na-an zaḫḫiyanun numu maḫḫan* . . . "I would have fought him, but when . . . me" KBo 3.4 iii 11, ed. AM 68f.; *ma-an INA* ᵁᴿᵁ*Ḫayaša pāunpat nuza* MU.KAM-*za šer tēpauēššanza ēšta* "I would have also gone to Ḫ., but the year had become too short" KBo 4.4 iii 22-23, ed. AM 124f.; *maḫḫanma ḫamešḫanza kišat ma-an INA* KUR ᵁᴿᵁ*Azzi taninumanzi pāun maḫḫanma* . . . "When spring came, I would have gone to set A. in order, but when . . . " ibid. iv 42-43, ed. AM 138f.; *nukan maḫḫan ANA* KASKAL ᵁᴿᵁ*Taggašta tiyanun ma-an iyan⸗niyanun numu eniššan kuit* LÚ.MEŠ ᵁᴿᵁ*Tag⸗gašta šēnaḫḫa piran tieškanzi numu* MUŠEN *arān* (var. *aran*) *ḫarta* "When I had stepped on the road to T., I would have proceeded. But, because the men of T. were (lit. are) laying an ambush for me, a(n oracle?-)bird had stopped me" KBo 5.8 i 14-17 with dupl. KUB 19.36:10-12, ed. AM 148f.; *ma-an INA* KUR ᵁᴿᵁ*Kalašma ukila pāun numukan šāru kuit* . . . "I would have gone in person to K., but because the booty . . ." ibid. iv 12-13, ed. AM 160f.; cf. further KUB 19.37 iii 49-53, ed. AM 176f.; KBo 2.5 i 5, ed. AM 180f.; ibid. iv 1-2, ed. AM 190f.; (Mašḫuiluwa quarreled with me and incited the land of P. and my Hittite subjects against me) *ma-an-mu menaḫḫanda ku[ruriyaḫta]* "He would have made war against me (§ But when I, His Majesty, heard . . .)" KUB 6.41 i 33 (Kup.), ed. SV 1:110f, and cf. ibid. i 46-48; LÚŠU.DIB-*ma-an UL manqa taštašiyait* "The prisoner would/should not have whispered/grumbled/ conspired(?) at all" KUB 14.17 ii 6, ed. AM 84f. *ma-a-an-kán damain kupiyatin kupta ma-an INA* KUR URU*Karanduniya penništa* "He would have plotted another coup, he would have driven to Babylonia, (but . . .)" KBo 3.6 iii 64-65 (Ḫatt. iv 33-35), ed. Ḫatt. 34f., StBoT 24.24f.; □ it is unlikely that *mān* means "if" here, since Ḫattušili's subsequent transfer of Urḫitešub was ostensibly in response to some clear indication of the latter's intentions to rebel; tr. Kühne/Otten, StBoT 16:38 "hätte er ein anderes Komplott (mit Erfolg) geschmiedet, so wäre er nach Babylonien gefahren", i.e., sub b 2′.

2′ in both protasis and apodosis of contrary to fact conditional sentences — **a′** *takku⸗man . . . ⸗man*: *išḫaḫru⸗šm[it⸗ši⸗šta ša]nḫun ták-ku-ma-na-<aš->ta UL-ma šan[ḫun* GAM-*an šarā⸗ma-]*⸢*a*⸣*-am-mu lālit ēpten* KUB 40.65 + KUB 1.16 iii 7-9 (OH/NS); for translation and discussion see *lala-* 1 a 1′, □ *takku⸗man⸗a⸗ta* is impossible because *kaštit⸗a⸗man* (KUB 14.1 obv. 12) shows that *⸗a* preceeds *⸗man*; cf. KUB 40.65 + KUB 1.16 iii 11-12 (OH/NS), early edition without KUB 40.65 in HAB 10-11.

b′ *mămman/mamman* (= *mān* + *man*) . . . *man*, or *man mān . . . ⸗man*, *mānman . . . man*: *ma-a-am-ma-an* (par. *ku-i-it-ma-an*) *dandukiš⸗naša* DUMU-*aš uktūri ḫūišwanza ēšta ma-na-aš-ta mān antuwaḫḫaš idāluwa inan arta* (par. *artariya*) *ma-na-at-ši natta kattawatar* "Even if mortal man were to live forever, and the evil sickness of man were to remain (lit. stand) also, would it not be a grievance for him?" KUB 30.10 obv. 22-3 (Kantuzili prayer, OH or MH/MS), with par. KUB 36.79 ii 48-50 (NS), different tr. in ANET 400; ⸢*ma*⸣*-an-kán ma-a-an* ⸢*A*⸣*NA* m*Attaršiya ḫuiš⸗wetenna kāštit⸗a⸗ma-an akten* "Even if you had survived A., you would have died of hunger" KUB 14.1 obv. 12 (MH/MS), ed. Madd. 4f.; for *mān . . . -(y)a* "even if" cf. *mān* 7d; *ma-am-ma-an-za-kán kuiški* É-*er tama*⸢*iš ar*⸣*nut ma-an zik UL aršanieše* "If someone else had confiscated/ appropriated (your) house, would you not be upset?" ABoT 65 rev. 5-6 (letter, MH/MS), ed. Güterbock, AnDergi 2 (1944) 390, 400, Rost, MIO 4 (1956) 345-47, HW^2 344a; *nušmaš* LÚ*auriyaluš* (var. LÚ.MEŠ*au*[. . .]) *kuit arantat ma-a-an-kán ma-a-an ANA* m*Pittaggatallipat* (var. omits *-pat*) *warpa teḫḫun ma-an-mu* LÚ*auriyaluš* (var. [LÚ*a*]*uriyatalluš*) *kuit ŠA* m*Pitaggatalli auer ma-an-mu UL duḫušiyait ma-an-mu* (over erased *ma-a-an-mu*) *piran arḫa tarnaš* "Because their (the enemy's) advance guards were standing (at their posts), and because, if I had tried to surround P., P.'s advance guards would have seen me, and he would not have waited for me, but would have slipped away before me, (so I turned my eyes in the opposite direction toward mPittapara)" KBo 5.8 iii 14-18 with dupl. KBo 16.8 iii 18-21 (Murš. II annals), ed. AM 156f. without dupl., tr. in Gurney, The Hittites 109; none of the *mān*'s or *ma-an*'s is found in the preserved parts of the dupl.; cf. *ma-[a]-an-ma-an . . . [. . . m]a?-an-ta . . . ma-an . . .* KUB 21.38 obv. 44-45 (letter of Pud.), ed. Helck, JCS 17.91.

c′ particle *man*, sometimes written plene (*ma-a-an*, *ma-a-na-*, etc.), in both protasis and apodosis, and without conj. "if" (*takku* or *mān*) in the protasis; from OS; that the protasis contains the particle, not the conj., seems clear from the fact that it is sometimes enclitic (*-ma-an*): EGIR-*an-ma-an kuwapi apēdaš ANA* NAM.RA.MEŠ *tiyanun ma-an* dUTU-*ŠI* EGIR-*an tiyanun ma-an-za* dUTU-*ŠI apūš* (var. *apūn*) NAM.RA.MEŠ *daḫḫun ma-a-na-aš* URU*Ḫattuši arḫa uwatenun* "Had I ever concerned myself with those deportees, I, My Majesty would have concerned myself and would have taken those deportees and carried them off to Ḫattuša" KBo 3.3 iii 6-9 (arbitration of Murš. II regarding Barga), ed. Friedrich, KlF (1930) 291, Klengel, OrNS 32 (1963) 37, 43; also enclitic *-man* in KBo 5.6 iii 53ff.; *ma-a-n[e- . . .] tayazzil piškir ma-an ḫūmantešpat maršer [n?]ašma* (NS var. [*ma?-a?-*]*ne*) LÚ.MEŠNÍ.ZU *kīšantati kāš⸗ma-an kūn ēpz[i k]āš⸗a⸗ma-an kūn ēpzi ma-an* LUGAL-*waš* GIŠx *peššir* KBo 6.2 ii 54-57 (Law § 49,

OS) with NS dupl. KUB 29.14 iv 4; often discussed and very difficult to understand, but clearly containing irrealis, cf. von Schuler, Kaškäer 9 n. 89, Souček, OLZ 1961:461f., and on the questionable sign Hoffner, FsGordon 84 n. 17 and Güterbock, FsOtten 75f.; *[m]ān UL-ma ma-an-ta* ᵐ*Attaršiyaš [U]L dalešta [m]a-an-t[ák-k]án ku[enta]* "Had (His Majesty) not (driven Attaršiya away), A. would not have left you alone; he would have killed you" KUB 14.1 obv. 4-5 (MH/MS), ed. Madd. 2f.; cf. ibid. obv. 11; *ammuk⸗ ma-an⸗wa kuwapi* DUMU-*YA ēšta ammuk⸗ma-an⸗wa ammel [R]AMĀNIYA ammella* KUR-*eaš tepnumar tametani* KUR-*e ḫatranun* "If I had a son, would I have written to another land about my own shame and that of my land?" KBo 5.6 iii 53-54, iv 1-2 (DŠ frag. 28), ed. Friedrich, KlF 291, Güterbock, JCS 10:96; [DUMU. LUGAL]-*ma[-an-wa-a]n-na-aš* (coll.) *kuwapi ēšta anzāš⸗ma-an⸗wa [d]amēdani* KUR-*e uwauen* KBo 14.12 iv 15-16 (DS frag. 28), correct the ed. JCS 10:97; *ma-a-na-an* LUG[AL.GAL *ammel*] *annawališ memišta* ÌR-*DUM-ma-na-an*[... -*t]a*? KUB 14.3 iv 55-56 (Taw.), ed. AU 18f.; *ma-a-an-* (var. *ma-an-*)*wa-ra-aš-mu-kán šulliyat [(ku)]⸗ wapi UL ma-a-an* (var. *ma-an*) *ḫandān* LUGAL. GAL *ANA* LUGAL.TUR *katterraḫḫir* "If he had never picked the quarrel with me, would they (the gods) have subjected a great king to a petty king?" KUB 1.4:42-43 + 674/v with dupl. KUB 1.9:6, ed. Ḫatt. 30f. iii 77-78, StBoT 24:22f. iii 76-77 (674/v on Plate III), (Ḫebat almost fell from the roof.) *[ma]-an tiyat ma-na-aš-kán šuḫḫaz katta mauštat* "Had she taken a step, she would have fallen from the roof" KUB 33.106 ii 8-9 (Ullik., NH), ed. Güterbock, JCS 6:20f.; *ma-an-za zik UL manga* (var. *UL ziqqa*) *wa[(šdul)]aš ēšta ma-an-kán mān ANA* ᵈUTU-*ŠI kuwapi* Ḫ[(UL-*wanni*)] *kittat ma-an-ta* ᵈUTU-*ŠI apiyapat arḫa peš⸗ šiyanun m[a-(an-ták-kán)]* É *ABIKA* KUR-*TUM-ya kinunpat arḫa daḫḫun [(m)]a-na-at] damēdani peḫḫun ANA* KUR-*TI-ia-ma-an tamain* EN-*an* DÙ-*nun* (var. *iyanun*) "(Because your father Mašḫuiluwa sinned, and you, Kupanta-ᵈLAMMA, were M.'s son,) even if you had not been guilty in any way (var. guilty too) (still,) if ever (*kuwapi*) it had occurred to My Majesty to harm (you) (lit. you had been set for harm to My Majesty), I, My Majesty, could have cast you out at that very time. Even now I could have taken your father's house and land from you, I could have given them to someone else and made another lord for the land" KUB 6.41 iv 27-31, dupls. KBo 4.3 iii 30-35, KBo 5.13 iv 19-24, KUB 6.44 iv 9-14 (Kup., NH), ed. SV 1:136f. with different tr.

c. potential, with pres.-fut. tense or a nominal sentence — **1′** expressing a possibility: *mānwamu* 1-*an* DUMU-*KA paišti ma-an-wa-ra-aš-mu* ᴸᵁ́*MUTIYA kišari* "If you give me one of your sons, he could/would become my husband" KBo 5.6 iii 12-13 (DŠ frag. 28), ed. JCS 10:94, cf. Friedrich, KlF 292; (Or if you think to yourself:) *a-ši-ma-an-kán* ZAG[-*aš* GAM-*an*] *niyari na-aš-ma-<ma->an-wa-kán uniuš* EN.MEŠ *:alla[llā] pānzi ú-uq-qa-ma-an-wa pēḫudanzi* "That province might 'turn' (i.e., change its allegiance), or those lords might defect and take me away with them!" (Don't try it.) KBo 4.14 ii 78-80 (treaty of Šupp. II), ed. Stefanini, AANL 20:43f. ("potrebbe, potrebbero"); cf. *mali-* v.

2′ in questions: (Seeing the Sungod approaching, the Stormgod says to his vizier: KUR-*ewa nik[ku] kuwapikki ḫarkan ma-an-wa* URU. DIDLI.ḪI.A *nikku kūwapikki dannateššanteš ma-a-an-wa* ᴸᵁ́ERÍN.MEŠ *nikku kuwapiki ḫul⸗ lanteš* "The land hasn't somehow been destroyed? The cities wouldn't have been laid waste somehow? The troops wouldn't have been defeated somehow?" KUB 24.8 ii 16-18 (Appu, pre-NH/NS), ed. StBoT 14:8-9; *mān* in ii 18 would be the rarer plene writing.

Enclitic *-man* was suffixed to the first word of the clause, following that word's own enclitics (e.g., *kāštit⸗a* + *⸗man* KUB 14.1 obv. 12, *kāš⸗man kūn ēpzi kāš⸗a* + *⸗man kūn ēpzi* KBo 6.2 ii 56f.), but preceding the chain of sentence particles (*-wa*, *-mu*, *-naš*, *-kan*, *-ašta*). The word *māmman* (MS), *mānman* (NH) contains the conj. "if" and the particle *man* in that order. *ma-a-am-ma-an* KUB 30.10 obv. 22 (OH?/MS), *ma-am-ma-an-za-kán* ABoT 65 rev. 5 (MH/MS), *ma-a-an-ma-an* KUB 21.38 obv. 44 (Pud.), IBoT 1.33:90 (oracle, NH), *ma-a-an-ma-an-wa-at-ta* KUB 15.12 i 5 (Ḫatt. III), *ma-a-an-ma-na-aš-mu* KUB 23.103 obv. 25 (Tudḫ. IV), questionable ⸢*ma*⸣-*ma-an-wa* KBo 15.1 i 14 (cf.

StBoT 3:112f., 119). The conj. "if" is occasionally written *ma-an* or *ma-na-*, and the particle written *ma-a-an* or *ma-a-na-*. The particle is often enclitic, while the conj. "if" is never enclitic. Exx. of *mān* + *man* as a single word compound were unknown to Friedrich in 1930 (KlF 289f.), when he maintained on the basis of plene vs. nonplene writings that the particle always preceded the conj. in the non-compounded exx. such as *ma-an-kán ma-a-an* (KUB 6.41 iv 28, KUB 14.1 i 12), *ma-a-an-kán ma-a-an* (KBo 5.8 iii 15), *ma-a-an ma-a-an* (KUB 14.3 ii 16), and even (in Korrekturnachtrag) "*ma-a?-an ma-an*" (KUB 21.38 i 44), actually wr. as one word; cf. also *ma-an ma-a-an* KUB 33.117 ii 7, (10), KUB 19.55 rev. 9, KBo 9.85:22. The existence of analogous *takku⸗man* (2′ a′), however, where it is clear that "if" precedes the particle, and of the compound *mammān*, where it is highly unlikely that the "if" conj. is enclitic to the particle, suggests that the plene vs. nonplene contrast is an unsatisfactory basis for determining the sequence particle + conj. Even in the exx. cited by Friedrich where the particle and conj. are written as two separate words, it is likely that the conj. precedes.

Güterbock (OrNS 12:154) pointed out that, as in other IE languages, the optative and potential are expressed in Hittite by a common morpheme. In Hittite that morpheme is *man*. It would appear that the optative usage of *man* is attested in the earliest texts, and that the irrealis usage demonstrated in b 1′ grew out of the optative usage of a 2′ b′. In fact one could equally well translate many exx. in b 1′ as "so-and-so wanted to do such-and-such, but . . . " The usages under b share most with a 2′. The negative of a 1′ (speaker optative) is expressed by *lē* and *man*, while the negative of a 2′ (subject optative) would seem to be expressed by *numan*/*nuwan* "can't/couldn't" or "won't/wouldn't". Cf. Hoffner, GsKronasser 38ff.

Ungnad in Sommer, Heth. II (1922) 52 (irrealis); Friedrich, KlF (1930) 286-296 (detailed study of irrealis and potentialis); Hrozny, JA 218 (1931) 313 (translated VBoT 2:2-3 as optative); Sommer, AU (1932) 73 n. 1 (on spelling *-ma-a-na-*); HAB (1938) 135f.; Friedrich, HE (first ed., 1940) §§275-77; Güterbock OrNS 12 (1943) 154 (optative use); Hoffner in GsKronasser (1982) 38-45 (speaker optative, subject optative, and negation of the latter by *nūman*).

mān; **1.** like (postpos.), **2.** just as, as (conj.), **3.** how (interrog. adv. in main clause), **4.** if, whether (conj. introducing an indirect question), **5.** when, whenever, **6.** while (?), as long as (?), **7.** if (conj. introducing a conditional clause), **8.** *mān* . . . *mān*, whether . . . or (whether), either . . . or, **9.** *mān* in incipits, when/if; written syll. or BE-*an* (mng. 7), and possibly GIM-*an* (see 1 c 3′).

1. like (postpos.), from OS
- **a.** in OH
  - **1′** in OS
  - **2′** in MS or NS
- **b.** in MH and NH prayers and rituals
- **c.** in myths, epics, and translations of Sum.-Akk. hymns (all NS)
  - **1′** comparison with subject
  - **2′** comparison with object
  - **3′** comparison with subject or object, *mān* alternating in the same copy with *maḫḫan* or GIM-*an*
    - **a′** in Ullik.
    - **b′** in the Cow and the Fisherman
    - **c′** in Signalement lyrique
- **d.** in descriptions of dreams, "(someone) like", "(something) like", all NH

2. just as, as (conj.)

3. how (interrog. adv. in main clause)

4. if, whether (conj. introducing an indirect question), from OH/MS
- **a.** single question
  - **1′** preceding the main clause
  - **2′** following the main clause
- **b.** double question, "whether . . . or (whether)"
  - **1′** preceding the main clause
  - **2′** following the main clause
    - **a′** with pret. in the *mān* clause
    - **b′** with pres. or nominal sentence in the *mān* clause

5. when, whenever (conj.), from OS
- **a.** with pret., "when"
  - **1′** in OH texts other than myths and epics
  - **2′** in myths and epics (all NS)
  - **3′** in other NS texts
- **b.** with pres.-fut. and in nominal sentences, introducing a single event, "when"
  - **1′** in OH
    - **a′** in OS
    - **b′** in OH/MS and NS
  - **2′** in myths and epics
  - **3′** in ritual and festival texts
    - **a′** in general
    - **b′** introducing a time of the year or day
- **c.** with the pres.-fut. (incl. the hist. pres.), introducing recurring (or potentially recurring) events, "whenever"

6. while (?), as long as (?), (OH)
7. if (conj. introducing a conditional clause), from OS
  a. with verb in pres.
    1′ in general
      a′ in OS
      b′ in OH in MS and NS
      c′ in MH
      d′ in NH
        1″ in hist. and legal texts
        2″ in myths and prayers
    2′ in contrasting conditions, "if . . . , but if"
  b. with verb in pret.
    1′ in prayers
    2′ in oracle questions
    3′ in letters
    4′ in rituals
  c. with periphrastic perfect
  d. with delayed -(*y*)*a*, "even if", "even though" (with pret. or in nominal sentences)
    1′ even if
    2′ even though
    3′ even though/even if (in broken context)
  e. *mān* "if" clause without apodosis
    1′ with pret., as an affirmation of the truth, with an implied self-curse if untrue
    2′ with pres.
      a′ as a promise, with an implied self-curse if it is not fulfilled
      b′ as a warning addressed to another person
  f. *mān* clause following the main clause
  g. *mān* and *takku* in the Laws and in omen protases
    1′ in the Laws
    2′ in omens
  h. *mān nattama*
  i. *mān* with its force continuing through a chain of clauses
  j. temporal and relative clauses inserted in conditional clauses, with repetition of *mān*
    1′ temporal
    2′ relative
8. *mān* . . . *mān*, "whether . . . or (whether)", "either . . . or"
  a. introducing clauses, "whether . . . or (whether)"
    1′ MH
    2′ NH
  b. distinguishing single words, "whether . . . or", "either . . . or"
  c. with the omission of *mān* in the second or a later item
  d. *mān* . . . *našma*, replacing *mān* . . . *mān*
9. *mān* in incipits (incl. colophons and catalog entries), "when"/"if"
10. *mān* with indefinite pronoun and indefinite adv.
  a. with indefinite pronoun
    1′ in OH
    2′ in MH and NH
  b. with adv. *kuwapi*, *kuwapikki*, *kuwatqa*

Without enclitic: *ma-a-an* passim.

With consonant-initial enclitics: *ma-a-an-ša-an* KBo 5.9 ii 30 (Murš. II) etc. passim; **with assimilation:** *ma-a-aš-ši* (= *mān⸗ši*) KBo 17.65 rev. 15 (MH?).

With vowel-initial enclitics: *ma-a-na-aš*, *ma-a-na-at* etc. passim; *ma-a-na-pa* KBo 12.8 i (9), 11 (OH/NS), KUB 25.16 i 1 (OH/NS) etc., *ma-a-na-aš-ta* KBo 20.26 + KBo 25.34 obv. 18 (OH/NS), KBo 20.32 iii 10 (OH/NS), KUB 31.127 i 39 (MH/NS) etc. □ note the identical spelling *ma-a-na-*/*nu-* sub *man* (optative and potential with enclitic pron.).

with enclitic *-a* "and": *ma-a-an-na*(-) . . . KUB 29.1 iii 33 (OH/NS), KBo 10.12 iv (6), 15, 27, KBo 3.4 iii 80, KBo 4.14 iii 64 (all NH) etc.

with enclitic *-wa(r-)*—with *-n-* preserved: *ma-a-an-wa* KUB 33.8 ii (11) (OH/NS), KBo 3.7 iii 10 (Illuyanka A, OH/NS), KUB 12.66 iv 12, (Illuyanka D), KUB 14.1 rev. 46 (MH), KUB 15.16 i 4 (NH) and passim in NH.

with *-n-* lost: *ma-a-u-wa* KBo 25.151:3 + KBo 26.136 obv. 13, rev. 2 (MS?), KBo 21.22:56 (MS), KBo 22.118 rt. col. 7 (NS), *ma-a-wa*(-) . . . KBo 3.7 i 25 (etc. in Illuyanka, OH/NS), ibid. iv 9 and dupl. KUB 17.6 iv 6 (w. var. [*m*]*a-a-an-wa-* . . . KUB 12.66 iv 12), KUB 17.9 i 4 (NS), KUB 36.45:2 (NS); *ma-u-wa* KBo 13.94:1 (NS), KUB 12.63 obv. 11, 21, rev. 7 (OH/NS), KUB 34.50:(4), *ma-wa*(*-an-na-aš*) KUB 7.57 i 5(?).

***ma-an-* . . . and *ma-n(a)-* . . .** (rare; all exx. NH and with enclitics): *ma-an*(*-kán*) KUB 30.42 iv 21 (against *ma-a-an*(*-kán*) in par. KBo 23.1 ii 19), *ma-n*(*a-ša-an*) KBo 16.54:16, *ma-n*(*a-at*) AT 125:15 (2x), *ma-an*(*-wa-za*) KUB 15.32 i 46, *ma-an*(*-kán*) KBo 17.65 obv. 41 (with var. *ma-a-an*(*-kán*) KUB 44.59 rev. 13), *ma-an*(*-ma-aš-ma-aš*) KUB 18.12 obv. 4, *ma-an*(*-ši*) KUB 32.49b ii 14, *ma-an*(*-ma-kán*) KUB 25.37 i 31.

with assimilation: *ma-a-am-ma-an* (= *mān⸗man*) KUB 30.10 obv. 18, 22 (OH/MS), KUB 30.28 obv. 20, *ma-am-ma-an*(*-za-kán*) ABoT 65 rev. 5 (MH/MS).

BE-*an*: KBo 4.14 iii 37 (treaty, Šupp. II), KUB 8.35 obv. 12ff., KUB 43.8 iii 2ff. (all omens, NS), KUB 5.1 i 32 etc., AT 454 i 16 etc. (both NH) and passim in oracles.

BE (without compl.): KUB 6.2 obv 9, 11, 23; BE(*-ma*) KUB 18.40 obv. 1(?) (NH).

Possibly **GIM-*an***: see mng. 1 c 3′.

mng. 5: [*ma*]-⌜*a*⌝-*an* ᵈ*A-nu-uš* ᵈ[. . .] "When Anu (and) [Enlil] . . ." KUB 34.12 obv. 1, followed by omens beginning *ták-ku* ᵈ*SI*[*N* . . .] "If the mo[on . . .]" (cf. the trace ibid. 14), corresponding to Akk. *enūma Anu Enlil* at the beginning of the series, followed by *šumma* (DIŠ) in individual omens, Virolleaud, Astrologie chaldéenne: Sin, I.

mng. 7: (Sum.) [a]ḫ (coll.; expected: ud).ta.a = (Akk.) *šum*[*-ma*] = (Hitt.) *ma-a-an* KUB 3.99 + KBo 1.50 ii 20 (Erimḫuš Bogh. C).

BE-*an* interchanges with *ma-a-an*, e.g. KUB 8.35 obv. 11 against 12ff. (BE = Akk. *ŠUMMA* "if"), but note that in the bilingual omens KUB 4.1 iii 15-iv 31 (OH/NS) BE (iii 15, 17 etc.) in the Akk. vers. corr. to *ták-ku* (iii 16, 19 etc.) in the Hitt. vers.

(Sum.) [o].du.gam = ("Akk.") *mu ma mi* = (Hitt.) *ma-a-an*/ [o].lú = *ḫu ḫa ḫi* = *ku-it*/ [o].dù.a.bi = *lu la li* = ⌜GIM⌝-

an, KBo 26.20 ii 39-41 (Erimḫuš Bogh. A). □ Obviously the Hittite is not a translation of the Sum. or Akk. In translating the Sum.-Akk. composition Signalement lyrique the Hitt. uses *mān* "like" (cf. below sub 1 c 3′ c′) to render metaphorical predication ("She is a . . . ") in the Sum. and Akk. texts. For occasional alternations with GIM-*an* see below sub 1 c 3′. For *m*[*a-a-an*] or *m*[*a-aḫ-ḫa-an*] = Akk. *kī* in KUB 1.16 i/ii 18-19 cf. *maḫḫan*, bil. sect.

1. like (postpos.; both nouns in the simile are in the same case), from OS; occasionally *mān* alternates with GIM-*an* and *maḫḫan*, see section c 3′; Sommer, AU 126 n. 1, HAB 75, Ehelolf, OLZ 1933:5, Güterbock, OrNS 12:154, Hoffner apud DeVries, Diss. 82; cf. *maḫḫan*, mng. 1 — **a.** in OH — **1′** in OS: "Come to meet me!" [*takku n*]*attama uwaši nutta ḫartaggan ma-a-an* / [*an*(?)-*da*(?) *š*]*i*(coll.)-*iš-ki-mi nu*(-)*tuḫḫiyattit ākti* "But [if] you do not come I shall keep [squee]zing(?) you like a *ḫ*.-animal (acc.), and you will die of suffocation(?)." KBo 7.14 obv. 4-6 (Ḫatt. I, OS); *nu* UR.MAḪ-*iš ma-a-an utn*[*e*(-) . . .] KBo 3.22:26 (Anitta, OS), ed. StBoT 18:10f.

2′ in MS and NS: [*šu*]*minzana* ÌR.MEŠ-*amman* UR.BAR.RA-*aš ma-a-an pang*[*ur*] 1-*EN ēštu* "But let your clan, my subjects, be one like the wolf's" KBo 3.27 (BoTU 10β): 15-16 (Ḫatt. I, OH/NS), □ ÌR.MEŠ-*a*(*n*)*⸗man* is gen. pl. agreeing with *šuminzan⸗a*; cf. [*šumenzan*?] *wētnaš ma-a-an pankuršeme*[*t* 1-*EN*] *ēšdu* KUB 1.16 ii 46 (Ḫatt. I, OH/NS), ed. HAB 8-9; ⸢*numu*⸣ DINGIR-*YA ḫu*⸢*iš*⸣*nut numu wašdulaš kat*[*t*]*an arḫa išḫi⸗yandan* LÚ-*an ma-a-a*[*n*] *arḫa lā* "Save me, O my god, and release me, (who am) like a man bound in sins" KUB 36.75 iii 9-11 (prayer, OH?/MS), ed. Lebrun, Hymnes 125, 130.

b. in MH and NH prayers and rituals: *nu karū* KUR ^{URU}*Ḫatti* ^{URU}*Arinn*[*aš*] / [*IŠTU* ^{d}UTU(?) *za*]*ḫḫait araḫzena* KUR-*e* UR.MAḪ *ma-a-an a-ar*[*-aš-ki-it*(?)] KUB 24.4 rev. 2-3 (prayer, MH/NS); *karūm*[*a* KUR ^{U}]^{RU}KÙ.BABBAR-*ti IŠTU* ^{d}UTU ^{URU}*Arinna araḫzenaš* ⸢*ANA*⸣ KUR.KUR.ḪI.A-*TIM* UR.MAḪ *ma-a-an šar⸗ḫiškit* "But formerly the Ḫatti-land, with (the help of) the Sungoddess of Arinna, used to rush upon the neighboring countries like a lion" KUB 24.3 ii 44-45 (prayer, Murš. II), ed. Gurney, AAA 27:30f., Lebrun, Hymnes 162, 170, cf. the older par. KUB 24.4 rev. 2-3 (above); "Let Nerik, the city, (be) on your mind! You were sitting on the knee of (your) beloved Tešimi, dreaming sweet dreams." *arāi* ^{URU}*Neriqaš* ^{d}U-*aš* ^{d}*Tešimešwata* GEŠTIN-*aš mureš milit ma-a-an kankanza* "Arise, O Stormgod of Nerik! Tešimi is hanging upon you like a honey-sweet cluster of grapes." KUB 36.89 rev. 56-59, (prayer in Nerik rit., probably Ḫatt. III but likely to have incorporated older material), ed. Lebrun, Hymnes 377f., cf. Ehelolf, OLZ 1933:3f., Haas, KN 156f.; cf. GUD-*un ma-a-an* KUB 30.36 ii 5-6 (rit., MH/NS) with par. KUB 30.34 iii 13, KBo 14.100:9-(10) + KUB 39.99:14-(15) (prayer in rit., NS); ^{DUG}*palḫi ma-a-an* ibid. 3 + 8; AN.ZA.GÀR *ma-a-an* KUB 41.4 ii 5 (rit., NH).

c. in myths, epics, and translations of Sum.-Akk. hymns (all NS) — **1′** Comparison with subject: LÚ-*nataršetkan ANA* ^{d}*Kumarbi* ŠÀ-*ŠU anda* ZABAR *ma-a-an ulišta* "His (Anu's) manhood blended with Kumarbi's interior like bronze" (i.e. as copper and tin blend to form bronze) KUB 33.120 i 25-26 (Kingship in Heaven, NS), translit. Laroche, Myth. 154, tr. MAW 156; *nuššikan arunaš* [. . . (*išḫuzziyaš pid*)]*i* TÚG-*aš ma-a-an anda pēdanza* "And the sea reached (lit. was brought) to his waistline (lit. to the place of his belt) like a garment" KUB 33.93 iv 24-25 (Ullik. I A iv 29-30) w. dupl. KUB 33.92 iii 15, ed. Güterbock, JCS 5:158f.; *naškan* ^{URU}*Kummiya* ^{GIŠ}KÁ.GAL-*aš piran*(!) ^{GIŠ}*šiyatal ma-a-an tiyat* "And he (Ullik.) took his stand in Kummiya in front of the gate like a *š*." KBo 26.65 i 21-22 (Ullik. IIIA), ed. without join JCS 6:18f.; cf. *nuwar*[*aškan*] NÍ.TE-*az arḫa* ^{GIŠ}*šiyatal ma-a-an watkut* "He sprang out of the body like a *š*." KUB 33.93 iii left 17-18 + right 28-29 (Ullik. I A iii 17-18), ed. JCS 5:152f.; ^{d}U-*aškan* ^{GIŠ}*tiyaridaš šarā gagaštiyaš ma-a-an watkut* "^{d}U jumped up into the cart like a *g*." KUB 33.106 iv 21 (Ullik. III A iv 21), ed. JCS 6:30f.; [*n*]*uššikan* GI-*aš IŠTU* ^{GIŠ}BAN *pari*⸢*yan*⸣ MUŠEN-*iš ma-a-an iyattari* "Like a bird his arrow flies across from the bow" KUB 36.67 ii 21-22 (Gurparanzaḫ), ed. Güterbock, ZA 44:86f.; *nuššikan išḫaḫru* [*par*]*ā* PA_5.ḪI.A-*uš ma-a-an aršanzi* "And his tears flow forth like streams" KUB 33.113 i 16-17 (Ullik II B i 29-30), ed. JCS 6:12f. □ the verb agrees with PA_5.ḪI.A-*uš* = *amiyaruš*, plur. nom. in -*uš*, not with the neuter *išḫaḫru*; cf., partly restored, KUB 36.25

iv 4-5, translit. Myth. 187; KUB 8.48 i 18 (Gilg.), ed. Friedrich, ZA 39:18f.; KUB 17.3 ii 4-5 (Gilg.), ed. ZA 39:20f., cf. Myth. 132; KBo 19.112:18 (Ḫedammu), ed. StBoT 14:44f.

2′ comparison with object: [... (obj.)] GI-*an ma-a-an zaḫḫuraiškizzi* "He snaps off [...] like a reed" KUB 33.120 ii 31 (Kingship in Heaven), translit. Myth. 156; NA$_4$-*anwaran* ⸢*ma-a-*⸣*an*(coll.) *paršanut* "Break him like a stone" ibid. 36; cf. ⸢TÚG-*an ma*⸣*-a-an* ibid. 73(coll.), 76; *nuza* ^{d}*Ku⸗marbiš* ZI-*ni kattan ḫattatar* ^{NA_4}NUNUZ *ma-a-an išgariškizzi* "Kumarbi fastens wisdom to his mind like a bead" KUB 33.98 i 9-10 with dupl. ^{d}*Kumarbišza* ZI-*ni pi-an ḫat*[*tatar daškizzi*(?)] *nat* ^{NA_4}*kunnan ma-*⸢*a*⸣[*-an išgariškizzi*] KUB 33.96 i 9-10 (Ullik. I), ed. JCS 5:146f.

3′ comparison with subject or object, *mān* alternating in the same copy with GIM-*an* and *maḫḫan*, cf. *maḫḫan* mng. 1 — **a′** in Ullik.: [*i*]*zzan* GIM-*an* ... *lalakuešan⸗ma⸗war⸗an* [*ma-a-an*?] ... [G]I-*an ma-a-an* ... MUŠEN. ḪI.A GIM-*an* ... KUB 33.93 iii left 21-24 + right 32-35 (Ullik. I A iii 21-24), ed. Güterbock, JCS 5:152f.; [*da*]*nnaran* TÚG-*an* ⸢*ma-a*⸣[*-an a*]⸢*rḫa*⸣ *šar⸗gannit* ... *ma*[*lt*]*ani*[*šaš*] *ma-aḫ-ḫa-an kar⸗p*[*išk*]*attari* KBo 26.65 i 16-19 (Ullik. III A i 16-19), ed. without join, JCS 6:18f., cf. *naš :maltaneš* GIM-*an šarā karpiškattari* KUB 33.106 iii 36-37 (Ullik. III A), ed. JCS 6:26f., and [(*:maldanišaš* GIM-*an k*)*a*]*rpeškittari* KUB 33.93 iv 26 with dupl. KUB 33.92 iii 16 (Ullik. I A iv 31), ed. JCS 5:158f.

b′ in The Cow and the Fisherman: UR. MAḪ-*aš* GIM-*an* ... *ḫūwanḫuešar ma-a-an* KUB 24.7 iii 24-26, ed. Friedrich, ZA 49:228f., cf. Hoffner, FsLacheman 192.

c′ in Signalement lyrique: *laḫpaš⸗ma⸗aš kurakkiš ma-a-an zinnanza* "She (my mother) is finished (i.e. perfect?) like a pillar of ivory (?)" RS 25.421:28-29, ed. Laroche, Ugar. 5:773, 775 (for the Akk. section see Nougayrol, ibid. 313, 315, 317, and CHD *:laḫpa-*); ^{GIŠ}KIRI$_6$*-aš⸗ma⸗aš* GIM-*an ilali⸗yan*[*za*] *dammetarwantit šūwanza* "She is like a desirable garden, filled with luxuriant growth" RŠ 25.421:36-37, ed. Laroche, Ugar. 5:774f.; ^{GIŠ}*šuini⸗laš⸗ma⸗aš* GIM-*an šeššuraš* ibid. 38-39; PA$_5$*-aš⸗ma⸗aš* GIM-*an* ibid. 44; LUGAL-*aš⸗ma⸗aš* GIM-*an* DUMU.MEŠ.NITA ibid. 57, cf. ibid. 62, 64; cf. above in bil. sec. and *maḫḫan*, bil. sec.

The alternation may indicate that GIM-*an* could be read **mān* (beside *maḫḫan*), or that *mān* and *maḫḫan* (wr. GIM-*an*) were used side by side as is the case with syll. *maḫḫan* above in c 3′ a′ (KBo 26.65 i 16-19). Cf. also mng. 2 for [*mā*]*ḫḫanda* alternating with *mān* "just as". For other exx. of GIM-*an* in literary descriptions not alternating with either *ma-a-an* or *ma-aḫ-ḫa-an*, cf. *maḫḫan* mng. 1 a 2′.

d. in descriptions of dreams, "(someone) like ...", "(something) like ..."; all NH: *nuwakan zašḫiya* DUMU.LUGAL *ma-a-an kuiški anda uit* "In (my) dream someone like a prince entered" KUB 31.71 iv 2-3 (queen's dream), ed. Werner, FsOtten 327f.; *eniušmawakan* ÉSAG.ḪI.A *karū ma-a-an šarā šannapilaḫḫanteš nuwa* ^{GIŠ}KA×GIŠ. ḪI.A *ma-a-an kueqa kittari* "The aforementioned silos/storage bins were completely emptied out as formerly, and something like K.s were put (there) (lit.: are lying)" ibid. 10-13; cf. ibid. 29-32; *nuwa zašḫiya ABUYA ma-a-an* EGIR-*pa* TI-*eššanza⸗pat* "In (my) dream (there) was (someone) like my father, even come to life again" KUB 31.77 i 8-9 (queen's dream); cf. *:šaruntin ma-a-an kuinki* ibid. 10; EGIR-*andamawazakan* ^{d}UTU-*ŠI* Ù-*an aušta nuwakan zašḫiya* ŠÀ ^{URU}TÚL-*na tuḫḫūwaiš ma-a-an kuiški kišanza* "Thereafter His Majesty saw a dream, and in the dream something like smoke was occurring in Arinna" KUB 5.24 ii 14-16 + KUB 16.31 ii 3-5 (oracle question).

2. just as, as (conj., not clause initial), from OS; cf. *maḫḫan*, mng. 2: ^{d}UTU-*uš* ^{d}IM-*aš ma-a-an uktūreš* LUGAL-*uš* SAL.LUGAL-*ašša QĀ⸗TAMMA uktūreš ašantu* "Just as the Sungod (and) the Stormgod are everlasting, so let the king and queen likewise be everlasting!" KBo 17.1 iii 6-7 (rit., OS), with dupl. KBo 17.3 iii 6-7 (OS), ed. StBoT 8:30f.; contrast the above with [*ma-a-a*]*ḫ-ḫa-an-da* (var. *ma-a-an*) ⸢^{d}⸣UTU-*uš* ^{d}IM-*aš nēpiš tē*[(*kanna*)] *uktūri* (var. [*uktu*]*reš*) KBo 17.1 iii 1f., dupl. KBo 17.3 ii 15-iii 1, ed. StBoT 8:30 w.n.1; *kāš* LÚ.U$_{19}$.L[U-*aš*] *ma-a-an karū naš* EGIR-*pa* [*apen*]*iššan ēštu* "Just as this person was before, let him be like that again!" KBo 26.136 obv. 6-7 (myth., OH?/MS?), cf. KUB 33.66 ii 21 (NS), translit. Laroche, Myth. 70; *šiunan* ^{d}UTU-*ui marnuwan ma-a-an šiēššara an<da> kulamtati ištazanašmiš*(sic) *karazmišša*(! text -*ta*) 1-*iš kišat kānat* ^{d}*šiunan* ^{d}UTU-*aš Labar-* [*našša*] *ištazanašmit*(sic) *karazzamišša* 1-*iš kišaru* "O Sungod of the gods! Just as *m.* and beer have been blended so that their 'soul' and their *k.* have become one, . . . let the 'soul' and *k.* of the Sungod of the gods [and of] the Labarna become one!" KUB 41.23 ii 18-21, (incant., OH?/NS), discussed by Ehelolf, ZA 43:176f., ed. Archi, FsMeriggi 2:37f. (some of whose readings we do not accept), cf. ibid. ii 22-24.

3. how (interrog. adv. in main clause), from OH/NS, cf. Otten MVAeG 46.1:20 note d, Sommer, OLZ 1953:11, cf. *maḫḫan*, mng. 4: ⌈*ki*⌉*nunawa ma-a-an iyami k*[(*uitwa kiš*)*at*] "Now, how shall I act? What happened?" KUB 33.24 i 42 (missing Stormgod, OH/NS), rest. from dupl. C: KUB 33.27:6 (MS), (var. B:[. . . *kuit*] *kīšat kuitwa* [*iyami*] "[What] happened? What [shall I do?]" KUB 33.22 ii (5)-6, translit. Laroche, Myth. 55, tr. MAW 146); ⌈*ma-a-an-w*⌉[*a iya*]*weni* KUB 33.8 ii 11 (Tel. myth), translit. Laroche, Myth. 40; GIM-*anwa* DÙ-*weni* (var.: *ma*[*ḫḫ*]*anwa iyawe*⌈*ni*⌉) *ma-a-an-wa iyaweni* "When (*maḫḫan*) we act, how (*mān*) shall we act?" KUB 7:1 iii 9-10 (rit., NH), with dupl. KBo 22.128 iii(!) 7, translit. Otten-Rüster, ZA 67:58; cf. also 7 e 2′ a′; see *maḫḫan* bil. sec. for *m*[*ān*] or *m*[*aḫḫan*] = Akk. *kī* in HAB.

4. if, whether (conj., introducing indirect question), from OH/MS — **a.** single question — **1′** preceding the main clause: *ma-a-an-mu-kán annaz-ma kartaz* [*k*]*ī inan gulšta ugatza āppa* ^{SAL}ENSI-*ta natta kuššanka punuššun* "I never even inquired through an interpretress of dreams if you (O my god) ordained this illness for me from the womb of (my) mother" KUB 30.10 rev. 20-21 (Kantuzzili prayer, OH/MS), ed. Lebrun, Hymnes 115, 117, cf. par. KUB 30.11 rev. 19-20 (MS) and KUB 31.127 iii 10-12 (NS).

2′ following the main clause: "Concerning what you wrote to me: 'Send (me) a man whom you trust'" *nuwakan* $^{[U]RU}$*Malitiyan* GAM *aušdu ma-a-an-wa-kán* [*am*]*mel* URU.DIDLI.ḪI.A ⌈*awan*⌉(?) *arḫa UL* [o o-*a*]*n*-⌈*te*⌉-*eš* "'and let him inspect (the city of) M. (to see) if my cities are not [. . .]'" KBo 18.24 iv 12-14 (letter to Šalmaneser I), ed. Otten, AfO 22:113; *našta* ^{DUG}*išnūr*[*eš k*]*ueaz IŠTU* GAD DINGIR-*LIM kariyanteš nat PĀNI* ^{LÚ}EN.É-*TIM šarā appanzi nu* ^{DUG}*išnuruš aušzi ma-a-an-kán* ÍB.TAK$_4$ *šarā uwan* "They hold up before the master of the house the cloth of the deity with which the kneading troughs were covered, and he inspects the kneading troughs (to see) if the residue (of dough) has risen" KBo 15.33 ii 32-34 (Kuliwišna rit., MS), ed. AlHeth 145f. □ for ÍB.TAK$_4$ see Archi, OrNS 44:329, who erroneously adds MEŠ, and AHw 968f. s.v. *rēḫtu*(*m*) and 1252 s.v. *šittu*(*m*) II; for the Boğazköy shape of TAK$_4$, cf. also ÍB.TAK$_4$-*z*[*a* . . .] KUB 49.61:7, LÚ.TAK$_4$.TAK$_4$ KBo 26.4 ii 8; *nuwa apāt UL IDI ma*[-*a*]-*an-wa-ra-aš IŠTU* ⌈ŠU (?)⌉.MEŠ-*ŠUNU imma kuitki* GÙB-*laḫ-ḫanzi* "If they thwart(?) them (the troops? i 16) somehow with their own hands(?), *that* I do not know" (?) KUB 48.118 i 17-18 (dream, NH).

b. double question, "whether . . . or (whether)", cf. mng. 8, contrast the syntax of the direct double question on which cf. -*ma* a 1′ b′ 4″ — **1′** preceding the main clause: *ANA* DINGIR.MEŠ-*ma-aš ma-a-an* ZI-*anza ēšta ma-a-an-ša-ma-aš U*[*L* ZI-*anza ēšta*] *ammukmakan ŠA* ŠEŠ-*YA kariyaš*[*ḫi ḫandaš*] *apūn memian iyanun* "Whether it was the wish of the gods or whether it was not, I did this thing out of concern for my brother." KUB 21.19 + 1303/u ii 27-30, ed. Otten, Puduḫepa 18 with n. 41; cf. in the same prayer KUB 14.7 i 3-5, ed. Houwink ten Cate, FsGüterbock 125; and cf. KUB 14.7 i 20-21 continued by KUB 21.19 ii 1-3, ed. Güterbock, SBo 1.13, all prayer of Ḫatt. III and Pud., ed. Sürenhagen, AOF 8:88-93; [(UDU.ḪI.A-*ma* MU.KAM)]-*li ma-a-an* 1 *ME* (var. KUB 15.16:10 adds UDU) *ma-a-an* 50 UDU *peškimi* [*UL ku*(*itki t*)]*uqqāri* "Whether I shall give one hundred or fifty sheep every year makes no difference" KUB 15.17 + KUB 31.61 i 8-9 (vow of Pud.), with dupls. KUB 15.16:(9)-10, 1421/u:6-7 and KUB 48.116 i 9-11, ed. without KUB 48.116 StBoT 1:16f.; UDU.ŠIR.ḪI.A-*ma ma-a-an ḫargaēš ma-a-an tankuwaēš UL kuitki tuqqari* HT 1 iii 7-9 (rit.); cf. *ma-a-an* . . . ⌈*n*⌉*ašma* . . . *našma* . . . *nu UL kuitki duggari* KUB 17.28 iii 23-25; (Please send me some oil) *nammamu ma-a-an uppāi kuiški ma-a-an-mu UL kuiški uppāi numu ṬUPPA*$^{Ḫ[I.A]}$ *ḫatrātten nu* *šiggallu* "Furthermore write me letters and let me know whether someone will bring me (any) or whether no one will bring me (any)!" KBo 18.2 rev. 8-12 (letter, NH).

2′ following the main clause — **a′** with pret. in the *mān* clause: *nu apāt kuit UL IDI* [LÚ *ṬĒMI*-*Š*] *U*(?) *ma-a-an udaš kuitki ma-a-an UL* "Since I did not know whether [hi]s [messenger(?)] brought something or not" KBo 2.11 rev. 11-12 (letter, NH), ed. AU 242f.; *nu UL šagga*[*ḫḫu*]*n ma-a-an-za* LUGAL KUR [URU]*Miṣri ANA* [*ABI*] *YA edaš ANA* KUR.KUR.MEŠ *šer a*[*rkuwar*(?)] *iyat ma-a-an-za UL kuitk*[*i iyat*] "I did not know whether the king of Egypt had made a p[rotest(?)] to my father about those countries or whether he had done nothing" KUB 31.121a ii 12-15 (prayer, Murš. II), ed. Güterbock, RHA XVIII/66:60; cf. KUB 23.103 obv. 21-22 (letter to Assyria, NH), ed. Otten, AfO 19:41.

b′ with present or nominal sentence in the *mān* clause: *nuzakan zašḫimuš kuiēš uškizz*[*i*] *naš memiškizzi ma-a-an-ši* DINGIR-*LUM* IGI.ḪI.A-*wa parā tekkušnuškizz*[*i*] *nušši ma-a-an* DINGIR-*LUM kattišši šešzi* "(The patient) will tell the dreams he has been seeing, whether the deity shows him (her) eyes or whether the deity sleeps with him" KUB 7.5 iv 6-10 (rit. against impotence, NH), tr. Goetze, ANET 350, cf. Götze, Ḫatt. 76; (The king writes to a man who has asked him how he liked the birds he had sent) "The birds you sent me were unfit to eat. I neither ate them" *ūḫḫun*-*aš UL* [*m*]*a-na-at* SIG₅-*anteš ma-na*[-*at UL*] "nor (even) saw whether they were good or [not]" AT 125:(11-)14-15 (letter, NH), ed. Ehelolf, ZA 45:74, Rost, MIO 4:340f.; *nu* [m][*Urḫi*-[d]]U-*upaš kuit apiya nan punuš ma-a-an kišan ma-a-an UL kišan* "Since U. is there, ask him whether (it is) so (or) whether (it is) not so" KUB 21.38 obv. 11-12 (letter of Pud. to Ramses II), ed. Helck, JCS 17:88; "Concerning that which Ammatalla said," *punuššūenima nāwi ma-a-an mem*[*ia*]*š ašanza ma-a-an maḫḫan* "we have not yet inquired whether the word (i.e., the statement of A.) is true or how (it is)" KUB 22.70 obv. 31 (oracle, NH), ed. Ünal, THeth. 6:62f., cf. AU 69; for other exx. of *mān maḫḫan* see 8 a 2′ and *maḫḫan* 3 c. □ Contrast the above with the syntax of the double direct question, which requires *-ma* in the second question (cf. CHD *-ma* a 1′ b′ 4″).

5. when, whenever (conj.), from OS; for delayed *-ma* in temporal *mān*-clauses see *-ma* f 2′ a′ 3″; similarly, *-a* "but" and *-*(*y*)*a* "and" also occur after the second word — **a.** with pret., "when" — **1′** in OH texts other than myths and epics (OS, MS, and NS): *našta* [d]IM-*unnima ma-a-an āššuš ēšta* "And when he (Pitḫana) was dear to the Stormgod" KBo 3.22:3 (Anitta, OS), ed. StBoT 18.12f.; cf. ibid. 45-46, 73, 76; [(*ma*)]-*a-an* DUMU.MEŠ [URU]*Ḫatti* LÚ.MEŠ *ILKI uēr* "When the people of Ḫatti (who were) *ILKU*-people came" KBo 6.2 iii 16 (Law § 55, OS), (NS dupl. KBo 6.3 iii 19 and KBo 6.6 i 24 also *ma-a-an*); *ma-a-an* MU.ḪI.A *ištarna pāir* "When years passed by" KBo 22.2 obv. 6 (Zalpa story, OS), ed. StBoT 17:6f.; *ma-a-an* [URU]*Tama*[*r*-*mara*] *arir* "when they reached T." ibid. 8; *ma-a-an* [URU]*N*⌈*ē*⌉*ša pāir* ibid. 15; [*ma*]⌈-*a*⌉-*an lukkattati* KBo 3.38 obv. 2 (Zalpa story, OH/NS), ed. StBoT 17:6f., cf. ibid. 7, 26; *ma-a-an* [URU]*Ḫattušama uwauen* "But when we came to Ḫ." KBo 8.42 obv. 5 (OS); [*m*]*a-a-an luktat* KUB 36.104 obv. 17 (OS) with NS dupl. KBo 3.34 i 19 (anecdotes); *ma-a-an ABI* LUGAL *IŠME* KBo 3.34 i 27 with dupl. KBo 3.35 i 3 (anecdotes, both OH/NS); cf. KBo 3.60 ii 6, iii 10, 13 (OH/NS), ed. Güterbock, ZA 44:104f., 108f.; KUB 40.5 ii 3 + KBo 22.4 ii 5 (OH/NS), ed. StBoT 17:60; KBo 3.1 i 20 (Tel. pr., OH/NS) and passim in Tel. pr.

2′ in myths and epics (all NS, some OH/NS): *ma-a-an* [d]IM-*aš* [MUŠ]*illuyankašša INA* [URU]*Kiš*-*kilušša arga*(-)*tīēr* "When the Stormgod and the dragon got into a fight in K." KBo 3.7 i 9-10 (Illuyanka, OH/NS), translit. Laroche, Myth. 6, tr. ANET 125, NERT 157 = RTAT 179, □ for *arga*(+)*tiya*- see Hoffner, BiOr 35:247 ad no. 55, and HW² 306f.; cf. in the same myth *ma-a-an* UD.20.KAM *pait* KUB 17.6 i 23; *ma-a-na-aš šalleštama* "But when he grew up" KBo 3.7 iii 6; *ma-a-na-aš pāit*-*a* "But when he went" ibid. 13; etc.; *ma-a-an* [d]*Kumarbiš ŠA* [d]*Anu* LÚ-*natar katta pašta* "When K. had swallowed A.'s genitals (lit. manhood)" KUB 33.120 i 26, (Kumarbi epic, NS), ed. Kum. 7 and *2, translit. Laroche, Myth. 154, tr. ANET 120b and MAW 157; *ma-a-an-za* [d]*Ku*[*ma*]*rbiš* ZI-*ni pí-an* GALGA-*tar* ME-*aš* "When K. had taken counsel with himself (lit. took wisdom before his mind)" KUB 33.98 i 10 (Ullik. I B, NS), ed. JCS 5:146f.; *ma-a-an šalliš arunaš uddar IŠME* "When the great Sea heard the words" KUB 12.65 iii 9 (Ḫedammu, NS), ed. StBoT 14:50f. line 14.

3′ in other NS texts: *ma-a-an* ^{URU}*Āššuwa ḫarnin[ku]n āppama* ^{URU}*Ḫattuši [uwa]nun* "When I had destroyed Aššuwa and returned to Ḫattuša (I cared for the gods)" KUB 40.62 + KUB 13.9 i 2-3 (edict, MH/NS); *ma-a-an* ^{m}*Tudḫaliyaš* LUGAL.[GAL] ^{URU}*Ḫattuši ārḫun* "When I, Great King T., arrived in Ḫ." KUB 23.11 iii 12-13 (annals of Tudḫ., MH/NS); *ma-a-an-za ABI ABIYA-ma [. . .] taninummanzi IṢBA[T]* "But when my grandfather undertook to organize [such and such country]" KUB 19.12 iii 12-13 (DŠ), ed. Güterbock JCS 10:62, cf. KBo 14.12 iv 8f. (DŠ), ed. JCS 10:97; *ma-a-an-ma INA* KUR ^{URU}*Kummanni-ma pāun* "But when I went to K." KUB 14.4 iii 23 (prayer, Murš. II), cf. ibid. 4-5; *ma-a-an-ma-kán* ⸢ŠÀ É.LUGAL⸣ *DĪNU ŠA* ^{f}*Tawannanna* ⸢GÉME⸣-*KUNU kiša[t]* "But when in the royal house the trial of your maidservant T. occurred" KUB 21.19 i 20-21 (prayer, Ḫatt. III), ed. Sürenhagen, AOF 8:88f., cf. KUB 14.7 i 16-17 etc. in the same text; *ma-a-na-aš punuššūenma* "But when we asked them" KUB 43.77 obv. 9 (depos.?, NH), cf. ibid. 13; *ma-a-an kūr⸢ur⸣aš* MU.ḪI.A-*aš* EZEN ^{URU}*Nerik* ^{URU}*Ḫaqqamiš⸢ši iš⸣šuwan daiēr* "When, during the war years, they began to perform the festival of Nerik in Ḫakmiš" KUB 28.80 iv 4-6 (NH colophon of a Ḫattic text), tr. Geogr 21; *ma-a-an memian memiyauanzi zennit našta . . . šunnai* "When he has finished speaking the incantation, he fills . . . " KUB 40.102 vi 6-9 (*ḫišuwaš* fest., NS).

b. with pres.-fut. and in nominal sentences, introducing a single event, "when" — **1′** in OH — **a′** in OS: "If someone injures a person and causes him to be sick, he will take care of him, and in his place he will give a person (who) will work in his household" *kuitmānaš lāzziatta ma-a-na-aš lazziattama* "until he recovers. When he recovers (he will give him 6 shekels of silver)" KBo 6.2 i 16-19 (Law § 10, OS), with dupl. KBo 6.3 i 27 (OH/NS) and par. KBo 6.4 i 24 (NH); *ma-a-an* ^{URU}*Arinna* 11 ITU-*aš tizzi* "When in A. the eleventh month arrives" KBo 6.2 ii 61 (Law § 50, OS; NS dupls. not preserved), cf. KBo 6.2 ii 7 (§ 33), iii 10 (§ 53), 60 (§ 71); "If oxen go onto a field and the owner of the field finds them, he may harness them for one day" *ma-a-na-aš-ta* MUL.ḪI.A-*eš uenzi nuš āppa išḫišši pennai* "when the stars appear (lit.: come) he must drive them back to their (lit.: its) owner." KBo 6.2 iv 12-13 (Law § 79, OS), with NS variant "He may harness them for one day" *kuitmanašta* MUL.MEŠ *uwanzi* "until the stars appear" KBo 6.3 iv 7; [(*tan) attaššiš* (*dāi ma-a-*)]*n-na attašši[š* (*aki*)] (var. *ma-a-an dān ABUŠU-ya aki*) "His father will take her (the son's widow). And when his father, too, dies . . . " JCS 16:21(q) iv 3 (= KUB 29.36 rev. 2) (Law § 193, OS), with dupls. KBo 6.26 iii 41-42 and KUB 29.34 iv 20 (both NS); *ma-a-an* ^{MUŠEN}*ḫāra⸢nan ḫuš⸣[(uwandan appanzi)]* "When they catch a live eagle" KBo 17.1 ii 5 (rit, OS) with dupl. KBo 17.4 ii 14 (OS), ed. StBoT 8:24f., line 19; "when" also StBoT 8 ii 15, 25, 51, iii 17 (cf. 6 a 2′), iv 11, 14; *ma-a-an lukkatta-ma* ibid. ii 44, iv 7, 24 □ for *mān* in other functions in this text see mng. 2 "just as" and mng. 7a "if" (OH); *ma-a-an lāḫḫa paiš[i]* KBo 17.22 ii 6 (Hitt. col. of bil., OS); *ma-a-na-aš-ta* NIN.DINGIR-*aš* LUGAL-*i ḫandāetta* "When the priestess joins the king" KBo 25.31 ii 11 (fest., OS), translit. StBoT 25 p. 79, cf. NS par. ibid. p. 81; cf. in other NIN.DINGIR fests.: KBo 25.33 + KBo 20.14 i 9 (OS), translit. StBoT 25 p. 87, KBo 25.49 rt. col. 9, 12 (OH/NS), KBo 20.32 iii 10, 13 (OH/NS); KBo 20.26 + KBo 25.34 obv. 18, 21 (fest. of Tetešḫapi, OS), translit. StBoT 25 p. 90; *ma-a-na-aš-ta* ZA.LAM.GAR-*az uizzi* KBo 23.74 ii 8 (KI.LAM fest., OS), cf. KUB 2.3 ii 11f., KBo 10.33 i 6 (same fest., NS); cf. in fragmentary OS fests.: KBo 25.84 i 6, translit. StBoT 25 p. 164, KBo 25.89 ii 6, translit. StBoT 25 p. 169; *ma-a-an* DUMU-*aš* ^{URU}*Mištūr[a]ḫa paizzi ma-a-na-aš* ^{URU}*Karikūriška āri* ^{LÚ}GUDU$_4$-*ša mēmai* "When the prince is going to M., (and) when he arrives at K., the 'anointed' priest says" (Ḫattic recitation follows) KBo 25.112 ii 16-17 (invoc. of Ḫattic deities, OS); *ma-a-an* DUMU-*aš INA* ^{URU}*Kākšat ḫuwašiya ANA* ^{d}UTU ⸢*ḫu*⸣*ēkzi* ^{LÚ}GUDU$_4$-*ša memai* KUB 28.75 iii 19-20 (OS) and passim in these invocations, ed. Laroche, JCS 1:187-216; *ma-a-an ABĪ tuliyaš ḫalzai* "When my father calls to the assemblies" KBo 22.1:16 (OS); *ma-a-an-ša-ma-aš ABĪ parnašma tarnai* "When my father lets you go to your house" ibid. 21-22.

b′ in OH/MS & NS: *ma-a-an* ^LÚ^*maya[nd]a⸗ ta[r kardit]ti . . . [ma-a-an-ma* ^LÚ^]ŠU.GI-*tarra karditti* "When (young) adulthood is in your heart . . . but when old age is in your heart . . . " KUB 1.16 iii 29-31 (bil. of Ḫatt. I, OH/NS), ed. HAB 12f. □ for ibid. 28-29 see below, 6′; *nu ma-a-an uwatteni* "When you (O gods) come" KBo 7.28:40 (prayer, OH/MS), ed. Friedrich, RSO 32:219, 222; cf. ibid. 45; *ma-a-na-an išḫaššiš⸗a wemiyazi* "but when its owner finds it (i.e. the stray animal)" KBo 6.3 iii 65 (Law § 71, OH/NS; in OS copy KBo 6.2 iii 60 only *ma-a-n[a-an . . .]*), contrast *takku* in iii 67; *ma-a-an-ma* LUGAL *andan parna uizzi* "But when the king comes into the house" KUB 29.1 i 50 (rit., OH/NS), ed. Kellerman, Diss. 12, 27; *ma-a-an pāišima* ibid. 51; "when" also in the NH second rit. ibid. iii 13-37.

2′ in myths and epics: *ma-a-an-wa ANA* É DAM-*KA pāiši* "When you go to the house of your wife" KBo 3.7 iii 10 (Illuyanka, OH/NS), translit. Myth. 9, tr. ANET 126; *[m]a-a-an-w[a] miyarima* "But when he grows up (?)" KUB 33.120 iii 11 (Kingship in Heaven, NS); *[ma]-⸢a⸣-an* ^d^UTU-*waš⸗a [per(an paiši)]* "But when you go before the Sungod" KUB 33.61 iv 1 (myth of Inara, OH/NS), translit. Laroche, Myth. 93, with dupls. KUB 33.60 rev. 2 (NS) and KUB 43.25:1 (OS).

3′ in ritual and festival texts — **a′** in general: *ma-a-na-pa ḫaššan[zi]* KBo 17.19 ii 14 (OS), translit. StBoT 25 p. 117; *ma-a-an ḫaššanzi* KBo 20.10 i 1 (OS), translit. StBoT 25 p. 131; for *ma-a-an* in OS fests. see also section 5 b 1′ a′; *[m]a-a-na-pa* ^É^*ḫalentūwa ḫaššanzi* "When they open the palace(?)" KUB 25.16 i 1f. (fest., OH/NS); *ma-a-an katterrima* ^É^*arkiwi* ⸢*ari*⸣ "But when he arrives at the lower *a.*-structure" KBo 10.24 iv 31-32 (KI.LAM fest., OH/NS), ed. Singer, Diss. 97, 320 (tr. differs), StBoT (forthcoming); *ma-a-an* LUGAL SAL.LUGAL *ešanda* "When the king and queen sit down" KUB 2.10 iii 14 (fest. of the month, OH/NS); *ma-a-an [tun]nakkišna ḫalziya* KBo 19.163 ii 37 (fest. with Ḫattic, OH?/NS); *ma-⸢a⸣-an* ^LÚ^GUDU~4~ *malduwar* ⸢*zi*⸣*nnizzi* "When the GUDU~4~-priest finishes the recitation" KUB 25.36 v 24-25 etc. (fest., MS); cf. *ma-a-an zinnanzi* KUB 11.25 iii 23 (fest., NS) and similar phrases passim in fests. and rits.; *ma-a-an* ^NINDA^*taparpašuš šarrumanzi taruptari* "When the dividing of the *t.*-loaves is completed" KUB 10.89 i 16f. (fest., OH/NS); and passim in rits. and fests.

b′ introducing a time of the year or day, cf. *maḫḫan* 5 b 2′ a′: *ma-a-an ḫa-mi-[i]š-kán*(sic)*-za* DÙ-*r[i]* "When it becomes spring" KUB 38.26 rev. 1 (cult inv., NH); *ma-a-an-⸢kán⸣ zēni* DÙ-*ri* "When it becomes fall (lit. in the fall)" KBo 2.7 rev. 12 (cult inv., NH), ed. Carter, Diss. 93, 100; *ma-a-an lukkatta* (with spelling variants) "When it dawns" passim, see *luk-* A b 1′; *ma-a-an neku⸢zzi⸣* "When evening comes" KUB 33.70 iii 2 (rit. for a missing deity, NS), translit. Myth. 102; *m⸢a-a⸣-an* GE~6~-*a[nza k]išari* "When it becomes night" KBo 11.14 iii 6 (rit., NS).

c. with the present-future (including the historical present), introducing recurring (or potentially recurring) events, "whenever": *ma-a-na-aš-t[a* ^d^UTU-*uš]/[karūwariwar n]ēpišaz šarā ūp[zi]* "Whenever in the morning the sun rises through the sky" KUB 31.135 obv. 6-7 (prayer, OH/MS), ed. Güterbock, JAOS 78:240 and AnSt 30:48, rest. from par. KUB 31.127 + KUB 36.79 i 39-40 (NS); *ma-a-na-aš* (var. *[ma]-a-na-ša-pa*) *laḫḫaz⸗ma* EGIR-*pa uizzi* "But whenever he returned (lit. returns) from a campaign" BoTU 23A i 8 (= KBo 3.1 i 7) (Tel. pr., OH/NS), with dupl. BoTU 23B (= KUB 11.1) i 7f., cf. Chrest. 182f., cf. KBo 3.1 i 17; *ma-a-an uwarka[ntan] antuḫšan uwanzi nankan kunanzi šanap atānzi* "Whenever they see a fat man, they kill him and eat him" KBo 3.60 ii 3-5 (legend, OH/NS), ed. Güterbock, ZA 44:104f.; *ma-a-an INA* É.GAL-*LIM zakkitī artari nuza* ⸢^LÚ^⸣Ì.DU~8~ ^GIŠ^TUKUL.MEŠ EGIR-*an kiššan kappūezi* "Whenever he stands at the door bolt in the palace, the gatekeeper enumerates the occupations as follows" KBo 5.11 i 1-2 (instr., MH?/NS), □ cf. Sommer, HAB 124; *nu ma-a-an kiššan taranzi* § *utniwa māu šešdu . . . nu ma-a-an māi šešzi nu* EZEN *purulliyaš iyanzi* "When(ever) they speak thus: 'May the country thrive and prosper' . . . and when(ever) it thrives and prospers, they celebrate the *p.*-festival" KBo 3.7 i 3-8 (introduction to Illuyanka, OH/MS), translit. Myth. 6, tr. MAW 151 □ Goetze, Kl.139 n. 4 and ANET 125, mistakenly read *numān* "no longer", cf. Güterbock, OrNS 20:331 with n. 1, Hoffner, GsKronasser 38-45, esp. 43, and CHD *numan*. In this and the following exx. recurrence of the event or action is possible but was not necessarily felt by the ancient writer and does not necessarily call for a translation "whenever". We indicate this by writing when(ever). *ma-a-wa* (var. G: [*ma*]-⌈*a-an-wa*⌉) *gi*[(*mra*)] *paimi* "When(ever) I go to the open country" KUB 17.6 i 18-19 (Illuyanka C, OH/NS), with dupl. B KUB 17.5 i 23 and G KBo 12.84:5. For *mān* "when(ever)" in the incipits of festival texts see below mng. 9.

6. while(?), as long as(?) (OH): *ma-a-an* LUGAL-*uš* SAL.LUGAL-*ša išpanti ašanzi uga*[(*n kē*)] *ḫūmanda* [*a*]*nda pētaḫḫe* "While the king and queen are seated at night, I bring all these things in" KBo 17.3 + KBo 20.15 iii 29-30 + KUB 43.32 iii 5-6 (OH/MS) with dupls. KBo 17.1 iii 29-30 and KBo 17.6 iii 21 (OH/OS), ed. StBoT 8:32f. revised StBoT 15:30; *ma-a-an attaš uttar paḫḫašta* [NINDA-*an ezza*]*šši wātarra ekušši* "As long as you (have to) keep (your) father's word, you shall eat [bread] and drink water" KUB 1.16 iii 28-29 (bilingual edict of Ḫatt. I, OH/NS), ed. HAB 12f., this is to be understood as "while you are young" in contrast to "when you are old," see sub 5 b 1′ b′; cf. *ma-a-an uddā*[*rmet p*]*aḫša*[*nutteni*] KBo 3.27 (= BoTU 10β) obv. 22 (edict of Ḫatt. I, OH/NS); *ma-a-an nāwi* "as long as (it is) not yet (so)" KUB 1.16 ii 43 (see HAB 71); *ma-a-an atte*[*š* (TI-*išwanteš*)] "As long as the fathers are living" KBo 3.67 iv 3 with dupl. KUB 11.1 iv 16 ([*ma*]-*a-na-aš at-ti-iš*), (Tel.pr., OH/NS), translit. BoTU 23 C and B.

7. if (conj. introducing a conditional clause), from OS — **a.** with verb in pres. — **1′** in general — **a′** in OS: *takku* LÚ.^{GIŠ}TUKUL *U* LÚ.ḪA.LA-*ŠU takšan ašanzi ma-a-né-za it*[(*alaweš*⸗*šanzi*)] *taz* É-*SUNU šarranzi* "If a ^{GIŠ}TUKUL-man and his partner dwell together (and) if they quarrel and divide their estate, (if (*takku*) there are ten persons on their grounds, the ^{GIŠ}TUKUL-man takes seven persons and his partner, three)" . . . *takku* NÍG.BA LUGAL *tuppi kuiški* <(*ḫarzi*)> *ma-a-an-za* A.ŠÀ.ḪI.A-*na k*[(*arūilin*)] *šarranzi U* NÍG.BA 2 *QATAM* LÚ.^{GIŠ}TUKUL *dāu* (var. D: *dāi*) *U* 1 *QATAM* LÚ.ḪA.L[(A-*ŠU dā*)*u*] (vars. *dāi*) "If someone (one of them?) holds a documented gift of the king, if/when(?) they divide the original field (holding), too, let the ^{GIŠ}TUKUL-man take (var. the ^{GIŠ}TUKUL-man will take) two parts of the gift, his partner, one" KBo 6.2 iii 7-11 (Law § 53, OS), with NS dupls. B: KBo 6.3 iii 9-14, D: KBo 6.6 i 12-18 □ "When they quarrel and divide their estate" would imply that this was to be expected; therefore "if" seems preferable despite the contrast of *takku*; in iii 10, "if" and "when" both seem possible; *mān* "if" in KBo 6.2(OS) contradicts previous opinions, e.g. Sternemann, MIO 11:251, Otten-Souček, StBoT 8:91 n. 3; *ma-a-na-aš kardimiyanza* "if he (the Stormgod) is angry" KUB 43.23 obv. 3 (prayer, OS); *ma-a-na-aš tamattama* KUR-*ya* "but if he is (gone) to another country" ibid. 5; *ma-a-an* LUGAL-*uš* SAL.LU[GAL-*ašša taranzi*(?, dupl. has *t*[*ezzi*]) (*ta* DUMU.MEŠ-*an parna paimi*)] *ma-a-an n*⌈*atta*⌉[⸗*ma tar*(*anzi nu natta paimi*)] "When (or: If) the king and the queen say (so), I go to the house of the princes; but if they do not say (so), I do not go" KBo 17.3 iii 17-18 (rit., OS), ed. StBoT 8:32f., rest. from dupls. KBo 17.1 iii 17-18 (OS) and KBo 17.6 iii 9-10 (*mān* lost in these copies), cf. [*ták-k*]*u nattama taranzi* KBo 17.1 iv 12 (OS), ed. StBoT 8:36f. □ in KBo 17.1 iv 12 (OS) [*ták-k*]*u*, not [*ma-a-a*]*n* is required by the traces; in IBoT 3.135:12 (OS) either [*ták-k*]*u* or [*ma-a-a*]*n* is possible; cf. StBoT 8:91f. for *mān*/*takku* in these passages; cf. [*m*]*a-a-an-kán kalulupišmi kānk*[*i*] "If he hangs it on their fingers", KBo 17.2 i 7 (OS), ed. StBoT 8:16f. in contrast to *iššāšma*[*š*] "in their mouths" ibid. 6, 8.

b′ in OH in MS and NS: *kinuna ma-a-an* DUMU-*aš ANA* SAG.DU LUGAL *uwaštai kuitki apašan* ⌈*A*⌉[*NA* ^{d}ÍD(?) *ḫ*]*alzāi naš pait*⌈*tu*⌉ *ma-a-na-aš parkuešzi nu šākuwattet ūš*[*kittu*(?)] *takku* ^{d}ÍD(-?)⌈*ia-ma-za*⌉(?) *mimmai na*<*š*> É⸗*ši*⸗*pat ēštu* "But now, if a prince sins in some way against the person of the king (and) he (the king) calls him to the [river (ordeal)], let him go. If he is cleared, let him see your eyes. But(?) if he refuses (to go) to(?) the river, let him remain (lit. 'sit') in his house." KBo 3.28 (= BoTU 10γ):10-12 (edict, OH/NS), ed. Laroche, FsOtten 186f.; *kin*[*una m*]*a-a-an* DUMU.LUGAL *kuiški waštai nu* SAG.DU-*az*⸗*pat šarn*⌈*ikdu*⌉ "But now, if any prince sins he must atone with his own head" KBo 3.1 ii 59, (Tel.pr., OH/NS), ed. Chrest. 190f.; *ma-a-an* DUMU-*ŠU* EGIR-*pa*(-)*anda uizzi* "If her son returns" (rather than "when") KBo

6.26 ii 4, with dupl. KBo 6.13 i 14-15 (Law § 171, both NS); *ma-a-an* in the Laws replacing *takku* of older mss. in § 40: KBo 6.3 ii 41 (NS) against KBo 6.2 + KBo 19.1 ii 22 (OS), § 27: KUB 26.56 ii 9 (NS) against KBo 6.5 ii 8 (NS) and KBo 6.3 ii 3 (NS), § 64: KBo 6.8 ii 1 (NS) against KBo 6.2 iii 43 (OS) and KBo 6.3 iii 48 (NS); *ma-a-n[(a-an)] ḫandaiš walḫzi zigan ekunimi da⌈i⌉ takkuwan ekunimaš walḫzi nan ḫandaš[i] dai* "If the heat hits him, put him in a cool place; if the cold hits him, put him in a warm place" KBo 3.23 obv. 5-8 (OH/MS), rest. from par. KUB 31.115:9-11 (NS), (admonitions of Pimpira), ed. Archi, FsLaroche 41-43 □ the par. KBo 3.23 rev. 9 with *takku* in the first clause (the second is broken) shows that "if" is meant in both cases, with *mān* as a modernization, against Archi, ("Quand . . . si") and Goetze, NHF 25 ("when . . . when"); *ma-a-an paizzi išpannit iškarḫi* URUDU*tapul-liannitta kuērzi ma-a-an-ša-ma-aš-t[a ēšḫar] šiyāri apē tandukiš tašmaš pāimi ma-a-an-ša-ma-aš-ta ē[š]ḫar UL šiyari apē* DINGIR.MEŠ-*iš tašmaš UL pāimi* "When he goes, I(sic) shall prick (them) with a pin, and he shall cut them with a (copper) dagger(?); if their [blood] spurts, they are mortals, and I shall march against them; if their blood does not spurt, they are gods, and I shall not march against them" KUB 31.1 ii 7-11 (Naramsin legend, OH/NS), ed. Güterbock, ZA 44:52f. □ note temporal *mān paizzi* beside conditional *mān* in the alternative results of the test; in the Akk. version (Gurney, AnSt 5:102), *šumma* in lines 66 and 67 is only restored; (Having been asked for assistance by Inar, Ḫupašiya replied) *ma-a-wa kattiti šešm[i nuw]a uwami kardiaštaš iyami* "If I may sleep with you, I shall come and fulfill your wish" KBo 3.7 i 25-26 (Illuyanka, OH/NS); (Inara instructed Ḫupa-šiya, saying) *ma-a-wa* (var. G: [*ma*]-⌈*a-an-wa*⌉) *gi[(mra)] paimi ziggawarašta* GIŠ*luttan[(za)] arḫa lē autt[i] ma-a-wa-ra-aš-ta arḫa-ma autti nuwaza* DAM-*KA* DUMU.MEŠ-*KA autt[i]* "When(ever) I go to the open country, do not look out of the window. But if you do look out, you will see your wife and children" KUB 17.6 i 18-22 with dupls. KUB 17.5 i 23-25 and KBo 12.84:5-6 + KBo 13.84:7-9 (Illuyanka) □ while *mā(n)-wa . . . paimi* is temporal, *mā(n)-wa . . . autti* is better understood as conditional, as is *mā(n)-wa . . . šešmi* in the first ex. from Illuyanka; for temporal *mān* with pret. and pres. in the same text see above sub 5 a 2′ and b 2′ respectively.

c′ in MH: (Twelve guards are standing and holding spears) *ma-a-an* 12 LÚ.MEŠ*MEŠEDI-ma šarā UL arta* "but if twelve guards are not available" (so that there are too many spears, they carry away the extra spears) IBoT 1.36 i 11-12, (*MEŠEDI* instr., MH/MS), ed. Jakob-Rost, MIO 11:174f., and passim in that text; *andamakan ma-a-an* URU*Ḫattušaz* LÚ*pitteyanza uizzi* "Furthermore if a fugitive comes from Ḫ." KUB 23.77:59 (treaty w. Kaška, MH/MS), tr. Kaškäer 121, cf. line 62; *nu ma-a-an kūš lingāuš(!) paḫḫašduma . . . ma-a-na-aš-ta kūš-a lingāuš šarradduma* "If you keep these oaths . . . but if you transgress these oaths . . . " KBo 8.35 ii 14-16, (treaty w. Kaška, MH/MS), tr. Kaškäer 111; *nu ma-a-an* LÚ.MEŠ URU*Paḫḫ[uwa kē uddār] ienzi nat ANA* dUTU-*ŠI* ÌR.MEŠ *ma-a-an* LÚ.MEŠ URU*Paḫḫuwa-ma kē uddār UL ienzi . . .* "If the men of P. do these things, they will be His Majesty's servants; but if the men of P. do not do these things, . . ." KUB 23.72 rev. 24-25 (Mita, MH/MS), tr. Gurney, AAA 28:37; cf. also *mān* "if" in KUB 14.1 (Madd., MH/MS) obv. 39, rev. 36, 46, 88; *mān UL* "if not, otherwise" ibid. obv. 4, 11; (The enemy is harvesting the crops. Go there.) *nuššan ma-a-an ḫalkēš aranteš naškan arḫa waršten* "And if the crops are ripe, harvest them (and bring them to the threshing floor. Let the enemy not damage them.)" Maşat 75/13:15-17 (letter, MH/MS), ed. Alp. Belleten 44:46f. □ the translation "ripe" for *arant-* is based on *ḫalki*ḪI.A-*aš karū aranteš* "The crops are already ripe" Maşat 75/15:6, ed. Alp, Belleten 44:42f. ("ist schon reif"); "already standing" (HW^2 207b "stehend") would not indicate that the grain is ready to be harvested since immature grain also "stands." *ma-a-an-mu* ZAG-*azma* GÙB-*za ḫuiy⌈ant⌉eš* "But if they are fleeing from me on the right and on the left" KUB 21.47 obv. 11 (treaty/protocol, MH/MS); *ma-a-an-mu idalauwanni-ya kuiš waggariy[a-wa]nzi šanḫazi* "And if someone with evil intent seeks to stir up a rebellion against me" KUB 21.47 obv. 18 + KUB 23.82 rev. 23; *ma-a-an šullīši-ma* "But if you quarrel" KUB 36.114 rt. col. 6 (MH/MS), ed. Carruba, SMEA 18:188f.; cf. also KBo 16.46 obv.? 13, 14, 16; KUB 31.103:23, 33, l.e. 1 (both MH/MS); *ma-a-na-at išḫanāš-a uttar* "But if it is a case of bloodshed" KUB 13.7 i 14 (legal text, MH/NS); *ma-a-na-aš ANA* dUTU-*ŠI* LÚKÚR *tuqqaš* LÚKÚR *ēšdu* "If he is an enemy to My Majesty he must be an enemy to you" KBo 5.3 ii 24 (Ḫuqq., MH/NS) and passim in Ḫuqq.; *ma-a-an* ᵈUTU-*ŠI-ma kuwapi apāšila laḫḫiyaizzi* "But if His Majesty at any time goes to war in person" KUB 26.17 i 4 (instr., MH/MS); *ma-a-an* ᵈUTU-*ŠI-ma mannin⸗kuwan* "But if His Majesty is near" KUB 13.2 i 20 (instr., MH/NS), ed. Dienstanw. 42; cf. ibid. iii 32; for incipits of MH rituals cf. *mān* 9.

d′ in NH — **1″** in hist. and legal texts: *mān⸗wa⸗mu* 1-*an* DUMU-*KA paišti* "If you will give me one (of) your son(s)" KBo 5.6 iii 12-13 (DŠ), ed. Güterbock, JCS 10:94; *ma-a-an* ᵈUTU-*ŠI apizza* KUR-*eza . . . laḫḫiyami numu ziqqa QADU* ERÍN.MEŠ [ANŠ]E.KUR.RA.MEŠ *kattan laḫḫiyaiškiši* "If I, My Majesty, go to war from that country . . . , you, too, with (your) troops and chariots shall go to war with me" KUB 21.4 + KBo 12.36 i 24-28 (Alakš.), ed. SV 2:66-69, cf. *la(ḫ)ḫiyai-*1 a; and passim in treaties; (after prescriptions for the maintenance of a temple) *ma-a-an-ma apēdani* URU-*ri* É.DINGIR-*LIM* DUMU ᵈU *UL ēšzi nukan ma-a-an ŠA* LUGAL *kuitki wetummar* EGIR-*an ēšzi nukan apāt parā šanḫanzi* "But if in that town there is no temple of the Son of the Stormgod (but) if instead(?) there is some royal building remaining(?) they shall sweep that" (and care for its maintenance) KUB 9.15 iii 9-12 (instr., NH); *ma-a-an-wa-kán ŠA* ᵈUTU-*ŠI* ḪUL-*lun memi*⌜*an*⌝ *našma* GÙB-*tar kuedanikki* [(*anda*) *i*]*šdammašteni nuwaran ANA* ᵈUTU-*ŠI* ⌜*mem*⌝[*išt*(*en*)] "If you hear from someone an evil word (i.e. slander) or something unfavorable concerning My Majesty, report him/it to My Majesty!" KUB 26.1 iii 47-50 (SAG 1 instr., Tudḫ. IV), ed. Dienstanw. 14, with dupl. KUB 26.8 iii 9-12, and in other instructions; *ma-a-an-wa ammel* EN-*UTTA šanḫeškiši nuwa kāša INA* ᵁᴿᵁ*Iyalanda kuit uwami nuwakan* ŠÀ ᵁᴿ[ᵁ*Iy*]*a⸗landa tuēl* UN-*an lē kuinki wemiyami* "If you desire my overlordship, since I am now coming to I., let me not find any of your men in I.!" KUB 14.3 i 17-19 (Taw.), ed. AU 2f.; *nuwaza ma-a-an* EN-*YA apē* MUŠEN.ḪI.A *malāši nuwamu* EN-*YA* EGIR-*pa ḫatrāu* "If you approve these birds, my lord, may my lord write back to me" (so that I may begin to make regular deliveries) AT 125:7-10 (letter quoted in letter), ed. Friedrich, OrNS 8:311f.

2″ in myths and prayers: *ma-a-an-*⌜*wa-ra-aš-ta*⌝ *āššuwazma pedaz parā uwami* "But if I come out through (his) 'good place'" KUB 33.120 ii 33-34 (Kingship in Heaven), translit. Laroche, Myth. 156f., cf. Kum. 38 □ this is said by a deity growing inside Kumarbi; cf. the preceding fragmentary alternatives ibid. ii 30 and 31-32; *našmakan ma-a-an* [*amm*]*ukma kuitki šarnikzel ḫanti išḫiyattēni* [*na*]*tmu tešḫaz memišten nušmašat piḫḫi* "Or, if you (O gods), however, enjoin upon me something as a separate (or special) restitution, tell it to me in a dream, and I shall give it to you" KUB 14.8 rev. 34-36 (2nd Plague Prayer of Murš.), ed. KlF 1:216 § 10.9 cf. *mān* 10; *ma-a-an* UN-*aš⸗pat atti anni* DUMU-*an šallanuzi nušši attaš annaš ŠA* ˢᴬᴸUMMEDA *UL imma pāi* "Even on a human level (*-pat*) if a person raises a child for the father and mother, will the parents not indeed give her what is due to a nurse?" KUB 14.7 iv 11-13 (prayer of Ḫatt. III and Pud.), ed. Sürenhagen, AOF 8:96f. □ for the force of the *-pat* cf. Hoffner, FsOtten 113f.; "His Majesty made the following vow to (the goddess) Kataḫḫa:" *ma-a-an-kán* ᵁᴿᵁ*Ankuwaš* URU-*aš išparzazi UL-aš dapianza* BIL-*ni nu ANA* ᵈ*Kataḫḫa* 1 URU-*LAM* KÙ.BABBAR DÙ-*mi* "If the city of Ankuwa is spared, (in that) it does not completely burn down, I shall make a silver town for K." KUB 15.1 iii 17-20 (vow, Ḫatt. III), ed. Hoffner, IEJ 19:178f., and similarly in other vows.

2′ in contrasting conditions, "if . . . , but if" (almost always w. *ma-* in the second "if" clause), cf. also *mān* b 4′: *nu* EN.SISKUR.SISKUR *ma-a-an* LÚ *našzan ŠA* ᵈIM ᴳᴵŠŠÚ.A *ešari* [*m*]*a-a-na-aš* SAL-*ma našzan ŠA* ᵈ*Ḫebat ANA* ᴳᴵŠGÌR.GUB *ešari* "If the client is a man, he sits down on the chair of Tešub; but if it is a woman, she sits on the stool of Ḫebat" KUB 29.8 i 58-60 (*itkalzi* rit., NS); *ma-a-an* 1-*ŠU UL ištamaš⸗tani* [*nu*? 2]-*ŠU-ma išta*[*mašten*] *nu ma-a-an* 2-*ŠU-ma UL ištamaštani nu* 3-*ŠU* 4[-*ŠU* 5-*ŠU* 6-*Š*]*U* 7-*ŠU ištamašten* "If you don't listen the first time, listen the second time; if you don't listen the second time, listen the third, fourth, [fifth, sixth], seventh time" KUB 15.34 ii 34-36 (evocation, MH/MS), ed. Zuntz, Scongiuri 504f., Haas-Wilhelm, AOATS 3:192f.; *nu kūn* EZEN *ma-a-an*

LUGAL-*uš INA* UD.3.KAM *tezzi nan INA* UD.3.KAM *ēššanzi ma-a-an INA* UD.7.KAM *našm[a]* UD.9.KAM *tezzi nan naššu INA* UD.7.KAM *našma* UD.9.KAM *ēššanzi* "If the king orders this festival for the third day, they perform it on the third day; if he orders it for the seventh or ninth day, they perform it either on the seventh or on the ninth day" KUB 9.10 rev. 3-11 (fest., NS); (At the end of the meal) LUGAL-*uš* GAD-*an arḫa peššiyazi ta ma-a-an* DUMU. MEŠ.É.GAL *kuezzi paršnan ḫarkanzi nat apizza peššiyazi nat* DUMU.MEŠ.É.GAL *dānzi ma-a-an-ma* [LÚ.MEŠ]*MEŠEDI kuezzi paršnan ḫarkanzi nat apezza peššiyazi nat* [LÚ.MEŠ]*MEŠEDI danzi nat ANA* LÚ.MEŠ [GIŠ]BANŠUR *pianzi* "The king throws away the napkin. If he throws it to the side where the palace attendants have squatted, the palace attendants take it; but if he throws it to the side where the guards have squatted, the guards take it; and they give it to the waiters (lit. table men)" KBo 4.9 vi 5-13 (AN.TAḪ.ŠUM fest., NS), tr. ANET 360, and in other parts of that festival, cf. Gonnet, Hethitica 4:79ff.; *nu ma-a-an* EN.SISKUR [LÚ]MAŠ.EN.KAK . . . *ma-a-na-aš* :*ḫappinanzama* KUB 17.24 ii 16f. (*witaššiyaš* fest., NS); *natzat ma-a-an malāi . . . ma-a-an-ma-za mar-kiyazima* KBo 2.4 l.e. 2 ff. (Nerik fest., NS); *ma-a-an aniur* DUMU.MEŠ LUGAL-*ya ḫūmanteš kattiš-mi tianzi . . . ma-a-an* LUGAL-*unma AḪITIŠU aniyanzi* KUB 32.123 ii 47f., 50 (Ištanuwa fest.), cf. ibid. ii 34ff.; [*m*]*a-a-an* [SAL]*tapriyašma* NU.GÁL KBo 7.45 i 11; *namma ma-a-an* SAL.LUGAL *apiya . . . ma-a-an* SAL.LUGAL-*ma UL apiya* KUB 12.12 vi 6, 8f. (both *ḫišuwaš* fest.); *nu ma-a-an ḫamešḫanza . . . ma-a-an gimmanzama naššu zēnanza* KUB 27.16 i 10-12 (fest. for Ištar of Nineveh); for *mān* in incipits of rits. see below mng. 9.

b. with verb in pret., cf. also 7d and 7 e 1′ — **1′** in prayers: *ma-a-an ammuk eniššan AQBI* "If I said so" KUB 14.4 iv 13 (Murš. II); (Kaššuliyawiya has sent you this figure of a woman as a substitute) *nu ma-a-an* DINGIR-*LIM kuitki k*[*a*]*ppūit nutta kāš* SAL-*TUM pidi artaru* "If you, O god, have counted something (against her), let this woman stand for you in (her) place!" KBo 4.6 rev. 14-15 (Murš. II), cf. StBoT 3:117; *ma-a-an-kán* [d]U DINGIR-*LUM* KUR-*TI kuiški* TUKU.TUKU-*nut* "If some god of the land has angered the Stormgod" KBo 11.1 obv. 14 (Muw.), ed. Houwink ten Cate, RHA XXV/81:106, 115, cf. ibid. obv. 16, 18, 29 (TUKU.TUKU-*nu-an ḫarkanzi*), 32, 40, rev. 12; *nu ma-a-an* DINGIR.MEŠ EN.MEŠ-*YA ABUYA šallakartaḫta ku*!-*e-ez-qa memiyanaz* "If my father offended the gods, my lords, with some matter" KUB 21.19 i 17-18 (Ḫatt. III and Pud.), ed. Sürenhagen, AOF 8:88f.; *kīwa kuit* [d]*SIN-aš* (var. adds: [*nep*]*išaza*) GI[(ZKIM-*aḫta*) *nuw*]*a ma-a-an ammel* ḪUL-*lu išiḫta* "Concerning this omen which the Moongod gave (var. adds: from the sky): if he has presaged evil for me" KUB 24.5 rev. 4-5 (prayer in substitution rit.), with dupl. KUB 36.93 rev. 9-10, ed. StBoT 3:12f., cf. ibid. 13-14 (restore KUB 24.5 obv. 9 and ibid. 32-33 + KUB 9.13:20-21 accordingly); cf. KUB 17.14 obv.! 17-23 (StBoT 3:56-59); *ma-a-an šumāš* DINGIR.MEŠ LÚ.MEŠ [GIŠ]ERIN-*aš* [DINGIR.MEŠ-*aš attaš* (*pait*)] "If [the father of the gods] went to you, O male gods of the cedar" KUB 15.34 iv 28 (prayer in evocation, MH/MS), with dupl. KUB 15.38 iv 14-15, ed. Zuntz, Scongiuri, 520f. and Haas, AOATS 3:204f.

2′ in oracle questions: *nu ma-a-an zilaš apēz kišat* "If the oracular sign happened for that reason" KUB 22.70 obv. 32, 43 etc., ed. THeth 6:62f., 66f.; *nu ma-a-an* DINGIR-*LIM apadda šer ANA* [d]UTU-*ŠI zankilatar kuitki šanḫta* "If you, O god, demanded some amends from His Majesty for that reason" KUB 22.70 obv. 64, ed. THeth 6:74f., and similar questions passim.

3′ in letters: *ma-a-an-ma-at-ši-kán karū-ma arḫa tatta natši* EGIR-*pa pā*[*i*] "But if you have already taken them (i.e. his house and vineyard, neut. pl.) away from him, return them to him" Meskene 127 + 107:20-21 (letter of Hitt. king, NH), courtesy E. Laroche; cf. KUB 14.3 iv 49-56 (Taw.), ed. AU 18f.; for other exx. with the verb in pret. cf. *mān . . . -ya* below 7d.

4′ in rituals: (Certain offerings are prescribed for the seventh day after the birth of a child) [*ma-a-an* TUR.NITA *mi*]*yati . . . ma-a-an* TUR.SAL-*ma miyati* "[If a boy] was born . . . but if a girl was born . . ." KBo 17.65 rev. 39, 43 (birth rit.), ed. Beckman, Diss. 169, 177; cf. [*ma-a-an*-(*na* TUR.SAL-*ma*)] *mi*[(*-i-ia-ri* . . .)] "but if a girl is born" ibid. obv. 34, rest. from dupl. KUB 44.59 rev. 4 in the same context.

c. with periphrastic perfect: *nu kūn* UN-*an ma-a-an* LÚ-*iš iyan ḫarzi* (var. *iēt*) . . . [*ma*]-*a-na-an* [SAL-*z*]*a*⸗⌈*ma*⌉ *iyan ḫarzi* "If a man has done (it to) (i.e., bewitched) this person . . . but if a woman has done (it to) him" KBo 12.126 i 13-16 + KUB 24.9 i 12, with dupl. KBo 11.12 i 16 (rit. of Alli, NH), ed. THeth. 2:22f.; *numuššan ma-a-an* DINGIR-*LAM* [(*kuiški ŠA* KUR ^{LÚ}KÚR) *š*]*arā tittanuwan ḫarzi* "If someone has aroused a god of an enemy country against me" KBo 15.21 i 18-19 with dupl. KBo 15.19 i 22-23 (rit.), followed, with *našma*, by pret. [*au*]*šta*, *tiyat*, *tēt*; cf. KBo 2.9 iv 13-14, KBo 5.1 i 41-42 (Pap.), KUB 29.7 obv. 4-5, rev. 27-28 (rest.), 34-35 (all incant. spoken in rits., NH); *ma-a-an* . . . TUKU.TUKU-*nu-an ḫarkanzi* KBo 11.1 obv. 29 (prayer, Muw.), cf. parallel use of pret. in the same text above sub 5 b 1′. *ma-a-an-kán* ŠÀ KUR-*T*[*I*] *akkiškittari nat ma-a-an kūruraš ku*[*iš*]*ki* DINGIR-*LIM iyan ḫarzi* "If people are dying in the country and if some god of an enemy (country) has caused (lit.: made) it" KUB 9.31 ii 43-45 (incipit of rit. of Uḫḫamuwa, NH), tr. Goetze, ANET 347. □ Note the different use of *ḫar*(*k*)- with part.: *ma-a-an*[-*w*(*a*)] DINGIR-*LUM* GAŠAN-*YA* ^{d}UTU-*ŠI IŠTU* MU.ḪI.A GÍD.DA TI-*nuan ḫaddulaḫḫan ḫarti* "If you, O goddess, my lady, will keep His Majesty alive and healthy for many (lit.: long) years" KUB 15.17 + KUB 31.61 i 3-4 (introduction to the Vow of Pud.), ed. StBoT 1:16f. with additional dupl. KUB 48.116 i 4-5.

d. *mān* with delayed -(*y*)*a*, "even if", "even though", (with pret. or in nominal sentences) Friedrich, SV 1:32f.; cf. *man* b 2′ b′ — **1′** even if: [*z*]*iqqan* KI-*aš* ^{d}UTU-*uš ma-a-an* ḪUL-*anni*⸗*ya* (var. *idalauwanni*⸗*ya*) [(*ui*)]*ēš kinunankan waḫnut nan* SIG₅-*in* MUŠEN-*in iya* "Even if you, O Sungoddess of the Earth, have sent it (the bee) for evil, change it now and make it into a favorable bird!" KBo 11.10 ii 25-27 with dupl. KBo 11.72 ii 29-30 (MH?/NS); (Let them look for the offspring of a daughter of Ulmitešub) *ma-a-na-aš araḫzini*⸗*ya* KUR-*e nan apezz*(*i*)*ya* EGIR-*pa uwadandu* "Even if he is in a foreign country, let them bring him back even from there" KBo 4.10 obv. 13-14 (treaty, Tudḫ. IV).

2′ even though: *tuk*[*m*]*a* [*i*]*štarkit nu irmali*⸗*yattat* [*nu*]*za ma-a-an irmalanzaš*⸗*a ēšta* ^{d}UTU-*ŠI-ma*[*t*]*ta* [*ANA*] *AŠAR ABĪKA tittanu*⸗*nunpat* "You fell ill and became sick. And even though you were sick, I, My Majesty, still installed you in the position of your father" KBo 5.9 i 14-17 (Dupp.), ed. SV 1:10f.; ^{m}*Urḫi*-^{d}U-*upaš*⸗*ma*⸗*mu ma-a-an* ḪUL-*ušš*⸗*a ēšta* "Even though U. was hostile toward me, (I did not remain silent about the matter of Mittannamuwa)" KBo 4.12 obv. 24-26 (Ḫatt. III), ed. Ḫatt. 42f., cf. SV 1:32; "Do you, My Brother, really have no woman? Did you, My Brother, not do it (viz., ask for a daughter of mine) for the sake of the brother-sister relation with me (lit.: my brotherhood (and) sisterhood)?" *nat ma-a-an iyat*⸗*ya* (*i-ia-at-ia*) *natkan ANA* LUGAL KUR ^{URU}*Karanduniyaš imma ḫandan*(!) "And even though you did it, it just corresponds to (the action of) the King of Babylonia. (Did he not take a daughter of the Great King of Ḫatti, the mighty king, for a wife?)" KUB 21.38 obv. 53-55 (letter of Pud. to Ramses II), ed. Stefanini, AttiAccTosc 29:12f., Helck, JCS 17:91f.

3′ even though/even if (in broken context): [*nuw*]*arat ma-a-an ištantanuši*⸗*ya* ŠU.MEŠ-*azmawarat kinun ēp* "Even though you are letting it tarry, grasp it now by (its) hands (or: with your hands)" KUB 48.122 i 3-4 (dream, NH). Because the preceding section is lost, it is not clear whether this is "even though" or "even if".

e. *mān* "if" clause, without apodosis — **1′** with pret., as an affirmation of the truth, with an implied self-curse if untrue: "You shall make a declaration before the god as follows:" *ma-a-an-wa-za kī ḫūelpi anzel* ZI-*ni ḫūdāk piyauēn našmawaraš* . . . *piyawen* DINGIR.MEŠ-*ašmawakan* ZI-*an zammurāuēn* "'If we have hastily given away these first fruits according to our own wishes, or have given them to . . . , and thereby have offended the will of the gods,'" (we shall be cursed) KUB 13.4 iv 48-52 (instr. for temple officials, pre-NH/NS), ed. Chrest. 164f.; *ma-a-an-ma-wa* ^{GIŠ}PISAN *iškallaḫḫun našmawa* . . . *našmawaza* . . . *našmawaza* ^{m}GAL-^{d}U-*aš kuitki dāš nuwarat UL memaḫḫun* (end of §) "If I have torn open the container or . . . or . . . or (if) GAL-[d]U has taken something and I did not report it, (then I'll be cursed)" KUB 13.35 iv 24-27 (depos., NH), ed. StBoT 4:12f.

2′ with pres. — **a′** as a promise, with an implied self-curse if it is not fulfilled: *piḫḫi⸗wa<r>atši ma-a-an-wa-aš-ši UL pi[ḫḫi]* "I shall give it to him. If [I] don't give (it) to him—" (I'll be cursed) (end of speech) KUB 12.60 i 21 (myth., OH/NS), translit. Laroche, Myth. 20 □ alternatively: "How [shall I?] not give (it) to him?" (above, mng. 3).

b′ as a warning addressed to another person: *našmakan ma-a-an* [d]UTU-*ŠI kuedani anda idālu ištamašti natmukan ma-a-an šannatti natmu UL mematti apūnnamu antuḫšan UL tekkuššanuši nan anda imma munnāši* "Or if you hear evil about My Majesty from someone, if you keep it from me and don't tell me and do not reveal that person to me and even hide him—" § (sc. "the gods will punish you") KBo 5.3 i 27-30 (Šupp. I treaty with Ḫuqq., MH/NS), ed. SV 2:108f. For other exx. of a *mān* clause without a main clause see Sternemann, MIO 11:412 and lit. quoted there, n. 67.

f. *mān* clause following the main clause: "I said to Lilauwanta: 'When (*kuwapi*) I do not go to His Majesty, what will/can Ḫešni do to me? He will not hit me (or: Will he not hit me?)'" [d]UTU-*ŠI-ma⸗wa⸗mu⸗kan UL* SAG.DU-*anpat kuerzi ma-a-an-wa UL paimi* "'But will not His Majesty cut my very (*-pat*) head off if I do not go?'" (Then we: Lilauwandaš, I, and the grandees went to Ḫattina before His Majesty . . .) KUB 31.68:11-15 (deposition, NH), ed. Stefanini, Athenaeum 40:23f.

g. *mān* and *takku* in the Laws and in omen protases — **1′** In the Laws: "If" introducing a law is always *takku*, from OS mss. to the late version, KBo 6.4. *mān* is used only in conditional clauses inside a law; for exx., including one in OS, see mng. 7 a-b.

2′ In omens: Most omen protases begin with *takku*. Here, too, *mān* may occur in the interior of a paragraph. At the beginning of an omen, *mān* is used instead of *takku* in the lunar eclipse omens listed in CTH 532 II (KUB 8.1 etc.) and CTH 533.12, 13 (KUB 34.10 with dupls. and KUB 34.11); in the mixed omens KBo 13.29 (CTH 544.2); in the physiognomic omens KUB 43.8 (CTH suppl. 543.3) with [B]E-*an* rev. 9, probably also KUB 43.9 (CTH suppl. 543.4) with [*ma-a-a*]*n-za-kán* in lines 7, 9; in the text of *iqqur īpuš* type, KUB 8.35 (CTH 545 II). Both *takku* and *mān* are found in CTH 535.2 with *takku* in B = KUB 8.25 i 7 and *ma-a-an-ša-an* in A = KUB 8.22 ii 6; and in the liver omens CTH 549 b and c (KUB 8.34 + KUB 43.13, KBo 10.7). In KUB 8.28 (CTH 535.4) only the colophon uses *mān*, against *takku* in the text, apparently a modernization by the copyist.

h. *mān nattama* (cf. *-ma* b 2′, above p. 94): "Let no one open the royal storage bins. Whoever opens them, seize him" . . . *nan* LUGAL-*waš āški uwatetten ma-a-an UL-ma uwadatēni nu* [ÉS]AG-*an* LÚ.MEŠ URU-*LIM šarninkanzi* "and take him to the king's gate (for judgment). But if you do not take (him there), the townspeople will make compensation for the storage bin" (and punish him who opened it) KUB 13.9 iii 7-11 (instr. Tudḫ., MH/NS), ed. von Schuler, FsFriedrich 447, 450, cf. Otten, FsLaroche 273ff.; instead of the full negative condition, simple *ma-a-an* (*Ú-*) *UL-ma* "but if not" is frequently used as a fixed idiom, e.g. KUB 13.27 obv.! 26 (Gašga treaty, MH), KBo 3.3 i 26 (edict, Murš. II) KUB 7.5 iv 14 (rit.), and especially in letters: Maşat 75/45:13, 75/10:10, 75/69:11 (all MH), ed. Alp, Belleten 44:38-42, KUB 31.101:24 (NH?), KBo 18.57:26 (NH); with different word order: *ma-a-an-ma Ú-UL* KUB 23.95:20 (letter, NH), ed. AU 262f., *ma-a-an-ma-wa UL* KBo 12.46 obv. 3.

i. *mān* w. its force continuing through a chain of clauses: *numukan ma-a-an apel kuiški ŠA* NAM.RA.MEŠ *ḫūwaizzi naš tuk kattan uizzi zigan UL ēpti nan ANA* LUGAL KUR [URU]*Ḫatti* EGIR-*pa U*[*L*] *pešti nušši kiššan imma ematt*[*i eḫ*]*uwa īt kuwapiwa paiši ammukmawatta lē šaggaḫḫi nukan NĒŠ* DINGIR-*LIM šarratti* "If one of those captives flees from me and comes to you, and (if) you do not seize him and do not return him to the king of Ḫatti and even say thus to him: 'Go wherever you (may) go, but let me not know you!'—(thereby) you will transgress the oath" KBo 5.9 ii 39-45 (Dupp., Murš. II), ed. SV 1:18f.; similar clauses passim in treaties and protocols; *ma-a-an kī⸗pat namma[ma] tamāi* NU.GÁL *kuitki nu* IGI-*zi* [SU.MEŠ SIG₅-*ru*] "If it is only this and there is nothing else, let the first [exta be favorable]" KUB 22.70 rev. 1 (NH), ed. THeth 6:82f. and passim in oracle questions; abridged to *ma-a-an kī⸗pat* KI.MIN, where KI.MIN "ditto" stands for "and (if) there is nothing else" KUB 18.24:13 and passim; [(*ma-a-an-na-a*)]*d-du-za* ^{d}UTU-*ŠI kuedanik*<*ki*> *memiyani* [(*parā ui*)]*yami našmatta tuēl* [(*kuedani*)]*kki memini punušmi* [(*nan l*)]*ē šannatti našmakan* (var. adds *ma-a-an*) *uttar* [(*kuedani*)]*kki markiyami* . . . "If I, My Majesty, dispatch you for some matter or (if) I ask you about a matter of your own, do not conceal it! Or if I deny something to someone . . ." KUB 26.1 iv 20-24 w. dupls. KUB 26.8 iv 8-12 and KUB 23.67:1-5 (instr., Tudḫ. IV), ed. Dienstanw. 15f. □ note that the dupl. repeats *mān* where the main text omits it; *našma* alone, without *mān*, introducing conditional clauses, occurs passim in these texts. For *mān* after *našma* in a different context, where *našma* introduces a different situation, see 7 a 1′ d′.

j. temporal and relative clauses inserted in conditional clauses, with repetition of *mān* — **1′** temporal: ^{d}UTU-*ŠI kēdani* MU-*ti INA* ^{URU}*Ḫatti* ŠE₁₂-*yazi ma-a-an-ma-kán kuitman* ^{d}UTU-*ŠI* ^{URU}KÙ.BABBAR-*ši šer ma-a-an-ma ANA* ^{d}UTU-*ŠI* ŠU-*aš waštulit UL kuitki* ḪUŠ-*weni nu* SU.MEŠ SIG₅-*ru* "His Majesty will spend the winter this year in Ḫattuša. If, while His Majesty is up in Ḫattuša, we have nothing to fear for His Majesty from a 'sin of the hand' let the exta be favorable" KUB 5.3 i 1-4 (oracle question, NH), cf. ibid. 15-18, 42-44, KUB 5.4 i 4-5, 19-20 etc. □ for the reading ḪUŠ see Güterbock, FsKraus 83-89; BE-*an-ma kuitman* ^{d}UTU-*ŠI* TA KASKAL ^{URU}*Aššur* ⌈EGIR-*pa*⌉ *uizzi* BE-*an-ma-kán uniuš* ZAG.ḪI.A *UL neantari ANA* ^{URU}*Ner*[*ik*] *UL* ḪUL-*uešzi* SIG₅-*ru* "If, until His Majesty returns from the journey (or: campaign?) to Assur, these border areas will not defect (so that) nothing evil will befall Nerik, let (the oracle) be favorable" KUB 5.1 iii 79-80 (oracle question, NH), ed. THeth 4:76-79; *ma-a-an IŠTU* ITU.6.KAM *IŠTU* UD.21.KAM *kuitman* ^{d}*SIN-aš zinnattari kuit⸗man* ITU.GIBIL *tiēzzi nu ma-a-an* ^{d}*SIN-aš aki* "If the moon is eclipsed (at any time) from the 21st day of the sixth month until the moon (phase) is completed (and) until the new month begins" KUB 8.1 ii 11-13 (NH) and similarly at the end of other monthly cycles in these eclipse omens: KBo 8.47 obv. 7-8 (with temporal *mān* instead of *kuitman*), KUB 8.1 iii 4-6 (with *irḫāitta* for *zinnattari*), KUB 34.7 rt. col. 10-12, KUB 8.5 + 11/y (ZA 62:233) 5-7.

2′ relative: *ma-a-an-na-mu* 2 ^{d}LUGAL-*manniš* 1 ^{d}*Alanzunnišša ANA* DINGIR-*LIM-kán kuiēš ginuwaz arḫa uwatten numu ma-a-an kūn* INIM-*an ištamašteni* "If you, the two Šar⸗rummanni-gods and the one Alanzunni-goddess, who came forth from the loins (lit. knee) of the god, listen to this word of mine" KUB 15.1 ii 28-30 (vow, NH).

Note that *mān* "if" does not exclude the sentence particle *-kan* (contra Stefanini, JNES 42:146b). Cf. KBo 17.2 i 7 (OS), KUB 23.77:59 (MH/MS), KUB 14.8 rev. 34-35 (Murš. II), KBo 11.1 obv. 14 (Muw.), KUB 15.1 iii 18-19 (Ḫatt. III), KUB 26.1 iii 47-50 (Tudḫ. IV).

8. *mān . . . mān* "whether . . . or (whether)", "either . . . or" — **a.** introducing clauses, "whether . . . or (whether)" For *mān . . . mān* introducing dependent interrogative clauses cf. 4 b — **1′** MH: "Even if they (the people of certain cities) are remiss in respect to so much as a fiber of wool" [*n*]*uš* ^{d}UTU-*ŠI kēzza zaḫḫiyami zik⸗uš apezza zaḫḫiya nuškan ma-a-an kuemi ma-a-nu-uš arnumi ma-a-an-mu-kán arḫama kuiški išparzazi* "I, My Majesty, shall fight them from here, you fight them from there! Whether I kill them or carry them off, if anyone escapes me" (you must fight him wherever he goes) KBo 16.47:8-11 (treaty, MH/MS), ed. Otten, IM 17:56f.; "(Whoever is an enemy for me shall be an enemy for you)" *nan laḫḫiya*[*tten*] *ma-a-na-aš* 1 LÚ-*LUM ma-a-na-aš mekkiš ma-a-na-aš* ERÍN.MEŠ *kuiški ma-a-na-at* KUR-*e kuitki ma-a-na-at telipurī kuitki ma-a-na-aš* URU-*aš kuišaš imma kuiš antūwaḫḫaš nan hūmanteš takšan karši zaḫḫiyad*[*du*]*mat* "Make war upon him! Whether it be one man, or many, or some army, or some country or some district, or a town—whatsoever person (it may be)—fight him faithfully all together!" KUB 21.47 obv. 14-17 + KUB 23.82 rev. 19-22 (treaty, MH/MS); *ma-a-na-at* LÚ.MEŠ.DUGUD-*TIM ma-a-na-at piran tiyanteš* LÚ.MEŠ.SIG$_5$-*TIM* "Whether they are dignitaries or high-ranking officers" IBoT 1.36 ii 48, 52-53 (instr. for guards, MH/MS); (Be very cautious about a woman of the palace) *kuišaš imma kuiš ŠA* É.GAL-*LIM* SAL (dupl. SAL-*TUM*) *ma-a-na-aš ELLUM ma-a-na*<(*-aš*)> SAL.SUḪUR.LÁ "Whatever palace woman she may be, whether free or a harem slave" KBo 5.3 iii 44-45 (Šupp. I treaty with Ḫuqq., MH/NS), ed. SV 2:126f., with dupl. KUB 19.24 + KBo 19.44 iv 31-32 (early NS), cf. SV 2:132; cf. NH par. KUB 26.1 iv 30-32 (Tudḫ. IV), with dupl. KUB 26.8 iv 17-19, ed. Dienstanw. 16; *nuššan* DINGIR-*LIM-iš apāš ma-a-an nepiši ma-a-na-aš taknī* "Whether that god is in the sky or whether he is on earth" FHG 1 ii 11-12 (prayer, MH?/NS), with par. KUB 36.75: 10-11 (MS) and KUB 30.11 rev. 4 (MS); *nuza* DINGIR.MEŠ LÚ.M[E]Š GIŠERIN-*aš* [*k*]*uwapi kuwa*[*p*]*i ma-a-an-za nepiši ma-a-an taknī ma-a-a*[*n-z*]*a* ḪUR.SAG.MEŠ [*ma*]-⸢*a*⸣-*an* ⸢TÚL.MEŠ⸣ *ma-a-an-za INA* KUR URU*Mittanni ma-*[*a*]*-an-za* KUR URU*Kinza* [KUR UR]U*Dunip* KUR URU*Ugarit* (etc.) "Wherever you male gods of the cedar are, whether you are in the sky or on earth, whether you are in the mountains or in the springs, whether you are in Mittanni, whether you are in GN$_1$, GN$_2$, GN$_3$" (etc.) (now return to Ḫatti-land) KUB 15.34 i 50-63 (evocation rit., MH/MS), with dupl. KUB 15.38:1-13, ed. Zuntz, Scongiuri 496f., Haas-Wilhelm, AOATS 3:186-89, cf. KUB 15.32 i 42, KUB 36.90 obv. 10-13 □ these are all nominal sentences with *-za* indicating 2nd person subject; sometimes the *-za* is deleted in the 2nd member of a contrasting *mān . . . mān* pair; note that Mittanni is set off from the rest of the GNs in the paragraph, which are lumped together by the deletion of *mānza*.

2′ NH: DINGIR-*LUM kuedani kuedani papranni piran arḫa piddaitta nušši ma-a-an nepiši paitta ma-a-an-kán* ḪUR.SAG-*i paitta ma-a-an-ša-an aruni paitta ma-a-an*⸢*-kán*⸣ 7 KASKAL.MEŠ *paitta* § *kinuna nepišaz e*[*ḫu*] etc. "O god, on account of whatever contamination you fled, whether you went to the sky or went to the mountain or went to the sea or went on the seven paths, return now from the sky (etc.)!" KBo 23.1 i 19-23 (rit., NH); *ma-a-na-aš* INIM LÚKÚR *ma-a-na-aš* (var. adds INIM) EN *DĪNI ma-a-na-aš* INIM É.LUGAL *kuiški* "Whether it was a plot of an enemy or a plot of an opponent at law or some plot of the royal house" (Ištar protected me from all) KUB 1.1 i 55-57, with dupl. KBo 3.6 i 46-47 (Ḫatt. III), ed. Ḫatt. 12f., StBoT 24:8f., cf. Chrest. 66f.; "Herewith we have dispatched the result of the oracles" *nukan* EGIR-*an tiya ma-a-an anda ēp ma-a-an maḫḫan* "Take care (of the matter): either include (it) or (act) however (you see fit)" KBo 18.140:3-8 (letter, NH), cf. 4 b 2′ b′ and *maḫḫan* 3 c; GIŠZA.LAM.GAR.ḪI.A *ma-a-an dammili pedi ma-a-an-kán* GIŠTIR-*ni anda tarnanzi* "they erect tents either on virgin soil or in a grove" KUB 17.28 iii 36-38 (rit., NS) □ since *-kan* here must indicate a clause boundary, this is an ex. of alternative clauses with the deletion of *tarnanzi* in the first.

b. distinguishing single words "whether . . . or", "either . . . or": "But if the owner of the arable land is living" *našma* É EN A.ŠÀ A.GÀR *ēšzi ma-a-an apēdani utnē ma-a-an damēdani* KUR-*e šaḫḫan UL ēššai* "or (if) there is a house(hold) of the owner of the field and ground, either in that country or in another country, he will not perform the corvée." KBo 6.4 iv 18-20 (late version of Laws § XXXVII, NH), ed. HG 56-59; *nankan ḫūtak* SAG.DU-*an* [*m*]*a-a-an* 1-⸢*ŠU*⸣ *ma-a-an* 2-*ŠU* GUL-*aḫzi* "He hits him (the patient) right away on the head, either once or twice" KUB 44.63 ii 6-7 (medical rit., NH), ed. StBoT 19:28f.; [*n*]*u* UDU.U$_{10}$ *kuiš ḫandānza ma-a-an armauwa*[*nza*] *ma-a-an šannapiliš nankan* É.ŠÀ-*ni andan ūnniyanzi* "The ewe which has been prepared, whether pregnant or not (lit.: empty), they drive into the bedchamber" KBo 17.62 i 19-21 (birth rit., MH or NH/early NS), ed. Beckman, Diss. 37, 39.

c. with the omission of *mān* in the second or a later item: LÚ*ḫuyanzaššašma*[*š* LÚ*pittiy*]*anzašša kuiš anda* [. . . *a*]*ri*(?) *ma-a-na-aš ELLU* ÌR GÉME *nan appiškitten* "A deserter and a fugitive who enters your [land(?)], whether a freeman (or) a male slave (or) a female slave, seize him." KUB 23.72 rev. 56-57 (Mita of Paḫḫuwa, MH/MS), tr. Gurney, AAA 28:38; *UNŪTUM-šamaš* *kuit* LIBIR.RA *ma-a-an UNŪT* [. . . *ma*]-⌜*a*⌝-*an* ^{GIŠ}GIGIR ^{GIŠ}UMBIN GAD ^{TÚG}*parnan karū kui*[*t da*]*tten nat* GAM-*an arḫa* GAR-*ru* "Let the old utensils which you [to]ok earlier be left aside, whether [. . .] utensils, or a chariot, wheel, linen (or) a *p.*-cloth" KUB 13.35 + KBo 16.62 iv 16-18 (depos., NH), ed. StBoT 4:12 (with gap disregarded); cf. KUB 15.34 i 50-63, above mng. 8 a 1′.

d. *mān . . . našma*, replacing *mān . . . mān*; cf. 7 i: (Let not the good perish with the evil) *naš ma-a-a*[*n*] 1-*EN* URU-*LUM našma*-*at* 1[-*E*(*N* É-*TUM našma*)] 1-*EN* LÚ *nu* DINGIR.MEŠ *apūnpat* 1-*EN ḫa*[*rnikten*(?)] "Whether it is a single town, or a single house, or a single person, O gods, destroy only that one" KUB 24.4 + KUB 30.12 rev. 11-13 (prayer, MH/NS), w. dupl. VBoT 121:(2)-3 and NH par. KUB 24.3 ii 57-59 (Murš. II), ed. Gurney, AAA 27:30f.; *nuzakan ma-a-an nakkiš* ^{d}*Telipinuš šer nepiši* DINGIR.MEŠ-*aš ištarna ma-a-an aruni našma ANA* ḪUR.SAG.MEŠ! *waḫanna pānza našmaza INA* KUR ^{LÚ}KÚR *zaḫḫiya pānza* "Whether you, O honored Telipinu, are above in heaven among the gods, or in the sea, or gone to the mountains to roam, or if you have gone to an enemy country for battle" (let this sweet cedar perfume call you back) KUB 24.2 obv. 7-9 (prayer, Murš. II), ed. Gurney, AAA 27:16f. □ Note that *-za* is not repeated with the following *mān* or *našma*, but occurs again with the final *našmaza*. Our tr. 'or if you have . . . ' seeks to reflect the resumption of *-za*; cf. another ex. in 8 a 1′.

9. *mān* in incipits (incl. colophons and catalog entries), "when"/"if": In rituals which prescribe means for counteracting or remedying certain conditions in persons, the *mān* clause is to be understood as conditional, e.g. *ma-a-an antu*-*waḫḫaš alwanzaḫḫanza nan kiššan aniyami* "If a person is bewitched, I treat him as follows" KUB 11.12 i 1-2 (rit. of Alli), ed. THeth 2:20f. and passim. We found no OS rituals beginning with *mān* "if". In MH/MS we noted KUB 32.115 i 1 (2Mašt.). Further exx. in MH/NS are KUB 12.34 i 2 (1Mašt.) and KBo 12.107 rev. 19 (colophon of rit. of Mašt. to expiate murder). For conditional *mān* from MS on see mng. 7 above.

In other types of rituals, *mān* must be understood as temporal, e.g. in the rituals for the construction of buildings: *ma-a-an INA* É.GAL-*LIM* GIBIL *ḫattalwaš* GIŠ-*ru tittanuwanzi* "When they install the door bolt in a new palace" KUB 2.2 ii 37-38 (beginning of Ḫattic-Hitt. bil., OH/NS), ed. HHB 65; *ma-a-an šamanaš kattan tiyanzi* "When they make deposits under the foundations" KUB 2.2 ii 36 (colophon, NH); in KUB 29.1 i 1 (OH/NS), the verb *wetezzi* demands the restoration of [*mān* . . .], cf. ibid. iii 13 (see Kellerman, Diss. 25, 32); in other rits.: *ma-a-an* LÚ-*an* LÚ.^{d}U-*nili aniyami* "When(ever) I treat a man in the manner of a 'Man of the Stormgod'" KUB 7.57 iv 2-3 + KUB 35.148 iv 26-27 (colophon of the rit. of Zuwi, NS), for a possible OH origin of this rit., incl. OS exemplars, see Neu, StBoT 25, p. 23.

In festival texts, which describe regularly recurring rites, the *mān* clause in the incipit/colophon must be temporal, not conditional, e.g. *ma-a-an* LUGAL-*uš* ^{URU}*Arinna ANA* EZEN *nuntaryašḫaš* [*p*]*aizzi* "When(ever) the king goes to Arinna for the *n.*-festival" KUB 2.9 vi 5-8, *ma-a-an* LUGAL SAL.LUGAL [*l*]*aḫḫaza uwan*[*zi*] "When(ever) the king and queen return from a voyage" KUB 25.14 vi 2-3, etc.

It has long been observed that some archaic features in NS festival texts point to an early date of the original composition. The OS festival texts (in StBoT 25) confirm the early existence of the genre. The temporal function of *mān* was preserved in festival incipits through NH. A dated late ex. is: *ma-a-an-za* (var. adds [*tab*]*ar*-*naš*) ^{m}*Tudḫaliyaš* LUGAL.GAL . . . ^{d}U ^{URU}*Ḫatti INA* GIŠ.ḪI.A ^{GIŠ}TÚG ^{É}*tarnui maninkuwan* EZEN.AN.TAḪ.ŠUM^{SAR} *ḫame*<(*š*)>*ḫi* DÙ-*zi* (var. *iyazi*) "When(ever) (the Tabarna) T., the great king (with full title and genealogy of Tudḫ. IV) performs the A. festival for the Stormgod of Ḫ. in the box grove near the bath house in the spring" KUB 20.63 + KUB 11.18 i 1-10, w. dupl. KUB 20.42 i 1-9, cf. the undated parallel KUB 11.22 vi 1-5.

Exx. for temporal *mān* in incipits outside festivals are: *ma-a-an* ERÍN.MEŠ-*an lenkiya peḫudanzi* "When(ever) they conduct the troops to (the place of) the oath" KBo 6.34 iv 18-19 (Soldiers' Oath, MH/NS), ed. StBoT 22:14f.; *ma-a-an* ^{URU}*Ḫattuši šalliš waštaiš kišari* "When in Ḫ. the great calamity occurs (i.e., the death of the king)" KUB 30.16 i 1 and passim in HTR; *ma-a-an* ŠÀ KUR ^{URU}*Ḫatti* [*akk*]*iškittari* [*na*]*t ṬUPPA ḫantī* [. . . ?] [*nu*? *m*]*a-a-an* ^{d}UTU ^{URU}*Arinn*[*a mu*]*gānzi nuššan* [. . .] *anda memiškanzi* "If/When people keep dying in Ḫatti-land, that (is) [written on(?)] a separate tablet; [and(?)] when they invoke the Sungoddess of Arinna, they recite [as follows]" KUB 36.80 iv 2-7 (prayer of Murš. II); *ma-a-an-za* SAL-*za armaḫḫi* "When(ever) a woman becomes pregnant" KBo 17.65 obv. 1 (birth rit., NS), *ma-a-an-za* SAL-*za ḫāši* "When(ever) a woman gives birth" KBo 17.60 obv. 1, rev. 12 (birth rit., MH/MS), both ed. Beckman, Diss., 163, 171 and 76f.; cf. KUB 30.29 i 1. Once with pret.: *ṬUP-3-PÍ* ᵐ*Palliyaš ma-a-an* LUGAL ᵁᴿᵁ*Ki*[*zzuwatna*] / [ᵈ]U(!) ᵁᴿᵁ*Kummanni ša*[*rā*] *tittanu*[*t*] "Three tablets of P.: when the king of K. erected (the statue of) Tešub of Kummanni" KUB 30.47 i 7-8 (catalog entry, NH), ed. CTH p. 183f., referring to the incipit of CTH 475 (KUB 7.20 i 1 and KBo 9.115 i 1) which has *kuwapi* instead of *mān*.

10. *mān* with indefinite pronoun (*kuiški*, *kuitki*) and indefinite adverb (*kuwapi*, *kuwa-pikki*, *kuwatqa*) — **a.** with indefinite pronoun — **1′** in OH: The Laws, including OS, after *takku* "if", have only forms of *kuiški*. With *mān* (all OH/NS): [(*k*)]*inuna ma-a-an kuitki* "But now, if (there is) something" KBo 3.40a (BoTU 14α) rev.! 7 with dupl. KBo 13.78 rev. 5; *kinuna ma-a-an* DUMU.LUGAL *kuiški* [(*waštai*)] "But now, if some prince sins" KUB 11.6 (= BoTU 23E) ii 5 (Tel.pr.), with dupl. KBo 3.1 (= BoTU 23A) ii 59, cf. Chrest. 190f., cf. KBo 3.1 ii (70).

2′ in MH and NH: *mān . . . kuiški* (etc.) predominates, *mān . . . kuiš* (etc.) is relatively rare: *nuwamu ma-a-an idālun memian kuiš* [*memai*] . . . *ma-a-an-wa* ⌈*ku*⌉*it kūrur ēpzi* "If someone [reports] an evil affair to me (I shall not [conceal it] from His Majesty but report it); if he begins some hostility", (I shall fight him) KUB 14.1 + KBo 19.38 rev. 45-46 (Madd., MH/MS), cf. KUB 23.72 rev. 63 (Mita, MH/MS); in the MH/MS instruction for the guard IBoT 1.36, forms of *kuiški* i 19, iii 35, iv 20, 22 occur as do forms of *kuiš* i 43, 57, 70, ii 64, 66, iii 42; in the instr. for the border commander (MH) *ma-a-an DĪNU-ma kuiš . . . udai* "but if someone brings a legal case" KUB 13.2 iii 21-22 (NS), ed. Dienstanw. 47f. occurs beside *ma-a-an* É.DINGIR-*LIM-ya kuitki zappiyatta* "and if some temple is leaking" ibid. ii 37-38, ed. Dienstanw. 46, and in a conditional clause introduced by *našma* (see above 7i) both forms occur side by side: *našmakan ANA* ᵈU *kuiški BIBRU* (var. [*BIB*]*RU kuiški*) *našmakan tamēdaš* (sic) DINGIR-*LIM* (var. has better reading: *tamēdani ANA* DINGIR-*LIM*) *kuedani UNŪTUM ḫarkan nat* ᴸᵁ́.ᴹᴱŠSANGA . . . EGIR-*pa iyandu* "or (if) some rhyton of the Stormgod, or a cult object of some other god is lost, let the priests . . . replace it" KUB 13.2 ii 39-41 (NS), with dupl. KUB 31.90 iii 9-10 (NS), ed. Dienstanw. 46; *andamatta ma-a-an BĒLU kuiški z*[*aḫḫiya*(?)] *uwanna ḫalzāi* "Furthermore, if some lord calls you to come for b[attle]" KBo 16.46:13 (treaty, MH/MS?); cf. ibid. 16; KUB 13.9 ii 3 (MH/NS); KUB 19.26 iv 4 (Šupp. I); KUB 21.41 iv 3-4 (Šupp. I); KUB 13.20 i 7, 13f., 20 (military instr. of a Tudḫ., MH/NS); the instr. for temple officials, KUB 13.4 and dupl. (pre-NH/NS), ed. Chrest. 148ff. has forms of *kuiški* in A = KUB 13.4 ii 76 (ed. Chrest. 156 ii 83), iii 23-24, 26-27, 48, iv 35, 61-62; forms of *kuiš* in A iii 68, iv 41 (with dupl. G = KUB 13.17 iv 4), in B = KUB 13.5 ii 11 (ed. Chrest. 152 ii 6) but with variant [. . . -*d*]*a-ni-*⌈*ki*⌉ KUB 40.63 i 17 (coll.) = J; in texts of Murš. II, Muw. and Ḫatt. III forms of *kuiški* are used throughout; exceptions are: [*ma-a*]-*an šarnikzel kuiš* "If there is some restitution (to be made)" KUB 14.8 rev. 30 (2nd Plague Prayer, Murš. II), ed. Götze, KlF 1:216f. § 10.7, *ma-a-an memiyašma kuiš iyauwaš* "but if there is some deed to be done" KBo 5.9 iii 7 (Dupp.), ed. SV 1:20f. (against many exx. with forms of *kuiški* in this treaty), ⌈*ma-a-an*⌉ DUMU.⌈MEŠ⌉ *kurimmuš-ma kuiēš peškanzi* "But if some people give orphans [to . . .]" KBo 11.1 rev. 3 (prayer, Muw.), ed. Houwink ten Cate, RHA XXV/81:109, 118, *ma-a-an-ma-kán ANA* DUMU-*YA*-⌈*ma*⌉ *kuedani* (erasure) [. . .] KUB 21.37 obv. 11 (Ḫatt. III); the treaty with Ulmitešub KBo 4.10 has forms of *kuiški* in obv. 46 (w. par. ABoT 57:28, 31), rev. 15, 16, but *ma-a-an* URU-*LUM kuiš našma AŠRU kuitki ANA* ᵐ*Ulmi-*ᵈU-*up . . . piyanna UL* ZI-*anza* "If he (His Majesty) does not wish to give some town or some place to U. (lit.: if some town or some place is not (in His Majesty's) wish for giving to U.)" rev. 18; KUB 14.3 (Taw.) has *mān . . . kuwatqa* ii 56-57 but *mān . . . kuedani* ii 63-64; in the instr. for LÚ.MEŠ.SAG, ed. Dienstanw. 8ff., all preserved exx. have forms of *kuiški*, (in KUB 26.1 ii 56 read *ku-iš*[(-) . . .] against Dienstanw. 12, and in ibid. iv 38 (Dienstanw. 16) *mān* is restored); the instr. KUB 26.12 etc., ed. Dienstanw. 22ff., has forms of *kuiški* throughout; KBo 4.14 (Treaty of Šupp. II) has *mān . . . kuedani* iii 64-65, elsewhere it has forms of *kuiški*, as do KBo 12.30 ii 8-9, 12-15 and ABoT 56 i 19 (both Šupp. II); in oracle questions forms of *kuiški* are the rule; an exception is *nukan ma-a-an INA* É.LUGAL *kuit ḫurtiyaš uttar nūwa* EGIR-*an* "And if some matter of a curse is still left over(?) in the royal house" KUB 22.70 rev. 24, ed. THeth 6:88f.; in rituals, forms of *kuiš* are more frequent than in the above text categories. Special cases: *ma-a-an ūqqa kuitki wašda*[*ḫḫu*]*n kuitat imma kuit waštul ma-a-an-na-aš-še-kán* DINGIR.MEŠ-*aš kuiš* ḪUL-*uwa*[(-) . . . ?] *piran* [*šan*]*ḫeški*[*zz*]*i* "If I committed any sin, whatever sin it (may be), and if someone of the gods plans evil because of (lit.: before) it . . ." KUB 43.72 ii 12–iii 1 (rit., OH?/NS), cf. *kuiški* etc. iii 9-13 where [*ma-a-an-š*]*e-kán* may be restored at the beginning of lines; *ma-a-an-kán* EME.ḪI.A *kuedani uwanzi* "If tongues come upon someone" KUB 7.1 iv 13 (NH), w. variants [*ku-e-da-ni-ik*]-*ki* in unpubl. dupl. Bo 1648 iv 3 (Istanbul) and *ku-e-da-ni-ki* KUB 30.48:13, in contrast to *mānkan . . . kuiški* KUB 7.1 iv 10-11 and par. KUB 43.52 ii 6-7.

b. with adv. *kuwapi*, *kuwapikki*, *kuwatqa*: Of these *mān kuwapi* is by far the more frequent. Exx. for *mān kuwapi* are KUB 13.27 obv! 9 (Gašga treaty, MH/MS), KUB 13.7 i 9 (Tudḫ., MH/NS), KUB 26.17 i 4 (instr., MH/MS) but [*ma-a*]-*an kuwatka* ibid. 9, IBoT 1.36 ii 63 (instr. for guard, MH/MS), KUB 13.2 i 15 (*BĒL MADGALTI* instr., MH/NS), KBo 16.50:9-10 (oath of Ašḫapala, MH/MS), KBo 5.3 i 35, iii 35 (treaty of Šupp. I with Ḫuqq., MH/NS), KUB 19.26 i 12 (Šupp. I), KUB 13.4 i 27, 28, 33, 50, iv 56 (temple officials, pre-NH/NS), but *mān . . . kuwapikki* ibid. iii 65; *mān . . . kuwapi* also in letters, instructions, rituals, cf. exx. under *mai-* 3; further exx. for *mān . . . kuwapikki*: KUB 30.39 obv. 6 w. dupl. KBo 10.20 i 7 (outline of AN.TAḪ.ŠUM fest.), Bo 2823 iii? 8 (rit.), ed. Otten ZA 65: 300, with dupl. IBoT 3.148 iv 39; *mān . . . kuwatqa* KUB 19.20 rev. 10 (letter, Šupp. I), KUB 13.20 i 12 (military instr. of a Tudḫ., MH/NS).

Hrozný, MDOG 56 (1915) 38 w.n.4 "wenn"; idem, SH (1917) 184 "wenn, als, sobald, seit; da"; Ungnad, ZA 36 (1925) 105 n. 1 (temporal use, mng. 5); Götze, OLZ 28 (1925) 238 (mngs. 5 and 7); Friedrich, SV 1 (1926) 32f. (mng. 7 d); Forrer, Forsch II/1 (1926) 23 "ob" (mng. 4); Hrozný, ArOr 1 (1929) 277, line 26 "comme" (mng 1 a); Götze, KlF 1 (1930, 2nd fasc. 1929) 211 § 5:3 "ob" (mng. 4); Friedrich, KlF 1 (1930) 289-92 (usage with *man*); Sommer, AU (1932) 66 (mng. 4); 126 n. 1 (mng. 1); Ehelolf, OLZ 36 (1933) 5 (mng. 1); Götze-Pedersen, MSpr. (1934) 58f. (temporal use, mng. 5); Sturtevant, Gl. (1936) "as, when, if" (bibliography); Sommer, HAB (1938) 75f. (mng. 1, also possible spelling GIM-*an*, 1 c 3′); 71 n.1 (temporal, incl. "while", mngs. 5 and 6); 96f. (mng. 8); 135 (*takku⸗man⸗ta* corr. to later *mān⸗man⸗*[*ta*], cf. *man*; Ehelolf apud Güterbock, Symb.Koschaker (1939) 31 n. 21 (mng. 7 e); Otten, Tel. (1942) 20f. with note d (mng. 3); Hahn, Lg. 20 (1944) 91-107 (shift from temporal to conditional); Friedrich, HW (1952) 134: (altheth.) "als", "wie", (neuheth.) "wenn, falls" with lit.; Sommer, OLZ 48 (1953) 11 (mng. 3); Sternemann, MIO 11 (1966) 234-62 (semantic), 381-90 (syntactic analysis); ibid. 412 on mng. 7 e; Otten-Souček, StBoT 8 (1969) 91f. (on "when/if" in that text); Haas, KN (1970) 194 (mng. 5 in NH); Neu, StBoT 18 (1974) 102f. (mngs. 1 and 5 in OH/OS text); Szemerényi, FsMeriggi[2] (1979) 620-21. For use as dating criterion see Kammenhuber, KZ 83 (1969) 268, 280f.; Neu-Rüster, FsOtten (1973) 240.

:manna- n.; see *:manna(n)-*.

:manā- Luw.v.; to see; NH.†

[^{m}*Naniy*]*anzašš⸗a⸗wa⸗za :ma-na-a*[*-ta*(?) . . .] "N., too, sa[w]" KUB 31.76 rev. 21 (depos., NH), ed. StBoT 4:26f. Because of the marker and the plene spelling with *-a-* this word is here kept apart from *manawa-* (q.v.) against Werner, StBoT 4:28. For the Luwian verb see DLL 67 (without tr.).

Starke, Kadmos 19 (1980) 145.

Cf. *mammana-*.

^{SAL}manaḫuerata- n.; (a cult functionary); NH.†

[. . .]x $^{SAL.MEŠ}$*ma-na-ḫu-e*(var.: *-i*)*-r*[(*a-ta-aš*) . . .] *akuanna pianzi* IBoT 3.74:6-7 with dupl. KUB 27.57 iii 6-7 (cult of Ḫuwaššanna) □ the context, though fragmentary, suggests that *m.* is pl. dat.

Laroche, DLL 176.

mannai- adj.; (describing a reed basket or box); NH.†

sg. nom. com. *ma!*(coll. shows sign as copied)*-an-na-iš* KBo 18.175 v 5, *ma-an-na*[*-iš*] KUB 42.17 rt. col. 8.

m. occurs twice at the beginning of paragraphs in inventories: 1 GIPISAN *ma!-an-na-iš* x[- . . .] KBo 18.175 v 5; ⌈1⌉ GIPISAN SA5 *ma-an-na*[*-iš*? . . .] KUB 42.17 rt. col. 8. In the inventories whose paragraphs begin with 1 GIPISAN, what regularly follows is a descriptive adj. or participle. The strange shape of the sign read *ma*! in KBo 18.175 v 5 is similar to the *ma* in ABoT 65 rev 13 [*Ú-U*]*L-ma-wa*[*-aš-š*]*a-an*.

mannāimmi-, :mannaimi- Luw. part in Hitt.; (meaning unknown); from MS.†

sg. nom. *:ma-an-na-i-mi-iš* KUB 44.4 rev. 16 + KBo 13.241 rev. 6 (NH); **pl. nom.** *ma-an-na-a-im-mi-in-zi* KBo 23.50 ii 23 (MS); **pl. acc.** *ma-an-na-*⌈*a*⌉*-*[*i*]*m-mi-in-za* KBo 23.51 + KBo 20.107 i 18 (MS), *ma-an-na-a-im-mi-in-z*[*a*] KBo 23.50 + 637/c (ZA 68:153) iii 32 (MS).

"(O dLAMMA of the Shield, my lord! Be pacified again!)" *kāša tuel* LÚ *ṬEMI* SURX.DÙ.AMUŠEN(erased?) *appantan antuḫšan* ⌈*A*⌉*NA* MUŠEN.ḪI.A *ḫūmandāš ḫaluki piewen nu aruta ma-an-na-a-im-mi-in-zi* UZUGAB.ḪI.A Ì*-anteš* MUŠEN.ḪI.A ⌈*u*⌉[*w*]*andu* "We have just sent out your own messenger, the falcon, (as?) a captive person with a message to all the birds. (So,) let the *a. m.* (and) the birds oiled(?) on (their) breasts come" KBo 20.107 + KBo 23.50 ii 20-24 (MS), translit. Otten-Rüster, ZA 68:153; cf. *nu* MUŠEN.ḪI.A [?] SIG5[*-ia*]*nduš aruta ma-an-na-a-im-mi-in-za* U[ZUGAB.ḪI.A] Ì*-antēšša uwati* "Bring the birds which are favorable, *a. m.*, and those oiled(?) on their breasts" ibid. iii 32-33; *:zunnimiš⸗ti :ma-an-na-i-mi-iš* "You are a *m. z.*" KUB 44.4 rev. 16 + KBo 13.241 rev. 6, taking Luwian *-ti* as the equivalent to Hitt. *-za* in nominal sentences.

(:)*mannai*(*m*)*mi-* according to its formation should be the participle of a Luw. verb **mannai-*. The verb *manā-* "to see" (q.v.) is known (Starke, Kadmos 19:142ff.), but its participle should be **manā*(*m*)*mi-*. To ignore this spelling distinction and translate the participle (:)*mannai*(*m*)*mi-* as "seen, visible, conspicuous" does not materially clarify its contexts. Kammenhuber, HW² 355, mistakenly reads *arutaman⸗naimmi-* (i.e. as a single word).

:manna(n)- n. or adj.; (mng. unkn.); NH.†

In an enumeration of foodstuffs to be used in the *witaššiyaš* festival: [. . . GIŠGEŠTI]N È.A *:ma-an-na-an parḫū*[*ena-* . . .] / [. . . UDU*iy*]*an⸗taš* SÍG*ḫuttul*[*i-* . . .] KUB 27.52:5-6; it is unclear from the broken context whether the enumerated items are accusatives, objects of a missing verb, or nominatives in a list and whether *m.* is a noun or an adj. modifying one of the nouns. It is probably a Luwian word, and as such is marked by the double wedge (which is wr. over an erasure).

Laroche, DLL 68 (without tr. or indication of stem or case).

[*ma-na-pí*] KUB 36.1:4 read *ba*(coll.)*-na-pí*.

GIŠmanapnalla n.; (a toiletry article); NH.†

1-*NUTIM* GIŠGA.ZUM *mān ŠA* GIŠTÚG *mān ŠA* KA×UD AM.SI 1-*NUTIM* GIŠ*ma-na-ap-na-al-la mān ŠA* GIŠTÚG *mān ŠA* KA×UD AM.SI "One set of combs, either of boxwood or ivory; one set of *m.*, either of boxwood or ivory" KUB 29.4 i 26-27 (rit., NH) with dupl. KUB 29.5 i 10-11, ed. Schw. Gotth. 8f.

Friedrich, HW 135; van Brock, RHA XX/71:118.

manawa- n. [neut.]; (object made of silver); NH.†

ANA INIM NA4*Y*[*AŠPU* Ù*-it memir* . . .] / *ḫališšiyandu* [. . . *UMMA* f*Ḫepa*-SUM] / 1 *ma-na-wa* KÙ.BABBAR[*-wa ANA* DINGIR-*LIM* GAL *pianzi*] "[They said in a dream] regarding the matter of the jasper stone: ['The . . .] let them plate, [and . . . ' Thus says Ḫ.:] '[They shall give] one silver *m.* [to the Great Deity]." KUB 15.5 ii 21-23 (dreams of the king), for the jasper cf. i 4. Whenever number + unit of weight or measure + measured object occurs clause initial, the consistent practice of Hittite scribes is to put the sentence particles after the measured object. There is no known instance of a particle interrupting this chain. For this reason we have not read 1 MA.NA⸗*wa* KÙ.BABBAR. What Werner (StBoT 4:26f. and 28) read *:ma-na-a*[*-wa*? . . .] in KUB 31.76 rev. 21 and identified with this word, is the Luw. verb *:manā-* q.v. *manawa-* appears to occur as a component of the name dU*-manawa* (NH no. 1259).

Friedrich, HW (1952) 135.

mānḫanda see *māḫḫanda*, *mānḫanda*.

mani- n. (com.); pus (or other exudate); NH.†

(Akk.) [*a*?-*d*]*a*?-[*a*]*m-mu* = (Hitt.) *iš-ḫar* "blood"/ (Akk.) ⌜*šar*⌝-*ku* "pus" = (Hitt.) *ma-ni-iš* KBo 1.51 rev. 17-18; (Sum.) [lú] šà-bi-šè-mud!-lugud!(text UZU.UD.BAD) = (Sum. pronunciation) lu-ša-bi-iš-ši-mu-li-ku-du = (Akk.) *ša* [...] = (Hitt.) ŠÀ-*ir*!-*kán ku*!-<*e*>*da-ni e-eš-ḫar ma-a-ni-it an*-[*d*]*a* [...] "in whose heart blood is [...] together with pus" KBo 1.39 ii 4-5 (proto-LÚ), ed. MSL 12, 216-17; the Sum. entry lacks a verb; possibly the Hittite is a nominal sentence. Cf. the similar entry in Old Babylonian Lu: (Sum.) lú-šà-úš-lugud-dé-dé = (Akk.) *ša li-ib-ba-šu d*[*a-ma*] *ù ša-ar-ka ma-lu*-[*ú*] "one whose heart is full of blood and pus" MSL 12, 185:52.

The tr. of *mani-* is based entirely upon the meaning of Akk. *šarku*, cf. CAD and AHw s.v. Perhaps *ma-a-ni* inserted after *inani*⸗*mu*⸗*za* in KUB 31.127 iv 2 (prayer, OH/NS) is this word.

manni- adj.? (meaning unknown); NH.†

IGI-*andazaškan šarḫiyat* ⌜*ma*⌝-*an-ni-iš* SAL-*iš*(?) SAL.ŠÀ.ZU KUB 44.4 rev. 27 + KBo 13.241 rev. 15 (birth ritual), ed. Beckman, Diss. 226, 228f., revised edition forthcoming in StBoT 29. □ From the complementation of SAL-*iš*, which here is probably singular nominative, it would seem that it is the Luwian word for "woman", *wanatti-*/*unatti-* (Starke, KZ 94:74ff.).

maniyaḫḫ- v.; **1.** to distribute (without dat.), **2.** to entrust (w. dat.), **3.** to hand over, turn over, allocate, allot, assign (w. and without dat.), **4.** to show, teach, **5.** to administer, govern, **6.** (with prev. *appa*) to hand over, deliver (all exx. NH), **7.** (with *idalawanni katta*) to subject to harm, or abuse (Tudḫ. IV); from OH.

act. pres. sg. 1 *ma-a-ni-ia*-⌜*aḫ*⌝-*mi* KUB 13.3 ii 16 (MH?/NS), *ma-ni-ia-aḫ-mi* KUB 31.71 iv 5 (NH); **sg. 2** *ma-ni-ia-aḫ-ti* KBo 4.4 iv 21, KBo 5.9 iii 19 (both Murš. II); **sg. 3** *ma-ni-ia-aḫ*-[(*ḫi*)] KUB 43.26 iv 3 (OS) rest. from KBo 17.74 iv 10 (MS), *ma-ni-ia-aḫ-ḫi* KBo 23.61:9 (OH/pre-NS), KBo 10:28 v 6 (OH/NS), KUB 33.106 ii 26 (NH), *ma-a-ni-ia-aḫ-ḫi* KBo 17.74 ii 31, iv 10 (OH/MS), *ma-ni-aḫ-ḫi* KBo 10.28 v 10 (OH/NS), *ma-ni-ia-aḫ-zi* KUB 13.27 rev.! 17, KUB 13.35 ii 2, KUB 23.1 iii 15 (both NH), KBo 22.125 i 7, KBo 24.93 iv 8, KUB 46.42 iv 7 (all NS), *ma-ni-i-ia-aḫ-zi* KUB 44.64 i 21 (NS), *ma-ni-aḫ-zi* KUB 51.28 left col. 6 (NS); **pl. 3** *ma-ni-ia-aḫ-ḫa-an-zi* KUB 10.13 iv 7 (OH?/NS), KUB 24.5 rev. 9, KUB 39.57 i 13, KUB 46.39 iii 17 (all NH), KUB 39.66 rev. 4, KUB 46.41:4, *ma-ni-aḫ-ḫa-an-z*[*i*] KUB 16.44 rev. 11 (NH), *ma-an-ni-ia-aḫ-ḫa-an-zi* VAT 8304 rev. 4 (Neu, IF 85:87f. n29).

pret. sg. 1 *ma-ni-ia-aḫ-ḫu-un* KBo 9.114:10 (OH/MS?), KBo 2.9 i 37 (MH/NS), KBo 4.4 iv 13 (Murš. II), KUB 13.35 iv 23, 32, HT 97:8 (both NH); **sg. 2** *ma-ni-ia-aḫ-ta* KUB 30.10 obv. 8 (OH or MH/MS); **sg. 3** *ma-ni-ia-aḫ-ḫi-iš* KBo 3.34 ii 2, iii (9) (OH/NS), *ma-ni-aḫ-ta* KUB 29.1 i 40 (OH/NS), *ma-ni-ia-aḫ-ta* VBoT 120 ii 9 (MH/NS), KUB 48.122 i 11, KUB 40.92 obv. 11 (all NH), *ma-ni-ia-aḫ-da* KUB 13.35 iv 22, KUB 12.25:3 (both NH); **pl. 3** *ma-ni-ia-aḫ-ḫi-ir* KUB 29.1 i 18, 21, 38, KUB 2.2 ii 43, KUB 33.106 i 4, KUB 42.100 iii 35 (all NH).

imp. sg. 2 *ma-ni-ia-aḫ* KUB 29.1 i 36 (OH/NS), KUB 7.8 ii 7, iii 5 (MH?/NS), KUB 26.12 iii 19 (NH); **sg. 3** [*ma-n*]*i-ia-aḫ-du* KBo 9.79:10 (rest. HW 3.Erg.23); **pl. 2** *ma-ni-aḫ-ten* KUB 29.1 ii 49 (OH/NS), *ma-ni-ia-aḫ-ten* KUB 13.4 i 63 (pre-NH/NS).

mid. pres. sg. 3 *ma-ni-ia-aḫ-ta-ri* KUB 36.32:1 (MH/MS).

mid. pret. sg. 1 *ma*[(*-ni-ia-a*)]*ḫ-ḫa-aḫ-ḫ*[*a-ti*(?)] KUB 36.98b rev. 8 rest. from KUB 26.71 obv. 21.

inf. *ma-ni-ia-aḫ-ḫu-u-wa-an-zi* KBo 16.17 iii 27 (AM), KBo 14.12 iii (19) (DŠ), and possibly in broken contexts *ma-ni-ia-aḫ-ḫu-wa-an-zi* KBo 20.75 rev. 4 and KBo 22.42 rev.? 17.

verbal subst. gen. [*m*]*a-ni-ia-aḫ-ḫu-u-wa-aš* KUB 46.42 iv 4 (NH).

part. sg. nom. com. *ma-ni-ia-aḫ-ḫa-an-za* KUB 24:12 iii 9 (NH): **nom.-acc. neut.** *ma-ni-ia-aḫ-ḫa-an* ibid. ii 23, KUB 44.47 ii 11.

iter. act. pres. sg. 1 *ma-ni-ia-aḫ-ḫi-iš-ki-mi* KUB 43.68 obv.? 12 (pre-NH/NS), KBo 16.47:7 (MH/NS); **sg. 2** *ma-ni-ia-aḫ-ḫi-iš-ki-ši* Bo 4171 + KUB 46.46 (ZA 68:271) i? 11, KBo 11.72 iii (24) (MH?/NS), KUB 36.19:(17), *ma-ni-ia-aḫ-ḫe-eš-ki-ši* KUB 21.29 i 9, KBo 22.250 i (8); **sg. 3** *ma-ni-ia-aḫ-ḫe-eš-ki-iz-zi* KBo 3.34 ii 28 (OH/NS), KUB 40.92 obv. (10), (16), Bo 4171 + KUB 46.46 i? 12, KUB 5.12 rev. 13; **pl. 2** *ma-a-ni-ia-aḫ-ḫi-iš-kat-te-ni* KUB 13.20 i 29 (MH/NS), *ma-ni-ia-aḫ-ḫe-eš-kat-te-ni* KUB 26.12 ii 13, iii 14 (Tudḫ. IV); **pl. 3** ⌜*ma-ni-i*⌝*a-aḫ-ḫe-eš-kán-z*[*i*] KUB 13.9 iii 4 (MH/NS), KBo 9.137 ii (6).

pret. sg. 1 *ma-ni-ia-aḫ-ḫe-eš-ki-nu-un* KBo 6.29 i 24, 30 (Ḫatt. III), KUB 33.82:(1); **sg. 3** [*m*]*a-ni-ia-aḫ-ḫe-eš-ki-it* KUB 19.3 i 17 w. dupl. KBo 16.6 iii (3) (Murš. II), KBo 3.6 i 24 (Ḫatt. III), *ma-ni-ia-aḫ-ḫi-iš-ki-it* KUB 19.29 iv 12, (9) (Murš. II), KUB 1.1 i 28 (Ḫatt. III), KUB 34.37 obv. 5, KUB 5.9 obv. 33 (NH), *ma-ni-ia-aḫ-ḫi*-[*i*/*eš-ki-it*] KBo 2.5 iv 20 (Murš. II); **pl. 2** *ma-ni-ia-aḫ-ḫe-eš-ki-it-ten* KUB 36.98b rev. 9 (OH/NS) var. of *ma-ni*-⌜*ia*⌝-*aḫ-ḫa-it-ten*; **pl. 3** *ma-ni-ia-aḫ-ḫe-eš-ki-ir* KBo 3.1 i 10 (OH/NS) w. var. *ma-ni-ia-aḫ-ḫi-iš-ki-ir* in dupls. KUB 11.1 i 10 and KBo 3.67 i 12.

imp. sg. 3 *ma-ni-i*[*a-aḫ-ḫi-i*]*š-ki-id-du* IBoT 1.30:6 (OH?/NS), [*ma-ni-ia-aḫ-ḫi-iš-k*]*i-id-du* in parallel KUB 48.13 rev. 14, [*ma-n*]*i-ia-aḫ-ḫi*-⌜*iš-ki-id-du*⌝ KUB 36.118:2 (MH/MS); **pl. 2** *ma-a-ni-ia-aḫ-ḫi-iš-ki-it-ten* KUB 13.20 i 31 (MH/NS); **pl. 3** *ma-ni-ia-aḫ-ḫi-iš-kán-du* KUB 36.118:11 (MH/MS), *ma-ni-ia-aḫ-ḫe-eš-kán-du* KBo 9.137 ii 13 (MS?).

mid. pres. sg. 3 [*m*]*a-ni-ia-aḫ-ḫi-iš-ki-it-ta-ri* KUB 36.32:3 (MH/MS), ⌜*ma-ni-aḫ*⌝-*ḫi*-⌜*iš*⌝-*kat*-[*t*]*a* KBo 8.42 rev. 12 (OH/OS?).

ending broken [*m*]*a-ni-ia-aḫ-ḫi-iš-ki*[-. . .] KBo 20.92 i 8; *ma-ni-ia-aḫ-ḫe-eš-k*[*i*-. . .] KUB 26.71 iv 7 (OH/NS).

1. to distribute (without dat.), obj. lands: DINGIR.MEŠ KUR.MEŠ *ma-ni-ia-aḫ-ḫi-ir* "The gods distributed the lands (but in Ḫattuša they placed the great throne, so that Labarna, the king, [might sit on it])" KUB 2.2 ii 43 (Hattic-Hittite bil., OH?/NS), ed. Laroche, RA 41 (1947) 74f., Schuster, HHB (1974) 66f.; [*mānšan ANA* ^{GIŠ}GU.Z]A *ABIYA ēšḫaḫati napa utnimit* (var. *utnē ḫūman*) *ma*[(*-ni-ia-a*)]*ḫ-ḫa-aḫ-ḫ*[*a-ti*?] / [*nat*? *ANA* DUMU.MEŠ-*YA*? *ḫ*]*enkun šumeš ma-ni-ia-aḫ-ḫe-eš-ki-it-ten* (var. *ma-ni-ia-aḫ-ḫa-it-ten*) "[When] I had sat down [on the thr]one of my father, I distributed my land (var. the entire land). I [al]lotted [it to my sons(?)] (saying): You govern!" KUB 36.98b rev. 8-9 (a text of Ammuna, OH/NS), w. dupl. KUB 26.71 i 20-22 □ restoration of OH *mān*⸗*šan* (vs. NH *mān*⸗*za*⸗*kan*) based on Tel.pr. OH/NS, restoration *-ḫ*[*a-ti*] based on *ešḫaḫa*(*t*)*ti* in the same line.

2. to entrust: LUGAL-*imamu* DINGIR.MEŠ ^{d}UTU-*uš* ^{d}IM-*ašša utnē* É-*er*⸗*mitta ma-ni-ia-aḫ-ḫi-ir* "The gods, the Sungod and the Stormgod entrusted the land and my house to me (as) king, (that I, the king, might protect them)" KUB 29.1 i 17-19 (foundation rit., OH/NS), ed. Kellerman, Diss. 11, 25 ("ont confié"), tr. ANET 357 ("entrusted") □ we concur with Goetze (ANET) and Kellerman, who have used the tr. "entrust" here, but different translations in i 21, 35-40; the latter occurrences we have treated below in mng. 2; "Now, if you (farmers of temple lands) are sowing grain, and if the priest does not send along a man to sow the seed," *šumašat aniyauwanzi ma-ni-ia-aḫ-ḫi*(coll.) "(and if) he (i.e., the priest) entrusts it (*-at*, i.e., the seed) to you for sowing, (and you sow much, . . .)" KUB 13.4 iv 13 (instr. for temple officials, pre-NH/NS), cf. differently Chrest. 162f.

3. to hand over, turn over, allocate, allot, assign (w. and without dat.) — **a.** without dat. — **1′** food and drink: "They take these things: one bull, two rams, . . ." *IŠTU* NINDA-*ma* KAŠ EN URU-*LIM mašiwan ma-ni-ia-aḫ-zi* "And as much bread and beer as the lord of the town allocates" KBo 22.125 i 3-7 (rit., NH), cf. KBo 24.93 7-8.

2′ supplies: *piyanawanz*[*i kuit*?] *IŠTU* É.GAL-*LIM ma-ni-ia-aḫ-ḫa-an-zi nušši pianzi* "They give (to him) [that which] they allocate from the palace for contributing" KUB 10.13 iv 5-8 (KI.LAM fest., OH?/NS), translit. Singer, Diss. 397 n. 10.

b. with dat. — **1′** lands and cities: *nutta kāšma* KUR ^{URU}*Ḫatti* EGIR-*pa dammešḫan ma-ni-ia-aḫ-ḫu-un* "I have handed over to you (Ishtar) the land of Ḫatti (which) again (has been) damaged" KBo 2.9 i 37 (prayer to Ishtar of Nineveh, MH/NS); *andamakan mān takšulaš* ^{URU}*Ḫatt*[*uši anda pa*]*izzi nušši kuin* URU-*an* ^{LÚ}*BĒL MADGALTI ma-ni-ia-aḫ-zi nuza ḫappar apiya ie*[*ddu*] "Furthermore, if someone from a friendly (country) goes into the land of Ḫatti, let him conduct trade there in the city which the governor of the border province assigns to him" KUB 13.27 rev! 16-17 + KUB 23.77:87 (treaty, MH/MS), tr. Kaškäer 122; [*nu*]*kan* ^{URU}*Aripšan zaḫḫiyaz katta*! (text: *UL* = *natta*) *daḫḫun* [*n*]*an* ^{URU}*Ḫattuši ḫūmantī šārui ma-ni-ia-aḫ-ḫu-un* "I took the city A. in battle, and turned it over to all the Hittites for plunder" KBo 4.4 iv 12-13, ed. AM 134f., cf. ibid. iv 21.

2′ persons (humans and deities): "On (any) day when the king's mind is troubled, (so that) I, (the king) call all you food personnel" *nušmaš* ÍD-*i ma-a-ni-ia*-⌜*aḫ*⌝-*mi* "I turn you over to the river (ordeal)" KUB 13.3 ii 14-16 (instr., MH?/NS), ed. Friedrich, MAOG 4:46, 48, tr. Laroche, FsOtten 185; *nušši* GÉME-*KA ma-ni-ia-aḫ* "Turn your (i.e. the god's) maidservant over to him (i.e. her husband), (so that she becomes a yoke-partner for him)" KUB 7.8 ii 7-8 (rit. to cure impotence, MH/NS), cf. ibid. iii 5; *ūkwar*⸗*anši* ^{d}LAMMA *ma-ni-ia-aḫ-ḫu-un* "I assigned him to him as a protective deity" KBo 9.114:10 (OH/MS?).

3′ years: LUGAL-*e*⸗*mu* DINGIR.MEŠ *mek*⸗*kuš* MU.KAM.ḪI.A-*uš ma-ni-ia-aḫ-ḫi-ir* "The gods allotted many years to me (as) king" KUB 29.1 i 21 (foundation rit., OH/NS), ed. Kellerman, Diss. 11f., 25f., tr. ANET 357.

4' trees: "Are you not my, the king's, friend?" *nuwamu ini* GIŠ-*ru ma-ni-ia-aḫ* "Allocate these trees to me, (and I will fell them. Ḫalmaššuit replies: Fell them! Fell!)" ᵈUTU-*uššatta* ᵈIM-*tašša ma-ni-ia-aḫ-ḫi-ir* "The Sungod and the Stormgod allocated them to you. (Come up now, you (trees), from this country)" ᵈU-*ašmaš* LUGAL-*i ma-ni-aḫ-ta* "The Stormgod allocated you to the king" KUB 29.1 i 35-40 (foundation rit., OH/NS).

5' animals: SAL.LU[GAL-*y*]*awa kuedaš* UN. MEŠ-*aš* ANŠE.GÌR.NUN.NA.ḪI.A *ma-⸢ni-ia⸣-aḫ-zi ītwašmaš pāi* "Go and give mules to those people to whom the queen allocates them!" KUB 13.35 ii 1-2 (depos., NH), ed. StBoT 4.6f.; *Ù-TUM* ᵈUTU!-*ŠI Ù-it* GIM-*an* ᵈUTU!-*ŠI* 10 UDU.ḪI.A ᴸᵁ·ᴹᴱˢ*gawanniyaš ma-ni-ia-aḫ-ta* "A dream of His Majesty: how His Majesty in a dream allotted ten sheep to the g.-men" KUB 48.122 i 10-13 (king's dream, NH).

6' food and drink: *ABI* LUGAL ᴰᵁᴳ*ḫarḫarān* x-x (var. GEŠTIN) *A!NA* ᶠ*Ḫištaiyara* ᵐ*Marat⸗tiya ma-ni-ia-aḫ-ḫi-iš* "The king's father allocated a *h.*-vessel of wine to H. and M." KBo 3.34 (= BoTU 12A) ii 1-2 (anecdotes, OH/NS), w. dupl. KBo 3.36 obv. 11f.

4. to show, teach (object shown or activity taught stands in acc., person seeing or learning in dat.) — **a.** to show (visually) (non-iter.): "In a dream someone like a prince came in and kept saying to me" *eḫuwatta ma-ni-ia-aḫ-mi ŠÀ É-TIKA-watakkan kuit neyattat* "Come, I will show you what has happened in your house" KUB 31.71 iv 4-6 (dream, NH), ed. Werner, FsOtten 327f.; (If some land or some refugee, wishing to go to Ḫatti, comes through your land,) "Put them well on the road" KASKAL-*anma INA* KUR ᵁᴿᵁKÙ.BABBAR-*TI ḫinga* "Give them the road to the land of Ḫatti!" (... if you do not set them on the way,) *INA* KUR ᵁᴿᵁḪattiyašmaš KASKAL-*an* UL *ma-ni-ia-aḫ-ti* "(if) you do not show them the road to Ḫatti, (then you transgress the oath)" KBo 5.9 iii 16-19 (Dupp.), ed. SV 1:20f. (tr. differs).

b. to show (mentally), teach: *nuš* ᵐ*Išputaš⸗inaraš ma-ni-ia-aḫ-ḫe-eš-ki-iz-zi* GI-*an* ᴳᴵˢUMBIN *ḫašḫaššuar* ᴳᴵˢTUKUL(!, text MA) *appatar* "Išputašinara was teaching (hist. pres.) them to scrape/smooth the arrow (and) ... (and) to hold a weapon" KBo 3.34 ii 28-29 (anecdotes, OH/NS); *innarāwantimamu pēdi iyauwa zikpat* DINGIR-*YA ma-ni-ia-aḫ-ta* "Only you, O my god, taught me (how?) to proceed in a ... place" KUB 30.10 obv. 8 (Kantuzzili prayer, OH or MH/MS), ed. Lebrun, Hymnes 112, 115 (tr. differs), tr. ANET 400; see parallel *innarawantimukan ḫaḫarranni ištar⸗n[a(*coll.)] *iyawar zikpat* DINGIR-*YA ma-ni-ia-a[ḫ-ta]* FHG 1 ii 19-20 (prayer to the Sungod, OH/NS); ᴸᵁNAR-*wamu kuitki ma-ni-ia-aḫ-⸢ḫe⸣-eš-ki-iz[-zi* x x] *karū* 3 *išḫamāuš* [*m*]*a-ni-ia-aḫ-ta* "The singer keeps teaching me things; already he has taught (me) three songs" KUB 40.92 obv. 10-11 (NH).

5. to administer, govern, command, (see also *maniyaḫḫai-* v.) — **a.** absolute use, without direct obj.: *našma šumeš kui[ē]š BĒLU*ᴴᴵ·ᴬ DUMU.MEŠ LUGAL *ma-ni-ia-aḫ-ḫe-eš-katte-ni* "Or you lords and princes who govern" KUB 26.12 iii 13-14 (instr. NH), ed. Dienstanw. 26; cf. also KUB 36.98b rev. 9 above under mng. 1.

b. lands, cities, border points — **1'** non-iter. exx.: "Then [he took?] his son, Šarrikušuḫ" *nušši* KUR ᵁᴿᵁ*Kargamiš* ᵁᴿᵁ[*Kargamišanna*] URU-*an ma-ni-ia-aḫ-ḫu-u-wa-an-[zi paiš] nan ḫanti* LUGAL-*un iy[at]* "He [gave] him the land of K. and the city [of K.] to administer. He made him a king in his own right." KBo 14.12 iii 17-20, ed. DŠ 95-96; "Aparru, the man of Kalašma, came before My Majesty in Ḫattuša. I drew him forth and made him a lord" *nušši* KUR ᵁᴿᵁ*Kalāšma ma-ni-ia-aḫ-ḫu-u-wa-an-zi peḫḫun* "I gave him K. to administer (and put him under oath)" KBo 16.17 iii 24-27 (ann. Murš. II), ed. Ehelolf, MDOG 75:66.

2' iter. exx.: [*nuš*]*šan* KUR-*e ḫūman Labarnaš* ŠU-*az ma-ni-i[a-aḫ-ḫi-i]š-ki-id-du* "Let the Labarna personally (lit. with the hand) administer the whole land" IBoT 1.30:5-6 (OH?/NS), cf. KUB 48.13 rev. 12-14; *nu utn[(ē)] ma-ni-ia-aḫ-ḫi-iš-ki-ir* (var. *ma-ni-ia-aḫ-ḫe-eš-ki-ir*) "(The emperor's sons) administered the lands" KBo 3.67 i 11-12 w. dupl. KBo 3.1 i 10 (Telepinu edict, OH/NS), ed.

Chrest. 182f.; [*ḫ*]*ūmanna zik ma-ni-ia-aḫ-ḫi-iš-ki-ši* (var. [*maniy*]*-aḫ-ḫe-eš-ki-ši*) [(*taknašma* ^{d}U)TU-*uš daganzi*]*paš* KUR-*e ma-ni-ia-aḫ-ḫe-eš-ki-iz-zi* "And you (O Sungod) govern everything, but the Sungoddess of the earth governs the land of the netherworld" Bo 4171 + KUB 46.46 i? 11-12 w. dupl. KBo 22.250 i 8, translit. Otten-Rüster, ZA 68:271; "My brother, Muwatalli, sat on the throne of his father" *ammukmašši piran* KUR.KUR.MEŠ *ma-ni-ia-aḫ-ḫe-eš-ki-nu-un* "But I administered the lands under him." (He gave me the lands of Ḫakpiš, Ištaḫara, Taraḫna, Ḫ[attinna] and Ḫanḫana . . .) *nušši kē* KUR.KUR.MEŠ *ḫū⸗man*[*ta pir*]*an ma-ni-ia-aḫ-ḫe-eš-ki-nu-un* "All these lands I administered under him" KBo 6.29 i 23-30, ed. Ḫatt. 46f.; KUR.UGU-*yamu mani⸗yaḫḫanni pešta nu* KUR.UGU!-*TI :taparḫa piranmatmu* $^{m.d}$*SIN*-^{d}U-*aš* DUMU ^{m}*Zidā ma-ni-ia-aḫ-ḫi-iš-ki-it* (var. *ma-ni-ia-aḫ-ḫe-eš-ki-it*) "He (Muwatalli) gave the Upper Land into my administration, and I ruled (*tapar-*) the Upper Land. But under me (*piran⸗ma⸗at⸗mu*) Arma⸗tarḫunta, the son of Zida, administered it (*mani⸗yaḫḫeški-*)" KUB 1.1 i 26-28 (Ḫatt. III), w. dupl. KBo 3.6 i 22-24, ed. Ḫatt. 8f., StBoT 24:6f.; □ Armatarḫunta is known from other sources to have ruled the Upper Land prior to Ḫattušili. But this text need not also be stating that temporal priority. The obvious shift from *:taparḫa* to *maniyaḫḫiškit*, the use of the specialized construction *piran* + dat. + *maniyaḫḫeški-* "to administer under someone", and the statement of Zuntz (Ortsadv. 84) that temporal "before" is expressed by *piran parā*, never by *piran* alone, have led us to conclude that A., who had previously ruled directly under the emperor, was subordinated to Ḫattušili and continued as the latter's deputy; cf. also the second ex. under 5 c; [*n*]*ammašmaš šumēš kuiēš BĒLŪ*$^{ḪI.A}$ [*ḫ*]*antezi auriuš ma-ni-ia-aḫ-ḫe-eš-kat-te-ni IŠTU* KUR ^{URU}*Azzi* KUR ^{URU}*Kaška IŠTU* KUR ^{URU}*Luqqā* "You lords who in the first place(?) govern the border points facing the land of Azzi, the land of Kaška, (and) facing the land of Lukka" (let no one intentionally cross the border) KUB 26.12 ii 12-15 (SAG 2 instr., NH), ed. Dienstanw. 24; *kāša* ^{m}*Ḫattu⸗šiliš* LUGAL.GAL *šummaš ANA* LÚ.MEŠ ^{URU}*Tiliura araḫzandaya kuiēš* URU.DIDLI.ḪI.A *zik* EN *MAD*<-*GAL*>-*TI kuiēš ma-ni-ia-aḫ-ḫe-eš-ki-š*[*i*] *ANA* LÚ.MEŠ ^{URU}*Ḫatti* LÚ.MEŠ ^{URU}*Gašgaya išḫiūl kišan išḫiyanun* "I, Ḫattušili, the Great King, have made a treaty as follows for you people of Tiliura and for the cities round about which you, O Governor of the Border Province, govern—both for Hittites and for Kaškaeans" KUB 21.29 i 6-10 (instr., Ḫatt. III), tr. Kaškäer 146.

c. obj. personnel, troops, etc.: "The troops of Ura and the troops of Mutamutaši will go [with] me on campaign" *māḫḫanmatmu ANA* ^{d}UTU-*ŠI* [*ašš*]*awēš nuš apeniššan ma-ni-ia-aḫ-ḫi-iš-ki-mi* "As they are good to me, My Majesty, so I will command them" KBo 16.47 obv. 6-7 (treaty, MH/MS), ed. Otten, IM 17:56f.; *ANA PANI ABIŠU-wa* ERÍN.MEŠ ANŠE.KUR.R[A.MEŠ . . . *ma*]*-ni-ia-aḫ-ḫi-iš-ki-it* "He commanded the infantry and chariotry under his father" KUB 19.29 iv 8-9, ed. AM 16-19; cf. also ex. under d.

d. obj. law (*šaklai-*): *BĒLŪ*^{MEŠ} *kuiēš* ERÍN.MEŠ ANŠE.KUR.RA.ḪI.A *auriuš ma-a-ni-ia-aḫ-ḫi-iš-kat-te-ni* "You lords who command the infantry, chariotry, (and) sentinel points" (remain loyal to the king! . . . As for the king's law (*šaklai-*), just as you value your own persons, your wives, children, and estates,) LUGAL-*uwaš šakliya genzu QĀTAMMA ḫarten nat* SIG$_5$-*in ma-a-ni-ia-aḫ-ḫi-iš-ki-it-ten* "in the same way value the king's law and administer it well!" KUB 13.20 i 28-31 (instr., MH/NS), ed. Alp, Belleten 11:392f., 407.

6. (with preverb *āppa*) to hand over, deliver (all exx. NH): *šup*[*p*]*a ḫūišawaza zeyandaza* EGIR-*pa ma-ni-ia-aḫ-ḫa-an-zi* "They hand over meat, (some) raw, (some) cooked" KUB 24.5 rev. 8-9 (royal subst. rit.), ed. StBoT 3:12f., cf. ibid. rev. 19; GUD-*yašmaš* UDU *šarnikzi*[*l*]*aš* EGIR-*pa ma-ni-ia-aḫ-zi* "And he hands over to them the compensatory ox and sheep" KUB 46.42 iv 7 (rit.), cf. ibid. 4; GUD-*ma* UDU.ḪI.A-*ya karū* EGIR-*pa ma-ni-ia-aḫ-ḫa-an* "The ox and sheep have already been handed over" KUB 44.47 ii 10-11 (fest.), cf. parallel KUB 25.41 iii (1-2); ^{m}*Ibri*-LUGAL-*mašwamu kue kue UNŪTE*^{MEŠ} EGIR-*pa ma-ni-ia-aḫ-da nuwarat udaḫḫun nuwarat ANA* ^{m}GAL-^{d}U EGIR-*pa ma-ni-ia-aḫ-ḫu-un* (Arlawizzi said:) "Whatever items Ibrišarruma handed over to me, I brought here and handed over to GAL-ᵈU" KUB 13.35 iv 21-23 (depos.), ed. StBoT 4:12f.; "Eyebrow, eyelash, beard . . ." *nuwarat alwanzaḫḫan [tuk* K]I-*aš* ᵈUTU-*i* EGIR-*pa ma-ni-ia-aḫ-ḫa-an ēšta* "They were delivered to you hexed, O Sungoddess of the netherworld" KUB 24.12 ii 21-23 (rit. with many scribal errors), cf. ibid. ii 3, iii 6-9; "They fill them with oil and honey" [*n*]*at ANA* ᵈUTU AN-*E* EGIR-*pa ma-ni-ia-aḫ-ḫa-an-zi* "They deliver them to the Sungod of heaven" KUB 39.57 i 12-13 (rit.); [*k*]*uitmawa ammuk* ᴸᵁ́SANGA *iēr nuwamu UNŪTE*ᴹᴱŠ [*k*]*ue* EGIR-*pa ma-ni-ia-aḫ-ḫi-ir nuwarat tittiyan* "The implements which were handed over to me, because they made me a priest, have been set up" KUB 42.100 iii 34-35 (testimony in cult inv., Tudḫ. IV).

7. (with *idalawanni katta*) to subject (i.e. hand over, deliver) to harm, injury or abuse (both exx. Tudḫ. IV): (Or if some Hittite man attaches himself to you, Šaušgamuwa,) *nuttakkan ŠA* ᵈUTU-*ŠI kuitki :kuggurniyawar* EGIR-*pa anda uda*⌜*i*⌝ *našmatakkan* ᵈUTU-*ŠI kuitki* ḪUL!-*anni katta ma-ni-ia-aḫ-zi* "And he recalls to you (lit. brings back in to you) something pertaining to My Majesty (which is) defamatory(?), or he subjects His Majesty to harm (abuse, malice?) (before) you in some way" KUB 23.1 iii 12-15 (treaty w. Šaušgamuwa), ed. StBoT 16:12f.; (If some Hittite subjects are unhappy about *šaḫḫan* obligations, and their spokesman says: 'I keep telling His Majesty, but he won't listen to me.') *nuwaza zik āššuš ḫalziyattari* ᵈUTU-*ŠI-mawakan* ḪUL-*wanni* GAM *ma-ni-ia-aḫ* "You call yourself dear (to His Majesty?/to me?). Subject His Majesty to harm!" KUB 26.12 iii 18-19 (SAG 2 instr.), ed. Dienstanw. 26; in order for there to be a practical advantage in this command, this must mean "To hell with the interests of the king! Let me off the hook!"

Melchert, Diss. 376, claims ᴸᵁ́AGRIG-*ḫi-iš* KBo 3.36 obv. 10 as a log. for *maniyaḫḫiš*, but without proof.

Götze, Ḫatt. (1925) 61f.; Laroche, RA 41 (1947) 75f.; HW (1952) 135; HW 1. & 3. Erg. s.v.; Kammenhuber, ZA 57 (1965) 197 n. 74; Neu, StBoT 5 (1968) 112; Oettinger, Stammbildung (1979) 41f., 458; Laroche, in Pouvoirs Locaux (1980, publ. 1982) 142f.

Cf. *maniyaḫḫa-*, *maniyaḫḫai-* n., *maniyaḫḫai-* v., ᴸᵁ́*maniyaḫḫant-*, ᴸᵁ́*maniyaḫḫtalla-*, *maniyaḫḫatar*, *maniyaḫḫiyatt-*, *maniyaḫḫeššar*, *maniyaḫḫiškattalla-*.

maniyaḫḫa- n. com.; deputy(?), confidant(?), agent(?); OH?/NS.†

[. . . *n*]*ankan* ᵈUTU-*i menaḫḫanda ēpmi nu*[-*o*] ᵈUTU-*i menaḫḫanda kiššan memaḫḫi kā*[*š*]*a tuel ma-ni-ia-aḫ-ḫa-aš-ti-iš nu kāš kui*[*t*] *memai nat zik šakti ziga kuit* [*mema*]*tti nat kāš šakki*(! text *šakti*) "I hold it (the puppy) toward the Sun(god) and speak as follows toward the Sun(god): 'This is your *m.* You know what he says, and he(!) knows what you say.'" KUB 35.148 iii 9-13 (rit. of a Zuwi, NS).

[*takku IZBU*(?) . . . -]x-*iššī ḫapātianteš* / [o o o o o o o] ⌜*Ú*⌝-*UL ma-ni-ia-aḫ-ḫa-aš* / [. . .] KBo 13.13 rev. 3-5 (omen, OH?/NS?), ed. StBoT 9:62f., 65ff.; from the angle of the lower horizontal of the trace one can exclude Riemschneider's reading *-ni-*; perhaps *ḫa-an*]-⌜*di*⌝-*iš-ši* "on its forehead"? *UL maniyaḫḫaš* (versus *maniyaḫḫaš* NU.GÁL) would be a negated predicate: "is not a *m.*" Also possible is a free-standing genitive: "is not (that) of a deputy(?)". *maniyaḫḫaš* cannot be a form of the verb *maniyaḫḫ-*, because of the ending *-aš*. One would expect any verb at the end of an omen to be future tense.

The *m.* must be a living being. The knowing of each other's word points to a meaning like "trusted one, confidant, deputy". The denominative(?) verb in *-ai-*, *maniyaḫḫai-* (with possible iter. *maniyaḫḫeški-*) "to govern, administer (from 'to be a deputy'?)" may derive from this noun.

Laroche, BiOr 11 (1954) 122 and RA 52 (1958) 188 (equates *m.* with the noun *maniyaḫḫai-*).

Cf. *maniyaḫḫ-*.

maniyaḫḫai- n. com.; **1.** administrative district, realm, **2.** administration, government, rule, **3.** (in a phrase with *išḫa-*): from OH.†

sg. nom. (? cf. below under mng. 1) *ma-ni-ia-aḫ-ḫa-iš* KBo 11.72 iii 23 (MH?/NS), [*ma-a-n*]*i-ia-aḫ-ḫa-a-iš* 243/v:6 (NS) (Neu, IF 85:87f. n. 29); **acc.** *ma-ni-ia-aḫ-ḫa-en* KUB 29.1 i 23 (OH/NS), KUB 19.26 i 23, *ma-ni-ia-aḫ-ḫa-i-i*[*n*] KBo 19.60:23, *ma-ni-ia-aḫ-ḫa-in* ibid. 22, [*m*]*a-ni-ya-aḫ-*<*ḫa*>*-in* KBo 3.21 ii 2 (OH?/NS); **gen.** *ma-ni-i*[*a-aḫ*]*-ḫa-ia-aš* KUB 31.127 i 20 (OH/NS), *ma-ni-ia-aḫ-ḫi-ia-aš* Mşt 75/104:14 (MH/MS), KUB 24.13 iii 22, KUB 22.27 iv

26 (NH), KBo 24.118 vi 11 (NH), KUB 50:82:(7); **d.-l.** *ma-ni-ia-aḫ-ḫi-ia* KUB 13.2 i 22, iv 9, (13) (MH/NS), KUB 34.37 obv. 8, [*ma*]*-a-ni-ia-aḫ-ḫi-ia* 243/v:9 (NS) (Neu, IF 85:87f. n. 29), *ma-ni-ia-ḫi-ia* KUB 13.2 ii 24.

pl. acc. *ma-ni-ia-aḫ-ḫa-uš* KBo 14.45:3 (Ḫatt. III).

1. (administrative) district, realm: [*n*]*umukan ma-ni-ia-aḫ-ḫa-uš dā*[*š*] "He took districts from me" KBo 14.45:3 (hist., Ḫatt. III), cf. Otten, AfO 19:224; URU.DIDLI.ḪI.A BÀD-*kan kuiēš ma-ni-ia-aḫ-ḫi-ia anda* "(Let the Governors of the Border Provinces keep account of) the fortified cities which are within (their) district" KUB 13.2 i 22-23 (*BĒL MADGALTI* instr., MH/NS), ed. Dienstanw. 42; *ma-ni-ia-ḫi-ia-ia-ták-kán kuieš* MUŠEN.ḪI.A-*aš luliyaš anda* "(Let) the bird ponds that are in your district (be well cared for)" KUB 13.2 ii 24, ed. Dienstanw. 45; cf. KUB 13.2 iv 9, 13 and KUB 13.1 iv 1, ed. Dienstanw. 51 and 62; *ḫalkueššarma ŠA* GAL *MEŠEDI ma-ni-ia-aḫ-ḫi-ia-aš udai* "He will bring the cult provisions of the district of the Chief of the Guard" KUB 22.27 iv 25-27 (oracle results, NH); "Have mercy, O Sungod!" *ḫūman* [*tuel*? dUTU?]-*aš ma-ni-ia-aḫ-ḫa-iš* KUR.KUR-*TIM zik* [*maniyaḫ*]*ḫiškiši* "Everything is [your] realm, [O Sungod]. You govern the lands." KBo 11.72 iii 22-24 (rit., NH).

2. administration, government, rule: LUGAL-*uemu ma-ni-ia-aḫ-ḫa-en* GIŠ*ḫulugannen* GIŠDAG-*iz arunaza udaš* "(Ḫalmaššuit) brought rule (and) the carriage from the sea to me, the king" KUB 29.1 i 23-24 (myth in rit., OH/NS), following tr. ANET 357; different tr. "(O) Trone, à moi, le roi, tu as apporté de la mer le char royal", Kellerman, Diss. 11, 26, cf. Starke, ZA 69:58f.; *našma*[*tazakan*] [*Š*]*A* LUGAL *ma-ni-ia-aḫ-ḫa-en našma ŠA* LUGAL [*š*]*a-ak-li*!*-in piran tepnuzi* "Or (if) he belittles the king's governing or the king's law before [you]" KUB 19.26 i 22-24 (decree, Šupp. I), ed. Goetze, Kizz. 14f.; cf. *nu* dEN.LÍL-*taršet tuk paiš* DINGIR.MEŠ-*naša wališḫiuwar* [*m*]*a-ni-ia-aḫ-*<*ḫa*>*-in-na tuk zinnit* KBo 3.21 ii 1-2 (hymn to Stormgod, OH?/NS), tentative tr. Güterbock, Oriens 10:359.

3. (in phrase with *išḫa-*) — **a.** LÚ*maniyaḫḫiyaš išḫa-* as a military-administrative title: *ŠA* É dUTU-*ŠI-mamu kuit* LÚ*ma-ni-ia-aḫ-ḫi-ia-aš* EN-*aš uttar ḫatrāeš kāwa* NU.GÁL *nat kuedani pedi nušmaš ḫatrāi natkan kattanda unniandu* "(Concerning) the matter of the district lord of the house of My Majesty, which you wrote to me: 'There is none here.' Write to them (the district lords) in the place where they are, and let them drive down (to you)" Mşt 75/104:13-19 (letter, MH/MS), ed. Alp, Belleten 44:50f.; LÚ.MEŠ *RABŪTIM* LÚ*ḪAZZIYANNI* LÚ*ma-ni-ia-aḫ-ḫi-ia-aš* EN-*aš . . . tarkuwanda* [I]GI.ḪI.A-*wa daḫḫun* "I (, the Old Woman) took (away from him) . . . the furious eyes of the nobles, of the *ḪAZANNU*, of the district lord" KUB 24.13 iii 21-26 (rit., NH), ed. Goetze, Tunn. 72f. (who translated LÚ*m.* and EN as separate titles); The determinative LÚ must be considered as belonging to the whole unit *maniyaḫḫiyaš išḫaš.*

b. *maniyaḫḫayaš išḫa-* (without det.) as a calque of an Akk. epithet of the Sungod: "To you alone is given a strong lordship" *ḫandānza ma-ni-i*[*a-aḫ*]*-ḫa-ia-aš išḫāš zi*[*k*] "You are the just lord of government" KUB 31.127 i 19-20 (prayer to the Sungod, OH/NS), ed. Güterbock, JAOS 78:239 and AnSt 30:45.

Sturtevant, FsPedersen (1937) 59; HW (1952) 135, HW 1. Erg. 13, HW 3. Erg. 23.

maniyaḫḫai- v.; to be in charge of, administer, govern, oversee, command; from OH/NS.

pret.(?) pl. 2 *ma-ni-*⌈*ia*⌉*-aḫ-ḫa-it-ten* KUB 26.71 i 22 (OH/NS).

[*mānšan ANA* GIŠGU.Z(*A ABIYA ē*)]*šḫaḫatti napa utnē ḫūman* (var. *utnimit*) *ma-ni-ia-*[*a*(*ḫ-ḫa-aḫ-ḫ*)*a-ti*?] / [*nat*(?) *ANA* DUMU.MEŠ-*YA ḫ*(*enkun*)] *šumeš ma-ni-ia-aḫ-ḫa-it-ten* (var. *ma-ni-ia-aḫ-ḫe-eš-ki-it-ten*) "[When] I had sat down on the thro]ne of my father, I distributed the entire land (var. my land). I [al]lotted it [to my sons(?)], (saying) 'You govern!'" KUB 26.71 i 21-22 (text of Ammuna, OH/NS) with dupl. KUB 36.98b rev. 8-9. Cf. *maniyaḫḫ-*, mng. 1 a and 5 a for the first clause and the variant.

The stem in *-ai-* is shown in *ma-ni-*⌈*ia*⌉*-aḫ-ḫa-it-ten* (OH/NS). The iter. in *-i/eški-* (vs. *-aiški-*) can belong to either *maniyaḫḫ-* or *maniyaḫḫai-*. Those iter. forms which are possible for either *maniyaḫḫ-* or *maniyaḫḫai-*, and which must be translated "administer, govern", have been assigned to *maniyaḫḫ-* mng. 5.

Oettinger, Stammbildung (1979) 366.

Cf. *maniyaḫḫ-*.

LÚmaniyaḫḫant- n. com.; (mng. unclear); MH/NS.†

kuišzan kēdaš LUGAL-*waš uddanaš karūš-šiyazi našza naššu* LÚ*arašiš munnāši nušši maškan pāi nuzata naššu* LÚ*ma-ni-ia-aḫ-ḫa-an-da-aš-ša* LÚ.ḪA.LA-*ŠU parā UL tarnai nezzan uddanī* EGIR-*an takšan UL appiyazi* KUB 13.9 iii 12-17 (instr.), dupl. KBo 27.16 iii 3-8, ed. Freydank, ArOr 38 (1970) 264ff. ("Untergebener?"), von Schuler, FsFriedrich (1959) 448, 450f., 453 ("Untertan?"), cf. Otten, FsLaroche (1979) 275, most of cited context obscure.

Cf. *maniyaḫḫ-*.

LÚmaniyaḫḫatalla- n. com.; administrator, deputy, governor; from OH/NS.†

sg. acc. LÚ*ma-ni-aḫ-ḫa-tal-la-an* KBo 3.34 ii 16 (OH?/NS), LÚ*ma-ni-ia-aḫ-ḫa-*⌈*tal*⌉*-la-an* IBoT 1.30:4 (OH?/NS), LÚ*ma-ni-ia-ḫa-tal-la-an* KUB 36.89 rev. 49 (NH).

"Aškaliya was lord in Ḫurma . . . Išpudašinara was a *ḫuprala*-man. Aškaliya, the 'man' of Ḫurma, took him" *šan INA* URU*Ullammi*! (var. *Ullamma*) LÚ*ma-ni-aḫ-ḫa-tal-la-an* (var. *ma-ni-ia-aḫ-ḫi-iš-kat-tal-la-an*) *iēt* "and made him (his) deputy/agent/administrator in Ullamma" KBo 3.34 ii 8, 15-16 (anecdotes, OH/NS), w. dupl. KBo 3.36 obv. 21-22 (NS); [*ši*]*uniyašmaza* KUR-*eaš* m*Labarnan* LUGAL-*un piran* LÚ*ma-ni-ia-ḫa-tal-la-an* DÙ-*at* "But in the gods' lands you made Labarna, the king, (to be) governor/administrator under yourself (*piran* + -*za*)" KUB 36.89 rev. 49 (rit. and prayer, NH), ed. Haas, KN 156f.; (The land belongs only to the Stormgod) *nuza* LÚ*Labarnan* LUGAL-*un* LÚ*ma-ni-ia-aḫ-ḫa-*⌈*tal*⌉*-la-an iyat* "(The Stormgod) made the Labarna, the king, (his) deputy/administrator. (. . . Let the Labarna keep administering the whole land with his hand!)" IBoT 1.30:3-6 (OH?/NS).

Götze, Ḫatt. (1925) 61 (Verwalter); Laroche, in Pouvoirs Locaux 143.

Cf. *maniyaḫḫai-* v., LÚ*maniyaḫḫiškattalla-*.

***maniyaḫḫatar** n. [neut.]; administration; NH.†

"My brother installed me in the post of Chief *MEŠEDI*-Guard" KUR.UGU-*yamu ma-ni-ia-aḫ-ḫa-an-ni pešta* "And he gave me the Upper Land to administer, (and I ruled [*tapar-*] the Upper Land)" KUB 1.1 i 25-27, ed. Ḫatt. 8f., StBoT 24:6f.

The Akkadogram *MUIRTUTU* has been kept apart despite Götze, Ḫatt. 60f. In the vocabulary KBo 1.42 the Akk. term *muʾerru* "commander, director" was tr. by Hitt. *watarnaḫḫanza*, (i 17), and Akk. *urtu* (**wuʾʾurtu*) "command, order" by Hitt. *ḫatreššar* (i 16). No words derived from the stem *maniyaḫḫ-* are used to tr. words containing the Akk. root *wʾr*. While Akk. *MUIR-TUTU* and Hitt. *maniyaḫḫatar* are similar in meaning, there is still insufficient evidence to determine if this Akk. word served as log. for *m.*

Götze, Ḫatt. (1924) 60f. ("Verwaltung").

Cf. *maniyaḫḫai-* v.

maniyaḫḫiyatt- n. [com.]; allotment(?), consignment(?), gift(??); MH/NS.†

"Decide well the cases of the land which you judge" *natzakan* . . . *ŠA* NINDA KAŠ *ma-a-ni-ia-aḫ-ḫi-ia-at-ti lē kuiški iyazi* "Let no one (of you) do it (i.e., make a judgment) . . . out of consideration for an allotment of bread and beer" KUB 13.20 i 32-34 (instr.), ed. Alp, Belleten 11.392-95, 407.

Götze, Madd. (1927) 79 ("Befehlsbereich?"); Alp, Belleten 11 (1947) 407 ("gain"), 413.

Cf. *maniyaḫḫ-*.

maniyaḫḫeššar n. [neut.]; allotment(?), consignment(?); pre-NH/NS.†

[LÚ].GIŠ.BANŠUR *ma-ni-ia-aḫ-ḫe-eš-šar pe*[*dai*?] "A table[-man] transports the *m.*" KBo 20.81 v? 14 (fest.).

The suggested tr. is based on the apparent derivation from *maniyaḫḫ-* mng. 3 "to allot, consign". In fest. texts the table-man usually carries food. Cf. also *maniyaḫḫiyatt-*.

Cf. *maniyaḫḫ-*.

maniyaḫḫiškattalla- n. com.; administrator, deputy; OH/NS.†

sg. acc. *ma-ni-ia-aḫ-ḫi-iš-kat-tal-la-an* KBo 3.36 obl. 22.

Replaces [LÚ]*maniyaḫḫatalla-* in the dupl. KBo 3.34 ii 16. Cf. [LÚ]*maniyaḫḫatalla-* for tr.

Götze, Ḫatt. (1925) 61 ("Verwalter").

Cf. *maniyaḫḫai-* v., *maniyaḫḫatalla-*.

man(n)ikuwan see *ma(n)ni(n)kuwan*.

manikuandaḫḫ- see **maninkuandaḫḫ-*, *mani-kuandaḫḫ-*.

manni(n)ni- n. [com.],; necklace; NH.†

sg. or pl. nom. *ma-an-ni-ni-iš* KUB 12.1 iii 14; **sg. acc.**(?) *ma-an-ni-ni-i[n]* KUB 18.24:27; **pl. acc.(?)** *ma-an-ni-ni-uš* KUB 42.84:8, *ma-an-ni-in-ni-uš* KUB 42.78 ii? 3.

1-*NUTUM ma-an-ni-ni-iš* KÙ.G[I GAR.R]A 1-*EN* GAB *KI-PU*(?)[- . . .] / *ṬURRU-ši* KÙ.GI *anda* 1-*E*[*N*] *awitiš* KÙ.G[I . . .] 8(?) *kuwalutiš* ZA.GÌN *anda* "One necklace-set, [se]t(?) with gold, one . . . [. . .] and a band(?) of gold is on it, one (with?) a gold *awiti*-monster [. . .] (and) eight blue *k*.'s on (it)" KUB 12.1 iii 14-16 (inv. of Manninni), ed. Košak, Linguistica 18:100, 103f.; 1-*NUTUM ma-an-ni-in-ni-uš* NUNUZ K[Ù. . . .] / AŠ.ME KÙ.GI *armanniuš* x[. . .] "One necklace-set (with) bead(s) of go[ld (or: silver?) . . .], gold sun disk(s), [gold/silver?] lunulae" KUB 42.78 ii 3-4 (inv. of Manninni); [x *T*]*APAL ma-an-ni-ni-uš anda* DIB-*anza* [. . .] KUB 42.84:8 (list of materials), ed. Košak, THeth 10:154f.; *ḫattallan* KÙ.GI *ma-an-ni-in*[-*ni*?- . .] 35/g obv. 7 (Kronasser, FsPagliaro 3:63); uncertain: [. . .]x *ma-an-ni-ni-i*[*n*? . . .] KUB 18.24:27 (oracle, NH); probably not KUB 22.37 rev. 4. It is conceivable that instead of translating "a necklace set", one could translate "a set of necklaces".

Cf. the PNs [m]Manninna, [f]Manina, and [m]Manninni NH and NH Suppl. no. 746-747.

manni(n)ni is a loanword (possibly Indo-Aryan through Hurr.) in New Hittite and in Akkadian (restricted to El Amarna, Qatna and Alalah) CAD M/1:211f.

Sommer, ZA 46 (1940) n. 5 (semantisch noch unklar, = *maninnu* in El Amarna, prob. Hurr.), HuH (1947) 94 (ein Schmuckstück); Kronasser, WZKM 53 (1956-57) 184f. (from Vedic *maṇi-* "Halsschmuck" + Hurr. *-nni-*); Mayrhofer, Kurzgefasstes etymologisches Wörterbuch des Altindischen 2 (1963) 556f., Die Indo-Arier im alten Vorderasien (1966) 19; Kronasser in FsPagliaro 3 (1969) 61-66. For further lit. cf. Mayrhofer, Die Arier im Vorderen Orient—Ein Mythos?, SÖAW 294/3 (1974) 68 s.v. *maninni*; Košak, Linguistica 18 (1978) 107.

[*maninku-*] For the form *maninkueš* cited in HW 135 see **maninkuwa-* and *maninkuešš-* v.

***maninkuwa-** adj.; near.†

1 *ME* [LÚ]KÚR ERÍN.MEŠ *warreš ma-ni!-in-ku-e-eš* "One hundred enemy auxiliary troops (were) near" KUB 23.55 iv 8 (frag. naming the Kaška); it is possible also to restore *ma-ni!-in-ku-e-eš*[-*ta*] and consider this a form of the verb *maninkuešš-*.

Even without the passage cited above, one would wish to posit an adjective **maninkuwa-* to explain the formation of the verb *maninkuwanu-* and the adv. *maninkuwan*. Cf. Neu, IF 85 (1980) 82. For the proposal of a stem *maninkuī-* see Weitenberg, Hethitica 1:38, 49f., Oettinger, Stammbildung 246 w. n. 16.

Cf. *ma(n)ni(n)kuwaḫḫ-*.

ma(n)ni(n)kuwaḫḫ- v.; **1.** to draw near, come/go near, approach (from OH), **2.** to shorten (NH).

pres. sg. 1 *ma-an-ni-in-ku-wa-aḫ-mi!* KUB 21.38 rev. 3 (NH); **sg. 3** *ma-an-ni-in-ku-wa-aḫ-ḫi* KUB 11.32 iii 26 (OH?/NS), IBoT 1.36 iii 72 (MH/MS), possibly also KUB 24.9 ii 18 (cf. s.v. *manninkuwaḫḫi*), *ma-ni-in-ku-wa-aḫ-ḫi* KUB 9.1 ii 13 (NH), KBo 11.43 i 29, KUB 41.41 v? 7, [*m*]*a-an-ni-ku-wa-aḫ-ḫi* KUB 43.13 iii 4 (NS); **pl. 3** *ma-ni-in-ku-wa-aḫ-ḫa-an-zi* KBo 21.34 ii 25 (MH/NS), Bo 2834 (StBoT 25 p. 161) rev? vi 1 (OH/NS); **pret. pl. 2** *ma-ni-in-ku-wa-aḫ-ten* KUB 17.14 i! 19 (NH).

verbal subst. nom.-acc. *ma-a-ni-en-ku-wa-aḫ-ḫu-wa-ar* KUB 43.72 ii 10.

1. to draw near, come/go near, approach (from OH) — **a.** with d.-l. or all.: *maḫḫanma* NIN.DINGIR *INA* [URU]*Wargatauwi ma-an-ni-in-*

ku-wa-aḫ-ḫi "But when the NIN.DINGIR-priestess approaches W., (they give her something to drink)" KUB 11.32 iii 24-28 (fest., OH/NS); cf. KBo 27.42 i 33-34 (KI.LAM fest.); *maḫḫanma* LUGAL-*uš* KÁ.GAL-*aš ma-ni-in-[k]u-wa-aḫ-ḫi* "When the king approaches the gate" KUB 41.41 v? 7 (fest.); cf. IBoT 1.36 iii 72 (*MEŠEDI* instr., MH/MS); *nu maḫḫan* DINGIR.MEŠ [URU]*Aštūriya ma-ni-in-ku-wa-aḫ-ḫa-an-zi* "When the gods approach A." KBo 21.34 ii 25 (fest., MH/NS); cf. KBo 20.23 obv. 2 with dupl. Bo 2834 rev? vi 1 (StBoT 25 p. 161:1); cf. also KBo 11.43 i 29, KUB 9.1 ii 13 (the latter NH); *ma-an-ni-in-ku-*⌜*wa*⌝*-aḫ-mi!-at?-ta* "And I will come near(er) to you" KUB 21.38 rev. 3 (Puduḫepa letter), ed. Helck, JCS 17:92f., cf. Sommer, AU 255 ("und(?) ich dir nahe kommen werde").

b. with Hittite case unmarked: *mān* [GIŠ]TUKUL-*anzama* KI.GUB *[m]a-an-ni-ku-wa-aḫ-ḫi* "But if the 'weapon' approaches the 'stand', (the man will survive)" KUB 8.34 iii 18-19 + KUB 43.13 iii 4 (KI.GUB omen, NS).

2. to shorten (NH): "If you upper gods have sought some evil against me," *numu* UD.ḪI.A ITU.ḪI.A MU.ḪI.A-*ya ma-ni-in-ku-wa-aḫ-ten* "and you have shortened my days, months and years" KUB 17.14 i! 17-19 (substitution rit., NH), ed. StBoT 3:56-59.

Sommer, AU (1932) 257 ("verkürzen, sich nähern, nahe sein").

Cf. *maninkuwan, maninkuwant-, maninkuwandaḫḫ-, maninkuešš-, maninkuwantatar.*

manninkuwaḫḫi n., sg. loc.?; nearby, in the vicinity; MH/NS.†

(The Old Woman takes up five loaves of bread, one vessel of beer, and a peg/stake of *karšani*-wood,) *naš araḫza paizzi ma-an-ni-in-ku-wa-aḫ-ḫi* ≪GIŠ≫ *tēkan paddāi* "She goes outside, and nearby digs (a hole) in the ground, (and puts the ritual materials in it)" KUB 24.9 ii 18, ed. THeth. 2:32f., cf. Güterbock, ZA 42:227. We interpret *m.* here as loc. sg. of a noun **manninkuwaḫḫa*- "vicinity" (cf. *alwanzaḫḫa-*, *maniyaḫḫa-*). But it is also possible to regard *m.* as pres. sg. 3 of the verb *manninkuwaḫḫ-*: "She goes outside, remains close by, and digs . . .".

Sturtevant, Language 14 (1938) 240; Laroche, RHA X/51 (1949/50) 21, 30 n. 18.

Cf. *manninkuwaḫḫ-*.

ma(n)ni(n)kuwan adv.; **1.** near (of place), nearby, **2.** near (of time); wr. syll. and *QERUB*; from OS.

ma-an-ni-in-ku-an KBo 6.2 i 48 (OS), KBo 19.44 rev. (32), 33 (NH), *ma-an-ni-ku-wa-an* KUB 10.78 i 7 (OH?/NS), IBoT 1.36 i 17 (MH/MS), *ma-an-ni-in-ku-wa-an* KUB 14.1 obv. 18, (26) (MH/MS), KBo 15.2 i 5, KBo 19.44 rev. 34 (NH), etc., *ma-ni-in-ku-wa-an* KBo 2.4 iii 7 (NH), KUB 24.3 i 27 (NS), etc., *ma-ni-en-ku-wa-an* KUB 36.65:2, KUB 48.123 i 17, KBo 10.12 ii 15, (17), *ma-ni-in-ku-u-wa-an* IBoT 1.33:111 (NH), KUB 8.55:(6), *ma-a-ni-in-ku-wa-an* KUB 40.2 obv. 30, *ma-ni-in-ku-u-wa-a-an* KUB 20.80 iii? 7(MH/NS), *ma-ni-in-ku-u-an* KBo 5.6 iii 36 (NH), *ma-an-ni-in-ku-u-wa-an* KBo 23.27 iii 23.

QÉ-RU-UB KUB 8.75 + KBo 19.10 i 28, KUB 9.17:27, KUB 26.43 obv. 36 and passim in this text and its dupl. KUB 26.50 (Tudḫ IV), VBoT 110:2, 6, 13, KBo 24.117 left col. 4, *QÈ-RU-UB* KUB 26.50 obv. 28 all NH.

(Akk.) [*ša* ZAG KUR-*ka qí*]-*ir-bu* KUB 3.7 obv. 7 (Aziru treaty), ed. Weidner, PD 70 (restored from parallel Tette treaty, KBo 1.4 ii 10: *ša* ZAG KUR-*ka qir-bu*) = (Hitt.) [*tu*]*ēl ANA* Z[AG *m*]*a-ni-en-ku-wa-an* "(Enemy lands which are) near your border" KBo 10.12 ii 15, ed. Freydank, MIO 7:361, 369; cf. also K. Riemschneider, StBoT 9:31 who sought a parallel for Hitt. "If a woman gives birth, and its (the child's) right ear" *paršenušuš [m]a-an-ni-in-ku-wa-an kitta[ri]* "is lying near its cheek(?)" KBo 13.34 iv 15-16 in Akk. *ina lētišu ṭeḫât* "(its ear) is near its cheek" Leichty, Izbu III 11.

1. near (of place), nearby — **a.** as predicate in a nominal sentence (cf. mng. 2): cf. bil. sec.; *mān* [d]UTU-*ŠI-ma ma-an-ni-in-ku-wa-an* "But if His Majesty is near" KUB 13.2 i 20 (*BĒL MADGALTI* instr., MH/NS), ed. Dienstanw. 42; *iyanzima kuwapi nu kuwapi ḫaršauwar ma-ni-in-ku-wa-an* NU.GÁL "Where do they make (the tent)? Where there is no cultivation nearby" KUB 12.58 i 16-17 (rit. of Tunn., NH), ed. Tunn. 8f.; cf. *UL-za QÉ-RU-UB* KBo 24.117 left col. 4 (NH).

b. with intrans. verbs — **1′** *ar-* (act.) "to come near": *maḫḫanma* DUMU.LUGAL *INA* [URU]*Kaštamma ma-ni-in-ku-u-wa-a-an ari* "But when the prince approaches (the city of)

K." KUB 20.80 iii? 6-7 (fest., MH/NS), cf. KUB 20.25 i 11-12 + KUB 10.78 i 6-7 (OH?/NS), Güterbock, JNES 20:92.

2′ *ar-* (mid.) "to stand (near)": 1 [LÚ]*MEŠEDI-ma kēz IŠTU* [LÚ]*MEŠEDI kuttaz* KÁ-*aš ma-an-ni-ku-wa-an arta kēzma IŠTU* LÚ.MEŠ. ŠUKUR.KÙ.GI *kuttaz* 1 LÚ.ŠUKUR.KÙ.GI (erasure in margin) KÁ-*aš ma-an-ni-in-ku-wa-an arta* "But one guard stands on one side by the wall of the guards near the gate, and one man of the gold spear stands on the other side by the wall of the men of the gold spear near the gate" IBoT 1.36 i 17-19 (*MEŠEDI* instr., MH/MS), ed. Jakob-Rost, MIO 11.174f., cf. Alp, Beamt. 7, Melchert, Diss. 291f.; cf. KUB 20.42 i 12 (fest.).

3′ *ki-* (mid.) "to lie (near)": cf. bil. section.

4′ *pai-* "to go (near)" — **a′** in general: *ANA* AN.ZA.GÀR EN É-*TI* GAŠAN É-*TI-ya ma-ni-in-ku*(dupl. adds -*u*)-*w*[(*a-an lē paizzi*)] "Let the lord of the house and the lady of the house not go near the tower (where the anger of the Stormgod has been nailed down)" KUB 7.13 obv. 31 (purification rit.), with dupl. KUB 46.56:18; *luttiya ma-ni-in-ku-wa-an UL pānzi* "They don't go near the window" Bo 3481 i 5-6 (fest.), ed. Haas, KN 292f.; cf. KUB 33.52 ii 2-3 (myth of Inara), with dupl. KUB 33.55 ii 8-9, translit. Myth. 88.

b′ with a sexual connotation: *nuwašši kuitman* [LÚ-*aš* (*ma-ni*)]-*in-ku-u-wa-an nāwi paiz*[*zi*] "Before [the man] has gone near to her" KUB 8.55 ii 6 (Gilg.), with dupl. KUB 8.51 rev. 8), ed. Otten, IM 8:104f., 122; *kuišaš imma k*[(*ui*)]*š ŠA* É.GAL-*LIM* SAL *mānaš ELLUM mana*<(*š*)> SAL.SUḪUR.LÁ *nušši ma-ni-in-ku-wa-an* (var. [*m*]*a-an-ni-in-ku-a*[*n*]) *lē tiyaši nušši ma-ni-i*[*n-ku*]-*wa-an* (var. *ma-an-ni-in-ku-*⌈*an*⌉) *lē pāiši memiyannašši lē mematti* ÌR-*KA-yašši* GÉME-*KA ma-ni-in-ku-wa-an* (var. *ma-an-ni-in-ku-wa-an*) *lē paizzi* "Do not step near or go near any woman of the palace, whether she is a free woman or a harem slave. Do not say a word to her, and do not let your male slave or female slave go near her" KBo 5.3 + KUB 40.35 iii 44-48 (Huqq. treaty, Šupp. I), with dupl. KBo 19.44 rev. 31-34, ed. SV 2:126f., 156; cf. KUB 26.1 iv 36f., 42f., (SAG 1 instr., Tudḫ. IV), ed. Dienstanw. 16.

5′ *šalik-* "force one's way (near)": *naš* DINGIR.MEŠ-*aš* [NINDA]*ḫarši* ⌈DUG⌉*išpantuzzi ma-ni-in-ku-wa-an šaknuanza šāliqa* "(If) he forces his way near the gods' bread and libation vessel (while) unclean" KUB 13.4 iii 79-80 (instr. for temple servants, pre-NH/NS), ed. Chrest. 162f., tr. ANET 209, cf. Neu, StBoT 5:148; cf. KBo 5.6 iii 36-38 (DS), ed. JCS 10:95, where the restoration *š*[*a-li-ik-ta*] is not certain.

6′ *tiya-* "to step (near), approach": TUR-*limat* ⌈*ma-ni*⌉-[*i*]*n-ku-wa-an lē tianzi* "Let them not step near the child" KBo 3.8 ii 8-9 (rit. of Ayataršа, pre-NH/NS); *nu ma-ni-in-ku-wa-an UL kuiški tiyazzi* "No one will step near (the silver and gold in the temple)" KUB 24.3 i 27-28 (prayer, Murš II), cf. KUB 24.1 ii 19 (prayer to Telepinu, Murš II); *QÉ-RU-UB* [URU]*Manaziyara tīēz*[*zi*] "He approaches the city of M." KUB 9.17 obv. 27 (fest. for the tutelary deities, NH); cf. *QÉ-RU-UB* GN KUB 26.43 obv. 40, 41, 43, etc. (Tudḫ. IV); *takku* [MUL]*leš*[*šall*]*aš* [d]*SIN-mi ma-ni-in-ku-wa-an tiyazi* "If a *leššallaš* approaches the moon" KUB 8.16 + KUB 8.24 iii 10-11 (celestial omens, NS); *nuza* [m]*Išputaḫšu* LUGAL [U]RU*Kizzuwatna* [. . . *m*]*a-*⌈*an-ni*⌉-[*i*]*n-ku-wa-an tīezzi* KUB 31.81 rev. 10-11 (Telepinu-Išputaḫšu treaty, NS).

7′ *uwa-* "to come (near)": *ma-ni-in-ku-wa-an-na-aš-mu UL-pat uit* "He didn't come near me at all" KUB 1.1 ii 50 with dupl. KBo 3.6 ii 31, ed. Ḫatt. 18f., StBoT 24:14f.

c. with trans. verbs — **1′** *aršanu-* "to make flow": [URU]*Ner*[*ikiwaran*] *ma-an-ni-in-ku-wa-an aršanut* "He made [it] flow near Nerik" KUB 36.89 rev. 13-14 (myth in rit., NS), Güterbock, JNES 20:92f., MAW 153, □ the obj. is the Maraššanta River.

2′ *ḫan-* "to draw (water)": *mān*[*atkan*(?) *tūwa*]*li*⸗*ma* KASKAL-*ši iyanzi*(!) *nu kišš*[*an mem*]*anzi wā*[*tar*]⸗*wa ma-an-ni-in-ku-wa-an ḫānumēni* "But if they do [it] on a [lon]g trip (lit. on a distant road), and(?) they speak thus: 'We will draw water nearby'. § (They will not draw water in the place where the Red River joins the Maraššanda River)" KBo 23.27 ii 25-30 (Hurr. rit., MS?), for the rest. of ii 25 cf. KBo 4.14 ii 57.

3′ *iya-* (act.) "to do, perform, make, construct": *arḫayanma apiyapat ma-an-ni-in-ku-wa-*

an ᴱ*kip*[(*pan*)] *iyanzi* "But separately, near that same place, they construct a *k*.-building" KBo 15.2 i 5-6 (subst. rit.), with dupl. KUB 15.2 i 8, ed. StBoT 3:56f.; [(*mānza*) *Taba*]*rnaš* ᵐ*Tudḫaliyaš* . . . [(ᵈU)] ᵁᴿᵁ*Ḫatti INA* GIŠ.ḪI.A ᴳᴵŠTÚG [(ᴱ)]*tarnui ma-an-ni-in-ku-wa-an* (var. *ma-ni-in-ku-wa-an*) EZEN AN.TAḪ.ŠUM^SAR *ḫamešḫi iyazi* "When the Tabarna Tudḫaliya . . . performs the ANTAḪŠUM festival in spring for the Storm-god of Ḫatti near the bath house among the box trees" KUB 20.42 i 8, w. dupl. KUB 20.63 i 9 (fest.).

4′ *ep-* "to seize": (If a slave runs away,) *nan āppa kuiški uwatezzi takku ma-an-ni-in-ku-an ē*[(*pz*)]*i* "and someone brings him back; if he seizes (him) nearby" (the owner gives the finder shoes) KBo 6.2 i 48 (Law § 22, OS), with dupl. KBo 6.3 i 56-57 (NS).

5′ *tarna-* "to let (come)": DINGIR-*LUM ANA* ᵈUTU-*ŠI* [. . .] ḪUL-*lu ma-ni-en-ku-wa-an UL tarnatti* "O goddess, (if) you do not let evil [. . .] come near His Majesty, (I will do the following)" KUB 48.123 i 16-17 (vow, Pud.); cf. *m. tarna-* in KUB 31.127 + ABoT 44 iv 8-10 (prayer, OH/NS).

6′ *waḫnu-* "to turn (something)": *nu* ᴳᴵŠ*ḫūlugannin* ᴱ*katapuznipat ma-an-ni-in-ku-wa-an waḫnuwanzi* "They turn the carriage near the *k*.-building" KBo 10.24 iii 18-20 (KI.LAM fest., OH/NS).

2. near (of time) (in nom. sentence): *akkan*[*na*]*šma* MU *karū ma-ni-in-ku-u-wa-an* "But is the year of (sc. the king's) death already near?" IBoT 1.33:111 (oracle, NH), ed. Laroche, RA 52:155, 159.

This adv. was probably formed from the neut. of the adj. *maninkuwa-*.

Götze, Ḫatt. (1925) 57ff. and Friedrich apud Götze, ibid. 59 n. 1.

Cf. *ma*(*n*)*ni*(*n*)*kuwaḫḫ-*.

ma(n)ni(n)kuwant- adj.; **1.** short, low, **2.** close; from OH/MS.

sg. nom. com. *ma-ni-in-ku-wa-an-za* KBo 21.6 obv. 7 (NS), *ma-ni-in-ku-wa-a-an-za* KBo 9.125 i 10 (NH); **acc. com.** *ma-ni-in-ku-wa-an-da-an* KUB 9.34 i 29, iv 7, HT 6 obv. (11) (both NH), *ma-ni-in-ku-wa-an-ta-an* KUB 9.4 ii 7 (NH), *ma-ni-in-ku-u-wa-an-da-an* KUB 7.53 iii 8 (NH); **abl.** [*ma-ni-i*]*n-ku-wa-an-ta-az* KUB 35.80:9 (MH?/NS).

pl. nom. com. *ma-ni-in-ku-wa-an-te-eš* KUB 1.1 i 14 and dupl. KBo 3.6 i (12) (Ḫatt. III), *ma-ni-in-ku-u-an-te-eš* KUB 1.2 i 13 (var. of preceding), *ma-an-ni-*⌈*in-ku*⌉*-wa-an-te-eš* KUB 24.5 obv. 22 + KUB 9.13:10 (NH), *ma-a-an-ni-in-ku-wa-an-*⌈*te*⌉*-eš* ibid. 23, [*ma-a*]*n-ni-ku-wa-an-te-eš* KUB 32.117 rev.! 5; **acc. com.** *ma-ni-ku-an-du-š*(*a*) KUB 12.63 obv. 25 (OH/MS), *ma-ni-ku-wa-an-du-š*(*a*) ibid. 30, *ma-an-ni-in-ku-wa-an-du-uš* KUB 36.38 rev. 3, [*man*(*n*)*-i*]*n-ku-u-wa-an-du-u*[*š*] KBo 12.94:2 (NS), [*man*(*n*)*i*(*n*)*-k*]*u-u-an-du-uš* KUB 50.4 iv 12 (NH); **nom.-acc. neut.** [*m*]*a-ni-in-ku-wa-an-da* KUB 24.13 iii 24, *ma-an-ni-in-ku-wa-an-da* KUB 24.9 iv 13 (MH/NS); **gen.** *ma-ni-in-ku-wa-an-ta-aš* KUB 21.27 + 546/u iii 16 (Sürenhagen, AOF 8:114) (Ḫatt. III).

1. short — **a.** of time (opp. of *daluki-* "long") — **1′** said of years: *ANA* ᵐ*Ḫa*[(*tt*)]*ušiliwa* MU.KAM.ḪI.A *ma-ni-in-ku-wa*(var. *-u*)*-an-te-eš UL-waraš* TI-*ann*[(*aš*)] "Ḫattušili's years are short. He is not one of (long) life." KUB 1.1 i 14-15 (Apology of Ḫatt. III), with dupl. KUB 1.2 i 13-14, ed. Ḫatt. 8f., 57-59, StBoT 24:4f.; *kēdaniyakan ANA* EN.SISKUR *idalu papratar alwazatar āštayaratar* DINGIR.MEŠ-*aš karpin NĪŠ* DINGIR-*LIM pangauwaš* EME-*an ma-ni-in-ku-u-wa-an-da-an* MU-*an arḫa QĀTAMMA ḫuittiya* "From this sacrificer withdraw in the same way evil, impurity, sorcery, . . . , the anger of the gods, the oath of the god, the tongue of the multitude (*pankuš*) (and) the short year (an early death?)" KUB 7.53 iii 5-8 (rit. of Tunn., NH), ed. Tunn. 18f. iii 39-42; cf. KUB 9.4 ii 7, KUB 9.34 i 29, ii 1, iv 7, KBo 9.125 i 10, HT 6 obv. 11 (all NH), KBo 11.14 i (2) (rit. of Ḫantitaššu, MH/NS), KBo 15.12:(12) (rit., NS), KBo 12.94:8 (incant., NS), cf. sub *mišari-*; [. . . *manink*]*u-u-wa-an-du-uš* MU.KAM-*uš* DÙ-*anzi*/[*naš INA* ᴱ*ḫ*]*ešti pēdanzi* KUB 50.4 iv 12-13 (oracle question, NH) □ perhaps the situation described here is the making of images of the years to be carried into the ᴱ*ḫešta* in the ANTAḪŠUM festival; however, there it is always singular and without the qualification "short" (IBoT 2.1 vi 8-11, KBo 13.169 left col. 3, KUB 20.33 i 1-3).

2′ said of days: ḪUL-*luš* GISKIM-*iš ma-an-ni-*⌈*in-ku*⌉*-wa-an-te-eš* MU.ḪI.A-*uš ma-a-an-ni-in-ku-wa-an-*⌈*te*⌉*-eš* UD.ḪI.A[-*uš*?] "bad omen, short years, (and) short days" KUB 24.5 obv. 22-23 + KUB 9.13:10-11 (royal subst. rit., NH), ed. StBoT 3:10f.

3′ said of time: *meḫurši ma-ni-in-ku-wa-an* "His time is short" KUB 6.3:21 (oracle, NH).

b. of height (opp. of *parku-* "tall, high"), (said of mountains): ḪUR.SAG.MEŠ *par-ga-u!-uš manikuandaḫten ma-ni-ku-an-du-ša pa[rganut-ten]* "Make the high/tall mountains low/short, and make the low/short ones high/tall" KUB 12.63 obv. 25 (rit. of Zuwi, OH/MS), cf. Pedersen, JCS 1 (1947) 60f.

c. of length (opp. of *daluki-* "long") — **1′** said of roads: *ma-ni-ku-wa-an-du-ša* KASKAL. ḪI.A-*uš* KUB 12.63 obv. 30 (rit. of Zuwi, OH/MS).

2′ said of ribs: *ma-an-ni-in-ku-wa-an-da* UZU.TI "short ribs" KUB 24.9 iv 13 (rit., MH/NS), ed. THeth 2:52f., cf. HAB 80 n. 1; cf. KBo 12.60:2; perhaps 1 *ma-ni-in-ku*[- . . .] KBo 12.60:3.

2. close: *pa(n)gauwaš [m]a-ni-in-ku-wa-an-da tarkuwanda* IGI.ḪI.A-*wa* "the close, furious look (lit. eyes) of the multitude (*pankuš*)" KUB 24.13 iii 24 (rit. of Allaituraḫi), ed. Tunn. 72f.; cf. also Haas/Thiel, AOAT 31 (1978) 108f. and Wegner, MDOG 113 (1981) 115 w.n. 13, who quotes the Muslim incantation against the evil eye "(protect) from the long eye and from the short eye". Others in the listing in Allaituraḫi have a "furious look", but only that of the *pankuš* is said to be "close", cf. *lala-* 4 a 2′.

Götze, Ḫatt. (1925) 57ff.; Friedrich apud Götze, Ḫatt. 59 n. 1; on usage 1 a cf. Hoffner, FsPope (forthcoming).

Cf. *ma(n)ni(n)kuwaḫḫ-*.

***maninkuandaḫḫ-, manikuandaḫḫ-** v.; to make short; OH/MS.†

a. (opp. of *taluganu-* "to make long"): *talugaušwa* KASKAL.ḪI.A *ma-ni-ku[-an-da-aḫ-ten]* "Make the long roads short" KUB 12.63 obv. 24 (rit. of Zuwi).

b. (opp. of *parganu-* "to make tall/high"): ḪUR.SAG.MEŠ *par-ga-u!-uš ma-ni-ku-an-da-aḫ-ten* "Make the tall/high mountains short/low" KUB 12.63 obv. 25.

Friedrich, OrNs 13 (1944) 208-10.

Cf. *ma(n)ni(n)kuwaḫḫ-* v., *ma(n)ni(n)kuwan* adv., *ma(n)ni(n)kuwant-* adj., etc.

maninkuwantatar n. neut.; shortness; NH.†

Only in a lex. text: (Sum. and Akk. columns broken away) *ma-ni-in-ku-wa-an-ta-tar-me-et* "my shortness" KBo 13.2 obv. 16, immediately preceded by the entry: *pargatarmet* "my tallness" ibid. 15.

Cf. *ma(n)ni(n)kuwant-* adj.

maninkuwanu- v.; to bring near(?).†

ma-ni-in-ku-wa-nu-ut Bo 6238:7 quoted without context by Neu, IF 85 (1980) 82.

Cf. **maninkuwa-* adj.

maninkuešš- v.; to be short; from OH?/NS.†

UD.KAM.ḪI.A-*ušši ma-ni-in-ku-e-eš-ša-an-zi* "His (the person's to be born) days will be short" KUB 8.35 obv. 3 (omen apod., OH?/NS); for *ma-ni!-in-ku-e-eš[-zi/ta]* KUB 23.55 iv 8, which may be this verb, see under **maninkuwa-* adj.

Götze, Ḫatt. (1925) 59 n. 1.

Cf. *ma(n)ni(n)kuwant-*, etc.

mannitti- n. com.; (a desirable condition in nature); from OH/MS.

sg. nom. *ma-an-ni-it-ti-iš* KUB 47.59:10 (NS), KUB 33.24 iv (22); **sg. acc.** *ma-an-ni-it-ti-i[n]* KUB 33.24 ii 10 (OH/NS), *ma-an-ni-it-ti-en* KUB 17.10 i 11 (OH/MS), KBo 2.9 i 23 (MH/NS); **sg. dat.?** *ma-an-ni-i[t?-ti?]* KBo 13.193:9 (NS).

a. in OH missing god stories: *ᵈTelepinuša arḫa iyanniš ḫalkin ᵈImmarnin šalḫiantien ma-an-ni-it-ti-en išpiyatarra pēdaš* "And Telepinu departed. He carried off grain, Immarni, *šalḫianti-*, *m.* and satiety" KUB 17.10 i 10-11 (OH/MS), translit. Myth. 30; cf. KUB 33.24 i 21, ii 10, iv 22 (OH/NS).

b. in a MH/NS prayer to Ishtar of Nineveh: *ANA* KUR ᵁᴿᵁ*Ḫattikan anda . . . šalḫittin ma-an-ni-it-ti-en annarenna uda* "Bring into the land of Ḫatti (growth of crops, vines, cattle, sheep and humans, and) *šalḫitti-*, *m.* and *annari-*" KBo 2.9 i 22-24; for discussion see sub *miyatar*, a.

c. in an incantation ritual: [. . . T]I-*tar ḫaddul[atar . . .] tarḫuilatar tarḫu*[- . . .] *šalḫittin ma-[annittin . . .]* "[Bring(?)] . . . life, heal[th,

. . .] prowess, . . . [. . .], *šalḫitti-*, *m.* [. . .]" KBo 23.3:2-4.

d. personified as a deity, seated with deities and given offerings: (After the seating arrangement of many of the Former Gods has been indicated,) EGIR(*-pa* erased) ᵈA.NUN.NA.KE₄-*ma* ᵈ*Kumarpiš* [*ēšzi* EGIR ᵈ*Kumarp*]*ima šalḫittiš ma-an-ni-it-ti-iš* ᴺᴵᴺᴰᴬ*zippinaza* TUŠ-[*z*]*i* "But behind the Former Gods Kumarpi [sits, and behind Kumarp]i *šalḫitti-* and *m.* sit by(?) the *z.*-breads" KUB 47.59:9-10 + KUB 39.97 obv. 15-16 (rit. for Former Gods, NS), cf. Otten and Rüster, ZA 68:155; (Offerings of sheep, oxen, birds and breads to the Former Gods) [. . . 1 MUŠEN] 1 ᴺᴵᴺᴰᴬ*ma*⸗*kaltiš ma-an-ni-i*[*t*?*-ti*? . . .] KBo 13.193:9 (rit., NS) □ since *m.* is elsewhere always paired with *šalḫitti-*, it is likely that in one of the nearby lacunas *šalḫitti-* occurred; the assumption that *m.* is to be restored as dat.-loc. in KBo 13.193:9 is based on the form [*kariy*]*ašḫi* ibid. 11 and *dummantiya* IBoT 3.83:4 and *nenganani* KUB 17.20 iii 7 in similar passages.

Haas/Wilhelm, AOATS 3 (1974) 31, 57 ("luwisch").

Cf. *šalḫitti-*.

manka adv.; in some way, in any way; NH.

ma-an-ga KBo 5.13 i 19, iv 20, KBo 4.3 i 37, KUB 6.41 iv 27 (copies of Murš. II texts).

ma-an-qa KUB 6.44 iv 9, KUB 14.17 ii 6, KBo 4.4 i 35, KBo 14.20 i 19 (copies of Murš. II texts), KUB 19.2 obv. (46), KUB 26.46 iii 62, KBo 3.6 iii 60, KUB 21.19 + 1193/u ii 25 (all copies of Hatt. III), KUB 24.7 iv 32, KUB 17.31 i 7, KUB 40.90 ii (2), 4, KUB 23.93 iii 10, KBo 18.88 obv. 7, KUB 23.107:(15) (not securely dated, but probably Hatt. III or later).

For *ma-*⸢*a*-⸣*-an-qa* KUB 6.41 iii 64 read *ma-a-an-ma* according to coll. Ehelolf apud AU 126 n. 1.

a. negated by *UL* and often in close proximity to optative/potential *man* — **1′** in same clause with *man*: *kinuna* ᵐPÉŠ.TUR-*aš kuit ABUKA waštaš zikmaza* ᵐ*Kupanta*-ᵈLAMMA-*aš ANA* ᵐPÉŠ.TUR-*wa kuit* DUMU-*ŠU ēšta ma-an-za UL ma-an-ga* (var. *UL zi-iq-qa*) *wašdulaš ēšta* "Now because Mašḫuiluwa, your father, sinned, since you, K., were M.'s son, even if you had not been guilty in any way (var. yourself guilty)" KBo 5.13 i 18-20 (Kup. treaty) with dupl. KBo 4.7 i 68, ed. SV 1:114f.; cf. *man* b 2′; ᴸᵁ́ŠU.DIB-*ma-an UL ma-an-qa taštašiyait* "The prisoner(s) would not have whispered/grumbled/conspired at all" KUB 14.17 ii 6, ed. AM 84f., broken context; *nukan mān* KUR ᵁᴿᵁ*Lala*[*nda d*]*apianpat lagāri nunnašat* GEŠPÚ!-*uwaš ta*[*r-aḫ-ḫu-u-wa-aš*] *ma-an-ma-kán* KUR.ḪI.A *ŠAPLI*<*TI*>*-ma lagāri nunna*[*šat man*(?)] *UL ma-an-qa iya*[*u*]*waš* [. . .] "If it is only all of Lalanda which falls, it will be for us (a matter) of overpowering (and) con[quering] (it). Were the Lower Land to fall, there would be nothing at all for us to do (or: would there be nothing at all for us to do?)" KUB 19.23 rev. 17-20 (letter), cf. AU 127, AM 244f., if *man* is not to be restored in the second clause then presumably the optative/unreal/ potential meaning of the *man* in the previous clause carried over.

2′ with no *man*-clause nearby: *ŠA* ŠEŠ-*YA* DUGUD-*anni* (var. *nakkiyanni*) *ḫandaš UL ma-an-qa iyanun* "Out of respect for my brother I took no action at all" KUB 1.8 iv 14 with dupl. KBo 3.6 iii 60 (=Ḫatt. iv 29-30), ed. Ḫatt. 34f., StBoT 24:24f; cf. also 922/v:8 (StBoT 24 Tafel IV = Ḫatt. iii 39), KUB 26.46 iii 62; same wording in Ḫatt. III prayer KUB 21.19 + 1193/u ii 24-25; *nu nammapat ANA* ŠEŠ-*YA ḫandaš UL ma-a*[*n-qa iyanun*] KUB 14.3 ii 55 (Taw., NH), ed. AU 10; *nan šannapili*[*n*? . . .] *UL ma-an-qa arḫa tarnaḫḫi* "In no way will I let him/her go [. . .] emptyhanded" KUB 23.93:9-10 (letter); [(*parāmaškan*)] *UL iyattari ma-an-qa* "But he will not (cannot, must not?) go out at all" KUB 17.31 i 7 (rit. of substitute king), restored from dupl. KBo 15.2 rev. 5, ed. StBoT 3:60f. □ note the unusual position of *manqa* following its verb, if correctly interpreted.

3′ with insufficient context to determine presence or absence of *man*: *UL ma-an-qa* KUB 40.90 ii (2), 4 (depos.).

b. negated by *numan*: (Because there was a plague in the land of Ḫatti,) *nu nūman ma-an-qa iyanun* [*nušm*]*aš laḫḫiyauwa*[*nz*]*i UL pāun* "I would/could not act in any way. I did not go to war against them, (and because I retreated before the plague, I stayed in GN)" KUB 34.33:5-6 + KBo 14.20 i 19-20 (Murš. II ann.), ed. Houwink ten Cate, JNES 25:169, 178; cf. *laḫ*(*ḫ*)*iyai-* 1 a and on *nūman* "would/could not" Hoffner, GsKronasser 38-45, where it is proposed that *nūman* was the negative for the "subject optative" construction of *man* (q.v.); its occurrence here with *manqa* reinforces the impression gained from the exx. cited above under a 1′ that this adverb had a particular appropriateness to clauses involving the optative/potential/unreal particle *man*.

c. not negated: (The fisherman says:) DINGIR.MEŠ-*wakan ma-an-qa* [o o o-]*yaḫḫat* "I may/might have [. . .]-ed the gods somehow" KUB 24.7 iv 32 (Cow and Fisherman story, NH), ed. Friedrich, ZA 49:230f.; another broken passage where the negative does not immediately precede *manqa* is: [. . .] SIG_5-*in ma-an-qa* [. . .] KBo 18.88 obv. 7 (letter); *apāškan* INIM-*aš* 1-*anki ma-an-qa nepiš*[*a*(-) . . .] KUB 14.3 iv 57 (Taw., NH), photo confirms Forrer, Forsch. 118 against AU 18, context and meaning unclear.

If one rejects Sommer's tr. "with respect to one's self" in favor of "in some way" (negated "in no way"), one is faced with the question: "How does *UL manka* differ in meaning from *UL kuitki* or *UL kuwatka*?" No sure answer can be given yet. But if there is more than mere coincidence in the frequent association of *manka* with the particle *man* and the negative *numan*, there might be a hint of the optative, potential or unreal ideas in its contexts.

Friedrich, SV 1 (1926) 159 ("irgendwie", negated "keineswegs"); Sommer, AU (1932) 125-127, 415 ("in Beziehung oder Rücksicht auf die eigene Person"); Götze, AM (1933) 242-45, 299 (*UL manqa* "nihil non, ohne weiteres, unbedingt, unter allem Umständen"); Pedersen, Hitt. (1938) 68-71; Benveniste, RHA V/36 (1939-40) 125ff. (*UL manqa* "nihilominus" "non . . . moins, néanmoins", "tout autant, pareillement, malgré tout"); Pedersen, RHA VII/45 (1945-46) 1f. (approved Goetze's "ohne weiteres", "unbedingt"); Friedrich, HW 136 (derived from *mān* "how" + *-ka/ki* in *kuiš-ki*, *kuel-ka*, etc., cf. the Luw. cognate *manuḫa* cited by Meriggi, AfO 10 (1935) 121 and Hawkins, AnSt 25 (1975) 124, 136).

manman see *man* b 2′ b′.

mant- see *manza*.

DUGma-an-ta[l(?)- . . .] see DUG*manz*[*i*(?) . . .].

(SISKUR)mantallaššammi- Luw.; designated for *mantalli*-rituals; NH.†

sg. nom. SISKUR*ma-an-tal-la-aš-ša-am-mi-iš* KBo 2.6 iii 20, without det. KUB 8.27 rev. (10).

f.d*IŠTAR-attiš kuwatta imma kuwatta šer* TUKU.TUKU-*uanza nan ariyaueni nankan* KASKAL-*ši tiyaueni mānma* GIDIM *UL* SISKUR*ma-an-tal-la-aš-ša-am-mi-iš* (par. omits det. SISKUR) SISKUR*mantalliya⸗za* (par. omits *⸗za*) *UL* BAL-*anti mānmat* GIDIM *UL šanḫti* "Whatsoever (the spirit of the deceased) Šauš⸗katti is angry about, we will investigate her (i.e., her intentions) by oracle and we will put her on the road (i.e., satisfy her ?). If the deceased (Šauškatti) has not been designated for *mantalli*-rituals, (then) he (the king) will not offer *m.*-rituals; if you, the deceased, do not seek them, (let the exta be favorable; result unfavorable)" KBo 2.6 iii 17-23 (oracle), cf. parallel KUB 8.27 rev. 8-12.

m. is the passive participle of a Luw. iter. verb **mantallašša*- "to designate for *mantalli*-rituals".

Güterbock, OrNS 25 (1956) 122; Laroche, DLL (1959) 68.

Cf. *manza*, *mantalli*-, :(SISKUR)*mantalli*-.

mantalli- adj. venomous(?), poisonous(?), rancorous(?) (modifying tongues); MH/MS.†

pl. acc. *ma-*⌈*an-ta*⌉*-al-li-i-e-e*[*š*] 2Mašt. i 22 (MH/MS) and dupl. *ma-an-da-al-li-*[(*i-e-e*)*š*] 46/r i 24 (NS).

"The Old Woman says:" dUTU-*i išḫāmi kāšawatta parā tittanunun ma-*⌈*an-ta*⌉*-al-li-i-e-e*[*š*] (dupl. *ma-an-da-al-li-*[(*i-e-e*)*š*]) EME.ḪI.A-*eš* "O Sungod, my lord, I have brought forward to you the venomous(?) tongues" 2Mašt. i 21-23, ed. Rost, MIO 1:348f., dupl. 46/r i 23-25, cf. *lala-* mng. 6; cf. perhaps :*ma-an-tal-li-iš* KUB 16.17 ii 17 (oracle), if the noun "tongues" stood in the lacuna following *kuit*, otherwise, perhaps to (SISKUR)*mantalli*-, q.v.

The SISKUR*mantalli*- (q.v.) seeks to heal an estrangement or antagonism between two persons, living or dead. Although the 2Mašt. ritual is not called a SISKUR*mantalli*-, it too serves this purpose. In 2Mašt. the bitter words which caused the estrangement are referred to by the expression *mantallieš* EME.ḪI.A-*eš* "*m.* tongues". In view of the existence of the word *manza* (stem *mant*-?), which appears to translate Sum. and Akk. words for saliva, venom or sorcery, it is possible that the adjective *mantalli-* means "characterized by (*-alli-*) venom, poison or bitterness". The NH noun SISKUR*mantalli-* seems to be based upon the MH adj. *mantalli-*.

Cf. *manza*, (SISKUR)*mantallaššammi-*, :(SISKUR)*mantalli-*, *matalli(ya)-*.

(:)(SISKUR)mantalli-, (SISKUR)maltalli- n. (Luw.); a ritual pertaining to rancor(ous words) (?); NH.†

com. sg.? nom.? :*ma-an-tal-li-iš* KUB 16.17 ii 17, [. .]*ma-an-ta-al-li-iš* KUB 51.74 obv.? 18; **Luw. pl. acc.** [SI]SKUR*ma-an-tal-li-ia-an-za* KUB 22.35 iii 7.

neut. pl. acc. SISKUR.MEŠ*ma-an-ta-al-li-ia* KUB 21.33 iv? 19, SISKUR*ma-an-tal-ia* KUB 22.35 iii 11, :SISKUR*ma-an-ta[l-li-ia]* KUB 16.32 ii 14, 19 (without marker), SISKUR*ma-an-tal-li-ia* KBo 2.6 iii 21 (with suffixed *-za*), KUB 8.27 rev. 11, KUB 5.6 iii 25, KUB 16.32 ii 9, 23 (NH), SISKUR*ma-an-tal-li-ia-≪aš≫* KBo 2.6 iii 30 (NH), SISKUR*ma-an-tal-li* KUB 16.32 ii 17, [SISKU]R*ma-al-tal!-⌈li⌉-ia* KUB 5.6 iii 36.

unclear *ma-al-ta-li* 34/p:1, [. . . *ma-a*]*l-ta-li-ia-aš* 34/p:3 (both Alp, TTKYayin VI/23:362), here or under *maltalli-*?

a. to act against evil talk or curses — **1′** between living persons: (It was determined that Mašḫuiluwa uttered many curses before His Majesty's Zawalli god which he had in Arzawa [iii 8ff.], so that both the god and he himself were bewitched [iii 18f.]. It was asked whether M. should himself go to Kuwatna, where certain rites were to be performed [iii 19-23]) *kuit⸗mankan* mPÍŠ.TUR-*aš* m*Zaparti*-ŠEŠ-*ša IŠTU* SISKUR *aranzi kuitman⸗ma⸗aš*(sic) SISKUR*ma-an-tal-li-ia* URUKÙ.BABBAR-*aš* URU*Arzawašša iwar ITTI* dUTU-*ŠI iyanzi* "until M. and Z. arrive with the offerings and until they(!) perform the *m.*-ritual with (*ITTI*) His Majesty in the manner of Ḫattuša and in the manner of Arzawa" KUB 5.6 iii 24-26 (oracle question, Murš. II); cf. *kuitma[n* mPÍŠ.TU]R-*aš IŠTU* SISKUR *ari kuitmanza* [SISKU]R *ma-al-tal!-⌈li⌉-ia* URUKÙ.BABBAR-*aš* URU*Arzawašš[a iwar]* ⌈*ITTI*⌉ dUTU-*ŠI* DÙ-*zi* ibid. 35-36.

2′ between a living and a dead person: In the 5th tablet of the oracle questions about Armatarḫunta and the woman Šauškatti, KBo 2.6, the section ii 37 - iv 23 concerns Šauškatti. The first question is about EME *ŠA* f.d*IŠTAR-atti* "the tongue (evil talk) of (i.e., concerning) Šauškatti" while she was alive. This indicates that at the time of the text she was deceased, and that the log. GIDIM, used frequently in the following paragraphs, refers to her. Another reason for her anger was slander uttered by her sons (ii 55, iii 6). When it is determined that there is no other ground, the text continues: "Whatever Šauškatti is angry about, we shall investigate her (i.e., her intentions) by oracle and put her on the road (i.e., satisfy her?)." *mān⸗ma* GIDIM *UL* SISKUR*ma-an-tal-la-aš-ša-am-mi-iš* (var. without det.) SISKUR*ma-an-tal-li-ia-za* (var. omits *-za*) *UL* BAL-*anti mān⸗ma⸗at* GIDIM (var. + *-iš*) *UL šanḫti* "But if the deceased (Šaušgatti) has not been designated for *m.* rituals, (then) he (the king) will not offer *m.* rituals; if you, O deceased, do not seek them (let the exta be favorable." Result: unfavorable, i.e. she does seek them) iii 17-23 w. var. KUB 8.27 rev. 8-12. Although the following lot oracle gives to the same queries a "yes" answer (i.e., she does not seek them) in 24-29, the text continues: f.d*IŠTAR-attiš kuit ITTI* dUTU-*ŠI* SISKUR*ma-an-tal-li-ia≪-aš≫* BAL-*uwanzi* SI×SÁ-*at nuza* dUTU-*ŠI ITTI* GIDIM SISKUR*ma-an-tal-li-ia* BAL-*anti mān⸗ma⸗za* DINGIR.MEŠ *ŠA* f.d*IŠTAR-atti* SISKUR*ma-an-tal-li-ia ITTI* dUTU-*ŠI* BAL-*uwanzi malān ḫarteni* "Since it was determined that Š. should offer a *m.* ritual with His Majesty, should His Majesty offer *m.* rituals with the deceased? If you, O gods, have approved of Š.'s offering a *m.* ritual with His Majesty, (let the first MUŠEN ḪURRI oracle be favorable and the second one unfavorable)" (Result: first favorable, second unfavorable, i.e., a "yes" answer) ibid. iii 30-35 □ Lines 41-45, giving details about the procedure, contain the phrase GIDIM-*ia šarā ašešanuwanzi* "they make the deceased sit up", presumably meaning an image of her: iii 44-45, 61.

b. Purpose not mentioned — **1′** One or both participants deceased: [. . .] GIDIM-*ia* SUD-*anzi* [*nu* d]UTU-*ŠI ANA* GIDIM IGI-*anda* [SIS]KUR*ma-an-tal-li-ia-an-za* ⌈BAL⌉-*anti ABI* dUTU-*ŠI-ia* SUD-*anzi nuza ABI* dUTU-*ŠI* m*Ḫalpa*-LÚ-*išša* 1-*aš* 1-*edani* IGI-*anda* SISKUR*ma-an-tal-ia* BAL-*anti šarnikzel ANA* GIDIM

SUM-*anzi ANA* DINGIR.MEŠ URU*Ḫalpa⸗ya šarnikzel šaknuwandaza parkuwayaza* SUM-*anzi* "[. . .] and they will invoke (lit. pull) the deceased, and His Majesty will perform the *m.* rituals vis-à-vis (*ANA* . . . *menaḫḫanda*) the deceased. Also the father of His Majesty they will invoke, and the father of His Majesty and Ḫalpaziti—each will perform the *m.* ritual vis-à-vis the other. They will give compensation to the deceased, also to the gods of Ḫalpa they will give compensation, from the soiled and from the clean." KUB 22.35 rev. 5-15 (oracle question, NH), ed. Archi, AOF 6:82. In the first part, His Majesty is living. The identity of the GIDIM is not clear because of the lacuna; Archi believes that it is the ghost of Ḫalpaziti, whose name appears in line 1′ without context. If this is correct, then the second ritual is between two deceased persons—but who then is the GIDIM (sg.) of line 12?

2′ Performer living, recipients probably living: *ANA* dUTU-*ŠI kuit ANA* DUMU.MEŠ m*Urḫi*-dU-*ub* :SISKUR*ma-an-tal*[*-li-i*]*a* IGI-*anda arḫa* BAL-*uanzi UL* SI×SÁ-*at UL-aš kuit* [dUTU-*Š*]*I* ḪUL-*aḫḫ*[*u*]*n* ḪUL-*aḫta⸗aš kuiš* UN-*aš naš nūwa kuit* TI-*za nu* ⸢*a*⸣[*p*]*el kuit* ZI-*za UL waršiyanza nu* SISKUR*ma-an-tal-li arḫa* K[IN-*u*]*anzi apiz UL* SI×SÁ-*at* "concerning the fact that it was determined by oracle that His Majesty should not perform a *m.*-ritual vis-à-vis the sons of U., because I, My Majesty, did not wrong them and the person who wronged them is still living, and since his mind has not been appeased, therefore it was determined not to carry out the *m.* ritual" KUB 16.32 + KUB 50.6 ii 14-18 (oracle, Tudḫ IV), rest. after ibid. 19-23 □ see HW² p. 86 for *arḫa aniya-*, here "auszuführen"; ibid. p. 137c and 138c about *apel.* Cf. KUB 16.41 + 7/v:18-20, if line 18 is to be restored [DUMU.MEŠ mU]rḫi-dU-*ub*, cf. *pedanzi* in line 20 (differently Ünal, THeth 3:173, 4:112).

3′ unclear: *kinunakan* GIM-*an ŠA* DINGIR.MEŠ URU*Ḫalpa uliḫiuš* UGU *u*[*da*]*nzi nušmašza* dUTU-*ŠI* SISKUR*ma-an-tal-li-ia* IGI-*anda arḫa* [BAL-*ti*] "But now, when they bring the *uliḫi*-s of the gods of Aleppo up (to Ḫattuša?), His Majesty will per[form] the *m.* ritual vis-à-vis them." KUB 16.32 + KUB 50.6 ii 8-9 (oracle question, Tudḫ. IV). □ It is not clear to whom or what *-šmaš* here refers. For *uliḫi-*, elsewhere with det. SÍG, see the discussion by Kronasser, Schw.Gotth. 45f.; it might be a head band. If it was considered divine the *-šmaš* could refer either to the *uliḫi*-s, or to the DINGIR.MEŠ. In either case this would be the only example of *m.* offerings not destined for living or dead humans. Since the passage is preceded by a section dealing with Tanuḫepa and separated from it by a double rule, *-šmaš* can hardly refer back to a plurality of persons; [. . .] x *anda ma-al-ta-li* SISKUR *ma-a*[*l-* . . .] / [. . .] É*ḫalinduwaš kueda*[*š*(?) . . .] / [. . . *ma-a*]*l-ta-li-ia-aš kišša*[*n*(?) . . .] 34/p:1-3, ed. Alp, TTKYayin VI/23:362f., here or under *maltalli-*?

One party may perform (*iya-*/ DÙ) it (KUB 5.6 iii 25f., 36) or offer (*šipand-*/ BAL) it (KBo 2.6 iii 30-33) "together with" (*ITTI*, i.e., vis-à-vis) the other. One party may offer (*šipand-*/ BAL, KUB 22.35 rev. 6-7, 10-11, or *arḫa šipand-*/ BAL, KUB 16.32 + KUB 50.6 ii 14-15) it "opposite" (*menaḫḫanda*/ IGI-*anda*, i.e. vis-à-vis) another. Or one may carry it out (*arḫa aniya-*/ KIN KUB 16.32 + KUB 50.6 ii 17, 23). According to KUB 5.6 iii 35-36 the *m.*-ritual was performed in Arzawa differently from in Ḫatti.

The *m.* ritual was performed to heal an estrangement or antagonism between two people, one of whom was usually deceased. The position of the marker wedges before SISKUR in KUB 16.32 ii 14 suggests that SISKUR was not a logogram, but a determinative. But even if the SISKUR is a determinative and *m.* a substantive, the semantic connection of NH SISKUR*mantalli-* to the MH adj. *mantalli-* is likely. For the designation of a SISKUR by a word denoting the evil to be removed compare *maršaya* SISKUR (cf. *marši-* adj.).

The writing *maltalli-* does not fit the suggested derivation from *manza* q.v. (stem *mant-*?). If the writing *mantalli-* was the older, *maltalli-* might have arisen from a semantic consideration that the ritual was promised (*malt-*). For the alternation of *l* and *n* cf. Kronasser, EHS 58f. (§ 49) and NINDA*makalti-*/*makanti-* q.v.

Otten, TR (1958) 136 (Totenopfer); Laroche, DLL (1959) 68; Laroche, BiOr 18 (1961) 84 (le rituel qu'on adresse aux 'Mânes'); Stefanini, JAOS 84 (1964) 30 (a type of sacrifice); Archi, SMEA 14 (1971) 211f.; id., AOF 6 (1979) 82; Ünal.

THeth 3 (1974) 166ff.; Del Monte, AION 33 (1973) 383; Ünal, Anadolu 19 (1975/76 [1980]) 175-183.

Cf. *manza*, (SISKUR)*mantallaššammi-*, *mantalli- matalli(ya)-*.

[mantišuya] in [. . .]x ERÍN.MEŠ *man-ti-šu-ia kuiš nankan* x[. . .] KUB 23.70 l.e. 1 (frag. of treaty, NS) may be emended to ERÍN.MEŠ KUR!-*TI-ŠU-ia* "and the troops of his land", cf. . . . *nukan* KUR-*TI-IA ištarna* x[. . .] ibid. l.e. 3; cf. ERÍN.MEŠ KUR-*TI-pat* KUB 23.103 rev. 25, ERÍN!.MEŠ KUR-*TI ti*-x[. . .] KBo 18.58 obv. 10.

manu(z)zi(ya); (city and mountain name which occurs in the divine name dU (or dIM) *manuzi(ya)* "storm god of M.")

In dU(-)*ma-nu-zi* KBo 20.60 v? 13, 15, there is no word space between U and *ma*. This DN is also written dU ḪUR.SAG *Ma-nu-zi-ia* (var. [dU] ḪUR.SAG URU*Ma-nu-zi-ia*) KUB 6.45 i 63 (w. dupl. KUB 6.46 ii 28), dU URU*Ma-nu-uz-zi-ia* KBo 11.5 i 8, dU (var. dIM) URU*Ma-nu-uz-zi-ia-ma* KBo 4.2 iii 49 (w. dupl. IBoT 2.112 obv. 10), dIM *Ma-nu-zi-i[a]* KUB 40.102 v 9. Cf. also *pappenna ma-nu-z[i-ya] [š]ipanti* KUB 20.95:2-3 (*ḫišuwaš* fest.), KUB 40.100 v 8-9; *ANA pappi ma-nu-zi* [. . .] KUB 40.102 ii 12 (*ḫišuwaš* fest.). The same DN ("Stormgod of M.") could be written with the Hurrian gentilic adj. *manu(z)⸗zuḫi* q.v. For the GN see RGTC 6:259f.

manu(z)zuḫi Hurr. gentilic adj. of the GN *Manu(z)zi(ya)*.

a. modifying the god Tešub (all refs. are in the *ḫišuwaš* fest.): dIM-*up ma-nu-zu!-ḫi* KUB 45.58 iv 11, 12, cf. dupl. KBo 17.98 4, 5; dU-*up ma-nu-zu-ḫi* KUB 12.12 v 30; dU URU*ma-a-nu-z[u-ḫi]* KUB 45.59 rev. 18.

b. modifying *tiyari* (all refs. in *ḫišuwaš* fest.): KUB 12.12 i 29, 32, KBo 24.76 left col. 16, KBo 15.37 ii 11; w. divine det.: d*tiyāri ma-a-nu-zu-ḫi* KUB 45.53 iii 6-7; cf. KUB 27.20:6; cf. d*tiyāri* URU⌜*ma-a*⌝*-nu-zu-ḫi* KUB 25.48 iv 16; d*tiyāri* <<DINGIR>> URU*ma-nu-uz-z[u-ḫi]* KBo 13.168 i 11.

c. modifying d*šurinni* (*ḫišuwaš* fest. only): d*šurinni ma-nu-zu-ḫi* KBo 9.133 obv. 13.

d. modifying "god(s)": DINGIR.MEŠ-*na ma-nu-zu-u-ḫi* KBo 17.98 v 23 (*ḫišuwaš* fest.); URU*ma-nu-zu-ḫi* DINGIR.MEŠ [. . .] KBo 11.2 ii 3 (rit. of Muwalanni); *enuš ma-nu-[zu-ḫi]* KUB 20.44:8.

manu(z)zu⸗nna (pl. in place of the expected **manuzuḫi⸗nna*: (GLH 167)) from KBo 15.48 ii 17, iii 17, (44), KUB 25.42 ii 19-20, iv (7), etc.

Haas and Wilhelm, AOATS 3 (1974) 108; Laroche, GLH (1979) 167.

manz- v. see *maz(z)-*.

manza n.; saliva(?), venom(?), sorcery(?); NH.†

In Syllabar A vocabulary KBo 1.45 obv.! 10: (sign pronunciation) [ú-uḫ] = (Sum.) [UḪ] = (Akk.) [. . .] = (Hitt.) *ma-an-za*, ed. MSL 3:53; in sequence of Hitt. entries *alwanzatar*, *iššalli*, *manza*, [*iš*?]*šallanza*, [o o]x-*ša-an-za*, all apparently translating Sum. UḪ and/or the Akk. translations thereof: probably *kišpu*, *ru'tu*, *rupuštu*, *illatu*, *imtu*, *uḫḫu*, *ḫaḫḫu* or *ḫurḫummatu*, words denoting saliva, spittle, phlegm, venom, poison, sorcery, etc. But even if the Akk. version had a word meaning "saliva" or "venom", Hittite Assyriologists often misunderstood the Akk. So the meaning of *manza* remains unclear.

The stem might be *mant-*, *manz-* or *manza-*. If it is *mant-*, it might be the base from which the adjective *mantalli-* was derived.

Cf. *mantalli-*, (:)(SISKUR)*mantalli-*.

GIŠmanzari, :manzari n. neut.; (object made of wood); NH.†

1 GIŠBAN 20 GIKAK.Ú.TAG.[GA . . .] 1 GIŠ*ma-an-za-ri* EGIR-*an* [. . .] 5 URUDU. GAL "one bow, twenty arrows [. . .] one *m.* [. . . -ed] on the back, five copper goblets" KUB 40.96 iii? 26-28 (inventory); *nuwa* m*Anuwanzaš* :⌜*ma*⌝*-an-za-r[i dāš(?)] / natkan šaštaš* É.ŠÀ-*n[i anda pedaš(?)]* "A. [took] a *m.* and [carried] it [into] the bedchamber" KUB 49.97:7-8 (oracle question, NH).

DUGmanz[i? . . .]; (a vessel); (OS).†

DUG*ma-an-z[i?- . . .]* KBo 25.51 ii? 7 (offering list),

translit. StBoT 25 p. 115. A reading DUG*ma-an-ta*[*l*- . . .] is also possible.

GADmanziti(ya?)- n.; potholder(?); NH.†

abl. GAD*ma-an-zi-ti-ia-za* KBo 11.2 i 11, KBo 11.4 i (11); **broken** GAD*ma-an-zi*-[*ti*- . . .] KBo 18.185:3.

nuza LUGAL-*uš* SISKUR *ḫalalenzi iyazzi* GAD*ma-an-zi-ti-ia-za* 1 GUNNI *kuptaš ANA* DINGIR.MEŠ *ABI* 1 GUNNI *kuptaš ANA* DINGIR.MEŠ LÚ.MEŠ *tuliyaš* "The king performs *ḫ*.-rituals. With a potholder(?) [he places?] one *kupta*-brazier for the ancestral gods, one *kupta*-brazier for the male gods of the assembly" KBo 11.2 i 9-12 (rit.), dupl. KBo 11.4 i 10-13; on *kupta*- see Güterbock, JNES 34:275f.

mar- v. see *mer*- v.

māra- n.; see *mara*(*i*)- n.

marra-, marri-, marriye-, marriya- v.; **1.** (intrans., mid. and part.) to melt (down), dissolve, stew or cook until tender, **2.** (trans. act.) to heat (something) up(?), bring to a boil(?), melt down(?); from OH.

act. pres. sg. 2 [*m*]*ar-ri-it-ti* KUB 43.60 iii 8 (OH?/NS); **sg. 3** *mar-ri-ia-az-zi* KUB 33.120 iii 72 (MH/NS).

mid. pres. sg. 3 *mar-ri-it-ta* KBo 17.18 ii 7 (OS), KBo 6.34 i 44 (MH/NS), [*m*]*ar-ri-it-t*[*a*(-) . . .] KBo 24.1 i 5, *mar-ri-ia-ta-ri* KBo 4.14 i 48 (NH), *mar*-[*ra*/*i*-]*at-ta-ri* KUB 1.13 ii 26; **pret. sg. 3** *mar-ra-at-ta-at* KUB 34.91 i (2), (3), (4), 5 (OH?/NS), [*ma*]*r-ra-at-ta-t*(*a-aš*) ibid. 7.

imp. sg. 3 *mar-ri-e-et-ta*<-*ru*> KBo 6.34 ii 3 (MH/NS), *mar-ri-it-ta-ru* KBo 27.12 ii 7 (MH/NS); **part. pl. nom.** *mar-ra-an-te-eš* KBo 10.34 i 11 (MH); **case uncertain** *mar-ra-an-ta-aš* KBo 3.13 rev. 16 (OH/NS).

1. (mid. and part.) to melt (down), dissolve, stew or cook until tender — **a.** of salt: *ḫaššī*≈*makan* MUN *mar*-[-*ra*/*i*-]⌈*at-ta*⌉-*ri ANA* DUG*NAMZITI*(coll. Potratz)-*ya* BULÙG AL. GAZ [*ma*]*rḫanuwamman* "Salt melts/dissolves on the brazier. Crushed malt is brewed/stewed in the fermenting vat" KUB 1.13 ii 26-28 (Kikkuli, NH), ed. Hipp.heth. 60f., cf. AU 188 n. 2, Madd. 73.

b. of mutton tallow: "He puts wax and mutton tallow into their hands and throws (some) into the *ḫappina*- (flame?/pan?) and says:" *kī* GAB.LÀL *maḫḫan šalliyaitta* (var. [*šall*]*iētta*) Ì!. UDU-*mawa* GIM-*an mar-ri-it-ta* "As this wax melts(?), as the mutton tallow dissolves/melts, (whoever transgresses the oath and acts deceptively toward the king of the land of Ḫatti,)" *naš* GAB.LÀL-[*aš*] ⌈*i*⌉*war šallittaru* (var. *šalliēttaru*) UZUÌ.UDU-*m*[*aw*]*a iwar mar-ri-e-et-ta*<-*ru*> (var. *mar-ri-it-ta-ru*) "let him melt(?) like the wax, let him melt/dissolve like the mutton tallow" KBo 6.34 i 41-ii 3 + KUB 48.76 ii 1-3 w. dupl. KBo 27.12 ii 3-7 (soldier's oath, MH/NS), ed. without dupl. StBoT 22:8f., tr. ANET 353.

c. of mutton: 1 UDU *šuppištuwaraš INA* DUGUTÚL *mar-ri-it-t*[*a*] "One . . . sheep stews/cooks in a pot" KBo 17.43 i 6 (rit., OH/OS?), cf. *mara*(*i*)- n.; cf. parallel KBo 17.18 ii 6-8.

d. of evils: [*mar-r*]*a-at-ta-a*[*t* . . . *ḫap*]*anzi mar*-⌈*ra*⌉-*at-t*[*a-at* . . .] *išḫaḫru mar-ra-at-ta-a*[*t* . . .] *mar-ra-at-ta-at šipan ma*[*r-ra-at-ta-at*] §[*g*]*amara*[*š*] KI.MIN *ḫarki* KI.MIN *in*[*an* KI.MIN *ma*]*r-ra-at-ta-ta-aš* KUB 34.91 i 2-7 (rit. in myth, OH?/NS); a similar list of evils occurs in KBo 23.4 (+ KUB 33.66) i 5-9 and KUB 33.66 ii 9-15 (OH/MS); in KUB 33.66 they are put into pots which sit in the sea.

e. (w. preverb *šarā*) of bread/pastry: "Six loaves of *ḫaršpawant*-bread, six [loaves of] thin [bread] of (i.e., made with) oil" 5 NINDA*šarā mar-ra-an-te-eš* "five breads/pastries melted(?)/glazed(?) on top" KBo 10.34 i 11 (enthronement rit., MH?), cf. KBo 21.23 i 3; cf. Hoffner, AlHeth 144f.; tr. of *šara* suggested by the composite 3 NINDA*še-er-ma*(coll.)-*ra-an-te-eš* KUB 9.2 i 19, Hoffner, AlHeth 182f.

2. (trans. act.) to heat (something) up(?), bring to a boil(?), melt down(?), obj. contents of a pot: *numu zik ḫurzakiši* DUGUTÚL KAŠ GAM-*an* [(space for 8 signs)] *nu apāš* DUGUTÚL-*aš mar*-⌈*ri-ia*⌉-*az-zi* "You continually curse me. A pot of(?) beer [. . .]. That pot will bring (its contents) to a boil(?)" KUB 33.120 iii 71-72 (myth, MH/NS), translit. Myth. 160, Neu, StBoT 5:112f. n. 1 ("und jener Topf geht in Stücke").

The translations "melt (down)" and "stew/cook" are meant to indicate that heat has been applied to the object, so that it undergoes a physical change. In modern terms we would say that it changes from a solid state to a liquid one. The solid salt dissolves in the hot water; the solid mutton tallow melts, when thrown into the *ḫappina-*. It is fitting that the action occurs in a ^{DUG}UTÚL (1c), since elsewhere cooking (*zanu-*) is done in a ^{DUG}UTÚL (cf. KUB 32.49b ii 19, KUB 23.34 i 27), and stews (TU$_7$.ḪI.A) are often contained in a ^{DUG}UTÚL. Salt which is "on the brazier/hearth" (*ḫašši*) in 1a is certainly being heated. Whether the *ḫappina-* is an "open flame" or a "pan", it is a location where there is heat. Friedrich by his translation "zerlassen" correctly recognized the role of heat in this action. The idea of heat appears to be present also in *marri-* "daylight(?)" "heat-of-day(?)" (= Akk. *ṢĒTU*) and *mar-ra-*[. . .], n., (= Akk. *ḫunṭu*?, in RS 25.421 obv. 35 qqv.

Friedrich, ZA 35 (1924) 163 n. 15 ("zerlassen?"); Götze, Madd. (1927) 73 ("zerkleinern"), 98 n. 12 ("zerlassen werden"); Sommer, AU (1932) 188 n. 2; Neu, StBoT 5 (1968) 112 ("zerstückeln?, zerkleinern?, zerlegen?, in Stücke gehen, entzwei gehen"); Oettinger, StBoT 22 (1976) 9, 30 ("zerlaufen").

Cf. *marra*[-. . .], *marri* adv., *marri* A n.

mar-ra[-. . .] n.; (something) cooked(?) or boiled(?); NH.†

In Hittite tr. of Sumero-Akkadian literary text: "She is an abundant harvest." *šep-pittaš⸗ma⸗aš mar-ra*[-. . .] "she is cooked(?) . . . of *šeppit*-grain" RS 25.421 obv. 35, ed. Laroche, Ugar. 5:774f. and 778; the Akk. vers. reads: *ebūru nuḫšu ḫunṭu saltu*, ed. Nougayrol, Ugar. 5:313, 315, 317.

Laroche restored *mar-ra*[*-tar*], a word which occurs nowhere else. Hoffner restored *mar-ra*[*-an*] and considered it a part. sg. nom. neut. from the verb *marra-* q.v. Since *marra-* (mid.) means "melt, dissolve, cook", it is possible that the Hittite translator mistook *ḫunṭu* (a quality of cereals) for *ḫunṭu*/*ḫumṭu* "heat".

Hoffner, AlHeth 79f., 144f.

Cf. *marra-* v.

māra(i)- n.; (an implement for lifting); OH.†

inst. *ma-a-ra-i-it* KBo 17.43 i 7 (OS).

1 UDU *šuppištuwaraš INA* ^{DUG}UTÚL *mar⸗ritt*[(*a* $^{LÚ.MEŠ}$*MURIDI-š*)*a*(coll.) . . .] *ma-a-ra-i-it* ⸢*kar*⸣*pan ḫarkanzi tan ḫaššan* (var. *ḫaššaš*) *pir*[(*an tianzi*)] "One . . . sheep is stewing in a pot. The food servers hold [. . .] lifted with a *m.* and place it before the braziers" KBo 17.43 i 6-7 (fest.), restored from dupl. KBo 17.18 ii 7-8, cf. Neu, FsRanoszek 86 ("Lanze(?)") □ the lacuna before *m.* contained the object of the verb *karpan ḫar(k)-*, which is resumed by the common gender pron. *-an* in the next sentence.

The stem could be *māra-* (cf. IGI.ḪI.A-*wait* KUB 35.148 iii 36) or *mārai-* (cf. the instr. *zalḫait* in IBoT 2.14 obv. 10).

marak- see *mark-* v.

maralli (Hurr. word of unkn. mng.); NH.†

Occurs twice in KUB 44.54, a magic ritual similar to that of Allaituraḫi: *nu* ^{LÚ}AZU *ḫurlili* x[. . .] *ma-ra-al-li memai* "The exorcist in Hurrian says [. . .] *maralli*" rev. iii 6-7; *nu* SAL.ŠU.GI [. . .] *ma-ra-al-l*[*i* . . .] ibid. ii 5-6.

Laroche, GLH s.v., listed without tr.

ma?-ra-an-ti-iš n.; (a material of value).†

In a list of offerings to Hurrian deities: (Various items such as combs, axes, and an eagle of black iron, gold, silver and wood,) ŠÀ.BA [. . . *ḪAṢṢ*]*INNU* GAL KÙ.GI ^{NA_4}ZA.GÌN ^{NA_4}TI AN.BAR.GE$_6$-*ya* [. . .] / *šermašša*[*n* . . . 1-*E*]*N ŠA* ^{NA_4}TI 1-*EN-ma ma?*(*ku?*)*-ra-an-ti-iš* KÙ.GI-*y*[*a* . . .] *piran š*[*a-* . . .] KUB 32.86 obv. 1-3 + KBo 20.103:2-4 + KBo 21.87 obv. 10-12. Other nouns in this position in the context are *laḫma-*, gold, silver, lapis lazuli, and wood, which suggests that this word denotes a valuable material such as wood, ivory, gems or precious metal. The sign as copied could be either *ku* or *ma*. 1-*EN-ma* shows that this word is a sg.

marapši-; (epithet of the Stormgod, probably Hurr.); NS.†

"The queen steps forward" *nukan* ^{LÚ}ḪAL *ANA PANI* ^{d}U *ma-ra-ap-ši* ^{d}*āpin kinuzi našta* ^{LÚ}AZU 1 UDU *ANA* ^{d}U *ma-ra-ap-ši šipanti nankan* ^{LÚ}AZU *ANA* ^{d}*āpi kattanda ḫad⸗dāi* § *nukan ēšḫar ANA* GAL *katta tarnai nat taknī ANA PANI* ^{d}U *ma-ra-ap-ši dāi* "the exorcist opens a pit in front of the Stormgod *m.*

and the exorcist slaughters a sheep into the pit. § He drains the blood into a cup and places it on the ground in front of the Stormgod *m.*" KUB 10.63 i 17-22 (fest. for Ištar of Nineveh, NS), ed. Vieyra, RA 51:88, 94, cf. Hoffner, JBL 86 (1967) 391, Wegner, AOAT 36:126. Probably Hurrian, cf. *purapši-* and *šinapši-*.

Wegner, AOAT 36 (1981) 126.

marra[tar] see *marra*[-. . .].

$^{(\text{GIŠ})}$**marāu-** n.; (a wooden object used as a seat); from OH.†

UGULA $^{\text{LÚ.MEŠ}}$ALAN.ZU$_x$ ^{GIŠ}*ma-ra-a-u*[-*i* (*ē*)]*šzi* "The foreman of the *ALUZINNU*'s is sitting on the *m.*" KBo 22.195 ii! 14 + KBo 22.224 obv. 4 (KI.LAM fest., OH/MS), restored from dupl. KBo 25.12 ii 18 (OS), ed. Singer, Diss. 90, 337, translit. Neu, StBoT 25:32; cf. *ma-ra-a-u-i ēšz*[*i*] 1256/v obv. 3 (Neu, StBoT 25:32 n. 85); 10 ^{GIŠ}*ma-ra-a-u* KBo 20.86:9 in a list of implements. Cf. the Luwian *ma-ra-a-wi$_5$-iš-ta* KUB 25.39 iv 1 (DLL 68, 167).

Cf. ^{GIŠ}*marawirali-*.

^{GIŠ}**marawirali-** n. (com.); (a wooden object); NH.†

In an inventory in context with ^{GIŠ}*ḫūpparalliš* and ^{GIŠ}PISAN there occurs 1 ^{GIŠ}*ma-ra-u-i-ra-liš* x[. . .] KUB 42.11 v 29, ed. THeth 10:34, 36. Since the *liš* sign can also be read *li$_x$*, one could possibly read ^{GIŠ}*ḫūpparalli* and ^{GIŠ}*marawirali* and consider both as neut.

Cf. ^{GIŠ}*marau-*.

:marḫ- v.; (mng. unkn.); late NH.†

pret. sg. 3 *:mar-ḫa-ta* KUB 1.1 iv 6 with dupls. *:mar-aḫ-da* KUB 1.4 iii 50 + Bo 69/256 iii 51 (StBoT 24, Plate III) and *:ma-*⌜*ar*⌝*-ḫa-ta* KUB 1.10 ii! 23.

^{m}*Šipa*-LÚ-*išma ammuk* IGI-*an*[(*da*)] *idaluš kuit ēšta UL-ašmu* IGI-*anda :mar-ḫa-ta* (var. B *:mar-aḫ-da*, F *:ma-*⌜*ar*⌝*-ḫa-ta*) "Because (or: Although) Š. was malicious toward me, he did not *m.* against/toward me" KUB 1.1 iv 5-6, w. dupl. B: KUB 1.4 rev. 49-50 + Bo 69/256 + 674/v iii 50-51 and F: KUB 1.10 ii 21-23 Apology of Ḫatt. III), ed. Ḫatt. 30f. ("hatte er mir gegenüber keinen Erfolg"), StBoT 24:22f., 76.

Götze, Ḫatt. (1925) 31, 98; HW (1952) 136; Kammenhuber, RHA XVII/64 (1959) 16f. (correctly disassociates this verb from $^{(\text{TU}_7)}$*marḫan*).

Cf. $^{\text{TU}_7}$*marḫa-*.

$^{(\text{TU}_7)}$**marḫa-** n.; (a kind of stew or cooked food); from MH?

sg. acc. *mar-ḫa-an* KBo 26.182 i 13, KUB 17.35 i 8, ii 21, iv 28, ⌜*mar*⌝*-ḫa-a-an* IBoT 2.5 obv. 14, $^{\text{TU}_7}$*mar-ḫa-an* KBo 2.13 obv. 15 (all NH); **sg. loc.** *mar-ḫi* KBo 15.36 + KBo 21.61 ii 6, 11 (MH?/MS?).

(He breaks bread for various gods) *našta mar-ḫi anda šūnizzi* [*šeraššan*] SAR.ḪI.A 3 *AŠRA dāi* "He pours (it) into the *m.*-stew and puts vegetables on top of it in three places" KBo 15.36 + KBo 21.61 ii 6-7 (rit., MH?/MS?) and compare ibid. 11-12. Often in cult inventories one finds the clause *mar-ḫa-an ippian tianzi* "they set out *m.* and *i.*" KBo 26.182 i 13 or *ippiyan mar-ḫa-an tianzi* KUB 17.35 i 8 or $^{\text{TU}_7}$*mar-ḫa-an :ippiya tiyanzi* KBo 2.13 obv. 15. For these passages see Carter, Diss. 106, 111, and passim.

Both Carter, Diss. 192f. and Archi, UF 5 (1973) 20 n. 62 consider $^{(\text{TU}_7)}$*marḫan* a participle of a verb "to stew" or "boil". The loc. form *marḫi*, however, shows this to be incorrect. The Luw. [*ma*]*rḫanuwamman* (q.v.) may derive from the same root as this noun. A possible connection w. Palaic *marḫa-*, *marḫant-* is considered by Kammenhuber, RHA XVII/64:16f.

[ma]rḫanuwamman(?); brewed(?); NH.†

ḫaššīmakan MUN *mar*[*r*]*attari ANA* ^{DUG}*NAMZITI* (coll. Potratz)-*ya* BULÙG AL.GAZ [*ma*]*r-ḫa-nu-wa-am-ma-an* "Salt is being dissolved (in water) on the brazier. Crushed malt (is) brewed(?) in(!) the fermentation vat (Then he gives them one cup of salt water and one cup of extract of crushed malt)" KUB 1.13 ii 26-30 (Kikkuli, NH), ed. Hipp.heth. 60f., cf. AU 188 n. 2, Madd. 73. KUB, followed by Potratz 72, read [*w*]*a-*; Otten (ZA 55:282 n.3) suggested [*ma*]*r-*; coll. is indecisive.

As it stands, the form presents difficulties for grammatical analysis. It might be a neut. sg. *a*-stem, *n*-stem or *nt*-stem. The assumed underlying verb **marḫanuwa-* would be a causativefactitive in *-nuwa-*, based on the same root as the noun (TU₇)*marḫa-* (a kind of stew or cooked food).

SÍGmarḫaši- see SÍG*mariḫši-*.

(GIŠ)māri-, GIŠmārit- n. com.; spear(?), javelin(?); from OH.

sg. acc. *ma-a-ri-in* KBo 25.28 iii? 5 (OS), KBo 10.2 ii 46 (OH/NS), KUB 44.16 ii 13, 15 + IBoT 3.69 ii 10 (NS), KBo 9.136 i 7 (NS), KUB 34.72 obv.? 4, GIŠ*ma-a-ri-in* KUB 10.17 ii 11, 13 (OH/NS), KUB 10.18 ii 15 (OH/NS), ABoT 13 i (6), 8 (NS), KUB 43.56 ii 16 (NS), KBo 22.189 ii 5, KBo 14.21 ii 29 (NH?), GIŠ*ma-ri-in* KUB 2.3 ii 7 (OH/NS), KUB 36.19:9 (MH/NS), KBo 22.189 ii 7 (NS), KBo 2.8 iii 19 (NH), *ma-ri-in* KUB 38.2 ii 25 (NH); **gen.** *ma-a-ri-ia-aš* KBo 13.119 iv 9 (NS); **loc.** GIŠ*ma-a-ri* KBo 4.9 iv 10 (NS), KUB 11.29 iv 12 + KUB 41.52 iv! 13 (NS); **abl.** GIŠ*ma-a-ri-ta-a[z]* KUB 43.56 ii 16 (MH?/NS).

pl. nom. GIŠ*ma-ri!-uš* KUB 42.100 iv 5 (Tudḫ. IV); **acc.** *ma-a-ri-uš* KBo 20.37 obv. 1 (OS), GIŠ*ma-a-ri-uš* KBo 17.12 rev. (2) (OS), KBo 10.23 vi (7) (OH/NS), KBo 10.25 vi (15) (OH/NS), KUB 11.34 iv 12! (MS?), KBo 10.18 rt.col. 9 (NS), KBo 8.56:(3) (NH), [. . . *m*]*a-a-ri-uš* KBo 20.20 obv.? 8 (OS), KUB 44.7 i 4.

GIŠ*ma-ri*ḪI.A KBo 10.37 i 9 (OH/NS) is possibly *IZ-MA-RI*ḪI.A "spears", cf. CAD A2:527f.

a. a weapon carried by humans — **1′** in ceremonies: "[The king leaves] the ten[t, hol]ding the lituus. Two palace attendants precede him" ŠÀ.BA 1-*EN* DUMU.É.GAL GIŠŠUKUR AN.BAR *ḫarzi* 1-*EN* DUMU.É.GAL-*ma* GIŠ*ma-ri-in* AN.BAR GIŠ*kalmuš* GIŠ*IŠTUḪḪA* GIŠ*mukarra ḫarzi* "Of these one palace attendant holds an iron ŠUKUR-spear, and one palace attendant holds an iron *m.*-spear, a lituus, a whip and a *mukar* (rattle?)" KUB 2.3 ii 1-8 (KI.LAM fest., OH/NS), ed. Singer, Diss. 364, 131; "The king goes into Inara's temple" 2 DUMU.MEŠ.É.⸢GAL⸣ 1 LÚ*MEŠEDI* GIŠŠUKUR A[(N)].BAR-*aš ḫarzi* 1 DUMU.É.⸢GAL⸣ AN.BAR-*aš ma-a-ri-in ḫ*[(*ar*)]*zi* LUGAL-*i piran ḫūiyanzi* [(L)]UGAL-*uš* AN.BAR-*aš ma-a-*⸢*ri-in*⸣ *ḫarzi* "Two palace attendants, one guard holds an iron ŠUKUR-spear, one palace attendant holds an iron *m.*-spear, (and) they precede the king. The king holds an iron *m.*-spear" KUB 44.16 ii 11-15 + IBoT 3.69 left col. 6-10 (fest. for all dLAMMA's, NS), with dupl. KBo 22.189 ii 3-8 (NS), ed. Lebrun, Hethitica 2:8, 11; cf. KBo 9.136 i 7, KUB 34.72 obv.? 4, KBo 25.28 iii? 5; "The king and queen are seated on the throne. A palace attendant comes in" GIŠŠUKUR GIŠ*ma-a-ri-in* GAD-*ya ḫarzi nu* GAD LUGAL-*i pāi* GIŠ*kalmušmakan* GIŠ*ma-a-ri-in* GIŠŠUKUR-*ya* GIŠDAG-*ti dāi* "He holds a ŠUKUR-spear, a *m.*-spear and a linen cloth. He gives the linen cloth to the king. The lituus, the *m.*-spear and the ŠUKUR-spear, however, he puts on the throne platform" KUB 10.17 ii 9-14 (ANTAḪŠUM fest., OH/NS); "A palace attendant carries a gold ŠUKUR-spear and a *mukar* (rattle?)" *natšan paizzi* GIŠDAG-*ti* LUGAL-*i* ZAG-*naz* GIŠ*ma-a-ri kattan dāi* "He goes and puts them with the *m.*-spear to the right of the king on the throne platform" KBo 4.9 iv 7-11 (ANTAḪŠUM fest., NS), tr. ANET 359, cf. ABoT 13 i 5-8 (NS); "While they are distributing the *taparwašu*-bread" nu LÚ.MEŠ URU*Anunu*⸢*mi*⸣*neš ḫ*[(*attili*)] SÌR-*RU* GIŠ*ma-a-ri-uš!-š*[(*a-an*)] *anda walḫannian*[*zi*] "The men of Anunuwa sing in Hattic and they strike the *m.*-spears together" KUB 11.34 iv 11-13 (*nuntarriyašḫaš* fest., MS?), with dupl. KBo 10.18:7-9 (NS); [LÚ.MEŠ U]RU*Anunuwa kattešmi iyanta* [*nu?* GIŠ*m*]*a-a-ri-uš anda walḫanianda* [*nu?* SÌ]R-*RU* "The men of Anunuwa walk with them, strike the *m.*-spears together and sing" KBo 10.25 vi 14-16 (KI.LAM fest., OH/NS), translit. Singer, Diss. 358; cf. KBo 10.23 vi 2-8, translit. ibid. 314.

2′ in historical texts: "I conquered the town of Ḫaššuwa in one year" . . . *nu* m*Tawannagaš ma-a-ri-*⸢*in*⸣ *arḫa peššer* "they threw away (i.e., discarded ??) the *m.*-spear of Tawannaga" KBo 10.2 ii 45-47 (ann. of Ḫatt. I, NS) □ the Akk. version has only [*i?-n*]*a?* URU-*lim* URU*Taunaga* [. . .] KBo 10.1 i 46.

b. a weapon of gods — **1′** held in the right hand of a statue of dLAMMA, whose left hand holds a shield: dLAMMA ⸢ALAM LÚ⸣ GUB-*an* IGI-*ŠU* KÙ.GI GAR.⸢RA⸣ ZAG-*za* ŠU-*za ma-ri-in* KÙ.[BA]BBAR *ḫarzi* GÙB-*za* ŠU-⸢*za*⸣ *ARĪTUM ḫ*[*ar*]*zi* "dLAMMA, statue of a man standing; his eyes are plated with gold. He holds a silver *m.*-spear in (his) right hand; he holds a shield in (his) left hand. (He stands upon a stag)" KUB 38.2 ii 24-26 (descr. of deities, NH), ed. Bildbeschr, 8f., tr. Jakob-Rost, MIO 8:176f.

2′ in other contexts: GIŠ*ma-ri!-uš* KÙ.BABBAR GAR.RA KUB 42.100 iv 5 (cult inv.,

Tudḫ. IV), ed. del Monte, OA 17:184, 187; *nuwa* GIŠ*m*[*a*]-*a-ri*-[*i*]*n* KÙ.GI ⌜*ŠA* DINGIR-*LIM* *danzi*⌝ "They take the gold *m.*-spear of the deity KBo 14.21 ii 29 (oracle question, NH); cf. [GI]Š*ma-a-ri-uš* ME-*anzi* KBo 8.56:3; *nuza* SAL. LUGAL 1 GIŠ*ma-a-ri-in dāi nu* Ì.UDU GIŠ*ma-a-ri-ta-a*[*z*](coll.) *dāi* KUB 43.56 ii 15-17 (MH?/NS).

Both the *māri-* and the GIŠŠUKUR are weapons of the spear type. Of English words available (spear, pike, javelin, lance) we have avoided "lance", because it suggests a weapon used from horseback. There is no evidence from texts that either the *māri-* or the GIŠŠUKUR were hurled (javelin). Indeed, in texts, no evidence has been found which might point to the military use of either. A pike is a particularly long thrusting spear held with two hands. The word "spear", although it can denote a thrusting weapon, is the least specific of the available terms. Until concrete evidence is available we think it best to refer to these as "*māri*-spear" and "ŠUKUR-spear". One reading of GIŠŠUKUR was *turi-* (Sommer, ZA 46:24ff.; Laroche, OLZ 1959:276; Popko, Kultobjekte 103f.), but the complementation GIŠŠUKUR-*an* (acc. sg.) in Hittite Law 101 indicates another reading. The GIŠ*turi-* is once used figuratively "to thrust forth, expel" (*parā šuwai-*) the "portentous thing" (*kallar uttar*) (KBo 4.2 i 69-70). This could indicate that the *turi-* was used for thrusting or prodding, if the figure of speech in the ritual reflects the actual use of the weapon. In the idol description (usage b 1′) the god dLAMMA holds a *māri-* in his right hand and a shield in his left. For examples of standing gods in the attacking posture with shield in the left hand and spear (or javelin?) in the upraised right hand see Helga Seeden, The Standing Armed Figurines in the Levant, Prähistorische Bronzefunde, Abteilung I, Band I, München, 1980, plates 112-116. The weapons have been lost from the Dövlek statuette (Bittel, Die Hethiter, figure 149), but it probably held a shield in the left hand and a spear in the upraised right hand. Other artistic representations of gods and kings show them with a long spear in one hand but never a shield in the other: cf. Bittel, Die Hethiter, figures 182, 183, 185, 201, 202, 203, 207, 239. This longer spear might be the *turi-* or GIŠŠUKUR. Note especially the longer spear used in Bittel, figure 182, to fight a lion at close quarters without a shield; and compare with this the GIŠŠUKUR which the hunter Kešši takes when he sets out with his dogs to go lion hunting (KUB 33.121 ii 11).

Sommer, AU (1932) 381 ("eine Trutzwaffe"); Von Brandenstein, Bildbeschr. (1943) 41f. ("eine Angriffswaffe, etwa Lanze"); Alp, TTKYayin VI/23 (1983) 43 n. 49 ("Sichel- bzw. Krummschwert").

(NINDA)**mari-** n.; bread stick(?); from OH.†

(In lists, number and case uncertain): *ma-a-ri-e-eš* KBo 25.56 iv 8 (OS), NINDA*ma-a-ri-e-eš* KBo 21.1 ii 14, 15 (MS?), 1143/v (4), NINDA*ma-ri-e-eš* KBo 21.1 i 8, 10 (MS?), [NIN]DA*ma-ri-i-e-eš* Bo 4045 left col. 1, [NIND]A*ma-ri-i-iš* KBo 21.2 i 7 (MS?), *ma-ri-iš* KUB 40.102 i 13, *ma-ri-uš* 147/v:8.

2 NINDA*šēnuš* ZÍD.DA ZÍZ *ŠA* 2 *UPNI* 4 NINDA*ma-ri-e-eš* ZÍD.DA ZÍZ *ŠA* 3 *UPNI* 50 NINDA*šēnus* ZÍD.DA ZÍZ TUR-*TIM tarnaš* 50! NINDA*ma-ri-e-eš* ZÍD.DA ZÍZ TUR-*TIM tarnaš* 2-*ŠU* 9 NINDA UMBIN.ḪI.A ZÍD.DA ZÍZ TUR-*TIM ḫimmaš* "Two figurine pastries (made of) two handfulls (of) wheat flour, four bread sticks(?) of three handfulls (of) wheat flour, fifty small figurine pastries (made of) one *tarna*-measure (of) wheat flour, 40/50! small bread sticks(?) (made of) one *tarna*-measure (of) wheat flour, twice nine small wheel-shaped pastries of wheat flour (as) models" KBo 21.1 i 8-11 (rit., MS), tr. StBoT 22:63; for measurements see Del Monte, OA 19:219ff., cf. KBo 21.1 ii 14-16; "The king goes [in] before Tešub of Manuzzi" *nu* 15 *kappiša* [ŠÀ].BA 3 *kugullaš* 3 *kellu* [3 *z*]*am*-*muran* 3 *šēnan* 3 *ma-ri-iš* "15 *kappiša*, including 3 *kugulla*-pastries, 3 *kellu*-pastries, 3 *z.*-pastries, 3 figurine pastries, (and) 3 bread sticks(?) are made. (He presents them to the god)" KUB 40.102 i 10-14 (*ḫišuwaš* fest., NS); 1 BÁN Ì.NUN *ma-ri-uš ḫul*[*i-* . . .] 147/v:8 (rit.).

In view of the Hittite practice of naming breads and pastries by objects of similar appearance, the *mari*-pastry might be a bread stick in the form of a spear. Its regular association with NINDA*šena-* "figurine pastry" and the occurrence of the word *ḫimma-* "model" in KBo 21.1 seem to confirm this.

Hoffner, AlHeth. 171.

Cf. *mari-* n.

TU7mari- n.; (a soup).†

kar-aš TU7*ma-a-ri*[(-) . . .] KBo 10.37 ii 50.

In that this follows *kar-aš*, it appears to be something to eat; perhaps this is a soup containing NINDA*mari-* q.v.

marri adv.; **1.** in the heat of emotion or passion(?), rashly(?), impetuously(?), **2.** (in *mekki marri*) exceedingly; NH.†

mar-ri (passim), *mar-ri-i* KUB 23.91:33.

1. in the heat of emotion or passion(?), rashly(?), impetuously(?): *nuza apūnna AŠŠUM* DAM-*UTTIM mar-ri UL daḫḫun IŠTU* INIM DINGIR-*LIM-zan daḫḫun* DINGIR-*LIM-anmu* Ù-*it ḫenkta* "I did not take her (Puduḫepa) in marriage in the heat of passion(?)/rashly(?). I took her at the command of the goddess. The goddess assigned her to me in a dream." KBo 6.29 i 18-21 (Ḫatt. III), ed. Ḫatt. 46f. ("aufs Geratewohl"); *mar-ri-ma-w*[(*atakkan UL kunanzi*)] "they will not kill you in the heat of emotion(?)/rashly(?)" KUB 8.79 rev. 18, with dupl. KUB 26.92:4 (letter, NH); [. . . *ANA*] dUTU-*ŠI* EN-*YA UL mar-ri ar-kuwa*[*r iyanun nu kūn*] ⌈INIM⌉-*an ANA* dUTU-*ŠI* EN-[*Y*]*A UL mar-ri AŠ*(coll.)[*PUR-un*] / [*UL mar-ri mema*]*ḫḫ*[*i*] *UL mar-ri ḫatreškimi* "I did not reply rashly(?) to Your Majesty, my lord. [And this] word I did not wr[ite] rashly(?) to Your Majesty, my lord. I do[n't speak rashly(?)]; I don't write rashly(?)." KUB 40.1 rev.! 1-3 (letter to the king, NH); [*k*]*ūn* INIM-*a*[*n ANA*] ⌈dUTU⌉-*ŠI UL mar-ri AŠPUR-un* "I didn't write this word to Your Majesty rashly(?)" ibid. left edge, left register 5.; *mān tūliyaš pedi mar-r*[*i*! . . .] "If in the place of assembly [someone speaks(?)] rashly(?)" KUB 33.110:5 (Ḫedammu, NH), ed. StBoT 14:48f. ("in eigenem Interesse"); restored freely by Sturtevant (Chrest. 158) in KUB 13.4 iii 36 [*mar-r*]*i i*[*šḫ*]*altuḫmeyanza*.

2. in the phrase *mekki marri* "exceedingly, very much": *nuza paḫḫūenaš uddanī mekkipat mar-ri paḫḫaššanuant*[*eš*] *ēšten* "Be exceedingly watchful in the matter of the fire" KUB 13.4 iii 54 (instr., pre-NH/NS), ed. Chrest. 160f.; *nu* É.MEŠ DINGIR.MEŠ *mekki mar-ri paḫḫašten nušmaš tešḫaš lē ēšzi* "Guard the temples very carefully. Don't fall asleep." ibid. iii 17-18, ed. Chrest. 156-59; *nuza ANA* INIM DINGIR-*LIM* [*me*]*kki mar-ri naḫḫ*[*ant*]*eš ēšten* "Be extremely mindful (lit., afraid) in a matter pertaining to a god" ibid. i 38, ed. Chrest. 148-49; contrast *mekki naḫḫanteš ēšten* (ibid. ii 24, 29, iii 44, 57), *mekki paḫḫaššanuwanteš ēšten* (ii 74), *mekki paḫḫašten* (iii 45); *nu* GUD-*uš* ⌈*mekki*⌉ *mar-*⌈*ri*⌉ SIG5-*t*[*at*] "The cow did exceedingly well" KUB 24.7 ii 52 (cow and fisherman story, NH), ed. Friedrich, ZA 49:224f., cf. Hoffner, FsLacheman 191; cf. *lazziya-* 3b.

If the heat of emotion, passion or anger is indicated by this adv., one might compare the verb *marra-* "to melt" and the noun *marra/i-* "daylight(?)", "heat-of-day".

Friedrich, ZA 36 (1925) 53 n. 1 ("von mir aus, nach eigenem Ermessen"); Götze, Ḫatt. (1925) 47 n. 19 ("aufs Geratewohl"), 140 ("eigenmächtig, auf eigene Faust", *mekki marri* "gar sehr"); idem, OLZ 1930:290 ("sehr"); Sommer, AU (1932) 188f. ("von sich aus, um seiner selbst willen").

Cf. *marra-* v.

marri A n., sg. loc.; daylight(?), sunlight(?), heat-of-day(?), heat(??); written syll. and Akk. *ṢĒTU*; NH.†

sg. loc. *mar-ri* KBo 15.2 rev. iv 7.

In the ritual for the substitute king: *parā-ma-aš-kan UL iya*[(*ttari manqa ṢE-TUM* x) . . .] / É-*ri kattanta peššiy*[*a-* . . . (*naškan*)] / *mar-ri* IGI-*anda* (var. *ANA ṢE-TI menaḫ-ḫanda*) *UL t*[*iyazi*?] "He doesn't go out at all. Daylight(?) [. . .] throws down [. . .] in the house. He does not step toward the daylight(?)" KBo 15.2 iv 5-7 with parallel KUB 17.31: 7-8, ed. Kümmel, StBoT 3:60f., 90. Possibly also in *uwat* IZI-*it mar*[*-ri-it*?] / x-*it paḫšanuwan ēš*[*du*?] (or *ēš*[*ten*??]) KBo 5.11 obv. i 23-24 rt. col.

Kümmel (loc. cit.) interpreted *ṢI-TUM* and *ṢI-TI* as Akk. *ṣītu*, which he translated

"Ausgang". As Kümmel realized, it is impossible to translate Akk. *ṣītu* as 'rising of the sun' without explicit mention of the sun. Interpreting the word as Akk. *ṣētu* 'light' also gives a possible sense (cf. Riemschneider, OrNS 40:477) and allows one to connect the Hittite counterpart with the verb *marra-*, *marriye-* "to melt" and the adverb *marri* "rashly(?), heatedly(??)".

Cf. *marri-* B.

marri- B n. (com.); (mng. unknown); NH.†

(Sum.) [o - o-]pap? = (Akk.) *i-ši-it-tù* (var. *i-še-et-tù*) = (Hitt.) *mar-ri-iš* KBo 1.44 + KBo 13.1 iv 14, with dupl. KBo 26.23:3, ed. StBoT 7:19 with n. 3, 22 (comments), MSL 17 Erim-ḫuš Bogh. A.

Regardless of the correct reading of the Sum. and Akk. columns, it is unclear how the Hittite scribe understood (and therefore translated) the ambiguously spelled Akkadian word. Possibilities, noted already by von Soden, StBoT 7:22, are: *išittu* "treasury, storehouse, granary", *išittu* "base, foundation", *isītu/esittu* "pestle", *ešītu* "confusion".

Otten and Von Soden, StBoT 7 (1968) 22; Riemschneider, OrNS 40 (1971) 477 (considers confusion with Akk. *ṣētu* "daylight", cf. *marri-* A).

marri-, marriya- v. see *marra-* v.

mariyani n. (sg. loc.); (a kind of field); OH?/NS.†

n⸢*uš*⸣ A.ŠÀ *ma-r*[*i-ia-ni-i*] *pētummēni nuš apiya ḫar*[*iyaweni*] "We will transport them (evil tongues) to a *m.*-field and bury them there. (And let them vanish from the sight of the gods.)" KBo 10.37 ii 10-12 (rit., OH?/NS); *k*[*āša* ḪUL-*la*]*muš* EME.MEŠ A.ŠÀ *ma-ri-*⸢*ia*⸣*-ni-i šuḫḫ*[*ā*]*i* "He is pouring the evil tongues on the *m.*-field" KBo 10.37 iii 21, cf. iv 24; pouring the contents of the *paddur* on the *m.*-field in iii 16-17.

All attested forms of this word seem to be dative-locatives. On the plene writing of allatives and locatives cf. Hoffner, JAOS 102:507-509. The language of KBo 10.37 has been modernized by the NS scribe. But it is still possible to see traces of its OH archetype in the sentence particle -(*a*)*pa* (i 34 etc.), enclitic possessive pronouns -*ši-* and -*šmi-* (i 25, 27, ii 17 etc.), nominal sentence with 2nd sg. subject without -*za* (iii 42), consistent -*uš* "them" (ii 11, iii 33, 37, iv 49).

(GIŠ)mariyawanna- n. neut.; (an architectural feature); MH/NS.†

sg. nom.-acc. *ma-ri-ia-wa-an-na* KUB 31.84 ii 3 (MH/NS), GIŠ*ma-ar-ia-wa-an-na* KUB 31.86 ii 3 (MH/NS); **inst.** *ma-ri-ia-wa-an-ni-it* KUB 31.84 ii 2, GIŠ*ma-ri-ia-wa-an-ni-it* KUB 31.86 ii 2 + KUB 48.104:11 (MH/NS); broken: GIŠ*m*[*a-* . . .] KUB 31.87 ii 8.

[. . .-*y*(*aš* AN.ZA.GÀR (over eras.) *šer arḫa*) o *gipeššar ēštu kattan*] *ar*!(text *pal*)-*ḫa-ma-aš* 6? (var. *katta*]*n*? *arḫayaš* 3) [(*g*)]*ipe*[(*ššar*)] *ēštu nammaš* [GI]Š*ḫeyawallit ma-ri-ia-wa-an-ni-it* (var. adds det. GIŠ) *anda waḫnuwanza ēštu ma-ri-ia-wa-an-na-ma-kán* (var. GIŠ*ma-ar-ia-wa-an-na-ma-*⸢*kán*⸣) *piran arḫa* 6 *gipeššar ē*[*št*]*u* (var. *ēšdu*) *parāmatkan* 5 *šekan uwan ēštu* "Let the tower of . . . be x *g.*'s around the top, but around the bottom let it be 6 (var. 3) *g.*'s (= 3 or 1.5 m.); and let it be encircled by a gutter and a *m.* Let the *m.* out in front (or: around the front?) be 6 *g.* (= 3 m.), but let it protrude(?) 5 *šekan*" KUB 31.84 ii 1-4 (*BĒL MADGALTI* instr., MH/NS) with dupl. KUB 48.104:10-12 + KUB 31.86 ii 1-5, ed. Dienstanw. 42 (without KUB 48.104), cf. Hoffner, BiOr 38 (1981) 651.

(SÍG)mariḫši-, :mariḫši-, SÍGmarḫaši-, SÍGmaršiḫ[. . .]- n. (com.); fuzz(?), loose threads(?), lint(?) (something of wool which adheres to linen or wool cloth); MH.†

sg.acc. SÍG*ma-ri-iḫ-ši-in* KUB 27.67 ii 27, iii 32, i (27) (MH/NS), :*ma-ri-iḫ-ši-in* KBo 13.109 ii 8 (MH/NS); **pl. nom.** *ma-ri!-iḫ-še-eš* KUB 15.42 ii 8 (MH/NS), KUB 43.58 ii (20) (MH/MS dupl. of preceeding); **broken:** SÍG*mar-ši-i*[*ḫ*?- . . .] HT 44 obv. 5, SÍG*mar-ḫa-š*[*i-*. . .] KUB 7.16 rev. 13 (NS).

(He takes a SÍG*ali-*, holds it out to the gods, and says:) *kāš* SÍG*ališ maḫḫan parkuiš nuššikan ma-ri!-iḫ-še-eš anda* NU.GÁL "As this *a.* is clean, having no *m.* in it, (you gods be likewise free (lit. pure) of evil words, oaths, curses, bloodshed, etc.)" KUB 15.42 ii 8-9 (rit., MH/NS), with dupl. KUB 43.58 ii 19-20 (MS); [*nu nam*]*ma* GAD-*an QĀTAMMA iyazi nu memai* [*kīm*]*a* GAD-*an maḫḫan* LÚ.MEŠTÚG *tannaran* [*aniy*]*anzi nuš-šikan* SÍG*ma-ri-iḫ-ši-in* [*arḫa*] *parkunuwanzi nat* *ḫarkišzi* "Further he treats a piece of linen in the same manner and says: As the cloth-finishers (fullers, etc.) make this linen plain (i.e., remove foreign matter), and remove the *m.* from it, so that it becomes white" KUB 27.67 ii 25-28 (rit., MH/MS); cf. ibid. i 25ff., iii 30ff.; GAD GIM-*an* LÚ.MEŠŠÀ.TAM *tannarantan* KIN-*zi nuššikan* :*ma-ri-iḫ-ši-in arḫa parku*<*n*>*uzzi nat ḫarkiēšzi* "As the chamberlains (LÚ.MEŠŠÀ.TAM) make the linen plain and remove the *m.* from it, so that it becomes white" KBo 13.109 ii 6-9 (same rit., MH/NS).

The LÚ.MEŠTÚG are usually thought to be fullers. The situation reflected in the KUB 27.67 passages might be the cleaning of linen prior to dyeing. The "chamberlains" in KBo 13.109 may function as overseers of the closets and storerooms, where items not in use (including clothing) are kept. Clothing must be cleaned before it is put away. Whatever impurities attach to clothes and keep them from looking *ḫarki-* "white" could be meant. The determinative SÍG "hair, wool" suggests "fuzz" or "lint". The word may be Luwian, as suggested by the gloss marker in KBo 13.109 ii 8. Cf. Luwian *ma-ra-aḫ-ši-wa-li-iš* KUB 25.39 iv 5 and DLL 68 (*mar(a)ḫši-* "sorte de laine").

Goetze in ANET 348 tr. KUB 27.67 ii 27 ("tufts"); Friedrich, HW 136 ("unreiner Bestandteil der Wolle(?)").

mārīš[. . .] n. neut.; (mng. unkn.).†

IGI.ḪI.A-*wakan Ú-U*[*L* . . .] / ⌈KA⌉[×U?]-*azkan* [. . .] / *idālu iššall*[*i* . . .] / *idālu ma-a-ri-i-i*[*š*- . . .] "Eyes n[ot . . .] From the mou[th(?) . . .] evil saliva [. . .] evil *m.* [. . .]" KBo 21.6 rev. 3-6 (rit., NS) □ KA[×U] was read in preference to KA[×ME] (= EME) because of *iššalli* in the following line.

marišḫi- Hurr. adj.; (mng. unkn.) NH.†

sg. *ma-re-eš-ḫi* KBo 20.126 ii 17, (19), *ma-ri-*⌈*iš-ḫi*⌉ KUB 45.81:11; **Hurr. pl. with anaphoric suffix** *-na ma-a-ri-iš-ḫi-n*[*a*] KUB 27.1 iii 3, ⌈*ma-ri-iš-ḫi*⌉*-i-na* KUB 27.1 ii 33 with dupl. *ma-r*[*i-* KUB 27.3 rt. col. 15, *ma-ri-iš-ḫa-n*[*a*] KBo 11.20 rt. col. 6.

1 NINDA.SIG *ma-a-ri-iš-ḫi-n*[*a*] DINGIR.MEŠ-*na* . . . TUŠ-*aš* KI.MIN (=*paršiya*) "Seated, he breaks one flat bread for the *m.*-gods . . ." KUB 27.1 iii 3-5 (fest. for Šauška of Šamuḫa), cf. ibid. ii 33-35; DINGIR.MEŠ-*na ma-ri-iš-ḫa-n*[*a*? . . .] KBo 11.20 rt. col. 6.

Laroche, GLH 168; Lebrun, Samuha (1976) 103.

GIŠ**mārit-** see (GIŠ)*māri-*, GIŠ*mārit-*.

mark- v.; **1.** to divide, separate, unravel, disentangle (yarn), **2.** to divide up, distribute, apportion (food and drink), **3.** to cut up, butcher (animals, i.e., their carcasses); from OH.

pres. sg. 1 *ma-a-ar-ka-aḫ-ḫi* KBo 17.3 iv 30 with dupl. KBo 17.1 iv (35) (both OS); **pres. sg. 3** *mar-ak-zi* KBo 8.77 obv. 4, KBo 15.25 rev. (13), Bo 6870 obv.? ii 5 (note HGG); **pl. 2** *mar-ak-te-ni* KUB 13.3 iv 25, 32, (39) (MH?/NS); **pl. 3** *mar-kán-zi* KUB 15.32 ii 22 (MH/NS), KUB 43.56 iii 15, 16, VBoT 24 ii 42 (both pre-NH/NS).

pret. sg. 3 *ma-ra-ak-ta* KBo 3.34 i 6, 10, ii 13 (OH/NS); **pret. pl. 3** *mar-ki-ir* KUB 33.114 iv 14 (NH), *mar-ke-e-*[*er*?] KUB 33.114 iv 15.

part. sg. nom. com. *mar-kán-za* VBoT 128 ii 9, Bo 1813 rt. col. 4 (Haas, KN 312); **sg. acc. com.** *mar-kán-ta-an* KBo 15.31 i 4!, 8, KUB 17.23 ii (25), *mar-kán-da-an* KUB 51.50 iii? 19; **sg. neut.** *mar-kán* KUB 13.5 ii 19 (pre-NH/NS); **inf.** *mar-ku-an-zi* 670/z. left col. 7 (StBoT 5:115 n. 8); **iter. supine** *mar-ki-iš-ki-u-wa-an* KUB 13.3 iv 23 (note that the iter. of *markiya-* is written similarly).

1. to divide, separate, unravel, disentangle (yarn): *gapinan kalulupizmit ḫaḫḫallit ma-a-ar-ka-aḫ-ḫi* "I separate the yarn from their fingers (*kalulupit*⸗*šmit*) with the *ḫ.*" KBo 17.3 iv 30 (rit., OS), w. dupl. KBo 17.1 iv 35 (OS), ed. StBoT 8:38f. □ the tr. "from their fingers" is based on the context (cf. KBo 17.3 iv 23-29); ablatival use of the instrumental case occurs in OH/NS: KBo 10.2 iii 18-19, cf. Melchert, Diss. 254f.; our ex. and KBo 17.3 i 14 (for which see Melchert, Diss. 166-68) provide OS exx.

2. to divide up, distribute, apportion (food and drink): URU[o o o -*u*]*kkima* NINDA.ERÍN.MEŠ *marnuanna ma-ra-ak-ta* . . . URU*Ḫa*[(*ttu*⸗*šima* ERÍN.MEŠ-*aš walḫi*)] *ma-ra-ak-ta* "In GN he distributed 'troops bread' and *marnuwa*-drink . . . but in Ḫattuša he distributed *walḫi*-drink to(?) the troops" KBo 3.34 i 5-6, 9-10 (anecdotes, OH/NS), restored from dupl. KUB 36.104 obv. 3-4, 7 (OS); *nuza* ZÍD.DA *mar-ak-zi* Bo 6870 obv.? ii 5, 22, rev.(?) 10 (translit. HGG).

3. to cut up, butcher (animals, i.e. their carcasses) — **a.** grammatical object is the entire carcass (or at least torso) — **1′** of an ox or sheep:

"(If you take away from the god a fattened ox or fattened sheep)" [(*šumaš⸗ma⸗z kui*)*n*] *mak⸗landan mar-kán ḫarteni* "and (you substitute) the emaciated one which you have (already) butchered for yourselves (*šumaš⸗ma⸗z*)" KUB 13.5 ii 19 (instr., pre-NH/NS), with dupls. KUB 13.4 ii 7, KUB 13.6 ii 2, ed. Chrest. 152.

2′ of a goat: MÁŠ.GAL-*makan ḫumandan mar-kán-z*[*i*] "They butcher an entire goat" VBoT 24 ii 42 (rit., MH/NS), ed. Chrest. 112f.; MÁŠ.GA[L-*ya*]*kan ḫūmantan pittalwan mar-kán-zi* "They butcher the entire goat 'plain'" HT 1 i 48 (rit.), translit. LTU 15; cf. KBo 15.31 i 4, 8, KBo 21.5:8.

3′ of a sheep: *maḫḫanmakan* UDU *arkuwanzi zinnanzi nu* ^{UZU}NÍG.GIG ^{UZU}ŠÀ *ḫappinit zanu⸗wanzi* UDU-*makan ḫūmandan mar-kán-zi* "When they finish gutting (i.e., removing the organs of) the sheep, they cook the intestines and heart with fire, but the entire sheep (torso) they butcher" KBo 19.142 ii 20-22 (fest. for Ištar of Mt. Amana); *našta* UDU.ḪI.A ≪SAL≫ *mar-kán-zi* "They butcher the sheep" KBo 5.1 i 28 (rit. of Papanikri, NH), ed. Pap. 4f.; cf. ibid. 35; KUB 10.63 i 27-28, KBo 15.25 rev. (13), KBo 23.95 obv. 1; KUB 32.123 iii 54, Bo 1813 rt. col. 4 (Haas, KN 312).

4′ of a *kakkapa*-animal: ^{URU}*Kuzurūi kaqqapuš ma-ra-ak-ta* "In Kuzuruwa he butchered *kak⸗kapa*-animals" KBo 3.34 ii 12f. (anecdotes, OH/NS), w. dupl. KBo 3.36:19, Singer, Diss. 244 tr. "distributed partridges".

5′ of a lamb: *nukan maḫḫan* $SILA_4$ BAL-*anti nammankan wappui katta ḫattai nu ēšḫar taknī katta tarnai* $SILA_4$-*makan arkanzi nammakan* $SILA_4$ *ḫūmandan pittalwandan mar-kán-zi* "When he offers a lamb, he slits it('s throat) down at the riverbank, and lets (its) blood (spill) on the ground; they gut the lamb, and they butcher the entire lamb('s torso) 'plain'" KBo 11.17 ii 12-18 (rit., NH); *našta* $SILA_4$ *pittalwan mar-kán-zi* "They butcher the lamb 'plain' KUB 17.23 ii 20 (rit., NS), cf. ibid. 25 □ for *pittalwant-* cf. the remarks at the end of this article; VBoT 128 ii 9, KUB 15.32 ii 22.

6′ of a dog: [*n*]*ammakan* UR.TUR *mar-k*[*án-zi*?] KUB 9.7 ii 3 (rit., NS), translit. LTU 79.

7′ of a pig: (They kill a pig and place thin breads with its blood) ŠAḪ-*ma ēššanzi* [*n*]*ankan pittalwan mar-kán-zi* "But the pig they 'treat' (= skin and gut?) and butcher it 'plain'" KUB 43.56 iii 14-15 (rit., MH?/NS), cf. ibid. 6.

b. grammatical objs. are the cuts of meat produced: (They immolate a goat, fill a cup with its raw intestines, mix its blood and fat with BA.BA.ZA and make ^{NINDA}*iduriš*. They cook its heart.) ^{UZU}GAB-*ma*[*kan*] ^{UZU}*wallaš ḫaštai* ^{UZU}*QATU-ya mar-kán-z*[*i*] "But they cut the brisket, shank (and) fore-quarter" KUB 32.128 ii 25-26 (EZEN *ḫišuwaš*. MH/NS), with dupl. KBo 15.49 i 12; possibly also KUB 13.3 iv 23 and KUB 33.114 iv 13-15.

Within the slaughtering and butchering terminology *mark-* occupies the following position: the initial act of extinguishing life is expressed with either *ḫuek-* "to slaughter", *šipand-* "to offer, sacrifice, immolate", or *ḫattai-* "to strike, cut, slit (throat)". After the blood is drawn off, the carcass is skinned and gutted and some of the extremities removed (the verb *ark-* seems to cover this entire process), cf. KBo 11.17 ii 16. Once (KUB 43.56 iii 4), the verb *ešša-* describes a step between draining the blood and butchering (*mark-*). The rest of the carcass, which constitutes a bare (*pittalwant-*, lit. 'plain', 'without skin and guts') torso can be cooked whole or butchered (KBo 11.17 ii 17). This cutting up of the torso into its component meat cuts (brisket, shank, loin, etc.) seems to be expressed by *mark-*. See especially the passages translated in 3 a 3′, 5′, and 3 b. [. . . *Q*]*ADU* SAG.DU.MEŠ GÌR. MEŠ *mar-kán*[-*zi*] (KBo 21.5:8) indicates that in this case the carcasses to be butchered (*mark-*) still possessed extremities. One could, therefore, butcher (*mark-*) a carcass without that carcass having been subjected to the action *ark-*. Thus we cannot agree with Kammenhuber (HW^2 300b) when she claims without reference to the slaughtering terminology that *ark-* means "tranchieren" ("carve up").

Sommer-Ehelolf, Pap. (1924) 20 ("(Opfertier) zerlegen", mng. 3); Kammenhuber, OLZ 1954:231 ("(Speisen oder Getranke) verteilen", mng. 2); Otten, StBot 8:39 (1969) ("(Faden) zerteilen", mng. 1); Ardzinba, Ritualy (1982) 62 ("sveževat'", i.e., Eng. "to skin").

markiya- v.; **1.** (act., w. *-za*) to disapprove of, object to, reject, refuse, find objectionable, unacceptable, find fault with, impugn(?), repudiate, (mid., without-*za*) to be rejected, objectionable, unacceptable, **2.** to forbid (act., without *-za*); from OH/NS.

act. pres. sg. 1 *mar-ki-ia-mi* KUB 26.1 iv 24, KBo 4.14 iii 3 (both NH); **sg. 2** *mar-ki-ia-ši* KUB 21.38 i 9 (Pud.), KBo 18.48 rev. (20) (NH), KUB 50.89 iii (5) (NH), *mar-ki-ši* KUB 21.38 ii 4 (Pud.); **sg. 3** *mar-ki-ia-zi* KBo 2.4 left edge 3, KUB 36.35 i (17) (both NH).

act. pret. sg. 2 *mar-ki-ia-at* KUB 5.6 i 9 (NH), KUB 21.38 ii 10 (Ḫatt. III, might be sg. 3); **sg. 3** *mar-ki-ia-at* KUB 31.66 ii 18 (Ḫatt. III?).

mid. pres. pl. 3 *[mar]-ki-ia-an-ta-ri* KUB 5.7 obv. 13 (uncertain but so StBoT 5:113 n. 2); **mid. pret. pl. 3** *mar-ki-ia-an-da-at* KUB 5.7 obv. 5 (NH); **imp. sg. 3** *[m]ar?-ki-ia-ru* KBo 3.34 ii 41 (OH/NS).

verbal subst. *mar-ki-ia-u-wa-ar* KBo 26.10 iv 8, KBo 26.11 rev. 6 (dupl. of preceding), KUB 26.8 ii 10 (all NH).

part. sg. nom. com. *mar-ki-an-za* KUB 5.1 iii 93; **sg. neut.** *mar-ki-ia-an* KBo 16.98 iii 9, (7), KUB 16.65 i 3, KUB 22.61 i (26) (all NH).

iter. pres. pl. 3 *mar-ki-iš-kán-z[i]* KUB 31.66 ii 26 (NH).

iter. inf. *mar-kiš-ki-wa-an-zi* KUB 40.1 rev! 25 (NH).

mar-ki-ia-u-wa-ar with Sum. and Akk. cols. broken KBo 26.10 iv 8 (Diri Bogh., NH), w. dupl. KBo 26.11 rev. 6.

1. to disapprove of, object to, reject, refuse, find objectionable, unacceptable, find fault with, impugn(?) — **a.** (act., with *-za*) — **1′** contrasted with *malai-* "to approve of" in the same context: see treatments of KUB 21.38 obv. 9, rev. 4, KUB 40.1 rev.! 25, KBo 2.4 left edge 3 sub *malai-* a 1′.

2′ without *malai-*, twice opp. *šanḫ-*: [(^{d}*Aš-erdu*)]*šwaza tuk* LÚ-*UTKA mar-ki-ia-[zi]* "A. is impugning(?) your manhood(?)" KUB 36.35 i 17 (Elkunirša, NH), rest. from dupl. KUB 36.34 i 7, ed. Otten, MIO 1:126f., tr. ANET 519, cf. Hoffner, RHA XXIII/76:8 w. n. 19; (Shouldn't I have communicated to my brother the word which I heard?) *kinunmamuza* ŠEŠ-*YA kuit mar-ki-ia-at [na]t UL namma iyami* "But now that my brother has (or: that you, my brother, have) expressed disapproval to me, I won't do it again" KUB 21.38 rev. 10-11 (Pud. letter), eds. Helck, JCS 17 (1963) 93 ("missbilligt hat"), Stefanini, AttiAccTosc. 29 (1964) 16 ("mi ha/hai respinto/rinfacciato"), 49 ("ha/hai obiettato"); *išḫiūllaza ŠA* ^{f}*Mizzulla iwar ma[r-k]i-ia-at nu išḫiūl ŠA* ^{URU}*Aštata šanḫta* "Have you (O god) rejected the prescribed (ritual) procedure in the manner of M. and preferred (lit. sought) the procedure of A.?" KUB 5.6 i 8-9 (oracle question, NH), cf. tr. in AU 276 ("hast . . . abgelehnt"); *ABUYA-muza piran UL kuiški mar-ki-ia-at . . . kuwatwaduza attašti[n . . .] piran mar-ki-iš-kán-z[i]* "No one found fault with my father in my presence . . . Why are they continually finding fault with your father in your presence?" KUB 31.66 ii 18, 25-26 (prayer, Ḫatt. III); *iwar* ^{m}*Temetti taparriaš IŠTU* DINGIR-*LIM mar-⌜ki⌝-an-za* NU.SIG$_5$-*du* "(If) command in the manner of T. is unacceptable to the deity, let it (i.e., the oracle) be unfavorable" KUB 5.1 iii 93 (Ḫatt. III), ed. THeth 4:80-81 ("abgelehnt") □ contrast the widespread use in oracle questions of *malan ḫarti* "(if) you (O deity) have approved" cf. sub *malai-* b; "Concerning what I have said: ' . . . '" *nuza uttar kuwatqa kuitki mar-ki-ia-mi* "Would I for any reason repudiate any word?" KBo 4.14 iii 1-3 (treaty, Šupp. II), Stefanini, AANL 20:44 ("rifiuterò"); DINGIR-*LUM-za . . . mar-ki-ia-an ḫarti* "If you, O deity, have found unacceptable (or: have disapproved of) . . ." KUB 16.65 i 2-3, KBo 24.126 obv. 18, (oracle questions, NH); cf. KBo 16.98 iii 7, 9, KUB 22.61 i 26; *mānza* DINGIR-*LUM* ALAM SAL-*TI mar-ki-ya-[ši]* DINGIR-*LUM* ALAM LÚ-*pat šan-ḫeškiši* ALAM SAL-*TI*-⌜*ma*⌝ *UL šanḫti nu* SU.MEŠ SIG$_5$-*ru* "If you, O god, are refusing the statue of a woman; (if) you, O god, are seeking the statue of a man, but you do not seek the statue of a woman, let the flesh(-oracle) be favorable" KUB 50.89 iii 5-7; *[arḫ]a mar-k[i?- . . .]* KUB 36.13 i 6 (Ullik. II B_2 i 6), ed. Güterbock, JCS 6:8-9 ("[I] refu[se(d) . . .]") in context following refusal of food, the broken context makes it impossible to determine whether *-za* was present.

b. to be rejected, objectionable, unacceptable (mid.; without *-za*): (We asked them again, and they said:) [NINDA.KUR$_4$.R]A UD-*MI-wa mar-ki-ia-an-da-at* "The daily bread (offerings) were unacceptable" KUB 5.7 obv. 5 (oracle questions, NH), tr. ANET 497 ("The daily [ration of] sacrificial loaves spoiled"), cf. Neu, StBoT 5.113 ("wurden unterlassen"); [. . .]^{m}*Kuḫšeš [ma]r-ki-ia-ru* "Let K. be rejected" KBo 3.34 ii 41 (anecdotes, OH/NS).

2. to forbid (act., without *-za*): *našmakan uttar [(kuedani)k]ki mar-ki-ia-mi* "Or if I forbid a thing to someone, (and I say to him: Don't ever (*kuwapikki*) do it again" KUB 26.1 iv 23-24 (instr. for eunuchs, NH), with dupl. KUB 26.8 iv 10, ed. Dienstanw. 16; "verbieten" suggested by Güterbock in Friedrich, HW s.v.

The presence or absence of *-za* makes an appreciable difference in the translation required for this verb. The same is true of the antonym *malai-* q.v.

Forrer, Forsch. I/2 (1929) 179 ("ablehnen"); Sommer, AU (1932) 161 ("abweisen" as antonym to *malai-*); Friedrich, OLZ 1936:308 ("missbilligen"); Goetze, JCS 13 (1959) 66 ("object, disapprove" as antonyms to *malai-* "approve"); Hoffner, RHA XXIII/76 (1965) 8 with n. 19 (in Elkuniršа text "impugn, insult").

[markišt-] HW 137; read *markišda*(coll.)*uwaš* in KUB 5.3 i 47 and see *markišta(i)-*.

markištaḫḫ- v.; to take (someone) by surprise(?), make a surprise attack on(?); NH.†

pret. sg. 1 *mar-⸢ki-iš-ta-aḫ⸣-ḫu-un* KBo 14.19 ii 24 (coll.); **pl. 3** *mar-ki-iš-ta-aḫ-ḫi-⸢ir⸣* KBo 26.121 ii 9; **broken**: *mar-kiš-ta-aḫ[-zi?]* KUB 26.52:5.

[namma?] INA KUR ^{ÍD}*Daḫar[a] mar-⸢ki-iš-ta⸣-aḫ-ḫu-un* (coll.) "[Thereafter(?)] I made a surprise attack(?) on the Daḫara River Land" KBo 14.19 ii 24 (annals of Murš. II),ed. Houwink ten Cate, JNES 25:175, 182, 189, utilizing HGG coll. ("I penetrated unobserved"); [o o *m]ān mar-kiš-ta-aḫ[-zi? ku⸗iški?]* / *[nu ap]āt AŠRU šalli pē[dan]* / *mān araḫzenaš* [. . .] / *mānaš antūriyaš an[tuḫšaš(?)]* / *ammukmašši UL* ÌR-*aḫ[ḫari(?)]* "[Furthermore(?)] if [someone(?)] makes a surprise attack(?), [and th]at place is the Great Pl[ace], whether he is a foreigner or a native per[son], I [will(?)] not ser[ve] him, [. . .]" KUB 26.52:5-9 (treaty frag., NH) □ for *šalli pedan* in the sense of Hittite royal domain see Ḫatt. iv 65; *[kiš]an lē memai [apē⸗wa⸗mu* . . .] *mar-ki-iš-ta-aḫ-ḫi-⸢ir⸣* "Let him not speak thus: They took [me] by surprise" KBo 26.121 ii 8-9 (myth frag., NH).

Götze, AM 239 ("dahinschwinden"); Houwink ten Cate, JNES 25 (1966) 182, 189 ("slip into, penetrate unobserved"; based on KBo 14.19).

Cf. *markišta(i)-*.

markišta(i)- v.; to take someone unawares(?)/ by surprise(?); NS.†

pres. sg. 3 *mar-ki-iš-ta-iz-zi* KUB 40.82 rev. 4 (NH), *ma-ar-ki-iš-da-a-iz-z[i!]* KUB 28.70 rev. 12.

verbal subst. gen. *mar-ki-iš-ta-u-wa-aš* KUB 9.4 iii 41, *mar-kiš-da-u-wa-aš* KUB 5.3 i 47 (coll.), *[ma]r-ke-eš-ta-u-wa-aš* KBo 13.99 obv. 8 (all NH), *[mar-ki-iš-ta-u]-⸢wa⸣-aš* KBo 17.54 i 13 (pre-NH/NS), *[mar-ki]-iš-da-u-wa*<*-aš*> KUB 9.34 i 25 (NH).

a. action of a deceiver: *[kui]škan NĪ[Š* DINGIR-*LIM šarratta*(?) . . . *n]u maršātar iyazi* [. . .] *aššu memiškiz[zi* . . .] *nu mar-ki-iš-ta-iz-zi n[u* . . .] *nan NĪŠ* DINGIR-*LIM appa[ndu]* "Whoever [transgresses(?)] an o[ath, . . .] and he practices deceit, [. . .] he always speaks well [of . . .], but he takes by surprise(?) [and . . .], let the oath deities seize him!" KUB 40.82 rev. 1-5 (protocol or treaty frag., NS).

b. action of a plague or disease: (In an enumeration of evils to be magically removed:) *mar-ki-iš-ta-u-wa-aš ḫinkan* <KI.MIN> (= *mū⸗daiddu*, cf. line 36) "Let it remove the death (plague?) which catches/takes one unawares(?)" KUB 9.4 iii 41-42 (Old Woman rit., NH), ed. Haas-Wilhelm, AOATS 3:56 with n. 1; also in KUB 9.34 i 25, KBo 17.54 i (13); (If a natural death [will come] on some of(?) ten or twenty men, and a general plague will not break out up in Ḫattuša,) ^{URU}KÙ.BABBAR-*zanaškan* GAM *pankuš mar-kiš-da-u-wa-aš* ÚŠ-*aš UL watkunuzzi* "and a general sudden death ("death which takes one unawares") will not make us flee down out of Ḫattuša, (then let the lot oracle be favorable)" KUB 5.3 i 47-48 (oracle question, NH), reading *markišdauwaš* from coll. in KUB 18.52, see comments on this passage in Götze, AM 239 ("dahinschwinden"), Haas-Wilhelm AOATS 3:56 (*markiš⸗tauwaš ḫinkan* "Schwindsucht"), on the immediately preceding context see Friedrich, SV 2:168.

c. unclear: *[m]ān* GA-*uš* (for GUD!-*uš*?) *ma-[a]r-ki-iš-da-a-iz-z[i!]* "If/when . . . takes (someone) by surprise" KUB 28.70 rev. 12 (rit.).

The proposed meaning of this difficult verb has been based on occurrences of *m.* and of the verb *markištaḫḫ-*.

Cf. *markištaḫḫ-*.

marlaḫḫ- v.; to make foolish; MS(?).†

[. . .] *mar-la-aḫ-ḫa-an*[- . . .] KBo 14.49:8 (letter fragm.?, MS?).

Since the attestation does not include the complete ending, it is possible that this is a passive participle (*marlaḫḫant-*) "foolish, dull-witted", rather than an example of a finite form of *marlaḫḫ-* "to make foolish".

Cf. *marlaiške-*.

marlaiške-, marliške- v.; to become crazed, mad; OH.†

iter. pres. mid. sg. 3 [*m*]*ar-la-iš-ki-it-ta* KBo 26.136 obv. 10, (11), (14), (15), [*m*]*ar-li-iš-ki-it-ta* ibid. 9.

"The Sun withdrew(?)/disappeared and left him at the edge of the river . . ." GUD-*uš mar-li-iš-ki-it-ta* UDU[-*uš m*]*ar-li-iš-ki-it-ta* ANŠE.KUR.RA-*u*[*š*] *mar-la-iš-ki-it-ta* ŠAḪ-*aš mar-l*[*a-iš*]*-ki-it-ta* UR.GI$_7$-*aš mar-la-iš-ki-i*[*t-ta*] / [o]-*ša*-x[o o] ⌈LÚ.U$_{19}$.LU⌉-*išša u-u*[*ḫ-ḫar-p*]*a-an-za apāšša mar-la-iš-ki-i*[*t-ta*] "The cow becomes crazed, the sheep becomes crazed, the horse becomes crazed, the pig becomes crazed, the dog becomes crazed [. . .], . . . the mortal is *u.*, and he too becomes crazed" KBo 26.136 obv. 8-11 + KBo 25.151:1, cf. repetition 13-16 (myth frag., OS).

Neu, StBoT 5 (1968) 113 ("schlapp/müde werden(?)").

Cf. *marlaḫḫ-*, *marlant-*, *marlatar*, *marleššant-*.

marlant- n.; fool, idiot; wr. syll. and ^{LÚ}LIL; NS.†

sg. com. nom. *mar-la-an-za* KBo 13.1 iv 2, 8, KBo 13.83:3 (NH); **com. acc.** *mar-la-an-da-an* KBo 13.34 iv 18; **gen.** ^{LÚ}LIL-*aš* KUB 43.37 iii 9; **broken** *mar-la-an*[- . . .] KUB 43.36:25.

(Sum.) [ḫu-ur] = (Akk.) [*li-il-lum*] = (Hitt.) *mar-la-an-za* KBo 13.1 iv 2 (Erimḫuš Bogh.); [gùn-gùn-a] = [. . .]x-*šu* = *mar-la-an-za* ibid. 8, ed. StBoT 7:19, MSL 17 (forthcoming).

"If a woman gives birth, and its (the foetus') right ear lies near the cheeks" [*I*]*NA* É.LÚ-*kan anda mar-la-an-da-an ḫaššanzi* "in the house of the man they will give birth to an idiot" KBo 13.34 iv 17-19 (omen), ed. StBoT 9:28-29, 31, 38, tr. of Akk. *šumma izbu* omen, *marlandan* translating ^{LÚ}LIL (= Akk. *lillu*, Leichty, Izbu p. 54:11); ^{LÚ}LIL-*aš iwar* [. . . *ḫar*]*nikzi* KUB 43.37 iii 9-10; in broken context KBo 13.83:3 (kingship of ^{d}LAMMA) and KUB 43.36:25.

Riemschneider apud Friedrich, HW 3.Erg. (1966) 23; Otten and von Soden, StBoT 7 (1968) 20; Riemschneider, StBoT 9 (1970) 38-39 (opposite of *ḫattant-* "wise").

Cf. *marlaiške-*.

marlatar n.; foolishness, idiocy, stupidity, folly; from MS.†

sg. nom.-acc. *mar-la-tar* KBo 4.14 ii 40, KBo 13.2 obv. 17, KBo 26.100 i 6, KUB 24.7 i 52, (55).

(Sum.) [. . . -mu] = (Akk.) [*li?-il?-lu?-t*]*i* = (Hitt.) *mar-la-tar-me-et* "my stupidity" KBo 13.2 obv. 17 (vocab.).

(Šupp. II warns a vassal not to rebel, saying:) *numukan* ZI-*ni mar-la-tar* [*lē daškiš*]*i*? "Towards me don't plan anything foolish (lit. don't take foolishness into the mind)" KBo 4.14 ii 39-40 (treaty, Šupp. II), cf. Riemschneider, StBoT 9:38f., comparing: *ḫattatar* ZI-*ni* (*piran*/*anda*) *daške-* "take wisdom into the mind"; *naš mar-la-tar pupuwa*[*latar iyaz*]*i*? *manatkan watkuan*[*zi*? . . . T]I-*nuzi ap*⸗ *panzima*[*š* . . .-]*ešuwar mar-la-*[*tar* . . .] "He [comm]its folly (and) adul[tery(?)], were they to elope, the [. . .] will [not] save [them]. Rather, the [. . .]-s will seize them. To be [. . .] is foolishness" KUB 24.7 i 52-55 (hymn to Ištar, NH), ed. Güterbock, JAOS 103:157, Archi, OA 16:306, 309 ("inettitudine"); [. . .-*š*]*amit mar-la-tar-ša-mi-it uš*?[- . . .] "their [. . .], their stupidity" KBo 26.100 i 6 (myth, pre-NH/MS).

Sommer, AU 184, 415 ("Unmännlichkeit, Schlappheit, Feigheit").

Cf. *marlant-*, *marlaiške-*.

marleššant- adj.; foolish, idiotic, demented; NH.†

sg. com. nom. *mar-le-eš-ša-an-za* KUB 14.3 iv 40; **neut. nom.-acc.** *mar-le-eš-ša-an* KUB 18.10 iv 32.

[. . .] KUR.KUR.ḪI.A-*ma kuit šamaleššan* ÌR.MEŠ-*kan mar-le-eš-ša-an* / [. . .] KUB 18.10 iv 32 (oracle question); [. . .] *mar-le-eš-ša-an-za* "[. . .] is foolish/demented" KUB 14.3 iv 40 (Tawagalawa letter, Muw. or Ḫatt. III), ed. AU 18f.

Forrer, Forsch. 1 (1926) 119, 195 ("Verräter"); Sommer, AU (1932) 19 ("feige"), 184 ("ignauus"), 415 ("(schlapp), feige"); Riemschneider, apud HW 3.Erg. (1966) 24 ("blöde werden").

Cf. *marlant-*, *marlaiške-*.

marliške- see *marlaiške-*.

marmarr(a)- n.; (a kind of terrain); from OH.†

sg. loc. *mar-mar-ri* KUB 17.10 i 12 (OH/MS); **pl. loc.** *mar-mar-aš* ibid., [*mar-m*]*ar-ra-aš* KBo 26.127 rev. 10 (OH/MS?).

(Telepinu went away) *ḫalkin . . . išpiyatarra pēdaš gimri wellūi mar-mar-aš andan* [d]*Telepinuša pait mar-mar-ri andan ulišta* "He carried off grain . . . and abundance of food into the steppe, the meadow (and) the *m.*'s. T. proceeded to unite with the *m.*, (and the *ḫalenzu* grew [lit. ran] over him)" KUB 17.10 i 10-13 (missing god myth, OH/MS), translit. Myth 30; cf. [[d] *Telepinuša*]*z šāit naššikan* [*ḫuman pedaš gimri wellui mar-m*]*ar-ra-aš naššan w*[*ellui marmarri andan ulišta*] KBo 26.127 rev. 9-11 (missing god myth, OH/MH?), for restoration of DN cf. ibid. 2.

While we do not wish to rule out Friedrich's equation of *marmarr*(*a*)- with [GIŠ]*mammarr*[*i*(-) . . .], the forms have been kept separate because the latter has no *r* in the first syllable, because its context within the missing god myth is different from *marmarr*(*a*)-, and because it bears the determinative GIŠ. Terms for terrain, such as *gimra-*, *wellu-*, and *luliyašḫa-*, do not bear the det. GIŠ. However in support of Friedrich, cf. *warḫueššar* without GIŠ and *tieššar* with GIŠ, both apparently meaning "forest". Otten's tr. "Moor" (Eng. "swamp, marsh") depends on his tr. of *ḫalenzu-* as a kind of algae, "duckweed" or the like. (HGG prefers *ḫalenzu-* = "foliage".)

Friedrich, HW (1952) 137 ("Dickicht??"); Otten, BagM 3 (1964) 95 ("Moor").

marnan A (or [GIŠ]*menan*?) n.; (mng. unkn.); NH.†

In a translation of an Akk. proverb: (Akk.) [. . .]x ⌜*dá*⌝-*al-ta tulli* / [. . .]x *mīnâ talqe* "You raised . . . , [. . .]. What did you obtain?" KBo 12.70 rev! iv 10-11 = (Hitt.) *attime* É-*erza wetet nat mar-na-an parqanut palḫaštimat* 9-*an ḫaštai* DÙ-⌜*at*⌝ *arḫamakan kuit datti* "O my father! You built for yourself a house and made it (as) high (as) a *m.* In width you made it nine 'bones'. But what will you take away (i.e., what will you obtain)? KBo 12.70 rev.! iii 10-12, ed. Laroche, Ugar. 5 (1968) 782f. iii 35-36, who read [GIŠ]*me-na-an*. Goetze (JCS 18 [1964] 91) read *mar-na-an* because of the existence of the glossed word :*marnan*, cf. :*marnan* B. Both [GIŠ]*me* and *mar* are possible (photo) in backwards leaning handwriting. In the Akk. vers. *dalta* "doorleaf" seems to be translated by the Hitt. *marnan* (or [GIŠ]*menan*). The Akk. vers. is too broken to deduce more. One could interpret the Hitt. vers. as giving the dimensions of the house, if *-at* "it" refers back to É-*er* "house". *marnan* and *ḫaštai* ("bone") could be units of linear measure. *ḫaštai* probably translates Akk. *eṣemtu*, which in Neo-Assyrian texts is a subdivision (probably 2/3) of a cubit (Postgate, Fifty Neo-Assyrian Legal Documents 71). This would make the house 6 cubits wide. But if *marnan* were a unit of measure, it should have a number before it. Since it doesn't, we might regard it as an object of known height used as a comparison ("You made it as high as a *m.*"). In such a clause the postpositional *maḫḫan* (cf. *nan* [GIŠ]AN.ZA.GÀR GIM-*an parganuši* KUB 24.7 ii 11) might be understood. In all other respects the construction is the same. Since in this proverb we do not know if the proportions of the father's house are supposed to be ridiculous, leading to the question "But what did you obtain?" (Akk.), we cannot use the width (6 cubits) of the house to predict its height (and therefore the height of a *marnan*). Since the semantic connection with the glossed :*marnan* B is unclear, we have kept the two entries separate and do not wish to exclude the possibility of reading [GIŠ]*menan* or of accepting the mng. "doorleaf" for it.

:marnan B Luw.(?) n.; (a duty or obligatory service); NH.†

In the Apology of Ḫattušili III: É-*erma kuit ANA* DINGIR-*LIM ADDIN* [(*nu ḫ*)]*ūmanza ANA* DINGIR-*LIM* :*kar!-na-an* :*mar-na-an* (var. *ma-ar-na-an-n*[*a*]) *ēššau* "In the house which I gave to the goddess let everyone perform *k.* and *m.* for the goddess" KUB 1.1 iv 79-80, w. dupl. 248/w:3, ed. Ḫatt. 38f., StBoT 24:28f.

The above translation assumes the more usual meaning "do, perform" for *ešša-* rather than the much rarer "make, construct". If the latter were intended, *ešša-* (usually having an iter. sense, as opposed to *iya-*) would imply repeated construction. With our interpretation *:karnan :marnan(a) ešša-* would be similar to *šaḫḫan ešša-*, *luzzi ešša-*, *mugawar ešša-*, *arkuwar ešša-*, SISKUR.SISKUR *ešša-*, *šaklain ešša-* and *išḫiul ešša-*.

[m]arnu- v. see *mernu-* v. and *kumarnu-* v.

marnuwa-, marnuwant- n. com. and neut.; (a kind of beer); OH and MH.

sg. nom.-acc. *mar-nu-an* KBo 17.35 iii 17, KBo 20.10 i 8, iii 5, KBo 20.11 iii 13, KUB 43.24:5, KUB 43.31 left col. 5, KBo 17.3 iv 20, KBo 25.13 ii 3, 6, 8 (all OS), KBo 21.70 i (13), 14 (OH/MS), KUB 12.8 ii (2), VBoT 58 iv 32, 44 (both OH/NS), IBoT 1.29 obv. 17, 31, 34 (MH?/MS?), KUB 2.2 iv 9 (NS), *mar-nu-wa-an* KBo 20.89 rev? 11 (OH or MH/MS), KUB 11.22 ii 9, 13, KUB 17.34 iv 6, KUB 25.32 ii 10, KUB 29.1 iii 16, 35, iv 28, KUB 31.57 i 21, KUB 41.23 ii (2), 4, 18, iii 9, KUB 48.77:2, VBoT 58 iv 21 (all OH/NS), KUB 41.8 iii 14 (MH/NS), KBo 13.178:(3), 10, 11, 14, KBo 22:238:4, 8, KUB 17.28 i (27), KUB 36.89 obv. 6, IBoT 2.90:8 (all pre-NH?/NS), *mar-nu-u-wa-an* KUB 10.39 iv 5 (OH/NS).

sg. com. acc. *mar-nu-wa-an-da-an* KBo 11.30 i 11, KBo 19.128 iii 5 (both OH/NS).

sg. gen. *mar-nu-wa-aš* Bo 3752 ii 8 (StBoT 25 p. 179) (OS), KUB 10.21 v 16, KUB 11.26 v 5, (both OH/NS), *mar-nu-an-da-aš* IBoT 2.121 rev. 5, KBo 25.84 i 10, KBo 25.88:19, KUB 43.30 ii 8 (all OS), KBo 23.74 ii 9, 10, KBo 23.91 rev. 9, KUB 25.36 ii 14, KUB 34.89 obv. 3 (all OH/MS), KBo 11.30 i 6, KUB 2.4 iv 13 (both OH/NS), *mar-nu-wa-an-da-aš* KBo 3.7 i 16, KBo 13.215:7, KBo 25.178 i 5 (*-wa*!-), KUB 2.3 ii 13, 18 (all OH/NS).

sg. inst. *mar-nu-an-te-et* KBo 21.72 i 13, KUB 11.28 iv 5 (both OH/NS), possibly *[marnuan]-te-et* KBo 13.248:26, *mar-nu-it* Bo 2329 ii 9f. (StBoT 13:38 n. 61).

a. In an OH/NS incantation where the properties of various beverages (*šieššar*, *marnuwan*, KAŠ.GEŠTIN, *walḫiyanza*) are mentioned, the phonetic similarity between *marnuwan* and the verb *mer-*/*mar-* "to disappear, vanish" is exploited in order to suggest that the beverage can make evils disappear, cf. [. . .] *mar-nu-wa[-an* . . .] *nu* ^{DUG}x-x-[. . .] *kāša mar-nu-wa-an [šieššarra(?)* . . .] *idalu uttar mērtu āššum[a uttar anda* KAR-. . .] ". . . Here (are) *marnuwan* [and beer(?) . . .]. Let the evil thing disappear, but [let] a good [thing be found(?) . . .]" KUB 41.23 ii 2-5 (OH/NS) with restorations based on ibid. iii 9-11.

b. mentioned together with many other beverages (cf. von Schuler AOAT 1:320) — **1′** with *šieššar*/KAŠ "beer": *šiunan* ^{d}UTU-*ui mar-nu-wa-an mān šiēššarra an<da> kulamtati ištazanašmiš karazmišša*(!) 1-*iš kišat* "O Sungod of the gods, as *m.* and beer have been blended, and their mind and *k.* have become one, (let the mind and *k.* of the Sungod of the gods and of the Labarna become one)" KUB 41.23 ii 18-21 (rit. OH/NS), ed. Ehelolf, ZA 43:176; also KUB 43.30 iii 19 (OS), IBoT 1.29 obv. 31, 34, 40-41.

2′ with KAŠ.GEŠTIN "'wine-beer'": KBo 20.32 ii 10 (KAŠ.GEŠTIN-*an*) (OH?/NS), KBo 20.11 iii 13 (OS), KUB 2.2 iv 9-10 (OH?/NS).

3′ with KAŠ.LÀL "mead(?)" or "sweet beer(?)": Bo 3752 ii 8 (StBoT 25 p. 179) (OS), KBo 24.109 + KBo 15.24 iii 10 (MH?/NS), VBoT 58 iv 32, 44 (OH/NS).

4′ with GEŠTIN "wine": KBo 13.175 rev. 4, KBo 17.1 iii 14-15 (both OS), KBo 20.88 i 5-6, KUB 25.36 ii 14, 15, Bo 4962 obv. 9 (Haas, KN 252).

5′ with *walḫi-*: KBo 10.31 iv 9-11.

6′ with KAŠ, GEŠTIN, *tawal-*, and *walḫi-*: KBo 13.114 ii 16-18.

c. held in many different types of container — **1′** DUG: KBo 13.175 rev. 4, KBo 16.76 iii 7 (cf. 3), KBo 17.31:6 (all OS), Bo 4962 obv. 9 (Haas, KN 252).

2′ ^{DUG}*ḫarši-*: KBo 25.13 ii 8 (OS), KUB 31.57 i 21 (OH/NS).

3′ $^{(DUG)}$*ḫuppar(a)-*: KBo 20.27:8, KBo 17.1 ii 10, KBo 25.23 rev. 8 (all OS), KUB 2.2 iv 9, KBo 20.32 ii 5 (OH??/NS), KBo 20.88 i 5.

4′ ^{DUG}*išnura-*: KBo 11.44 iv 12.

5′ *išpantuzziaššar*: KUB 43.30 ii 8 (OS), translit. StBoT 25 p. 76f., KBo 13.215 rt. col. 7-8 (OH/NS).

6′ ^{DUG}*KUKUB*: KBo 13.114 ii 17 (MH/NS), KBo 25.77:10; ^{DUG}ḪAB.ḪAB: Bo 4074:5 (StBoT 15:26).

7′ *luli-* "vat": cf. sub *luli-* 3 a.

8′ ^{DUG}*palḫi-*: KBo 3.7 i 16 (OH).

9′ ^{DUG}*šigga-*: KUB 17.28 i 26-27 (NS).

10′ ^{DUG}*taḫakappi-*: KUB 25.36 ii 14 (OH/MS), IBoT 2.90:7-8.

11′ *taḫaši-*: KBo 20.66:5 (OS), KBo 16.68 ii 2, iii 14-15, (OH/MS).

12′ *tapišana-*: KUB 34.93 obv. 11.

13′ DUG.ḪI.A *urāš:* KUB 11.26 v 5.

d. drunk in the cult: by the king (KUB 25.36 ii 12); by the king and queen (KBo 21.70 i 12-13, KBo 4.9 vi 27-30); by the congregation of worshippers (KUB 25.36 ii 12-16, KUB 25.1 i 60-61, KBo 4.9 vi 1-4), cf. von Schuler, AOAT 1:319-20.

e. is intoxicating: One may infer this from the effects of drinking *m.* seen in Illuyanka, first version. When the goddess Inara spreads the banquet for the Serpent in KUB 17.5 i 7-12 in which he and his offspring drink their fill (*neza ninkēr* i 12) and cannot go back into the hole, she serves the same beverages which are mentioned explicitly earlier in the story (KBo 3.7 i 14-18), which included wine, *mar-nu-wa-an-da-aš* (i 16), and *walḫi-*; cf. von Schuler, AOAT 1:320.

f. offered to a god to slake his thirst: [. . .]x *mar-nu-an kitta* [. . .]x-*i eku nuza nik* "*m.* has been put there [. . .] Drink and slake your thirst" KUB 43.31 left col. 5-6 (OS).

g. distributed by officials: cf. KBo 3.34 i 5-6 translated sub *mark-* mng. 2; supplied for festivals by the ^{LÚ}AGRIG's: KUB 36.89 obv. 6, KUB 25.31 + 1142/z obv. 17 (ZA 62:234), and in connection with the KI.LAM festival, cf. Singer, Diss. 262 with n. 3.

h. dipped/drawn (*ḫan-*) KBo 13.178:3 (OS), libated (*išpant-*/*šipant-*) KBo 17.3 iii 15 (OS), and poured (*laḫuwai-*) KUB 2.3 ii 26-27, VBoT 3 v 21; von Schuler, AOAT 1:319.

i. left as an offering at the sacred "places": EGIR-*ŠU IŠTU* KAŠ *mar-nu-wa-an-te-et AŠRI*$^{ḪI.A}$ *irḫa*[*izzi*] KUB 41.50 iii 5 (NS).

The overwhelming majority of occurrences of this beverage name occur either in OS texts or in cultic texts in the OH tradition (mostly OH/NS). The very few exx. which may be NH rather than OH/NS are in texts dealing with aliments necessary to celebrate festivals and rites which continue the OH (almost always Ḫattian influenced) religious traditions. The religious texts represented by the references cited above are those classified by Laroche as CTH 323 (The missing Sungod), 415, 612, 627, 633, 646, 648-9, 671, 674, 676, 681, 725, 730, 732, 739, all with evidence of Ḫattic religious and often linguistic influence. The word does not occur in religious texts relating primarily to Hurrian deities.

Von Schuler, AOAT 1:317, has pointed out that *marnuatum* in the Old Assyrian texts from Cappadocia is the same word as Hittite *marnuwan, marnuwant-*. Since this *marnuatum* was made from a cereal (CAD M 1:284), it was probably a kind of beer. It then makes sense, as Singer, Diss. 263, has pointed out, that *marnuwan* was distributed not by the ^{LÚ}ZABAR.DAB, who distributed wine, but by the ^{LÚ}AGRIG, who distributed the other beverages.

The spellings without the glide *-wa-* are predominantly found in texts of OS and MS, whereas those with the glide are usually in NS texts.

Friedrich, HW 137 posited two stems, *marnu-* and *marnuwant-*, the latter neuter. No form, however, requires the stem *marnu-*. Von Schuler, AOAT 1:317ff., recognized that the forms attributed to *marnu-* could also belong to a stem *marnuwa-*. Otten, StBoT 13 (1971):38, followed Friedrich and von Schuler in interpreting *marnu*(*w*)*an* as nom.-acc. neuter of the stem *marnu*(*w*)*ant-*, although by 1971 Otten knew of the two occurrences of *marnuwandan* (sg. com. acc.). The form *marnu*(*w*)*an* served as both subject of intransitive verbs (nom.) and object of transitive ones (acc.), which points to a neuter of either *marnuwa-* or *marnuwant-*. But since the *marnuwandan* forms show that *marnuwant-* was com. gender, we assume that the neut. *mar-nu*(*w*)*an* forms belong to the stem *marnuwa-*. It was the stem *marnu*(*w*)*ant-* which was taken up into the Old Assyrian *marnuatum*.

Zimmern, FsStreitberg (1924) 433 n. 5; Steiner, RLA 3 (1966) 307; von Schuler, AOAT 1 (1969) 317ff.; Otten, StBoT 13 (1971) 38; Singer, Diss. (1978) 262 with n. 3.

marnuwala- adj.; invisible(?); OH.†

sg. acc. com. *mar-nu-wa-la-an* KUB 43.60 i 29 (OH/NS).

"'The soul is great.' 'Whose soul is great?' 'The mortal soul is great.' 'And what road does it follow (lit. have)?'" *uran* KASKAL-*an ḫarzi mar-nu-wa-la-an* KASKAL-*an ḫarzi* "It follows (lit. has) the great road; it follows (lit. has) the invisible(?) road." KUB 43.60 i 29 (dialogue in rit., OH/NS).

According to its formation *marnuwala-* is an adj. in *-ala-*, derived from *marnu-*/*mernu-*, "to cause to vanish". For another ex. of a derivative in *-ala-* based on a *-nu-* caus. cf. *arnuwala-* "resettled person", from *arnu-* "to transport". Thus, "the road which makes (things) disappear" or "the road which has been made invisible", (for the latter see KBo 13.101 rev. 14-15, treated s.v. *mer-* and *mernu-*). Note also the DN ^{d}*Ma*[*r-nu?-w*]*a-la* KUB 35.135 rev. (6), 15.

Cf. *mer-*, *mernu-*/*marnu-*.

marnuwant- see *marnuwa-*.

(:)marša- adj. (Hitt. and Luw.); **1.** unholy, unfit for sacred use, **2.** treacherous(?); from MH.†

com. sg. acc. *mar-ša-an* KBo 5.2 i 4, 5 (MH/NS); **neut. sg. (acc.)** *mar-ša* ibid. iv 64; **Luw. neut. sg. (nom.)** *:mar-ša-aš-ša* KBo 4.14 ii 59 (NH), (for Luw. neut. sg. nom.-acc. in *-ša* see HHL 172-6 and Carruba, GsKronasser 1-15).

1. unholy, unfit for sacred use: "If a man is in a consecrated state (*šuppi*)" *nušši* NINDA-*an mar-ša-an kuiški adanna pāi našmašši* UZUÌ *mar-ša-an adanna pāi* "And someone gives him unholy bread to eat or unholy fat to eat; (or someone gives him bewitched bread or fat to eat; or someone gives him bread or meat from a mausoleum to eat or blood from a woman's body to drink)" KBo 5.2 i 3-9 (rit., MH/NS), ed. Ḫatt. 88; cf. *mān* UN-*aš šup*<*p*>*iš nušši mar-ša kuiški kuitki pāi* ibid. iv 64-65.

2. treacherous(?): ". . . If the lords turn against the king or the king gets sick, or the king goes off on a distant campaign" *našmat* GIM-*an ašān imma :mar-ša-aš-ša mēḫur* "or whatever sort of treacherous time it be" KBo 4.14 ii 56-59 (treaty, NH), ed. Meriggi, WZKM 58:88, Stefanini, AANL 20:42f. ("un tempo calamitoso") and see pp. 63f. (discussion), Carruba, GsKronasser 5.

Two areas of meaning can be ascertained in Hittite words based on the root **marš-*: (1) profaneness, unholiness, and (2) deceitfulness, dishonesty. Both meanings are attested for *marša-*, *maršaḫḫ-*, *maršanu-*, and *maršešš-*. *maršaštarri-* has only meaning (1), while *maršant-*, *maršatar* and *marše-* have only meaning (2). The two meanings probably derive from a common source, but we do not know what that was. According to Laroche, RHA X/51:23-25, it was the notion of falseness. The second meaning proposed for *maršant-*, "unfit, poor (quality)" (describing a cow), may derive from "deceptive", meaning that in the spring the cow looks better than she really is.

Götze, Ḫatt. (1924) 88 (*marša-* "schlecht"); Friedrich, SV 1 (1926) 80 (*marša-* "schlecht, verdorben"); Laroche, RHA X/51 (1949-50) 23-25 (*marša-* "faux, trompeur"; "corrompu, de mauvais aloi"); Goetze, JCS 13 (1959) 68 (*marša-* "deficient, of bad quality"); DLL 69 (*maršašša* = gén. adj.); Meriggi, WZKM 58 (1962) 88 (*maršašša-* "gefährlich (eigentl. 'faul')").

Cf. *maršaḫḫ-*, *maršant-*, *maršanu-*, *maršatar*, *maršaštarri-*, *marše-* v., *maršešš-*.

maršaḫḫ- v.; **1.** to desecrate, **2.** to make treacherous; from MH.†

part. sg. nom.-acc. *mar-ša-a-aḫ-ḫa-an* KUB 29.8 i 39 (MH/MS), *mar-ša-aḫ-ḫa-an* KBo 5.4 obv. 28, KBo 5.13 iv 8 (both Murš. II).

1. to desecrate: *mānwa* *ŠA* DINGIR.MEŠ KÙ.BABBAR KÙ.GI *našma* NA$_4$.ḪI.A *našma* *UNŪT* <GIŠ>TÚG *kuiški mar-ša-a-aḫ-ḫa-an našma papraḫḫan kuēz imma kuēz uddanaz mar-ša-aḫ-ḫa-an ḫarzi* "If someone has desecrated or defiled, or desecrated by whatsoever means (?), the deities' silver and gold, or gems, or utensils made of boxwood(?)" KUB 29.8 i 37-40 (rit., MH/MS).

2. to make treacherous: *namma antuḫšatarra* [*k*]*uit mar-ša-aḫ-ḫa-an nukan AWĀTĒ*^{MEŠ} *kattan piddāeškanzi* "Further, since humanity is treacherous, (if) rumors circulate . . ." KBo 5.13 iv 8-9 (Kup.), ed. SV 1.134f. lines 16f., identically in KBo 5.4 obv. 28 (Targ.), ed. SV 1.56f., KBo 21.5 iii (31) (Alakš.), w. dupl. KUB 21.1 iii (16), KUB 21.4 i (40), ed. SV 2.68f.

Friedrich, SV 1 (1926) 80 ("verderben"); Laroche, RHA X/51 (1949-50) 23-24 ("faux, trompeux, mensonger").

Cf. *marša-* adj. and disc. there.

maršanašši-, maršaunašši-(?) n. com.; (an oracle bird); NH.

sg. nom. *mar-ša-na-aš-ši-iš* KUB 5.25 iv 25, iii (2), KUB 5.18 rev.? 13, KUB 18.5 i 14, 18, KUB 5.22:39, 45, KUB 18.56 iii (25), KUB 49.19 iii? 30, *mar-ša-na-aš-ši-eš* IBoT 1.32 obv. 26, [*ma*]*r-ša-na-aš-še-iš* KUB 22.7 obv.? 12, *mar-ša-na-ši-iš* KUB 49.44:4, 8, *mar-ša-ú-na-aš-ši-i*[*š*] KUB 49.28 rt. col. 5; **sg. acc.** *mar-ša-na-aš-ši-in* KUB 5.17 ii 22, KUB 18.5 i 23, 26, KUB 18.9 iii 16, IBoT 1.32 obv. 25, KUB 22.41 rev. (8), KUB 49.19 iii? (14), 29, 34, *ma*[*r*]-⸢*ša-an-na-aš-ši-i*⸣[*n*] KUB 18.5 + KUB 49.13 i 21.

pl. nom. *mar-ša-na-aš-ši-iš* KBo 16.98 ii 19, KUB 18.2 ii? 21, KUB 49.11 iii 18, KUB 49.50:6, *mar-ša-na-aš-ši-uš* KUB 18.56 iii (21), (25), [*mar-š*]*a-na-ši-uš* KUB 49.44:9; **pl. nom. with ending broken** KUB 49.5 i (7); **pl. acc.** *mar-ša-na-aš-ši-uš* KUB 16.43 obv. 12; **pl. nom. or acc.** *mar-ša-na-aš-ši-uš* KUB 22.63:5, (6), KUB 22.65 ii 17.

a. coming (*uwa-*) toward the observer singly (e.g., KUB 5.22:39) and in pairs (KUB 18.2 ii 21, KUB 22.30 rev.? 6, KBo 16.98 ii 19); flight described as EGIR UGU SIG_5-*za uwa-* KUB 22.51 obv. 7-8, KUB 22.7 obv.? (12), KUB 5.17 ii 22-23, IBoT 1.32 obv. (26); EGIR(-*an*) GAM/*katta kuš*(*tayati*) *uwa-* KUB 5.22:39, KUB 18.2 ii? 21, KUB 18.5 i 18-19; *pi*(*r*)*an kuš*(*tayati*) *uwa-* KUB 5.18 rev.? 13, KUB 5.25 iv 25-26; *pi*(*r*)*an* SIG_5-*za uwa-* KBo 16.98 ii 19-20, KUB 5.22:45, KUB 5.25 iii (2)-3, KUB 22.30 rev.? 6-7, KUB 49.11 iii 18; ÍD-*an pariyan tar-u-an uwa-* KUB 18.5 i 24.

b. going (*pai-*) from the observer: flight described as [. . .] *aššuwaz pai-* KUB 18.5 i (26)-27; *pi*(*r*)*an arḫa pai-* IBoT 1.32 obv. 26, KUB 5.25 iv 27, KUB 22.65 ii 18, KUB 5.14:7, KUB 5.17 ii 22-24, KBo 16.98 ii 20, KUB 49.19 iii 30; 2(-*an*) *arḫa pai-* KUB 22.51 obv. 8, KUB 18.2 ii 22, KUB 5.22:39(?), 46, KUB 22.30 rev.? 7-(8), KUB 18.56 iii 22, 24, 26-27; [. . .] *tar-u-an pai-* KUB 18.5 i 25.

c. hiding: *naš munnaitta* KUB 18.5 i 27.

d. retracing its path (lit. took itself back): [*nuza mar-š*]*a-na-aš-ši-iš* EGIR-*pa* ME-*aš* KUB 49.19 iii 17, cf. Ünal, RHA XXXI:38.

e. observed (*auš-*, *ušk-*, *ĪMUR*, *NĪMUR*): singly KUB 5.17 ii 22, KUB 18.5 i 23, 26, etc.; and in groups 3 *maršanaššiuš ḫaštapinn*[*a*] KUB 16.43 obv. 12).

f. observed in association with other birds — **1′** *ḫaštapi-*: KUB 16.43 obv. 12.

2′ *ḫara-*/Á^{MUŠEN} ("eagle"): KUB 18.9 iii 16-17, KUB 18.5 i 20ff., KUB 5.22:45, KUB 49.19 iii 29.

3′ *aramnant-*: KUB 22.63:5.

4′ *šulupi-*: KUB 18.56 iii 21, 25, IBoT 1.32 obv. 25.

Laroche, RHA X/51:25 (connects the bird name to the family of words *marša-*, *maršaḫḫ-*, etc.). *maršanašši-* appears to be a Luw. gen. adj. in *-ašši-*. The single instance of *mar-ša-ú-na-aš-ši-i*[*š*] KUB 49.28 rt. col. 5 may be a mistake.

maršankuwaš n.; (a fruit); NH.†

^{GIŠ}*INBĒ ḫ*[*ūman* . . .] ^{GIŠ}*šammama* ^{GIŠ}[. . .] ^{GIŠ}ŠENNUR *kalak*[*tar parḫuenaš* . . .] *mar-ša-an-ku-wa-aš a*[*r*?- . . .] *šuppeš ḫap*[*puriyaš* . . .] § *kī hūman a*[*r*?- . . .] KBo 23.48 obv.? 4-9 (rit., NH); *mānmašši apāšm*[*a* . . .] *nu mar-ša-an-ku-wa-aš aw*[*an* . . .] *nat ANA* GAB.LÀL [. . .] *nat ŠA* GAB.LÀL [. . .] Bo 4588 rev.? 5-8 (frag. of med. rit., NH), ed. StBoT 19:35.

The *m.* is a 'fruit' since it occurs in the list headed: ^{GIŠ}*INBE ḫ*[*ūman*] "all fruits". But in Hittite the fruit category included nuts (cf. ^{GIŠ}*šammama-*, which according to Güterbock, JAOS 88:70f., is a kind of nut). That *m.* lacks the GIŠ det. could be either accidental, (cf. *ḫappuriya-* which occurs with and without GIŠ), or because it was not thought of as being a tree or shrub (such as *parḫuena-*, *galaktar*, etc.).

The gram. case of *maršankuwaš* cannot be determined in either occurrence. The stem could be *maršanku-*, *maršankuwa-*, *maršankuwaš-*, or it could be the genitive of a verbal subst. (nom. *-war*, gen. *-waš*) from **maršank-*.

maršant- adj.; **1.** deceitful, dishonest, treacherous, **2.** unfit, poor (quality); from OH/NS.

sg. com. nom. *mar-ša-an-za* KBo 3.34 ii 20 (OH/NS), KUB 43.8 ii 10b, KUB 4.3 obv. 13 (NH); **com. acc.** *mar-ša-an-ta-an* KUB 31.115:20 (OH/NS); **neut. nom.-acc.** *mar-ša-an* KBo 23.115 obv.? 3; **pl. com. nom.** *mar-ša-an-te-eš* KBo 16.54:19, 20, KUB 19.23 rev. 11, KUB 21.5 iii 52 (all NH), *mar-ša-an-te-(m)eš* KUB 21.1 iii 37 (NH); **neut. nom.-acc.** *mar-ša-an-da* KBo 12.45:4 (pre NH/NS).

In the bilingual KUB 4.3 the Akkadian corresponding to Hittite *mar-ša-an-za* GUD-*uš* in obv. 13f. has been lost—see below sub 2.

1. deceitful, dishonest, treacherous: (Išputaš-inara said to Aškaliya) *mar-ša-an-za-wa zik* "You are deceitful!" KBo 3.34 ii 20 (anecdotes, OH/NS); "When you [come] into a town somewhere, call together the artisans and elders [and] speak to them as follows" [o] *ḫattalwalliš mar-ša-an-te-eš* [LÚ.ME]Š *ŠA* É-*ya mar-ša-an-te-eš* [*nušm*]*aš* GEŠTIN-*an daškanzi* [o o o o] *menaḫḫanda wātar* [*laḫ*]*ūwanzi* "Are the doorkeepers deceitful? Are the [peopl]e of the estate deceitful? Do they keep taking wine for themselves and pour out water in its place?" KBo 16.54:16-22 (instr., NH), ed. Riemschneider, ArOr 33:337f.; ÌR.MEŠ-*ŠU-maššši kuiēš* LÚ.MEŠ [URU]*Arzauwaya nat mar-ša-an-te-eš* (var. *mar-ša-an-te-(m)eš*) *nu mān* [m]*Kupanta*-[d]LAMMA-*an kuiški idaluwanni šanḫzi*, "Those who are his servants and the Arzawans are treacherous— if someone (among them) should seek evil against K." KUB 21.5 iii 51-53 (Alakš.), ed. SV 2:72f., with dupl. KUB 21.1 iii 36-38; *manmakan* LÚ.MEŠ [URU]*Lalandama kuiēš* URU.DIDLI.ḪI.A *ārrū*[*ša*] *pāir nu* UN.MEŠ-*uš mar-ša-an-te-eš* "But if people of Lalanda, namely some towns, have defected(?), the people are treacherous" KUB 19.23 rev. 10-11 (letter, NH); cf. *mar-ša-an* UN.MEŠ-*tar* KBo 23.115 obv. 3; BI-*aš* UN-*aš mar-ša-an-za* "That man (is) *m*." KUB 43.8 ii 10b (apodosis of physiognomic omen), ed. Riemschneider, Omentexte 244f.

2. unfit, poor (quality): *mar-ša-an-za* GUD-*uš ḫamešḫipat* SIG$_5$-*ri* "Particularly in the spring (even) a poor ox may look good" KUB 4.3 obv. rt. 13-14 (bil. wisdom text, NH), ed. Laroche, Ugar. 5:781, cf. Hoffner, AlHeth 17. Of the Akk., KUB 4.3 obv. left 14 preserves only *i-dam-mì-i*[*q*] corresponding to this phrase, while Nougayrol, Ugar. 5:279 restores the duplicate RS 22.439 iii 11 as [. . . GUD ḪUL SI]G$_5$? *i-na ši-i-ma-ni*. However, *m.* might indicate that the true condition of the ox was obscured in the spring-time and that it appeared deceptively healthy.

Friedrich, SV 1 (1926) 80 ("schlecht"); Laroche, RHA X/51 (1949-50) 24 ("traître, faux frère"); idem Ugar. 5:781 ("gâté").

Cf. *marša-* adj. and disc. there.

maršanu- v.; **1.** to desecrate, to profane (opp. (*appa*) *šuppiyaḫḫ-* "(re)consecrate"), **2.** to falsify; from OH/MS.

pres. sg. 3 *mar-ša-nu-zi* KUB 7.52 obv. 5, KUB 30.11 rev. 9, *mar-ša-nu-uz-zi* KUB 30.10 rev. 13 (MH/MS), KUB 36.75 ii (19) (OH/MS).

part. sg. com. nom. *mar-ša-nu-an-za* KUB 16.39 ii 12; **neut. nom.-acc.** *mar-ša-nu-an* KUB 16.27 obv. 4, KUB 16.39 ii 7, *mar-ša-nu-wa-an* KUB 16.38 iv 3, KUB 16.39 ii 25, KUB 18.27 obv.? 17, KBo 11.1 obv. 35 (all NH); **pl. com. nom.** *mar-ša-nu-an-te-eš* KUB 16.34 i 2, KUB 16.39 ii 2, 19, iii 7 (both NH), *mar-ša-nu-wa-an-te-eš* ibid. ii 31, KUB 16.27 obv. (2) (both NH).

1. to desecrate, profane (opp. (*appa*) *šuppiyaḫḫ-* "(re)consecrate"): [*m*]*ānzakan* [d]U [URU]KÙ.BABBAR-*ti* [d]LAMMA [URU]KÙ.BABBAR-*ti* DINGIR.MEŠ *ḫapalkiyaš* [ŠÀ] É.⌈MEŠ⌉ DINGIR.MEŠ *UL kuēzqa mar-*⌈*ša*⌉*-nu-an-te-eš* "If you, O Stormgod of Ḫatti, (and) you, O Protective Deity of Ḫatti, (and) you gods of iron are not desecrated by anything [in] the temples" KUB 16.34 i 1-2 (oracle, NH); [*ANA* [d]UTU-*ŠI k*]*uit* SAL.LUGAL *maršaštarriš ar*[*iyašešnaza* SI×SÁ-*at*] / [*nat kuēz*] *imma kuēz mar-ša-nu-an-te-eš* ⌈*e*⌉[*šer*] "Since desecration [concerning His Majesty] (and) the queen [has been determined by oracle, by wh]atsoever [they wer]e desecrated" KUB 16.39 ii 1-2 (oracle question, NH), ed. HTR 108f. (w. different restoration), restored after [*ANA* [d]UTU-*ŠI kui*]*t* SAL.LUGAL *maršaštarriš ariyašešnaz*[*a* SI×SÁ-*a*]*t* / [*nat kuēz i*]*m*<*ma*> *kuēz*! *mar-ša-nu-an-te-eš* [*eše*]*r* ibid. ii 18-19 and [*AN*]*A*! [d]UTU-*ŠI kuit* SAL.LUGAL *maršaštarriš ariy*[*ašešnaza* SI×SÁ-*at*] / [*n*]*at kuēz imma kuēz mar-ša-nu-wa-an-*[*te-eš ešer*] KUB 16.27 obv. 1-2; "But if some mountain or *šinapši*-building, some holy (*šuppa*) place, is harmed (ḪUL-*aḫḫan*), . . . I, [My Majesty], will make it right again. . . ." *mānna mar-ša-nu-wa-an kuitki* *nat šekkanzi maḫḫan nat QĀTAMMA* EGIR-*pa šuppiy*[*aḫḫanzi*] "And if something is desecrated, they will reconsecrate it in the way that they know" KBo 11.1 obv. 32-35 (prayer, Muw.), ed. Houwink ten Cate, RHA XXV/81:107, 116f.; [*mān⸗z*]*akan zik* ^{m}*Tutḫališ* (sic) ŠÀ É.NA$_4$.DINGIR-*LIM IŠTU* GUD UDU *wašd*[*ul*]*awandaza* [*UL ku*]*ēzqa mar-ša-nu-an-za* "[If] you, Tutḫali (sic), have not been desecrated in the mausoleum (lit. divine stone house) by some sin-bearing ox (or) sheep, (then may the exta be favorable)" KUB 16.39 ii 11-12 (oracle question, NH), cf. ibid. ii 29-31; [. . . *k*]*uiški IŠTU* NÍ.TE-*ŠU mar-ša-nu-wa-an ḫarz*[*i*] "Has someone desecrated [. . .] with his body?" KUB 18.27 obv.? 17 (oracle, NH).

2. to falsify: ^{LÚ}DAM.GÀR-*ša* ⸢LÚ-*iš*⸣ ^{d}UTU-*i* ^{GIŠ}*ēlzi ḫarzi nu* ^{GIŠ}*ēlzi mar-ša-nu-uz-zi* "And the merchant man holds the scales toward the Sungod but falsifies the scales. (But what have I done to my god?)" KUB 30.10 rev. 12-13 (prayer, MH/MS), ed. Güterbock, JNES 33:326, cf. KUB 30.11 rev. 9-10, KUB 36.75 ii 18-20.

Otten, ZA 46 (1940) 219 n. 2 ("die Waage fälscht"); Laroche, RHA X/51 (1949-50) 23 ("fausser", participle in the sense of "victime d'une fraude"); idem, RHA XV/60 (1957) 10 ("frustrer"); Otten, HTR (1958) 109 ("hintergehen").

Cf. *marša-* and disc. there.

marša(š)tarri-, maršaštarr(a?)-, marza⸗(š)tarri- n. com.; desecration, profanement, sacrilege (opp. *šuppeššar* etc.); from MH/MS.

sg. nom. *mar-ša-aš-tar-ri-iš* KUB 26.12 iv 36, KBo 12.116 rev. 5, KUB 16.39 ii 1 (NH), KUB 29.8 i 41 (MH/MS), *mar-ša-aš-tar-re-eš* KUB 5.9 obv. 9 (NH), KUB 16.39 iii (6), KUB 8.40:14 (here?), [*ma*]*r-ša-tar-ri-iš* KUB 18.29 i? 8, *mar-š*[*a*]*-tar-re-eš* ibid. 12 (scribal error both times?), *mar-za-aš-tar-ri-iš* KUB 18.27:19 (NH); **acc.** *mar-ša-aš-tar-ri-in* KBo 23.1 i 6 (NH), ABoT 29 ii 21, (28) + ABoT 28:4, (11) (=KBo 23.1 ii 21, (28)) (NH), KUB 30.42 iv 23 (NH), KUB 16.34 i 16 (NH), ⸢*mar-š*⸣*a-aš-tar-*<*ri*>*-in* KUB 16.34 i 9; **gen.** *mar-ša-aš-tar-ra-aš* KUB 5.10 obv. 19 (NH), KUB 30.63 v? (6) (NH), KUB 5.9 obv. 29 (NH); **d.-l.** *mar-ša-aš-tar-ri* KBo 13.64 obv. 14, rev. 4, 13, AT 454 i 22, ii 7, iv 13 (both NH), *mar-za-aš-tar-ri* KUB 49.89 rt. col. 12, *mar-za-tar-ri* KUB 50.44 ii 6; **pl. d.-l.** *mar-ša-aš-tar-*[*r*]*a-aš* KUB 18.35:9 (NH).

"We questioned the temple servants and they said," (The temple servants have contact with servants of the mausoleum) "but they do not bathe (afterwards), and even (*-pat*) walk into the temple" DINGIR-*LUM aši* ⸢*mar-š*⸣*a-aš-tar-*<*ri*>*-in išiyaḫta* "O deity, have you indicated *this* sacrilege?" . . . "We questioned them further and they said, 'A do[g] went into the bakery . . . and the daily bread offering [was defiled?.] Also, the baker saw a dead person, but he did not bathe.' He was called to the te[mple]" DINGIR-*LUM aši mar-ša-aš-tar-ri-in išiyaḫta* "O deity, have you indicated *this* sacrilege?" KUB 16.34 i 5-10, 13-16 (oracle questions, NH); *IŠTU* É.GAL-*LIM-mamu kuit* INIM *mar-ša-aš-tar-ra-aš ḫatrāir INA* É.DINGIR-*LIM* ^{d}*IŠTAR* ^{URU}*Ninuwakan mar-ša-aš-tar-ri-iš* SI×SÁ-*at* "Regarding their writing me from the palace about the matter of sacrilege—(namely that) a sacrilege was determined by oracle (to exist) in the temple of Ištar of Nineveh—(we questioned the temple personnel. They said, 'A dog came up in the gate-house and reached the *ambašši*-s. They killed it right in the gate-house.' Are you, O deity, angry about that?)" KUB 5.10 i 19-23 (oracle question, NH); cf. KBo 13.64 obv. 10-15; *m.* as an object of oracle questions also in Meskene 74.57+:5-7 and Meskene 74.92+:6-7 (courtesy E. Laroche) "If someone has profaned/desecrated (*maršaḫḫ-*) or defiled (*papraḫḫ*)—profaned by whatsoever means—the deities' silver (and) gold or gems or boxwood(!) utensils(?)" *nuššan apāš mar-ša-aš-tar-ri-iš paprātarra kēdaš ēšdu* "Let that profanement and defilement be on these (viz. the scapegoats mentioned in line 30). (Let the silver, gold, gems and boxwood(!) utensils(?) be pure (*parkui-*))" KUB 29.8 i 37-43 (rit., MH/MS); for KUB 16.39 ii 1f., 18f. and KUB 16.27 obv. 1f. see *maršanu-*; [*m*]*ān ANA* É.GAL.SAL.LUGAL *mar-ša-aš-tar-ri-iš UL kuiški ēšzi* "If there is no desecration (attributable) to the queen's palace" KUB 5.9 obv. 1-2 (oracle question, NH), cf. ibid. 9 with *ANA* É.GAL É ^{d}UTU-*ŠI*(! text: *-aš*) "(attributable) to His Majesty's palace"; *mān kūšpat mar-ša-aš-tar-ra-aš waškuš* "If these alone are the sins of desecration" ibid. 29; *nušmaš šuppešni* [IGI-*an*?]*da tišḫanteš ēšten mānnakan ANA* LÚ.SAG [*kue*]*danikki* ḪUL-*luš mar-ša-aš-tar-ri-iš* "(You eunuchs) be diligent(?) [abo]ut the consecrated state, and if some eunuch has an evil unconsecrated condition (and he nears the king's person, that falls under the oath)" KUB 26.12 iv 34-37 (instr., NH), ed. Dienstanw. 29; *mān* ᵈ[U?] (or DINGIR-[*LUM*]?) / [INIM?-*a*]*z kuēzga kartimmiyauwanz*[*a*] / [*našm*]*ašši mar-ša-aš-tar-ri-iš-ma kui*[*ški*] / [*pira*]*n*! *iyanza našmaššikan* [. . .] / [*kuitki ḫ*]*arkan*ᵃⁿ *nan* SAG.[GEMÉ.ÌR . . .] / [. . . EGI]R-*pa m*[*u*⸗*g*]*ai*[*zzi*] "If [the Stormgod?] is angry about some[thing], or some sacrilege has been committed before him, or [something] of his(?) has been destroyed, (his?) servants will entreat him to return" KBo 12.116 rev. 3-8 (rit. colophon), rest. after KUB 8.71:11-15 (cat., NH), translit. CTH p. 187; *mānkan INA* É.DINGIR-*LIM anda šup*[*p*]*ai pedi kuin imma kuin mar-ša-aš-tar-ri-in wemiyanzi* "If they find desecration, of whatsoever sort, in the temple, in a consecrated place, (this is the ritual for it)" ABoT 28:2-5 + ABoT 29 ii 19-22 (=KBo 23.1 ii 19-22) (colophon of rit., NH), ed. Lebrun, Hethitica 3:144, 151f.; cf. KBo 23.1 ii 25-28 and i 3-6 (incipits); cf. KUB 30.42 iv 21-24, HSM 3644 (JCS 19:33):4-6, w. dupl. KBo 7.74:6-7, KUB 30.63 v? 4-7 (all cat.).

Friedrich, ArOr 6 (1934) 361 n. 9; Laroche, RHA X/51 (1949-50) 24-25 ("fraude"); Goetze, JCS 13 (1959) 68-69 ("flaw, deficiency, fault").

Cf. *marša-* adj. and disc. there.

maršatar n. neut.; fraud, treachery, deception, deceit, dishonesty; from OH.†

sg. *mar-ša-tar* KUB 13.4 iv 62 (pre-NH/NS), KUB 13.17 rev. 22 (pre-NH/NS), KBo 3.1 iii 46 (OH/NS), *mar-ša-a-tar* KUB 11.1 iii 11 (OH/NS), KUB 40.82 rev. 2 (NS).

"Let them bring (the sacrifice) to the gods as it was selected from the corral (or) fold. Let them not exchange it later on the road" *mānmakan* ŠÀ KASKAL-*NI* ᴸᵁ́SIPA.GUD *našma* ᴸᵁ́SIPA.UDU *mar-ša-tar kuiški iyazi* "But if some shepherd or cowherd contrives deception on the road (and turns aside the fattened ox or sheep . . . and they put a lean one in its place)" KUB 13.4 iv 59-65 (temple instr., pre-NH/NS), ed. Chrest. 166f.; [*kui*]*škan NĪ*[*Š* DINGIR-*LIM šarratta*? . . . *n*]*u mar-ša-a-tar iyaz*[*i* . . .] "He who [transgresses(?)] the oat[h of the god] and commits treachery" KUB 40.82:1-2 (protocol or treaty fragm., NS); [. . .] *mar-ša-tar* (var. B: *mar-ša-a-tar*) *ēššanzi nuššan ilašni parā n*[(*aššu* 1 *gipešša*)]*r našma* 2 *gipeššar* ⸢*ḫa*⸣*minkiškir našta u*[(*tnē ēšḫar akkušk*)]*ir* KBo 3.1 iii 46-48 (Tel.pr., OH/NS), with dupls. B: KUB 11.1 iii 11-13 and C: KBo 3.67 iii 4-6, ed. Archi, FsLaroche 45.

Friedrich, SV 1 (1926) 81 ("Schlechtigkeit, schlechte Handlung"); Laroche, RHA X/51 (1949-50) 23 ("fraude").

Cf. *marša-* adj. and disc. there.

maršaunašši- see *maršanašši-*.

:maršazan; (mng. unkn.); NH.†

[. . .]x *peškir nu :mar-ša-za-an š*[*a* . . .] KUB 50.69:5 (oracle question, NH).

Cf. the Luw. neut. *maršašša* sub *marša-* adj.

***marši-** adj.; (mng. unkn.); from MH.†

neut. pl. acc. *mar-ša-ia* KBo 17.65 rev. 5, (7), 8 (MH?/NS); **sg. or pl. gen.** *mar-ša-i-ia-aš* KBo 16.97 obv. 34 (MH/MS).

a. in a birth ritual: *ŠA* SAL.MEŠ ⸢ŠU⸣.GI *mar-ša-ia* SISKUR.SISKUR.MEŠ [*šipanti*] . . . [*na*]*m*⸢*maza* EGIR⸣-*anda ŠA* ᴸᵁ́AZU *m*[*ar*]-*ša-ia* SISKUR.SISKUR.MEŠ *šipanti* [*maḫḫanmaš ŠA*] ᴸᵁ́AZU *mar-ša-ia* SISKUR.SISKUR.MEŠ *ašnuzi* "[She performs] the *m.* rites (for removal of profanement/desecration(?)) of the Old Women. . . . Again afterwards she performs the *m.* rites of the exorcist, [but when] she completes the *m.* rites [of] the exorcist" KBo 17.65 rev. 5-8 (MH?/NS), ed. Beckman, Diss. 166f., 175 with no tr. proposed.

b. in an oracle question: *ŠA* SISKUR.SISKUR *mar-ša-i-ia-aš* "Is it (a problem) of the *m.* rites?" KBo 16.97 obv. 34 (MH/MS).

The birth ritual passage cited in **a** has to do with rites performed for the personnel attending a pregnant woman. If *m.* belongs to the word family of *marša-* in which there is present a nuance of impurity, profaneness or desecration, the SISKUR may be meant to remove that profanement or desecration from the personnel. The attested forms could also be from a stem *maršaya-* or *maršai-*.

Beckman, Diss. (1977) 213.

Cf. *marša-* adj., *maršant-*, *maršaḫḫ-*, *marše-*.

marše- v.; to be/become corrupt, dishonest, deceitful; OH.†

("If a *ḫippara*-person steals, there is no compensation. . . . His own person(?) is liable") *mān[e t]ayazzil piškir man ḫūmantešpat mar-še-e-er [n]ašma* LÚ.MEŠNÍ.ZU *kīšantati* "if they were accustomed to give (compensation for?) theft, they would all become dishonest or they would become thieves" KBo 6.2 ii 54-56 (Laws, § 49, OS), ed. HG p. 32f.; [(*mān appezziyanma* ÌR.MEŠ DUMU.MEŠ.LUGA)]L ⌜*mar*⌝*-še-e-er* (var. ⌜*mar*⌝*-še-eš-še-er*) "But when later the subjects/servants of the princes were(?) (var. became) corrupt/dishonest (they began to consume their estates)" KUB 11.1 i 20-21 (Tel. pr., OH/NS), with dupl. KBo 3.1 i 20-21, ed. Chrest. 184f. i 21-22.

Laroche, RHA X/51 (1949-50) 24 ("tremper dans une fraude").

Cf. *marša-* adj. and disc. there.

SÍGmaršiḫ[- . . .] see SÍG*mariḫši-*.

(GIŠ)**maršikka-** n. [com.]; (a tree or its fruits); from OH.†

sg. nom. ⌜GIŠ⌝*mar-še-eq-qa-aš* KBo 18.193:11 (NS), GIŠ*ma-a-ar-ši-ig-ga-aš* KUB 33.9 iii 13 (OH/NS); **acc.** GIŠ*ma-ar-ši-iq-qa-an* KUB 29.1 iv 22 (OH/NS), Bo 3092 obv. 5; **broken** *ma-ar-ši-ga-*x[. . .] KBo 17.47 obv. 5 (pre-NH/MS?), GIŠ⌜*mar-ši*⌝*-ik*[- . . .] KUB 42.101:7 (NS).

nu GIŠ*artartin* GIŠ*ma-ar-ši-iq-qa-an-na tianzi* "They put (out) *a.* and *m.* (and say as follows, 'As they cultivate these, so may their descendants care for (lit. cultivate) the king and queen'" KUB 29.1 iv 22-25 (rit., OH/NS), ed. Schwartz, OrNS 16:38f., Kellerman, Diss. 19, 31, Otten, Tel. 37-38 n. 4 ("einen *maršiqqa*-Baum stellt man auf"), HW² 343 ("sie stellen hin") □ for *aršai-* v. see HAB 151f., contrast HW² s.v., cf. Otten, ZA 71.218; GIŠḪAŠḪUR*-anza ŠA* dx[. . .] GIŠ*ma-a-ar-ši-ig-ga-aš Š*[*A* d . . .] KUB 33.9 iii 12-13 (Tel. Myth 3rd vers., OH/NS), ed. Otten, Tel. 37, translit. Laroche, Myth. 46; in broken context [. . . GI]Š*ḫatalkišni* 1 *ma-ar-ši-ga-*x[. . . GIŠ*a*]*lkištana*[- . . .] KBo 17.47 obv. 5-6 (rit., pre-NH/MS?); ⌜GIŠ⌝*mar-še-eq-qa-aš* GIŠ[*ḫ*]*atalkišnaš* KBo 18.193:11 (list of materials for rit., NS), ed. Werner, Symb.Böhl 394; [GIŠ*ḫa*]*talkišnaš* GIŠ⌜*mar-ši*⌝*-ik*[- . . .] KUB 42.101:7 (list of materials for rit., NS).

The (GIŠ)*maršikka* is listed together with the apple tree, the hawthorne, and the *arta(r)ti-*.

Otten, Tel. (1942) 37-38 n. 4; Friedrich, HW (1952) 138; Hoffner, EHGl (1967) 43 (w. n. 58), 91; Neumann, KZ 84 (1970) 141 ("eine Feigenart"); Ertem, Flora (1974) 135-36.

maršešš- v.; **1.** to become desecrated, profane, unholy (opp. of *šuppešš-*), **2.** to become corrupt, dishonest, deceitful; from OH.†

pres. sg. 3. *mar-še-eš-zi* KUB 29.8 ii 22 (MH/NS), *mar-ši-eš-zi* KUB 30.50 v 9 (NH); **pret. pl. 3.** ⌜*mar*⌝*-še-eš-še-er* KBo 3.1 i 20 (OH/NS), *mar-še-eš-šir* KUB 26.33 iii 10 (Šupp. II); **broken** *mar-še-iš-ša-an*(-)[. . .] KBo 8.78 rev. 7.

1. to become desecrated, profane, unholy (opp. of *šuppešš-*): "When the patient finishes bathing, they pour that w[ater i]nto an empty wash basin, either of pottery or of bronze, which is not damaged(?). Then (if) it happens that it (the basin) is mixed with the (other) utensils (no harm is done, since) *UL kuwatqa mar-še-eš-zi UL-maš kuwatqa šuppešzi* "It becomes neither profane (unfit for sacred use) nor holy (fit for sacred use) in any way (by the above procedure)" KUB 29.8 ii 17-23 (rit., MH/MS); *mān* TUR.SAL *tabriyaš INA tabritī šer mar-ši-eš-zi nu tabriša maḫḫan šuppiyaḫanzi* "How they consecrate the *tabri* when a *tabri*-girl becomes desecrated upon a *tabri* (menstruates?)" KUB 30.50 v 8-10 (cat., NH), ed. CTH p. 167.

2. to become corrupt, dishonest, deceitful: *mān apezziyanma* ÌR.MEŠ DUMU.MEŠ. LUGAL ⌜*mar*⌝*-še-eš-še-er* (var. ⌜*mar*⌝*-še-e-er*) "But when later the subjects/servants of the princes became (var. were(?)) corrupt/dishonest" KBo 3.1 i 20 (Tel.pr., OH/NS) with dupl. KUB 11.1 i 20 see *marše-* v.; cf. LÚ.MEŠ URU*Ḫat-ti mar-še-eš-šir* KUB 26.33 iii 10 (oath, Šupp. II).

Laroche, RHA X/51 (1949-50) 24 ("devenir faux, trahir"), CTH (1971) p. 167 ("se souiller"); Watkins, TPS 1971:74.

Cf. *marša-* adj. and disc. there.

[GIŠ*mar-ši-it-ti*] KUB 30.31 i 6 read *kat!-mar-ši-it-ti*.

[maršeddu] HW 138, HW 3.Erg.24 read ^{GIŠ}*MEŠEDDU*.

maršuḫlitašši-; (an extispicy term).†

In an extispicy: [. . .]-*eš mar-šu-uḫ-li-ta-aš-ši-eš* ^{GIŠ}ŠÚ.A-*ḫi* GÙB-*an* "[The . . .]s (are) *m*., the 'seat' is on the left" KUB 16.29 obv. 31 □ For ^{GIŠ}ŠÚ.A-*ḫi* = *kešḫi* as a technical term in extispicy see RA 64:137.

m. looks like a Luw. genitival adj. in *-ašši-* from a Hurr. term in *-uḫli-*.

Laroche, RA 64 (1970) 135.

marta[- . . .]; (mng. unkn.); NS.†

EGIR-*andama* 2 *mar-ta*-x[. . .] / *āški parā udanz*[*i* . . .] VBoT 114 obv. 10-11 (rit. frag.); the trace after *-ta-* is a single Winkelhaken, which might be *-a*[*ḫ*-, *-š*[*i*-, *-a*[*r*- or the like. The trace excludes *martappa-*; an alternative reading ^{GIŠ}*me-ta*-x[. . .] is unlikely (coll.).

martappaš; (mng. unkn.); NH.†

ma?-ar-tap-pa-aš in a one word indented entry on the lower edge of the rev. of the cult inventory KUB 38.32. In the copy the first sign is drawn more like a *ku*.

[mar-ti].

What appears to be [. . .-]*kán mar?-ti* GIM-*an* x[. . .] in the copy of HT 24 obv. 4 (*ḫišuwaš* fest.) should be read *kán-ga*!*-ti* GIM-*an* x[. . .]; there is a column divider left of *kán* (coll.).

marwai- Luw. adj., (mng. unknown; perhaps a color word); NH.†

nu-za a-da-an-zi nu EN.SISKUR *a-ku-wa-a*[*n-na* . . .] (= A iii 2) / *nu* ^{d}*I-ia-ar-ri-in* 3-*ŠÚ e-ku-uz*[*-zi* . . .] (= A 3-4) / (no § in B) *ŠA* ^{d}*I-ia-ar-ri* DINGIR.MEŠ *mar-wa-a-in-zi* (var. [*ŠA* ^{d}*I-ia-a*]*r-ri* ^{d}7.7.BI) [x-*ŠU ekuzi*] (= A 5-6) / (no §) EGIR-*an-ta-ma nam-ma* ^{d}*I-ia-ar-ri-in* 1-*ŠU* [. . .] / [. . .]x.UD *ekuzi* (= A 7-9) "They eat. The client [requests(?)] something to drink. He drinks (to) ^{d}Yarri three times. [He drinks(?) (to)] the *marwai-* gods of Yarri (var.: the Heptad of Yarri) [. . .] times. And afterwards [he drinks(?) (to)] Yarri once more. He drinks (to) [. . .]" Bo 1582 (translit. HGG after note of Ehelolf) ii 9′-13′ (B), with dupl. KUB 7.54 (A) iii 2-9; □ The correspondence is more likely to be understood as a descriptive adj. "the . . . gods of Yarri" rather than as a literal translation of ^{d}7.7.BI (Akk. *Sibitti*) "The Heptad". For the awesome appearance of the *Sibitti*, the companions of Erra, cf. Cagni, L'epopea di Erra (Roma, 1969), Tablet 1, esp. lines 23ff.

The earlier identification of ÍD.SA$_5$ "Red River" with ^{ÍD}Maraššanta (the Classical "Halys", Turkish "Kızıl Irmak") was first proposed by Forrer, SPAW 1919:1039, and advocated subsequently by Güterbock, JCS 10 (1956) 116 note b. On the basis of this equation one proposed SA$_5$ "red" = **marašša-* = Luw. *mar*(*r*)*ušša-*, related to the Luw. v. "to redden" (cf. Oettinger, Stammbildung 385). This equation must now be given up on the basis of *nu* ÍD.SA$_5$ *AN*[*A*] ^{ÍD}*Maraššanda kuedani pēdi anda imm*[*i*]*škittari* "In the place where the Red River mixes with (i.e., flows into) the Maraššanda River" KBo 23.27 ii 28-29, cf. KBo 12.94:3-5, cf. Otten, StBoT 17 (1973) 21f. With the collapse of the equation one must now cautiously reassess contextual evidence. Even the inner Luw. connection of *marwa*(*i*)- to *maruša-* should be viewed with skepticism. It is highly probable that the words *marwai-* (adj.), *marwai-* (v.), *maruwammi-* (part. of *marwai-*), and *mar*(*r*)*uwašḫa-* are derived from the same root. If, as Laroche (DLL 69) suggests, *maruša-* is iter. of the verb *marru-* / *maruwai-*, one could associate the part. *:marušam*(*m*)*e-* with the above words. Two problems confront this solution. What would be the sense in the iter. here (cf. on *:marušam*(*m*)*e-*)? And, how can one explain the form *marušašaš* in IBoT 1.31 i 16, which appears to be a noun or adj.?

(:)*marušam*(*m*)*e-* modifies garments in contexts where the other garments mentioned are qualified by color words. *marušaš*(*a*)-, if the immediately preceding word is *ḫarkiaš* "white", might also be a color word. In the passages where other words of this group occur it is possible, but not necessary to think of a color. We can say then that the group of Luwian and Hittite words related to *marwai-* could denote a color. But it is not yet possible to identify that color.

Cf. :*maruwai-* v., *marruwammi-*, ⁽ᴺᴬ⁴⁾*ma(r)ruwašḫa-*, :*marwatani*, (:)*marušam(m)e-*, *marušaš(a)-*.

:maruwai- Luw. v.; (mng. unknown); NH.†

pret. sg. 3 :*ma-ru-wa-a-*⌜*it*⌝ KBo 6.29 ii 12.

(Ḫattušili III wrote:) "I held up my hand to my lady Ištar of Šamuḫa, and my lady Ištar of Šamuḫa helped me" *šarazzi katterraya anda* :*ma-ru-wa-a-*⌜*it*⌝ *nu nepiš tekanna katkattenut* "She . . . -ed above and below; she shook heaven and earth" KBo 6.29 ii 11-13 (shorter version of Ḫatt.), ed. Ḫatt. 48f.; main version (Ḫatt. iv 16ff.) lacks these lines. In broken Luw. context: [. . . *m*]*ar-ru-ut-ti* / [. . .] *mar-ru-ut-ti* / [. . .] KUB 35.124 ii 3-5. For another possible ex. of this verb with prev. *anda* in broken Hitt. context see the separate entry :*marwatani*. The participle of :*maruwai-* is treated separately sub *marruwammi-*.

Götze, Hatt. (1925) 49 ("scheiden"); Friedrich, HW 138 ("durcheinander mengen(?)"); Güterbock, Or NS 25 (1956) 122f. ("blacken(?)" or "mix up(?)"), idem, JCS 10 (1956) 116 note b ("redden(?)"); Laroche, DLL (1959) 69 ("rougir(?)"); Oettinger, Stammbildung (1979) 385 ("rot machen").

Cf. *marwai-* adj., *maruwammi-*, *mar(r)uwašḫa-*.

marruwammi- Luw. part.; (mng. unknown); NH.†

[. . .]x ᴰᵁᴳUTÚL-*in mar-ru-wa-am-mi-in* KI.MIN KUB 35.148 iv 12 (incantation in rit. of Zuwi of Angulluwa); the verb expressed by KI.MIN ("ditto") cannot be determined because of broken context.

Laroche, DLL 69.

Cf. *maruwai-* v.

⁽ᴺᴬ⁴⁾ma(r)ruwašḫa- n. com.; (a mineral imported from Cyprus); NH.†

sg. acc. *mar-ru-wa-aš-ḫa-an* KUB 8.38 + KUB 44.63 iii 10 (KUB 44.63 iii 2), 11, 15, [ᴺ]ᴬ⁴*mar-ru-wa-aš-ḫa-*⌜*an*⌝ KUB 42.18 right col. 5; **case unclear** *ma-ru-wa-aš-ḫa-aš* KUB 11.15:2.

In a paragraph of an inventory mentioning stones or minerals (det. NA_4): [ᴺ]ᴬ⁴*mar-ru-wa-aš-ḫa-*⌜*an*⌝ x[. . .] KUB 42.18 right col. 5, ed. Rosenkranz, ZA 57:247, Košak, THeth 10:30f., cf. Burde, StBoT 19:34; [. . .-]*da ma-ru-wa-aš-ḫa-aš* [. . .] KUB 11.15:2 (small frag. of unknown nature); (If a person's eyes become diseased, so that . . . ;) *našmaš išḫaḫru iyau*[*wa*]*n*(?) *mar-ru-wa-aš-ḫa-an*[. . . (verb) . . .] *unima mar-ru-wa-aš-ḫa-an šar*[*ā* ᵁ]ᴿᵁ*Alašiyaz a*[*rnuan*]*zi tāwišši* ˢᴵᴳ*ḫandal*[*a*-o] *maḫḫan nammašš*[*i*] *puppušatari nan t*[*arn*]*āi nan ki-na-iz*!*-zi nammankan pūwāizzi nuk*[*a*]*n ANA* GAL ZABAR GEŠTIN-⌜*an*⌝ *lāḫuwāi uniya mar-ru-*[*w*]*a-aš-ḫa-an menaḫḫanda peš*-*šiazzi nan anda ḫarnamniyazzi* "or (if) he (the patient) [lacks(?)] tears, *iyauwan*, (and) *m.*, they b[rin]g up from Cyprus that *m.*-mineral as a woolen *ḫ.* for his eye. Next it (the *m.*?) is repeatedly ground for him (-*ši*). He (the practitioner) . . . -s it (the *m.*), and . . . -s it. Next he grinds it (again). Into a bronze vessel he pours wine. And that *m.* he throws in together with (the wine), and mixes it up" (and applies it to him either by day or by night . . . and when he applies it to him, he wipes away the tears and *šipa-* with hot water.) KUB 8.38 + KUB 44.63 iii 10-17 (medical rit.), ed. StBoT 19:30ff.; Burde here assumes that what is brought from Cyprus is a reddish mineral, perhaps copper-bearing. With the collapse of the ÍD.SA₅ = ᴵᴰMaraššanta equation (see disc. s.v. *marwai-*, adj.) there remains no compelling reason to translate *m.* as "redness" or "red substance". Cyprus was famous for copper, but all copper salts even in dilute solutions are known to attack mucous membranes (the tissue surrounding the eyes). The *uni*-*ma* (11) shows that the *m.* in 10 is also the mineral, not "redness" as a condition of the eyes. But if so, does line 10 contain one clause or two? Does the sufferer lack tears, *iyauwan* and the medicine *marruwašḫa-*? Then [*Ú-UL ḫar-zi*] would have to be restored on the right edge. Or should one read the line *našmaš*<*ši*> *išḫaḫru iya*[*uwa*]*n marruwašḫan*[*-ma Ú-UL ḫarzi*] "(The patient) has tears and *i.*; but he has no *m.*"? No solution is totally satisfactory. Since *nammašš*[*i*] in line 12 begins a new clause, and temporal *maḫḫan* is normally not delayed to the end of its clause, we have interpreted *maḫḫan* as comparative and associated it with the preceding verb *a*[*rnuan*]*zi* "they bring up". The mode of application of this preparation is indicated only by the rather non-specific verb *anda tarna-*. Burde thinks the preparation was put as drops into the conjunctival sac of the eye (StBoT 19:33).

An abstract formation in -*(a)šḫa-* based upon Luw. *maruwai-*.

Laroche, RHA XVI/63 (1958) 113 n. 67, idem, BSL 53/1

(1958) 195 n. 3; Burde, StBoT 19 (1974) 33f.; Berman, KZ 91 (1977) 234; Starke, KZ 93 (1979) 256. All the above authors assume a basic meaning "redness".

Cf. *marwai-* adj., *maruwai-*, v.

:marwatani (mng. unknown); NS.†

:ma-ar-wa-ta-ni-ma-za anda [. . .] KUB 36.89 rev. 26 (prayer, NS), ed. Haas, KN 152f., 171; cf. DLL 69 (without tr.). It was interpreted as a loc. of a noun by Haas, but it is just as likely to be a Luw. 2 pl. pres. of the verb *marwai-*, which occurs with a preverb *anda*. For another 2 pl. form in the immediate context see *šummaš⸗at* DINGIR. MEŠ *iyatte*[*n* . . .] ibid. rev. 20.

(:)marušam(m)e- Luw. part.; (perhaps a color word); NH.†

sg. nom. com. *ma-ru-ša-me-eš* KUB 42.16 iv? 2, *:ma-ru-ša-mi-iš* Meskene 74.57:30f. (courtesy E. Laroche); **pl. nom. com.** *ma-ru-ša-me-iš* KUB 42.16 iv? 3; **pl. neut.** *:ma-ru-ša-am-ma* KUB 22.70 rev. 11, (12), [*:m*]*a-ru-ša-ma* KUB 42.60:2, [*ma-r*]*u-ša-ma* IBoT 3.110:6; **with endings broken** *ma-ru*[- . . .] IBoT 3.110:9, KUB 42.16 ii 2, iv 5, 6.

Always modifies garments: TÚG.GAL KUB 42.16 iv? 2; TÚG.GÚ IBoT 3.110:9; KUB 42.60:2(?); TÚG.GÚ(.È.A) *ḪURRI* KUB 22.70 rev. 11, KUB 42.16 iv? 5; TÚG.GABA KUB 42.16 iv? 6; TÚG. GAD.DAM.MEŠ KUB 22.70 rev. 12; TÚG*KAR⸗KU* KUB 22.70 rev. 11; TÚG*ikkuwaniya* KUB 42.16 ii 2. Other garments mentioned in the same contexts are qualified by color words, e.g. BABBAR KUB 22.70 rev. 10-12, KUB 42.60:3; BABBAR, *ḪAṢARTI*, *ḪAŠMANNI* KUB 42.16 iv? 1-12; BABBAR and *ḪAŠMANNI* ibid. ii 1-8, etc.

Güterbock, Or NS 25 (1956) 122f. ("dunkel?", "bunt?"), JCS 10 (1956) 116 note b ("red").

Cf. *marwai-* adj.

marušaš(a)- (mng. unknown); NH.†

In an inventory text: 1 GIPISAN SA_5 GÌR NU.GÁL *ḫar-*(or: *hur-*)*ki-aš ma-ru-ša-ša-aš* IBoT 1.31 obv. 16., ed. Goetze, JCS 10:32ff., comment on p 37, Košak, THeth 10:5f. Goetze read *ḫurkiaš* and understood *m.* as describing a wheel (*ḫurki-*). Güterbock (JCS 10:116 n. b) followed by Košak (THeth 10:8f.) read *ḫarkiaš marušašaš* and understood both as genitives. If the red GIPISAN contained items of two colors, white and *m.*, we could have here the two color words without *-a* "and" or explicit noun. Another possibility is that *m.* is a noun, "one red reed basket/ hamper(?) (which) has no foot, of (i.e., containing) white *m.*"; cf. [*m*]*a-ru-ša-ša* [. . .] KUB 42.23 obv.? 13 (inv.).

Cf. *marwai-* adj.

marzai- v.; to scatter(?) (once with prev. *arḫa*); MH.†

pres. sg. 3 *mar-za-a-iz-zi* KBo 24.43 i 15, 16 (MS?), KUB 15.31 ii 61, iii 45 (MH/NS), KUB 15.32 iv 36 (MH/NS), *mar-za-iz-zi* KUB 15.32 ii 27 (MH/NS).

Always takes bread as its object: 3 NINDA. SIG.MEŠ-*ma paršiya nat āpiyaš* DINGIR.LÚ. MEŠ-*aš pariyan* EGIR-*paya mar-za-iz-zi* NINDA.Ì.E.DÉ.A *memal išḫū*[(*wai*)] *šipantiya* "He breaks three thin breads and scatters(?) them forwards and backwards for the male gods of the pit. He pours (into the pit) sweet cake(s) and meal, and libates." KUB 15.32 ii 26-28 w. dupl. KUB 15.31 ii 29-31 (rit. of drawing paths, MH/NS), ed. Haas/Wilhelm, AOATS 3:158f.; 3 NINDA.SIG.MEŠ[-*ma-* o *p*]*aršiya* [*nu* DIN(GI)]R.LÚ.MEŠ-*aš pariyan mar-za-a-iz-zi* EGIR-*paya* [*mar-za*]*-a-iz-zi šipantiya* KUB 15.31 iii 44-45 (w. dupl. KUB 15.32 iv 5), ed. AOATS 3:164f.; *nu* LÚAZU 6 NINDA. KUR_4.RA.ḪI.A *tarnaš* [. . . *paršiya*?] *nammaš arḫa mar-za-a-iz-z*[*i* . . .] *mar-za-a-*⌈*iz*⌉*-zi nu ḫurlil*[*i kiššan memai*] KBo 24.43 i 14-16 (rit., MS?).

marza(š)tarri- see *marša(š)tarri-*.

maša- n. com.; locust, swarm of locusts; from MH/MS; wr. syll. and $BURU_5$.†

sg. nom. [*m*]*a-ša-aš* KUB 8.1 ii 17, BUR[U_5]-*aš* KBo 10.6 i 6, $BURU_5$ KUB 8.1 iii 3; **acc.** *ma-a-ša-an* KUB 24.1 iii 17 (NH), $BURU_5$-*an* KBo 12.94:8; **gen.** *ŠA* BUR[U_5] KBo 10.6 i 7.

pl. acc. $BURU_5$.ḪI.A KUB 24.2 rev. 11 = KUB 24.1 iv 8 (NH); **gen.** *ŠA* $BURU_5$.ḪI.A KUB 30.42 i 18; **unclear** $BURU_5$!.ḪI.A-*aš* KBo 14.84 iv 3; $BURU_5$.ḪI.A KBo 26.117:3.

idalun ta[*paššan*] *ḫinkan kaštan* (erasure) *ma-a-ša-an-na* KUB 24.1 iii 16-17 is parallel to *idalun tapaššan* [*ḫin*(*kan kāštanna*)] $BURU_5$.ḪI.A-*ya* ibid. iv 7-8, restored from dupl. KUB 24.2 rev. 10-11 (Gurney, AAA 27 (1940) 74). See usage c below.

a. in letters: *INA* URU*Qašqa[m]awa ḫalki*ḪI.A-*uš* BURU5.ḪI.A *ēzzašta* "But in Kaška a swarm of locusts ate the crops" Maşat 75/15:7-8 (MH/MS), ed. Alp, Belleten 44 (1980) 42f.

b. in omen apodoses: KUR-*e anda*/[*m*]*a-ša-aš parāi* BURU14.ḪI.A *karāpi* "A swarm of locusts will appear(?) in the land and will devour the crops" KUB 8.1 ii 16-17, ed. AlHeth 93, Riemschneider, Omentexte 102, 105; a fresh collation supported Otten apud Hoffner, AlHeth 93 w.n. 323, against Riemschneider, KZ 90:149, showing alignment of [. . . *m*]*a-* in line 17 to the right of the [*m*]*a-* in line 16. But, since a Glossenkeil is not attested elsewhere for *maša-*, (what precedes *ma-* in KUB 24.1 iii 17 are traces of an erased sign), and since the slight extra space available in line 17 could have contained a longer *ma-*, there is insufficient evidence for positing a Glossenkeil for *maša-*; KUR-*e anda* BURU5 *arāi* "A swarm of locusts will arise in the land" ibid. iii 3 □ Hitt. *arāi-* probably tr. Akk. *itbī-ma*, which is commonly used in Akk. omen apodoses, cf. AHw 1342 s.v. *tebû* 4 d; for *parāi* see AlHeth. 87f.

c. in prayers: *IŠTU* KUR URU*Ḫatti⸗makan idalun ta*[*paššan*] *ḫinkan kaštan* (erasure) *ma-a-ša-an-na a*[*rḫa uiya*?] "But from the land of Ḫatti [drive] o[ut] the evil f[ever], plague, famine and locusts" KUB 24.1 iii 16-17, ed. Gurney, AAA 27:22f., cf. AlHeth 93; *nu idalun tapašš*[(*an*) *ḫink*]*an kāštanna* (erasure) BURU5.ḪI.A-*ya apēdaš ANA* KUR.KUR[.ḪI.A L]ÚKÚR *pāi* "give bad fev[er(?), pla]gue, and famine and swarms of locusts to those enemy lands KUB 24.2 rev. 10-11, w. dupl. KUB 24.1 iv 7-8, (prayer of Muršili II to Telipinu), ed. Gurney, AAA 27.32f.; cf. *ḫinkan* [o o o]-x BURU5 [. . .] KUB 23.124 iv 42 (plague prayer of Muršili II), ed. Götze, KlF 1:250-51, and cf. KUB 15.34 ii 47, w. dupl. KBo 8.70:9-10, ed. Goetze, JCS 11:111 ("fate"), cf. Ünal, Belleten 41 (1977) 463 w. n. 99.

d. in catalogues (of rituals): *mān* BUR[U5]-*aš kuedani* URU-*ri kišanza nu apēdani* URU-*ri* *ŠA* BUR[U5] SISKUR DÙ-*anzi* "If a swarm of locusts occurs in any city, they perform the ritual of the locust swarm in that city" KBo 10.6 i 6-7, ed. CTH pp. 184-85; DUB.1.KAM *ŠA* BURU5.ḪI.A *ḫukmaiš QATI* "one tablet: incantation of the locust swarms—finished" KUB 30.42 i 18, ed CTH pp. 162-63.

e. in an incantation: [Ḫ]UL-*un irman* ḪUL-*un ḫulla*[*nzain*(?) . . .] BURU5-*an mišaran maninkuwan*[*dan* MU-*an . . . a*]*runaš anda ēp*[*du*] "[Let] the sea keep bad illness, evil rebell[ion(?)], the locust, the *m.*-insect and the short [lifespan]" KBo 12.94:7-9 (NH).

f. in an inventory: 1 BURU5 KÙ.GI "1 locust (made of) gold" KUB 42.11 i 10.

Gurney AAA 27 (1940) 74; Hoffner, AlHeth (1974) 92-93; Riemschneider, KZ 90 (1976) 149-51; Ünal, Belleten 41 (1977) 463-64.

maššayašši- adj.; (describing garments); NH.†

In a broken context of an inventory: [. . .] 7 TÚG.ERÍN.MEŠ *maš*(or: *pár*?)-*ša-ia-aš-ši-iš* KBo 18.175 vi 15. This might be the genitival adj. of a Luwian noun. Since it modifies garments, and a garment TÚG*maššiya-* exists, we read the first sign *maš* rather than *pár*. Cf. THeth. 10:12, 17, 227.

LÚ!**maššanāmi-** n.; (a functionary in a festival).†

[(. . . LÚ.M)]EŠ É dI[M 2 L)]Ú.MEŠ É dLAMMA *ša*[(*rlaimiaš* 4 S)]AL.MEŠ*ḫaḫḫala*[(*l⸗ leš*)] ⌜1⌝ LÚ*ma-aš-ša-na-a-mi-i*[(*š*)] 1 LÚ*palaššiš* 1 [(LÚ*wāu*)]*īš nat* 12 LÚ.MEŠ*BĒ*[(*L* DINGIR.MEŠ)] ". . . men of the temple of the Storm-god, 2 men of the temple of LAMMA-The-Exalted, 4 *ḫ.*-women, 1 *m.*-man, 1 *p.*-man, 1 *w.*-man. These (lit. they) are 12 'lords' of the gods." (They call them all into the house.) KBo 14.89 + KBo 20.112 i 2-4, with dupl. KBo 20.68 i 6-9, ed. Otten, IM 19/20:86f. The form appears to be derived from the Luw. noun *maššana-* "deity" plus a suffix *-ami-*; cf. Hittite LÚ*šiuniyant-*.

ma-ša-ni-ia-a[š?(-) . . .]

In a broken context of a letter: *kāš*[*a . . .*] / *ma-ša-ni-ia-a*[*š*?(-) . . .] / *anda ḫa-*x[. . .] KBo 18.87 rev. 2-4 (NH). Although the Luw. word *maššani-* "god" is always written with a double *š* elsewhere, one might consider this an exceptional writing of the gen. adj. *maššan(iy)ašši-*; cf. DLL 69.

***mašḫuil-** or ***mašḫuiluwa-** n. com.; mouse(?); NH.†

Deduced from the PN written ᵐPÉŠ.TUR (*-u*)*-wa-* and syll. ᵐ*Mašḫuiluwa-*. *m.* could be Hittite or Luwian. It is attested to date only in this PN but not as a Hittite common noun. See PÉŠ.TUR in the Sumerogram sec.

Friedrich, SV 1:95; Götze, ZA 40 (1931) 65-70; NH no. 779.

maši-; (interrog. or indef. rel. pron.); **1.** how many (interrog. pron.), **2.** however many, however much (indef. rel. pron.); from OH/NS.

sg. com. acc. *ma-ši-in* KUB 29.51 i 12 (NS).

pl. com. nom. *ma-ši-e-eš* KUB 1.16 iii 44, (OH/NS), KUB 5.1 i 60 (Ḫatt. III), KUB 34.11:4 (NS), KUB 35.116:8, *ma-ši-i-e-eš* KUB 5.6 ii 40 (NH), KBo 24.93 iii 21.

pl. com. acc. *ma-ši-e-eš* KUB 5.1 i 79, 88, KUB 27.1 i 8 (all Ḫatt. III); **case uncertain** because of broken context: *ma-ši-e-eš*! KUB 15.6 ii 25; *ma-ši-ú-u*[*š*? . . .] KBo 9.109 rev. 4.

pl. com. acc. (with pronominal inflection) *ma-še-e* KUB 10.52 i 8 (2x) [HW 138: pl. neut.].

pl. d.-l.(?) *ma-ši-ia-aš-š*(*a*) KUB 32.123 iv 38 (NH).

1. how many (interrog. pron.): *nu ma-ši-e-eš* MU.ḪI.A *pāir* [*ma-ši-eš-š*]*a-kán ḫuwāer* "How many years have passed, and [how man]y (of the offenders) have escaped (their fate/punishment)?" BoTU 8 (=KUB 1.16) iii 44-45 (edict, Ḫatt. I/NS), ed. HAB 14f., cf. 164-67.

2. however many, however much (indef. rel. pron. or adj.) — **a.** with resumptives — **1′** pron. *-a-*: URU[(*-az*) . . .] *ma-ši-e-eš pānzi* [(*nuška*)*n* . . .] *kunan*[*zi*] "[The . . . -s] will kill however many go [. . .] from the city [. . .]" KUB 34.11:4-5 (apodosis to a lunar eclipse omen, NS), dupl. KUB 8.7:3-4; *nukan INA* ᵁᴿᵁ*Zitḫara ma-ši-i-e-eš* DINGIR.MEŠ ŠÀ ⸢É⸣ [DINGIR-*LIM nat ḫ*]*ūmandušpat* SIxSÁ-*antat* "However many deities are in the temple in Zitḫara, they all were determined by oracle (as having caused the king's illness)" KUB 5.6 ii 40-41 (oracle question, NH), ed. AU 280f.

2′ pron. *apā-*: *nu ma-ši-e-eš gimruš laḫḫiyan ḫarzi . . . nuza apēdaš gimraš šer . . .* "however many regions he has traveled in . . . for those regions . . ." KUB 27.1 i 8, 10 (Hurr. cult, NH), cf. *la*(*ḫ*)*ḫiyai-* v. 1 c.

b. without resumptive: *ma-še-e ma-še-e* ᴺᴵᴺᴰᴬ*takarmuš* LUGAL-*uš paršiya* 1/2 NINDA ᴸᵁ́.ᴹᴱŠSAGI *U* 1/2 NINDA ᴸᵁ́.ᴹᴱŠNAR *daškanzi* "The cupbearers and the singers each take half of however many *t.*-loaves the king breaks" KUB 10.52 i 8-10 (fest. frag.), ed. HAB 165 with n. 1, where it is pointed out contra Sturtevant (Lg 10:272f.) that the noun is com. gender. *mašē* has the pronominal com. pl. nom. ending here used as acc.

c. *maši- imma*: ⸢*nukan*⸣ *ma-ši-e-eš imma* UD.ḪI.A *andama* SIxSÁ-*ri naškan* UGU GUB-*ri* "He (the king) will stay up there however many days are determined by oracle" KUB 5.1 i 60-61 (oracle question, Ḫatt. III), ed. THeth 4:42f.; *nukan ma-ši-e-eš imma* UD.ḪI.A UGU *pēdai* "(regardless of) how many days he will spend up there (he will come back down in front of Nerik)" KUB 5.1 i 88 (oracle question, Ḫatt. III), ed. THeth 4:46f.; cf. ibid. 79; *nuššan ari*⸗*rauwanzi ma-ši-i-e-eš i*[*mma* U]D.KAM.ḪI.A *anda ḫandanda* KBo 24.93 iii 21-22 (fest.).

d. [. . .]x *ma-ši-ia-aš-ša* § [. . .]x NU.GÁL SÌR.ḪI.A⸗*ya*⸗*šmaš kue ēšzi* KUB 32.123 iv 38-39 (Laluppiya fest.) □ if the sentence continues over the paragraph line, one could tr. "And to however many [. . . -s] there is no [. . .], the songs which are theirs . . ."; the *-šmaš* could refer back to *mašiyaš*; the broken context makes every interpretation uncertain.

Repeated *mašē mašē* and the construction with *imma* establish a functional parallelism to *kui-* (HAB 166).

Hrozný, CH (1922) 115 ("combien il vole"); Götze, NBr (1930) 35 (quantitative relative and demonstrative, "wieviel", "etliche"); Sommer, HAB (1938) 164-66 (interrog. and indefinite relative pron.; demonstrative use "ist . . . nicht nachweisbar").

Cf. *mašiyan, mašiyanki, mašiyant-, mašiwa-, mašiwan, mašiwant-.*

ᵀᵁ́ᴳ**maššiya-** n. (com.); (a garment); NH.

sg. nom. ᵀᵁ́ᴳ*ma-aš-ši-ia-aš* KUB 22.70 rev. 10 (NH), ᵀᵁ́ᴳ*maš-ši-ia-aš* KBo 2.32 obv. 8, KUB 41.21 i (14), KBo

18.184 rev. (7), ^{TÚG}*maš-ši-aš* KBo 18.175 i 8, KBo 18.179 rev. v(?) 5, KBo 18.181 rev. 11, KUB 42.16 ii 3, iii 6, KUB 42.17 left col. 2, and passim in inventories; abbreviated writings ^{TÚG}*ma-ši* NBC 3842 (JCS 10.102) obv. 14, 16, rev. 13, ^{TÚG}*maš* ibid. obv. 21.

Goetze (Cor.Ling. 54) suggested that *m.* alternates with ^{TÚG}ŠÀ.GA.DÙ in roughly similar listings of articles of men's attire. Friedrich, HW 1.Erg. 13, accepted the idea, but the similarity of some of these lists to the others is slight, making this equation questionable.

a. colors — **1′** white KUB 22.70 rev. 10, KBo 18.175 i 8, KUB 42.16 iii 6, KUB 42.17 left 2.

2′ blue-green (Akk. *ḪAŠMANNU*) KBo 18.184 rev. 7, KUB 42.16 ii 3, KUB 42.17 right col. 10, KUB 42.84 obv. 9.

3′ blue (ZA.GÌN) KBo 18.181 obv. 1.

4′ green (Akk. *ḪAṢARTU*) KUB 42.51 rev.? 6!, NBC 3842 obv. 2 (JCS 10:101).

b. has a hem/edge/fringe (Akk. *SISSIKTU*): (in a list of items removed from a person by a sorcerer for use against him) *mānši* ^{TÚG}*maš-ši-ia*[(*-aš*)] *kuiški* ^{TÚG}*SISIKT*[*UM* (var. ^{TÚG}*maš-ši-ia-aš* $^{TÚG(coll.)}$[*SISIKTUM kuiški*]) *dāš*] "If someone [took] the hem of his *m.*-garment" KUB 41.21 i 14 (rit., NH) restored from dupl. KBo 2.32 obv. 8.

c. weight (or price?): 2 $^{TÚG!}$*maš-ši-aš* ŠÀ.BA 1 1 MANA 20 GÍN 1 1 MANA 13 GÍN NBC 3824 rev. 9-10, ed. Finkelstein, JCS 10:101-2, cf. ibid. obv. 20, rev. 4, 13.

d. (other): 3 ^{TÚG}*maš-ši-aš* ŠÀ.BA 1 ZA.GÍN 2 LÍL-*aš* "three *m.*-garments, of which one is blue, and two are 'of the field'" KBo 18.181 obv. 1 (inv., NH).

Goetze in Cor.Ling. (1955) 54 ("waist-band", = ^{TÚG}ŠÀ.GA.DÙ); Finkelstein JCS 10 (1956) 103 w. n. 7, 8 ("cummerbund"), HW 1.Erg. (1957) 13 ("Tuchgürtel?" oder "Shawl?").

mašiyaḫ[. . .]; (mng. unkn.).†

[. . .]x *kuiš* MUŠEN-*iš* [. . .] / [. . .] KÁ.GAL *ma-ši-ia-aḫ*-x[. . .] KUB 34.92:5-6 (rit. frag.); the trace after *-aḫ-* might be *-ḫ*[*i* or *-t*[*en*.

mašiyan adv.; as much as, as many as; from OH/NS.†

ma-ši-ia-an KBo 6.10 ii 20 (OH/NS), KUB 40.1 rev! 40 (NH).

a. resumed in main clause by *apeniššuwan* "that many, that much" (NS): *takku* SIG$_4$ *kuiški tayēzzi ma-ši-ia-an tayēzzi andašše*≪*ašše*≫ (var. q$_2$ *antayašše*) *apēnišūwan* (var. q$_2$ *apenišša*[*n*?]) *pāi* "If someone steals bricks, he shall give to him (the owner) in addition as many as he steals" KBo 6.10 ii 20-21 (Laws § 128, OH/NS), ed. HG 68f., dupl. KUB 29.28 (JCS 16:18 = q$_2$, OS):10; cf. ⌜*takku*⌝ *ḫūššielliyaz pu*[(*ru*)]*t kuiški daīyazi* [*mašiyan* (*d*)]*āiyazzi andašeya* (var. o$_3$ *andanapa*) *apēniššūwan pāi* "If someone steals mud/mortar from a *ḫ.*, he shall give in addition to it [as much] as he steals" KBo 6.11 i 18-19 (Laws § 110, OH/NS), ed. HG 62f., dupl. KUB 29.23 (o$_3$, NS):14.

b. resumed in main clause by *apeniššan* "in the same way" (OS): cf. above under a, Laws § 128 in q$_2$ (OS); cf. HW^2 180.

c. [. . .] / *kūn ma-ši-ya-an* UN-*an ŠA* ^{d}UTU-*Š*[*I* . . .] "As much as His Majesty's [. . . -ed/-es] this man" KUB 40.1 rev! 39-40 (letter, Tudḫ. IV or Šupp. II); the clause may begin with *kūn*, since this text contains many exx. of asyndeton; apparently the adv. *mašiyan*, when it occurs non-initially, can come between the demonstrative adj. and its noun; cf. *kāš⸗wa maḫḫan* URUDU KUB 2.2 i 6, *kāš maḫḫan* GUD-*uš* KUB 12.58 iv 8, *kāš⸗man kuwapi me*[*miaš*] KUB 21.40 iii? 24 (cf. 22), *kūn kuin* DUMU-*an* KUB 23.127 iii 9.

Cf. *maši-*.

mašiyanki relative adv.; however many times; from MH.†

a. resumed by KASKAL-*ši* KASKAL-*šipat*: *tūriyanzimaš ma-ši-ia-an-ki nu* KASKAL-*ši* KASKAL-*šipat INA* 7 IKU.ḪI.A *anda penneškizzi* "But however many times they hitch them up, each time he drives them seven IKU's" KBo 3.5 ii 13-15 (Kikkuli hipp., MH/NS), ed. Hipp.heth. 88f.; cf. already HAB 164 □ the usage of *-pat* here is discussed by Hoffner, FsOtten 108.

b. no explicit resumptive: *nuza* ᵈUTU-*ŠI* EZEN.MEŠ *ma-ši-ia-an-ki* MU.KAM-*ti iyazi apūnma* EZEN *šakuwaššaranpat ēššanzi* "However many times in a year His Majesty performs festivals, they perform that festival only in the proper way" ABoT 14 iii 12-15 (oracle questions about festivals, NH); a parallel passage in the dupl. KUB 50.34 ii 1 has *ma-⌜ši-ia-an-ti⌝*, cf. *mašiyant-*; □ on *šakuwaššaranpat* cf. Hoffner, FsOtten 110.

Götze, NBr (1930) 35 ("etliche Mal" on a); Sommer, HAB (1938) 164 ("so oft" on a).

Cf. *maši-*.

mašiyant- adj.; **1.** (sg. loc. as adv.?) however many times (?), **2.** (pl.), (uncertain mng.); from MH/NS.†

sg. loc. *ma-ši-ia-an-te* KUB 4.1 iii 10 (MH/NS), *ma-⌜ši-ia-an-ti⌝* KUB 50.34 ii 1; **pl. nom. com.** *ma-ši-ia-an-te-eš* KUB 36.48:5.

1. (sg. loc. as adv.?) however many times(?): They make offerings to the gods, and) *ma-ši-ia-an-te-ma-aš-ma-aš āššu nu apeneššuwan* (var. [*a*]*pēniššu*[*wan*]) *akuwanzi* "they drink however many times it seems good to them" KUB 4.1 iii 10-11 (rit., MH/NS), (Otten/Rüster, ZA 67:59 n. 8) □ an emendation *ma-ši-ia-an-ki!-* was proposed by Götze, NBr 35f., accepted by Sommer, HAB 165 n. 1, cf. HW² 180, but not emended by Otten/Rüster, ZA 67:59; the unemended form was considered by Sturtevant, Lg. 10:272f., to be a neut. of *mašiyant-*; [*nuza* ᵈUTU-*ŠI*] EZEN.ḪI.A *ma-⌜ši-ia-an-ti⌝* / [MU.KAM-*ti iyazi apūšma* EZEN.Ḫ]I.A *šakuwaššaruš*⸗*pat ēššanzi* "However many times(?) [in a year His Majesty performs] festivals, they shall perform [those fes]tivals only in the proper way" KUB 50.34 ii 1-2 (oracles about festivals), restored from a parallel passage from the dupl. ABoT 14 iii 12-15, which, however, has the variant *ma-ši-ia-an-ki* for *ma-ši-ia-an-ti*, see *mašiyanki* b.

2. (pl.; uncertain mng.): *nuwarat mekki*[(-) . . .]/ *ma-ši-ia-an-te-eš da*[- . . .]/ 2 *gipeššar kiš*[*a*(-) . . .] KUB 36.48:4-6 (frag. of unknown nature).

The adv. *mašiyan* (q.v.) was identified by Friedrich (HW 138) as neut. nom.-acc. sg. of the stem *mašiyant-*, but it could also be from a stem **mašiya-* (thus Götze, NBr. 35) which we have posited as *maši-*.

Cf. *maši-*, *mašiyanki*.

mašiwa- v.; to do/make so much(?); NH.†

imp. pl. 3 *ma-ši-wa-an-du* KBo 18.133 obv. 3.

⌜*nu-ut*⌝*-ta* DINGIR.MEŠ *iyata*[*š*(coll.) . . .] / [o o]x *ma-ši-wa-an-du išḫūwandu* "May the gods of abundance make so much(?) [. . .] for you (and) pour (it) out" or "May the gods make so much [. . .] of abundance for you (and) pour (it) out" KBo 18.133 obv. 2-3 (letter). The *-du* is clear from the photo and cannot be this scribe's *-ma*. It is possible that *ma-ši-wa-an-du*<*-uš*> should be read, but the preceding word is lost in the lacuna; for *iyataš* cf. line 8.

Cf. *maši-*.

mašiwan adv.; **1.** as much as, as many as, how much, how many, as many times as, **2.** how many (times), **3.** *mašiwan mašiwan* "however numerous"; from OH/MS?.

ma-ši-wa-an KBo 25.109 iii 9 (MS?), KBo 23.113 iii 19 (NH), and passim, *ma-a-ši-wa-an* KUB 25.27 i 15, (11?).

1. as much as, as many as, how much, how many — **a.** *mašiwan* resumed in the following main clause by *apeniššuwan*: *nu* NINDA KAŠ UDU *ma-ši-wa-an* [EN URU-*LIM*] *maniyaḫzi nu apenišūwan* [. . .] "As much bread, beer and (as many) sheep as the [lord of the town] allocates, that many [they will give]" KBo 24.93 iv 7-9 (fest., NS); "The man-of-the-Stormgod puts the Stormgod and the god [. . .] on his(!) table." *nu ANA* DUMU É.GAL *ma-ši-wa-an* [*āššu*(?) *nuš ap*]*eniššuwan ekuzi* "He drinks (to) them as many times as seems [good] to the palace official" KBo 25.109 iii 9-10 (rit., MS?), for *ma-ši-wa-an āššu* see KBo 17.67:8; [. . .] *ma-ši-wa-an ANA* EN.SISKUR ZI-*anza* [. . . *apeniššu*]*wan pāi* KUB 39.76 obv. 1-2; cf. KBo 14.91:7-10.

b. *mašiwan* resumed by *apeniššan*: LIBIR.RA.MEŠ-*mawamu ma-ši-wa-an* ZI-*anza nuwaza apēniššan dašganun* "And I was taking for myself as many of the old ones as I wished" KBo 16.62 + KUB 13.35 i 43-44 (depos., NH), ed. StBoT 4:6f.; ᵀᵁᴳ*parnaš* LIBIR.RA-*mawa kuiš nuwamu ma-*

ši-wa-an ZI-*anza nuwaza apeniššan daškinun* ibid. i 48-50; cf. KUB 34.98:8-9, rest. from unpub. dupls. Otten/Rüster, ZA 72:146.

c. *mašiwan* resumed by something other than a correlative adv. — **1′** main clause follows *m.* clause: *nukan ma-ši-wa-an* ^TÚG^*šeknuš* GAM *appanzi natza* ^SAL^AMA.DINGIR-*LIM dāi* KUB 44.4 rev. 20-21 + KBo 13.241 rev. 9, cf. Otten, ZA 64:47; EGIR-*ŠU* NINDA.KUR$_4$.RA BA.BA.ZA LUGAL-*uš ma-ši-*[*wa-an*] *lamniyazi nan paršiyanzi* KUB 41.35 ii 8-9 (fest. frag.); *nu ma-ši-wa-an* SI×SÁ-*ri namma ANA* KUR *P*[*išaiša* . . .]*ziladuwa* GAM-*an ḫamankmi* KBo 23.113 iii 19-20 (oracle question, NH); *kinun ma-ši-wa-an* [*ANA*] EZEN *zēni* EZEN Ú.BURU$_{14}$-*ašša peškanzi UL-kan waqqari*(!) KUB 42.100 iii 24-25 (cult inv., Tudḫ. IV); "The patient gives 8 sheep" ŠE?-*ya ma-ši-wa-an pāi* ^LÚ.MEŠ^MUŠEN.DÙ-*ia kuiša IŠTU* É-*ŠU* 1 NINDA.KUR$_4$.RA *dāi* "And (regardless of) how much grain(?) he gives, each of the bird-watchers takes one thick-bread loaf from his house" KBo 12.96 iv 5-7 (rit., MH/NS); GUD.ḪI.A-*ma* UDU.ḪI.A *IŠ*⌜*TU*⌝ x[. . . *m*]*a-ši-wa-an lamniyan nankan apēz arḫa iyawen*[*i*] KBo 21.37 rev.? 5-6 (rit. of Kizzuwatna), cf. *lamniya-* 3; *namma* NINDA KAŠ *ma-ši-wa-an ANA* EN.SISKUR.SISKUR *ā*[*ššu*] KBo 24.45 obv. 14 (rit.); cf. KBo 17.65 obv. 55; *ma-ši-wa-an ḫikkirmaḫiya pankur* "(May Labarna's (and) Tawannanna's offspring and years be) as numerous as a clan in a *ḫ.*" KBo 13.49:9-11; *nu ḫūetar ma-ši-wa-an u*[-. . .] *nat uwami ANA BELTĪYA za*[- . . .] KBo 13.62 obv. 18-19 (letter to queen, NH); KI.LÁ.BI-*ŠU*-⌜*yat*⌝ *ma-ši-wa-an nat iyanpat ēšdu* "And let it be indicated (lit., made) how much its weight is" KUB 13.4 ii 34-35 (instr., pre-NH/NS), ed. Chrest. 154f. ii 41-42.

2′ main clause precedes *m.* clause: *IŠTU* É.GAL-*LIM-ma kī danzi* (list of items) *ma-ši-wa-an-ša-an ḫaššī anda ḫandaittari* (end of paragraph) KUB 29.1 iv 4-8 (rit., OH/NS), ed. Kellerman, Diss 18, 31; *nu kī danzi* (list of items) *IŠTU* NINDA-*ma* KAŠ EN URU-*LIM ma-ši-wa-an maniyaḫzi* KBo 22.125 i 3-7, tr. s.v. *maniyaḫ-* 3 a 1′; NINDA.KUR$_4$.RA *paršiyanzi ma-ši-wa-an* LUGAL-*uš lamniyazi* KBo 4.13 iv 33-34; cf. KUB 10.22 i 20-21; *aššanumaš⸗ma* [*ma-a-ši-w*]*a-an lamniyanzi* KUB 25.27 i 10-11, cf. ibid. 15, KBo 26.152 rev. (5) (all cult texts).

2. how many times!: *numu* ^d^*IŠTAR* GAŠAN-*YA ma-ši-wa-an* [(*da*)]*tta numu šallai pedi ANA* KUR ^URU^*Ḫatti* LUGAL-*eznani* [(*ti*)]*ttanut* "Ištar, my lady, how many times you 'took' me (= helped me)! And you installed me in the Great Place in kingship over the land of Ḫatti" KUB 1.1 iv 64-66 w. dupl. KBo 3.6 + KUB 19.70 iv 25-27 (Apology of Ḫatt. III), ed. NBr 32f., StBoT 24:28f. ("wie oft").

3. *mašiwan mašiwan* "however numerous": [. . . *p*]*ankuršet ma-ši-wa-an ma-ši-wa-a*[*n* . . . *apeni*]*ššan ašantu* "Let the . . .-s be however numerous his clan is" KUB 36.107:5-6 (OH/MS?).

Götze, NBr. (1930) 35 ("wieviel"), Friedrich, HE 1 (1960) § 123b ("wie gross, wieviel").

Cf. *maši-*.

mašiwant- adj.; equal in size or amount to, as much/little as, as big/small as; from MH.

sg. com. nom. *ma-ši-wa-an-za* KUB 19.20 rev. 17 (Šupp. I), KUB 21.27 iii 40 (Ḫatt. III), *ma-a-ši-wa-*[*a*]*n-za* KUB 31.71 iv 36 (Ḫatt. III).

sg. com. acc. *ma-ši-wa-an-ta-an* KBo 16.47:8 (MH/MS), 1684/u:8 (+ KUB 23.72 obv. 42) (JCS 28:61 and ZA 67:54) (MH/MS).

sg. neut. nom *ma-ši-wa-an* KUB 33.120 iii 35.

pl. com. acc.(?) *ma-ši-wa-an-du*<-*uš*>(?) cf. *mašiwa-* v.

(Bring all the persons and goods) [*āppa* ^SÍG^*maišt*]*an ma-ši-wa-an-ta-an lē apteni* "Do not [with]hold so much as a fiber of wool" 1684/u + KUB 23.72 obv. 42 (Mita text, MH/MS), ed. Hoffner, JCS 28:61, cf. above s.v. ^SÍG^*maišta-*; [*m*]*ān* ^SÍG^*maištanna ma-ši-wa-an-ta-an waštanzi* "Even if they (the people of Ura and Mutamutašši) are remiss in respect to so much as a fiber of wool," (You and I will make war on them) KBo 16.47:8-9 (treaty, MH/MS), ed. Otten, IM 17:56f.; [. . . (x-*ki šalli mā*)]*l* KUR-*e ma-ši-wa-an* ". . . (is?) great, the [*ma*]*l* (is?) as big as the land" KUB 33.120 iii 35 with dupl. KUB 36.1 right col. 12 (Kingship in Heaven, NS), cf. above sub *māl* d; *kappišmawa* ⌜*da*⌝*lugaš*[*ti*] ŠU.SI *ma-a-ši-wa-*[*a*]*n-za* "But the small one, in leng[th] is as big as a finger" KUB 31.71 iv 35-36 (queen's dream, NH); *nu uwami ANA* ^d^*Liliwani* GAŠAN-*IA* ALAM KÙ.

BABBAR *ŠA* ^{m}*Ḫattušili* ^{m}*Ḫattušili ma-ši-wa-an-za* SAG.DU-*SU* ŠU.M[EŠ-*Š*]*U* GÌR.MEŠ-*ŠU ŠA* KÙ.GI *iyami* "I will come and make for DN, my lady, a silver statue of Ḫ., as big as Ḫ., its head, hands, and feet of gold" KUB 21.27 iii 39-41 (prayer, Pud.); cf. [. . .]-*ma pit/patturiš ma-ši-wa-an-za* "the size of a *p.*" KUB 19.20 rev. 17 (letter, Šupp. I).

mašiwant-, like *ḫumant-*, follows its noun.

Götze, NBr (1930) 35.

Cf. *maši-*.

maškan- n. neut.; **1.** bribe (given to officials), **2.** gift, propitiatory gift (given to gods); from MH/MS.

sg. nom. *maš-kán* KUB 15.11 ii 19 (NH).
sg. acc. *ma-aš-ka-an* KBo 16.25 i 9 (MH/MS), KUB 13.9 iii 14 (MH/NS), *ma-aš-ga-an* KUB 13.2 iii 26 (MH/NS), *ma-aš-kán* KUB 29.39 iv 10 (NH), *maš-kán* KBo 11.10 ii 24 (MH?/NS), KUB 14.14 rev. 8, 20 (Murš. II), KUB 22.57 obv. 5, 6, 15 (NH) and passim in NH oracles.
sg. abl. *maš-kán-na-*[*az*] KUB 14.14 rev. 13 (Murš. II).

1. bribe (given to officials); always in instr. texts and written *ma-aš-*. . . : [*nu* LÚ.KÚR-*an a*]*rḫa lē kuiški tarnai nuza ma-aš-ka-an dā*⌈*i*⌉ "Let no one let the [enemy] escape and take a bribe." KBo 16.25 i 8-9 + KBo 16.24 i 19-20 (instr., MH/MS); (Whoever keeps silent about these matters of the king, if either you, as his colleague, conceal them) *nušši ma-aš-ka-an pāi* "and he gives a bribe to him (or: for it [your silence?]), (or if . . .)" KUB 13.9 iii 14 (instr., MH/NS), ed. von Schuler, FsFriedrich 448, 450, 453, Freydank, ArOr 38:264-66.; (When the governor of the border-province participates with local officials in judicial proceedings, he is instructed:) *ma-aš-ga-an-na-za lē kuiški dāi DĪNAM šarazzi katteraḫḫi lē katterra šaraz*<*zi*>*yaḫi lē kuit ḫandan apāt īšša* "And let no one take a bribe. Let him not make the stronger case the weaker one, nor make the weaker case the stronger one. Do what is just." KUB 13.2 iii 26-28 (Bel Madg., MH/NS), ed. Dienstanw. 48, comments on 57; *ma-aš-kán* in the broken context KUB 29.39 iv 10 (market protocol, NH) probably also represents this usage, cf. *ḫannuan dāiš* "he began to adjudicate" in iv 8.

2. gift, propitiatory gift (given to gods); always in NH prayers, oracle questions, and vows, and always written *maš-kán* — **a.** an advance payment as a pledge to placate the deity until proper ceremonies can be undertaken: "We will make peace with him again" *nammašši arkuwar tiyauwaš šer maš-kán za*[*nk*]*ilatar* SUM-*anzi kuitman* ^{d}UTU-*ŠI uizzi nutta* ^{d}UTU-*ŠI* KASKAL-*šiaḫzi* "Next they will give him a gift and reparation for presenting a defense, until His Majesty comes, and His Majesty will 'put you on the way'" (Will you, O god, set your mind at rest through that?) KUB 22.57 obv. 14-16 (oracle question, NH), tr. differently HW[2] 313; "[. . .] I never gave, but now [. . .] I have sent to the god 25 persons. [. . . On one side] I put [x] persons, on the other I put 7 persons. I shall send [them(?) . . .] to the god" *nat ANA* DINGIR-*L*[*IM*] *maš-kán ēš*[*du*] GIM-*annakan* ^{d}UTU-*ŠI laḫḫaz šarā* SIG_5-*in uizzi* "Let it be a propitiatory gift for the god. But when His Majesty comes up (to Ḫattuša) from the campaign safe and sound, . . ." KUB 15.11 ii 15-20 (queen's vow, NH); EZEN *išuwašma* EZEN *ḫiyarraš kueda*[*š*] *ANA* DINGIR.MEŠ *ēšzi nušmaš pedišši maš-kán pianzi* "To the gods to whom an *i.*-festival and a *ḫ.*-festival is (due), shall they give them a propitiatory gift in it's place?" KUB 18.23 iv 2-3 (oracle question, NH).

b. given to offended gods along with other reparations in order to assuage their anger: (We will make good the neglected festivals) GAM-*anna maš-kán zankila*<*tar*> SUM-*qaweni ANA MANTADŪTI-kan* UN-*an parā* [*n*]*eyaweni* EGIR-*azzama maš-kán zankilatar* SUM-*weni* "and along with it we will keep giving (iter.) the propitiatory gift and reparation. We will send a man as a pledge(?), and afterwards we will give the propitiatory gift (and) reparation" KUB 22.57 obv. 5-7 (oracle questions, NH); cf. obv. 15; although no abstract noun formation in *-ūtu* is yet attested for Akk. *mandattu*, this seems the most likely interpretation; the person sent is to guarantee subsequent payment of fines; the usual Akk. word for this is *manzazānūtu*, (see CAD M1:233); *maš-kán-na zankilatarra IŠTU* É.LUGAL SUM-*anzi* SISKUR-*ya IŠTU* É.LUGAL ⌈SUM⌉-*anzi* . . . ^{d}UTU-*ŠI-yaššikan šer* *ma*! *ldai* "And they will give a propitiatory gift and reparation from the king's house, and they will give an offering (SISKUR) from the king's house . . . His Majesty will make a vow to that effect" KBo 24.126 rev. 7-9 (oracle question, NH); cf. rev. 14-15; (They will make good the vows which are to be made good) *kattanna zankilatar* SUM-*anzi maš-kán-na-kán* BAL-*anzi* "And along with it they will give reparation and offer a propitiatory gift" KBo 2.2 iv 9-10 (oracle question, NH); also with BAL (*šipant-*) in KUB 50.35 rev? 24; (O ᵈAMAR.UTU, they will do the following for you:) ᴸᵁ́*ĀŠIPU-kan mukiššar dāi* . . . *nu ANA* DINGIR-*LIM* SISKUR SUM-*anzi maš-kán-na-ši* SUM-*anzi* "The exorcist will compose (lit., put) an evocation . . . and they will give an offering to the deity, and give a propitiatory gift to him" KUB 6.13 + KUB 18.62:6-8 (oracle question, NH), cf. ibid. lines 13-16; [*zankil*]*atar* SUM-*anzi ITTI* ᵈUTU-*ŠI-mat* [. . .]x *ŠA* É.GAL-*LIM maš-kán pēdanzi* "They will give reparation, and together with His Majesty [. . .] they will convey it as the propitiatory gift of the palace" KUB 16.77 ii 41-42 (oracle question, NH); *ziqqa* KI-*aš*! ᵈUTU-*uš kūn* NIM.LÀL-*an kuin uiēš nutta kāša* LUGAL-*uš* SAL.LUGAL-*aš kēl ŠA* NIM.LÀL *maš-kán kūn* SISKUR *peškanzi* "The king and queen are giving you this offering as a propitiatory gift regarding this bee, which you, O Sungoddess of the Earth, have sent." (If you sent it for evil, change it now and make it a bird portending good.) KBo 11.10 ii 21-24 (rit., MH?/NS), cf. Haas, UF 13 (1981) 113; cf. KBo 11.72 ii 26-28 (passages from duplicate); (Because the bloodguilt for Tudḫaliya has now come upon me) *nat ammuqqa IŠTU* É-*TIYA šarnikzilaz maš-kán-na-*[*az*] / *šarnenkiškimi* "I will make restitution for it (-*at*) together with my household, with restitution and a propitiatory gift." (So let the soul of my gods, my lords, be appeased) KUB 14.14 rev. 13-14 (PP1), ed. Götze, Pestgeb. 172-73 ("Sühne ableisten").

The word denotes a gift made in order to secure someone's favor. In usage 1, the gift is regarded as decidedly improper. Therefore we have translated those passages "bribe". In usage 2 the gift is altogether proper. There our translation "propitiatory gift" is meant to express the religious context and the purpose of the gift. *m.* is the direct object of the verbs *pāi-* 'give, pay', *šipant-* 'offer', *pēda-* 'convey', and *dā-* 'take'.

Götze, Pestgeb. 190-92 ("Sühne, Sühngabe"); Friedrich, HW (1952) 138 ("Gabe, Bestechung, Schweigegeld"); Laroche apud HW 138 (proposed to read *parkan* as *maškan*); Freydank, ArOr 38 (1970) 264f.

Cf. *maškiške-*.

maške- v. see *ma-* v., *maškiške-*, *park-* v.

maškiške- v.; to give presents; OH/MS.†

nušmaš arū[*š*]*gazi ma-aš-ki-iš-ga-zi nu-uš-*≪*ma-*≫*ši-kán QĀTAMMA* ⌈*mi*⌉*yauēš ēšten* "He is showing reverence and giving presents to you (gods). So be mild to him in return!" KBo 20.34 rev. 7-9 (rit.).

Since the context requires an action which is ingratiating, a connection with the noun *maškan* (q.v.) "present, bribe," is plausible.

Cf. *maškan-*.

[*mašta-*] see *parta-*.

[*maštai-*] see *partai-*.

[*maštaimi-*] see *baštaimi-*.

[ᴷᵁŠ*mašduggani-*] see ᴷᵁŠ*parduggani-*.

[:*maššunti*(-)] see :*paršunti*(-).

[ᴳᴵŠ*mašušta*] Ertem, Flora 161, read ᴳᴵŠTUKUL-*šušta*.

[*mad-*] v. see *ma-* v., *maz*(*z*)-.

matalli(ya)-; (meaning unclear); NH.†

EN.SISKUR-*yašamašza ma-tal-li-ia*[- . . .] KUB 46.40 obv. 10 (rit.); EGIR-*ŠU-maza* EN. SISKUR *ANA* 2 DINGIR.MEŠ IGI-*anda ma-tal-li-ia* [ᴸᵁ́*parl*]*ašalla* x[. . .] / *aniyanzi* KUB 46.38 ii 12-13 (rit.); [EN.SISKUR-*za ANA* 2 DINGIR.MEŠ IGI-*and*]*a*? *ma-tal-li-ia* ᴸᵁ́*par-lašalla* [. . . *ar*]*ḫa aniyanzi* KUB 46.42 ii 15-16 (rit.); all refs. are found in the same ritual (CTH 495).

Because of the mention of TUKU.TUKU-*aš gangati* in KUB 46.40 obv. 11 and KUB 46.38 ii

13 it is possible that this ritual deals with the appeasing of angry parties. Two deities and one client (EN.SISKUR) are mentioned. There is some chance therefore that *matalliya-* is the same word as *mantalli(ya)-* q.v.

[^{GIŠ}*matanḫarišša-*] is to be read ^{GIŠ}PÈŠ *tanḫarišš[a]* in KBo 24.40 obv.(?) 8 despite the lack of word space in the copy. Cf. Pap. 6*-7*, Hoffner, EHGl 44 n. 63, AlHeth 116, Ertem, Flora 166. The same words are found in KBo 5.1 ii 24 (rit. of Papanikri), where the copy shows space.

mattaraši; (mng. unknown); Hurr.; NH.†

1 NINDA.SIG *naḫnazu ma-at-ta-ra-ši* KI.MIN KUB 27.1 ii 25 (fest.).

Listed in GLH 169 s.v. *matta-*.

[^{GIŠ}*matnani*] Ertem, Flora 161, 473/e:7 cited without context, possibly Akk. *MADNANU.*

:mataššu- n. or adv.; (mng. unclear); NH.†

"The votive gifts which are to be made good they will make good, and along with it they will give the reparation and offer the propitiatory gift" *ANA* DINGIR-*LIM-yakan :ma-ta-aš-šu UL* BAL-*anzakir kinunmakan* BAL-*anzakiuwan tianzi* "They were not offering *m.* to the deity, but now they are beginning to offer" KBo 2.2 iv 11-14 (oracle question), ed. Hrozný, BoSt 3:54f., Kammenhuber, MIO 3:47f.; [. . .]x *:ma-ta-aš-šu lē i-ia-at-t[a]*-x "Don't do/make [. . .] *m.*" or "Let him/her not go [. . .] *m.*" or "Let the *m.* not go [. . .]" KUB 15.3 i 3 (queen's dreams and vows); coll. showed that the horizontal of the trace after *-t[a]-* is lower than in the copy and could be the beginning of either *ni* or *ri*.

See HW 322, DLL 70.

[*ma-at-ša-at*] KBo 6.26 iii 8 (Law § 184) is probably to be emended to *MA-AD-DÁ!-AT*, a stative sg. 3 fem. from Akk. *madādu*, q.v., see Friedrich, HG 112.

^{NINDA}ma-du[-. . .]; n.; (a kind of bread or pastry).†

[*I*]*NA* É ^{d}IM 5 NINDA.SIG.MEŠ 1 ^{NINDA}*ma-du[-. . . š]ermašš⸢a⸣n* ŠE.GIŠ.Ì *išḫuwān* "in the temple of the Stormgod five flat breads, one *m.*-bread [. . .] with linseeds sprinkled on top" KBo 8.91 rev. 3-4 (Kizzuwatna rit.).

In view of the occasional use of GNs in bread names (Hoffner, AlHeth 209f.) one should perhaps compare ^{URU}*Maddunašša* (RGTC 6:266) along with the element *maddu-* in PNs (NH nos. 352a, 793, 794).

mau- v.; see *mauš-*.

mawalli- adj.; (mng. unkn.); NH.†

sg. acc. com. *ma-wa-al-li-in* KUB 31.66 iv 14.

"Although my father (Muwatalli) gave instructions about the chariotry (lit. horses): 'Let them not leave behind any chariotry'" ^{m}NU.^{GIŠ}KIRI$_6$-*išmazakan* ANŠE.KUR.RA *ma-wa-al-li-in tališta* "It was ^{m}NU.^{GIŠ}KIRI$_6$ (who) left behind for himself *m.*-chariotry, (I didn't know it. But when I heard it, . . .)" KUB 31.66 iv 13-15 (prayer of Urḫitešub), ed. Houwink ten Cate, FsGüterbock 131, 133, who tr. "a 'chariot-*mawallis*' (a type of detachment?)". One could also tr. "chariotry (and) *m.*" or "chariotry (as) *m.*" Contrast *⸗za⸗kan dala-* in line 13 with *⸗kan dala-* in lines 11-12 and 20.

Perhaps with DLL 70 s.v. *mauwa* this is to be related to the Luwian number *mauwa* "four", cf. HE § 129.4. Cf. also van Brock, RHA XX/71 (1962) 112 ("soit un cheval de quatre ans, soit un cheval de quadrige").

māuwani- Luw. v.; (an action of horses); NH.†

[o o o o o o DAN]NA *ma-a-u-wa-ni-in-ta* "They (i.e., the horses) . . . -ed [. . .] *DANNA*" KUB 29.55 i 22 (hipp.), ed. Hipp.heth. 152. Note the other Luw. 3 pl. pret. verb forms in the preceding context.

Connecting this verb with Luw. *mauwa* "four": Otten, Luv. (1953) 27f.; Laroche, DLL (1959) 70; Kammenhuber, Hipp.heth. (1960) 153 n. c, 208 n. 4; differently: Rosenkranz, WO 2 (1956) 287ff.

mauš-, mau-, mu- v.; to fall (usually w. local particle: *⸗kan, ⸗šan, ⸗ašta*); from OH/MS.

act. pres. sg. 1 [*mu*]*-u-uḫ-ḫi* KUB 43.60 i 33 (OH/NS), *mu-uḫ-ḫi* ibid. i 34; **sg. 3** *ma-uš-zi* KUB 30.29 i 5 (pre-NH/NS), KUB 8.1 ii 13, iii 6, KUB 29.9 ii (7), 10, (13), KUB 4.72 obv. [b] 3, KUB 34.22 i 4, 6 (all NS), *ma-a-uš-*

zi KUB 8.36 iii 10 (NH).

pret. sg. 3 *ma-uš-ta* KBo 12.85 iii 5 (MH/NS), KUB 28.5 obv. 10b, 11b, KUB 28.4 obv. 16b, 17b (NS), KUB 33.120 ii 40 (pre-NH/NS), KUB 6.29 obv.? 4, *ma-a-uš-ta* KBo 12.75:8 (NS); **pl. 3** *ma-ú-ir* KBo 21.22:4, 5 (OH/MS), *ma-uš-še-er* KUB 27.29 iii 16 (MH/NS), KBo 19.145 iii 31 (NH), KBo 19.80 rt. col. (12) (NH).

act. imp. sg. 3 *[m]a-uš-du* KBo 13.260 iii 38 (NS).

mid. pres. sg. 2 *ma-uš-ta* KUB 1.16 iii 52 (OH/NS); **sg. 3** *ma-uš-ta-r[i]* KBo 9.107 rev. 5, (13) (NS?), *[m]a-uš-ta-ri* KUB 45.79 obv. 8.

pret. sg. 1 *ma-uš-ḫa-ḫa-at* KUB 1.1 iii 24, KUB 19.67 i (17) (both Ḫatt. III); **sg. 3** *ma-uš-ta-at* KUB 33.106 ii 9, KUB 17.1 ii 5 (NH), KUB 33.114 i 18 (NS).

mid. imp. sg. 3 *[m]a?-uš-ta-ru* KBo 13.260 iii 41 (NS), assuming that this last line of the col. is indented.

part. sg. com. nom. *ma-uš-ša-an-za* KUB 4.1 iv 26 (NS), KUB 5.7 rev. 28 (NS); **sg. neut. nom.** *ma-uš-ša-an* ibid. rev. 27; **infin.** *ma-uš-šu-u-wa-an-zi* KUB 33.106 ii 8 (NH).

iter. act. pres. sg. 3 *ma-uš-ki-iz-zi* KUB 7.53 i 5 (NH); **pret. sg. 3** *ma-uš-ki-i[t(-) . . .]* KBo 9.83 rev. 5 (NH), *ma-uš-ke-e-e[t(-) . . .]* KUB 23.14 iii 8, (10) (NS?), the last two forms possibly being mid.

iter. mid. pres. sg. 3 *ma-uš-ki-it-ta-ri* KUB 31.86 iii 2 (MH/NS), *[ma?-u]š-kat-ta-ri* KBo 10.47g iii 18 (NS); **pret. sg. 3.** *ma-uš-ki-it-ta-at* KUB 48.124 rev.? 16 (NS), *ma-uš-ki-ta-at* ibid. rev.? 17, 18.

Plene writings of initial *ma-*: *ma-a-uš-zi*, *ma-a-uš-ta*.

a. without associated adverbs — **1′** literal: — **a′** of a person: ÍD-*p[a mu]-u-uḫ-ḫi luli[ya] mu-uḫ-ḫi* "I will fall into a river, I will fall into a pond" KUB 43.60 i 33-34 (myth in rit., OH/NS); note that this clause lacks *-kan*.

b′ of a celestial phenomenon: "[If] a 'big star' in the sky develops a tail (*talukešš-*), and is scattered, and furthermore comes together(?)" *[pa-aḫ-ḫ]ur?-kán nepiši* ZAG-*az ma-uš-zi* "[fi]re falls to the right in the sky" KUB 8.24 ii 5-7 (star omen, NS), cf. ibid. 10-12.

c′ of the moon: ᵈ*SIN-ašwakan nepišaz ma-uš-ta naškan šer* KI.LAM-*ni ma-uš-ta* "The moon fell from heaven. It fell on the gate house" KUB 28.4 obv. 16b-17b (myth, NS), ed. Kammenhuber, ZA 51:109, 113, translit. Laroche, Myth 15, tr. ANET 120 (reading *kilamni*); cf. KUB 28.5 obv. 10b-11b (ibid.).

d′ of fetuses: "If a woman's children keep dying" *našmaššikan* ᵁᶻᵁ*šarḫūwandama ma-uš-ki-iz-zi* "or if her fetuses keep miscarrying (lit. falling)" KUB 7.53 i 4-5 (rit., NH), ed. Tunn. 4f.

2′ metaphorical, "to fall, perish, suffer defeat" — **a′** w. expressed subject: *mānšan nepiši* MUL.ḪI.A *anda šiššandari natkan katta mumianzi* ERÍN.MEŠ-*kan ma-uš-zi* "If in heaven stars collide(?) and fall down, the army will suffer defeat" KUB 8.22 ii 6-8 (star omen, NS), ed. StBoT 5:156; cf. KUB 8:1 ii 13 (NS); KBo 13.15:10 with dupl. KUB 34:7 rt. col. 6 (both lunar eclipse omens, NS); KUR-*e-kan ma-uš-zi* "The land will fall" KUB 8.24 rev. 6 (star omen, NS); a similar phrase without *-kan*: KUR URI *ma-u[š-zi]* "The land of Akkad will fall" KUB 8:2 rev. 10 (lunar omen, NS); SAG.GEMÉ.ÌR.MEŠ-*kan ma-uš-z[i]* "The domestic servants will fall" KUB 34:22 i 6 (animal omen, NS); MÁŠ.ANŠE *ma-uš-zi* "The herds will fall" KUB 8.3 rev. 2 (lunar omens, NS).

b′ without expressed subject (impersonal use): *zaḫḫiyakan pangawi* ERÍN.MEŠ-*ti ma-uš-zi* "There will be a fall (defeat) in battle for the entire army" KUB 8.1 iii 6 (lunar eclipse omens, NS); cf. KUB 4.72 obv. [b]3 (liver model, OS or MS); *[n]ašmakan* ERÍN.MEŠ-*ti pangarit ma-u[š-zi]* KBo 8.47 obv. 11 (lunar eclipse omen, NS).

b. with associated adverbs and preverbs — **1′** *anda*: *[p]arā-aš tiyazi [n]aškan anda alallā [m]a-uš-du āppa-ma-aš tiyazi [n]aškan anda warišiyaš [pa]ḫḫuenašša šeli [m]a-uš-ta-ru* "(If) he walks forward, let him fall into treachery; (if) he walks backward, let him fall into a pile of *w.* and fire" KBo 13.260 iii 36-41 (incant., NS), cf. StBoT 5:114.

2′ *āppa*: (Let the offerings for the gods be ready for them!) *nuššan paraya [lē] naitti* EGIR-*payakan lē ma-uš-ta* "Do not postpone(?) (them). Do not fall behind" KUB 1.16 iii 51-52 (edict, Ḫatt. I, OH/NS), ed. HAB 14-15 "nachlassen".

3′ *āppan*: *nuššikan idalāuwanni* EGIR-*an UL* ⌜*namma ma-uš*-⌝*[(ḫ)]a-ḫa-at* "I did not fall back into maliciousness against him" KUB 19.67 i 16-17, dupl. KUB 1.1 iii 22-24 (Ḫatt. III), ed. Ḫatt. 24-25, StBoT 24:18f.; see StBoT 5:114-15 with n. 8.

4′ *arḫa*: "We questioned the temple personnel, and they said" *ANA* DINGIR-*LIM*-*wakan* 1 *ŠUR* IGI *arḫa ma-uš-ša-an* MÁŠ. GAL.ḪI.A-*yawašši kuiēš tūriyanteš nukan ANA* 1 MÁŠ.GAL KUN *arḫa ma-uš-ša-anza* "One of the deity's eye-brows has fallen off. Also, the tail of one of the billy-goats which are harnessed for him has fallen off" KUB 5.7 rev. 27-28 (oracle question, NH), tr. ANET 498.

5′ *katta* — **a′** with ablative — **1″** of persons: "When Ḫebat saw Tašmišu" *nukan* ᵈ*Ḫepaduš šuḫḫaz katta ma-uš-šu-u-wa-an-zi waqqareš* [*m*]*an tiyat manaškan šuḫḫaz katta ma-uš-ta-at* "she almost fell down from the roof. Had she taken a step, she would have fallen down from the roof. KUB 33.106 ii 7-9 (Ullik. IIIA, NH), ed. Güterbock, JCS 6:20f.; *mānkan antuḫšaš lagāri našmaškan* ⸢ᴳᴵˢGIGIR⸣-*az katta ma-a-uš-zi* "If a man topples over or falls down from a chariot" KUB 8.36 iii 9-10, ed. StBoT 19, 38f. and Laroche, CTH p. 189f., see *lak-* mng. 4 a.

2″ of stones: [(*k*)]*uē*[(*zzatka*)]*n u*[(*ēr*)] *ānteš* [NA₄.ḪI.A (*kuēzzatkan* ḪUR.SAG)-*az*] *katta ma*-⸢*uš-še-er*⸣ [(*ānteš* NA₄.ḪI.A)] "Where did they come from, the hot stones? From what mountain did they fall down, the hot stones?" KBo 19.145 iii 30-31 (myth in rit., NH), with dupl. KUB 34.101:3-5, ed. Laroche, RHA XXVIII:59 and Haas-Thiel, AOAT 31:302f.; cf. KUB 17.1 ii 5 (Kešši).

3″ of a clay figurine: *ANA* GUD IM *kue*[*dani*] *ŠA* KUR LÚ.KÚR *ŠUM-an kitt*[*a*] *naškan* ᴳᴵˢ*arkammiyaz* EGIR-*an katta ma-uš*-[*zi*] "The clay ox on which there is the name of an enemy land falls down behind from the *a*." KUB 20.77 iii? 4-7 (fest.).

4″ of celestial bodies (w. ⸗*ašta*): *takku INA* ITU KIN.ᵈINANNA *našta* MUL-*aš nepišaz katta ma-uš-zi* "If it is the month of Ululu, and a 'star' falls down from the sky" KUB 8.25 i 7-8 (celestial omen, NS), cf. Weidner, AfK 1 (1923) 2; cf. [*mānašt*]*a* [*n*]*epišza* MUL GAL *katta* [*ma-uš*]-*zi* KUB 8.22 ii 3-4 (celestial omen, NS); cf. also KUB 43.2 iii 1-3 (star omen, NS) with dupl. KUB 34.15:4-6; cf. a 1′ b′.

b′ without ablative — **1″** of plaster: *ḫāniš*⸗⸢*šuwa*⸣*rmakan k*[*uit katta*?] *ma-uš-ki-it-ta-ri* "The plaster which is falling [down]" KUB 31.86 iii 1-2 (Bel Madg., MH/NS), ed. Dienstanw. 45, rest. after dupl. *ḫaniššuwarmakan kuit awan katta mummīetta* KUB 13.2 ii 16.

2″ of a newborn (w. -*šan*): (The midwife prepares stools and cushions for the delivery) TUR-*aššan kuwapi katta ma-uš-zi* "when the child (is about to) fall down (i.e. be delivered) (the woman sits down on the stools)" KUB 30.29 i 1-16 (rit., pre-NH/NS), ed. Güterbock, Oriens 10:356 and Beckman, Diss. 20f.; *maḫḫanmaz* SAL-*za ḫā*[*ši kattaššan*?/*nuššan*?] TUR-*aš ma-uš-zi* "When the woman is giving birth and the child is falling [down] (they wave this ewe over the woman's [head?/body?] three times)" KBo 17.62 i 21-23 (rit., NS); cf. *nuššan* TUR-*aš kat*[*ta ma-uš-zi*] ibid. i 4; cf. a 1′ d′ (of fetuses).

6′ *kattan*: KBo 12.75:8 (myth.); KBo 21.22 (4), 5 (OH/MS).

7′ *parā*: [. . .]x *arrirranza* [. . .]x-(!)*ši parā ma-uš-ša*[-*an-za*(?)] [. . .]x-*anza* "(some part of an object) has been scraped, its [. . .] has fallen out, [and its . . .] has been [. . .]" KUB 6.29 obv. 3-5 (oracle question, NH).

8′ *šarā*: KBo 19.80 rt. 12 (hist., NH).

9′ *šer*: *tak*⸢*ku* ELLAG 2 *kiša nu*!*kan*⸣ 1-*aš* 1-*edani šer ma-uš-ša-an-za* "If there are two kidneys and one is fallen on the other" KUB 4.1 iv 26 (omen, NS), tr. of Akk. BE ELLAG 2-*ma ri-it-ku*!-*bu* "If there are two kidneys, and they lie (pl.) on each other" ibid. iv 25. KUB 29.10 ii 6 (omen), ed. Güterbock, AfO 18.80; KUB 28.4 17b, see a 1′ c′ above.

Weidner, AfK 1 (1923) 2-3 (= *maqātu* in Akk. omens); Goetze, Tunn. (1938) 41-42; Sommer, HAB (1938) 175.

Cf. *mumiya-*.

maz(z)-, manz- v.; to withstand, resist, offer resistance, endure; dare to (with inf.); from OH.†

pres. sg. 2 *ma-za-at-ti* KBo 4.14 iv 60 (Šupp. II); **sg. 3** *ma-az-zé* KBo 7.14 i 8 (OS), *ma-az-zi* KUB 31.147 ii 28, (31), *ma-az-za-az-zi* KUB 12.60 i (7) (OH/NS), KUB 13.4 iii 76 (pre-NH/NS), KUB 33.97 i 15, 16, *ma-az-za-zi* KUB 43.62 ii? 4, KUB 41.4 iii 13, *ma-za-zi* KUB 13.5 iii 45 (pre-NH/NS), *ma-an-za-az-zi* KUB 33.120 i 21

(NH); **pl. 1** *ma-az-zu-u-e-ni* KBo 12.126 i 24 (MH/NS).

pret. sg. 2 *ma-az-za-aš-ta* KUB 14.1 obv. 62 (MH/MS); **sg. 3** *ma-az-za-aš-ta* KBo 5.6 i 8, 29, KBo 16.8 ii 37, KBo 3.4 ii 30 (all Murš. II), KUB 23.59 ii? 4, *ma-za-aš-t[a?]* KUB 19.16 rev.? rt. 7.

verbal subst. gen. *ma-az-zu-wa-aš* KUB 33.120 i 32 (NH).

a. negated — **1′** with *natta* (Akk. *UL*) — **a′** w. *menaḫḫanda*: *nušši* ^{LÚ}KÚR *zaḫḫiya menaḫḫanda namma UL kuiški ma-az-za-aš-ta* "not one of the enemies gave further resistance in battle against him" KBo 5.6 i 7-8 (DŠ), ed. Güterbock, JCS 10:90.

b′ object in acc.: *nu [z]ik* ^{m}*Madduwattaš nam[ma* ^{m}*A]ttariššiyan UL ma-az-za-aš-ta nušši piran arḫa tarnaš* "But you, O Madduwatta, offered Attarššiya no further resistance; you fled from him" KUB 14.1 obv. 62 (MH/MS), ed. Madd. 16-17, cf. *manmu UL duḫušiyait manmu piran arḫa tarnaš* KBo 5.8 iii 17-18 (AM 156); ^{d}*Kumarbiš* ^{d}*Alaluwaš* NUMUN-*ŠU* ^{d}*Anui menaḫḫanta zaḫḫain paiš* ^{d}*Kumarbiyaš* IGI.ḪI.A-*wa UL namma ma-an-za-az-zi* ^{d}*Anuš . . . naš piddāiš* "Kumarbi, Alalu's offspring, gave battle to Anu; and Anu cannot withstand the eyes (i.e., threatening gaze?) of Kumarbi, . . . and he fled" KUB 33.120 i 19-22 (myth, NH), ed. Kum. *2, 6-7, tr. ANET 120; *nu aru[nan . . . (UL)] kuiški ma-az-za-az-[zi]* "No one can withstand the Sea(god)" KUB 12.60 i 6-7 (myth, OH/NS), restored from dupl. KUB 33.81 i! 4 (MS).

c′ case of obj. ambiguous: "I went to Apaša, the city of Uḫḫaziti" *numu* ^{m}*Uḫḫa*-LÚ-*iš UL ma-az-za-aš-ta našmukan :ḫūwaiš* "and U. offered me no resistance, but fled from me" KBo 3.4 ii 30-31, ed. AM 50-51; [*numu* ^{LÚ}KÚR?] *UL namma ma-az-za-aš-ta [numu . . . z]aḫḫiya UL tiy[at]* "[The enemy] offered [me] no further resistance; he did not come [against me] in battle" KBo 16.8 ii 36-37 (Ann. Murš. II), ed. Otten, MIO 3:167-68; ^{fD}*Aranzaḫit UL ma-az-zu-wa-aš* "(I impregnated you) with A., the irresistible" KUB 33.120 i 32 (Kingship in Heaven myth, NH), translit. Myth. 51, tr. MAW 157.

d′ object is infinitive: [*mā*]*n apāšma memiyauanzi UL ma-az-za-az-zi* (var. *ma-za-zi*) *nu* ^{LÚ}*arišši memāu* "But if he doesn't dare to tell (his superior), let him tell his fellow (servant)" KUB 13.4 iii 76-77 (instr., pre-NH/NS) w. dupl. KUB 13.5 iii 45, ed. Chrest. 160-61; (in a ritual the "mortal" says:) *UL-wa namma ma-az-zu-u-e-ni* "We don't dare any longer" KBo 12.126 i 24 (rit., MH/NS), ed. THeth. 2:24-25, inf. obj. is implied; [. . .]x *uwanna UL ma-za-at-ti* "You do not dare to see/look at [. . .]" KBo 4.14 iv 60 (treaty, Šupp. II), ed. Stefanini, AANL 20:49, 76.

2′ with *lē*: *nan lē ma-az-zi* "Let him not withstand him/it" KUB 31.147 ii 28, cf. 31; [*l*]*ē ma-az-za-zi* KUB 41.4 iii 13.

b. not negated: (Someone came in battle against the king, and) [. . .] ^{m}*Li*-KASKAL-*iš ma-az-zé* "L. offers resistance" KBo 7.14 i 8 (Syrian campaigns of Ḫatt. I, OS); [. . .] *tuegganza ma-az-za-zi* "The body will resist [. . .]" KUB 43.62 ii? 3-4; cf. also *natkan ma-az*[- . . .] KUB 39.78 rev. 15 claimed for this verb by Haas and Thiel, AOAT 31.163.

Although the inflection of this verb resembles that of *ed-* and *išpart-*, and Friedrich, HW 139, entered it under the stem *mat-*, no form of the verb has a *t*, even in forms where it might have been expected (e.g., *mazzuwaš* and *mazzuweni*). The reading *ma-t[e-er]* KBo 3.13 (=BoTU 3) obv. 18 (Güterbock, ZA 44:70f., 75, Oettinger, Stammbildung 208) is highly questionable from the traces in BoTU 3 and KBo 3.13. Contrast the trace after *ma-* with the *te* sign in line 21. The *ma-du* found in KUB 30.10 rev. 6 certainly is not this verb, cf. *ma-* v. We have concluded therefore that the stem was *maz(z)*-.

Hrozný, HKT (1919) 186 n. 4; Götze, Madd. (1928) 125f.; Sommer, AU (1932) 335; Laroche, OLZ 1955: 225, RHA XXIII/76 (1965) 51f.

Cf. *:mazalla*, *:mazzallaša-*.

(TÚG)mazakanni- n. com.; (a garment), NH.†

sg. nom. ^{TÚG}*ma-za-ga-an-ni-iš* KUB 42.14 rev. 4, KUB 42.84 obv. 3!, ^{TÚG}*ma-za-kán-ni-iš* IBoT 1.31 obv. 7, KUB 42.64 rev. 14, ^{TÚG}*ma-za-ga-an-ni-eš* KUB 42.59 rev. 17; **pl. acc.** ^{TÚG}*ma-za-qa-an-ni-uš* KUB 12.1 iii 18; **broken** ^{TÚG}*ma-z[a- . . .]* KUB 31.67 iii 11, ^{TÚG}*ma-za-ká[n- . . .]* KBo 9.87:6.

a. Usually in lists of garments — **1′** colors: SA_5 "red" KUB 42.14 rev. 4, KUB 42.59 rev.? 17,

HAŠMANNI "blue-green" KUB 42.84 obv. 3.

2′ ornamented with gold: 1 *ma-za-kán-ni-iš* KÙ.GI GAR.RA KUB 42.64 rev. 14; 2 ^{TÚG}*ma-za-ga-an-ni-uš* KÙ.GI *šakantamenzi* "2 *m.*-garments (with) appliqué(?) of gold, (on one there [is a . . . pattern], on the other there are 30 pomegranates)" KUB 12.1 iii 18, ed. Košak, Linguistica 18:104.

b. in a fragment of a dream text: *kūn* ^{TÚG}*ma-z*[*a-kán-ni-in* . . .] KUB 31.67 iii 11.

:mazalla (Luw.) adv.; tolerantly(?); NH.†

nu mān ^{LÚ}*araš* ^{LÚ}*aran ANA* INIM SAL-*T*[*I šer*] / *:ma-za-al-la aušzi ANA* LUGAL-*ma UL mema*[*i*] / *nan anda munnaizzi* "If someone looks tolerantly(?) on his fellow with respect to the matter of women, and doesn't tell the king, and hides him" KUB 21.42 left edge left col. 3-5 (instr., NH), ed. von Schuler, Dienstanw. 30.

Laroche, DLL (1959) 71; von Schuler, Kaškäer (1965) 151.

Cf. *maz*(*z*)-, *mazzallaša*-.

mazzallaša- (Luw.) v.; to tolerate(?), condone(?); NH.†

Luw. mid. pres. pl. 2 *ma-az-za-al-la-ša-du-wa-ri* KUB 21.29 iv 13.

(Take care of the families left behind in the city by defectors to the Kaška) *m*[*ān*] *šumešma* LÚ.MEŠ URU-*LIM ma-az-za-al-la-ša-du-wa-ri ku*[*in*/*t*?]*ki* "But if you men of the city tolerate/condone(?) someone/something, (what will it turn out to be for you?)" KUB 21.29 iv 13-14 (treaty with Urikina), tr. and comments by von Schuler, Kaškäer 148 ("Wenn ihr Leute der Stadt aber etwas inkorrekt (dabei) handelt(?)"). 151; Otten apud von Schuler, ibid. ("sich ausserhalb des Gesetzes bewegen").

Laroche, DLL 71 suggested "tolérer?", which von Schuler, Kaškäer 151 rightly notes accords with a possible derivation from the verb *mat*- "aushalten", for which verb, however, we posit a stem *maz*(*z*)- q.v.

Cf. *maz*(*z*)-, *mazalla*-.

mazeri- n. com.; (a marking on the exta); occurs only in oracle texts; often abbr. *ma-zé* and *ma-zé-eš*; NH.

sg. nom. *ma-zé-re-eš* KUB 16.29 obv. 16, 21, KUB 22.31 obv. 14, KUB 46.37 obv. 25 (2x), 49, rev. 2, *m*[*a-z*]*é-re-eš* KUB 46.37 obv. 31, *ma-zi-ri-iš* KUB 46.37 rev. 2, *ma-zi-r*[*i-iš*/*eš*] KUB 46.37 rev. 23, *ma-z*[*i-ri-iš*/*eš*] KUB 46.37 rev. 23, *ma-zé* KUB 6.2 obv. 36, KUB 22.31 obv. 9, KUB 22.52 obv. 5, KUB 22.54:10, [*m*]*a-zé* KUB 22.54:13, *ma-zé-eš* KUB 6.39 obv.? 2; **acc.** [*m*]*a-zé* KUB 6.2 obv. 26.

a. modified by *kunna*- "right": *ma-zé-re-eš* ZAG-*naš* "The *m.* (is) a right (one)" KUB 46.37 obv. 49 and passim in this text; cf. KUB 16.29 obv. 21, KUB 22.52 obv. 5, etc.

b. contrasted with *entiš* GÙB-*aš* "The *entiš* (is) a left (one)": *entiš* GÙB-*aš ma-zé-re-eš* ZAG-*aš* "The *entiš* is a left (one); the *m.* is a right (one)" KUB 16.29 obv. 16; cf. KUB 22.31 obv. 9 and 14.

c. other occurrences: *zul-ki*[*š*! *m*]*a-zé ḫarzi* "a *zulki*- holds a *mazeri*-" KUB 6.2 obv. 26; *m*[*a-z*]*é-re-eš* "(there is) a *mazeri*-" KUB 46.37 obv. 31.

This is probably the same word as Hurrian *mazeri*, *maziri* "help", and perhaps to be equated with Akkadian *rīṣu* "help" and "(a part of the exta)" (Laroche, Ugar. 5:456).

Laroche, RA 64 (1970) 137; GLH 169.

^{É}mazki(ya)- see ^{É}*makzi*(*ya*)-.

-mi-, -ma- enclitic poss. pron.; my; from OS; wr. syll., and Akkadographically -*YA* (and -*Ī* in ^{d}UTU-*ŠI* = *ŠAMŠĪ*, *A-BI* "my father" KBo 22.1:16, 21 (OS), and *BE-LÍ* "my lord" KUB 14.15 iv 21).

sg. nom. com. -*miš*: passim; -*mi-eš*: KUB 36.35 i 15; -*me-iš* KBo 13.2 obv. 6, 13; -*mi-š*(*a*) KBo 3.28:22 (OH/NS). **sg. voc.** -*mi*: *iš-ḫa*(-*a*)-*mi* KUB 31.127 i 1 (OH/NS), KUB 31.147 ii 17 (MH/NS?); -*me*: *atti*⸗*me* KBo 12.70 rev.! 10b; -*met*: KBo 3.34 i 22 (OH/NS); -*mit*: KBo 11.14 ii 4 (MH/NS), KUB 33.106 iv 10 (NS).
sg. acc. com. -*man*: with assimilation *n* + *m* > *mm*: *tu-ik-kam-ma-an* KUB 30.10 obv. 14 (OH/MS), *ad-dam-ma-an* KBo 3.44:9 (OH/NS); with assimilation and single writing of *m*: *at-ta-ma-an* KUB 29.3:6 (OS), KUB 43.31 left col. 4 (OS), *ša-a-a*[*k-l*]*i-ma-an* KUB 30.10 rev. 24 (OH/MS), DUMU-*la-ma-an* KUB 1.16 ii 4 (OH/NS), KBo 11.14 ii 5 (MH/NS), etc.; with the acc. ending only on the pron.: *addaš*⸗*ma-an* KUB 29.1 i 26 (OH/NS); -*min*: ^{LÚ}*ḫalugatallan*⸗*mi-in* VBoT 1:12 (MH/MS); with the acc.

ending only on the pron.: *attaš⸗mi-in* KUB 14.11 ii 22 (NH/NS).

sg. nom.-acc. neut. *-met*, *-mit*: GIŠTUKUL-*li-me-et* KBo 6.2 ii 24 (OS), É-*ir-me-et* KUB 1.16 iii 18 (OH/NS), É-*ir-mi-it* KBo 10.2 i 20 (OH/NS); with doubling of *m* after vowel: *me-e-ni-im-me-et* KBo 3.22:52 (OH/NS) *ut-ni-im-me-et* KBo 3.27 obv. 23 (OH/NS); with assimilation *n* + *m* > *mm*: ⌈*pé-e*⌉*-ra-am-mi-it* KBo 3.22:79; with assimilation and single writing of *m*: *ša-aḫ-ḫa-me-et* KBo 6.2 + KBo 19.1 ii 24 (OS), *ša-aḫ-ḫa-mi-it* KBo 6.3 ii 38 (OH/MS), *pé-e-da-mi-it* KUB 31.130 rev. 5 (MH/MS).

sg. gen. *-maš*: *attaš⸗ma-aš* KBo 3.22:10 (OS), KBo 3.28 ii 17 (OH/NS), 1193/u iii 13 (+ KUB 21.19 iii 45) (NH/NS); *-man*: with assimilation and single writing of *m*: *ḫu-uḫ-ḫa-ma-an* KUB 1.16 iii 40 (OH/NS), DUMU-*la-ma-aš-š*⌈*a-an*⌉ ibid. 62.

sg. dat.-loc. *-mi*: *kiššari⸗mi* KBo 17.3 i 15 (OS), *šiuni⸗mi* KUB 30.10 obv. 13, rev. 17 (OH/MS), *katti⸗mi* passim; with doubling of *m* after vowel: *kat-tim-mi* KBo 3.22:77 (OS), KBo 22.2 rev. 6 (OS); *-mit*: *paltani⸗mi-it* KBo 3.13 rev. 15 (OH/NS), *kišširi⸗mi-i*[*t*] KBo 3.29:5 (OH/NS).

sg. all. *-ma*, with doubling of *m* after vowel: *pár-nam-ma* KUB 1.16 iii 18 (OH/NS).

sg. inst./abl. *-mit*(?): KBo 3.13 rev. 14 (OH/NS).

pl. nom. com. *-miš*: KUB 1.16 iii 33 (OH/NS).

pl. acc. com. *-muš*: KUB 1.16 ii 28, KUB 43.75 obv. 17 (OH/NS), KUB 43.68 obv.? 6 (MH/MS); *-miš*: *tuzziuš⸗mi-iš* KUB 19.37 iii 10 (NH).

pl. nom./acc. neut. *-met*, *-mit*: *uddār⸗me-et* KUB 1.16 iii 46, etc. (OH/NS), *uddār⸗mi-it* ibid. ii 56, *šākuwa⸗me-et* KBo 3.28 ii 9 (OH/NS), IGI.ḪI.A-*mi-ta-wa* (*⸗mit⸗a⸗wa*) VBoT 58 i 41 (OH/NS).

pl. gen. *-man*: with assimilation *n* + *m* > *mm*: ÌR.MEŠ-*am-ma-an* KBo 3.27: 10, 15 (OH/NS).

dUTU-*ŠI* = Akk. *šamšī* "My Sun(god)" (My/Your/His Majesty) with Hittite complements in OH/NS, MH and Šupp. I: **sg. nom.** dUTU-*ŠI-iš* KBo 16.25 i 46, iv 62; **sg. voc.** d!UTU-*me-et* KBo 3.34 i 22 (OH/NS) (see below c 2′ b′); **sg. acc.** dUTU-*ŠI-in* KBo 19.58:12 (MH/MS), KBo 5.3 iv 45, i (15) (Šupp. I treaty w. Ḫuqq.), KUB 21.41 iv 9 (Šupp. I); **sg. d.-l.** dUTU-*mi* VBoT 1:13 (see d 6′), dUTU-*ŠI-mi*(-x?) KUB 8.81 iii 12 (MH/NS) (see below d 6′).

In the nom. and acc. exx. *-iš* and *-in* may be complements to the pronoun which is written Akkadographically by the *-i* of *šamšī*. The underlying forms of the possessive pronoun would have been *-miš* and *-min*. dUTU-*ŠI-aš* KUB 33.24 ii 7 (Stormgod myth) is probably a faulty writing for "Sungod," as is the nom. dUTU-*ŠI* ibid. 3.

For NUMUN dUTU-*ŠI-KU-NU* KUB 1.16 ii 44 (Ḫatt. I) cf. HAB 71f.

(Sum.) ⌈á⌉-mu-šè = (Akk.) *a-na i-dì-ia* = (Hitt.) *kuššani⸗mi* "for my wage" KBo 1.42 i 23 (Izi Bogh. A, NS), ed. MSL 13.133 as line 33, cf. CAD I/J 16; (Sum.) [. . .] = (Akk.) [. . .]-*ru-ru-ia* "my . . ." = (Hitt.) *katkattimaš⸗me-iš* "my agitation/trembling" KBo 13.2 obv. 6 (NS); (Sum.) [. . .] = (Akk.) [*šu-ut-t*]*i* = (Hitt.) *tešhaš⸗me-iš* "my dream" ibid. 13; (Sum.) [. . .] = (Akk.) [. . . .]-*ti* = (Hitt.) *muwatallatar⸗me-e*[*t*] ibid. rev. 9; (Sum.) [. . . . .] = (Akk.) [. . .]-*ru-ti* = (Hitt.) TUR-*tar⸗me-et* ibid. 10.

(Akk.) *a-wa-te*MEŠ*.ti-ia* BoTU 8(= KUB 1.16) iv 70 = (Hitt.) *ud-da-a-ar-m*[*e*]*-e*[*t*] ibid. iii 71 (Ḫatt. I, NS), ed. HAB 16f.; (Akk.) AMA-*mi* (*ummī*) = (Hitt.) *annaš⸗mi-iš* "my mother" RS 25.421: 32, 52 (Ugar. 5:444f.); (Akkadogram) *A-BA-Y*[*A*] KUB 14.8 obv. 25 = *at-ta-aš-mi-in* (acc. sg. by context) in dupl. KUB 14.11 ii 22 (PP2, Murš. II), ed. Götze, KlF 1:210f. with note m. Cf. also b 1′.

a. In OS - **1′** sg. nom. com. *-miš*: d*ši-i-uš-mi-iš* "my god" KBo 3.22:47 (Anitta), ed. StBoT 18:12f. ("mein Gott Šiu") with commentary pp. 119-131 □ With Starke, ZA 69:47-65 we take the word as a common noun; cf. the form d*ši-ú-šum-m*[*i-in*] (< *šiun⸗šummin*) ibid. 39, (41), d*ši-ú-na-šum-mi-iš* KUB 26.71 i 6 (NS), dupl. of line 57; *a-aš-šu-uš-mi-iš* "my dear (one)" KBo 17.22 ii 14 (Hitt. vers. of a lost Ḫattic prayer, translit. StBoT 25:207 □ here *⸗miš* "my" is more likely than *⸗šmiš* in view of the voc. [dUT]U-*i* SAL.LUGAL "O Sungoddess, queen" of ii 13. Probably not sg. 1 in KBo 17.3 ii 13 (StBoT 8:28f. ii 56 with n. 9).

2′ voc. *-mi*: (no OS exx.).

3′ sg. acc. com. *-man*: *nu āppa at-ta-ma-an* dIM-*a*[*n . . .*] "Again [I shall praise] my father, the Stormgod" KUB 29.3: 6, rest. after the NS dupl. *nu* EGIR-*pa ad-da-aš-ma-an* dU-*an walluškimi* KUB 29.1 i 26, ed. Kellerman, Diss. 21, 11, 26 □ *attaman* = **attamman* < **attan⸗man*; *attašman* of the NS copy is formed after the nom. *attaš⸗miš* without declension of the noun, see below c 3′; cf. [d]IM-*an at-ta-*[*m*]*a-an* KUB 43.31 left col. 4.

4′ sg. nom.-acc. neut. -(*m*)*met*/*-mit*: *me-e-ni-im-me-et nēḫ*[*ḫun*] "[I] turned my face" KBo 3.22:52 (Anitta), ed. StBoT 18:12f.; *kī* GIŠTUKUL-*li-me-et kī⸗ma ša-aḫ-ḫa-me-et* "this is my craft, but that is my *šaḫḫan*-duty" KBo 6.2 + KBo 19.1 ii 24 (Laws § 41, OS), ed. HG 28f. with NS dupl. KBo 6.3 ii 44 and variant *ša-aḫ-ḫa-ni-mi-it* KBo 6.5 iv 2 (NS); cf. *ša-aḫ-ḫa-me-et* KBo 19.1 ii 19 (§ 40, OS), ed. AfO 21:2, with var. *ša-aḫ-ḫa-mi-it* KBo 6.3 ii 38 (MS); [*e-e*]*š-ša-ri-mi-it* "my figure" KBo 20.49:5 (prayer) or sg. loc. (without context); ⌈*pé-e*⌉*-ra-am-mi-it* "in front of me" KBo 3.22:79 (Anitta, OS), ed. StBoT 18:14f., with NS dupl. KUB 36.98b rev. 6 *pé-ra-a*⌈*-am*⌉*-mi-i*[*t*].

5′ sg. gen. *-maš*: [ᵐ*Pi*]*tḫānaš at-ta-aš-ma-aš āppan* "after my father P." KBo 3.22:10 (Anitta), ed. StBoT 18:10f., cf. ibid. 30; Akkadogram *AWAT A-BI-IA* KBo 22.1:4, 6, 31.

6′ sg. (dat.-)loc. *-mi*: *ki-iš-ša-ri-mi dāi* "he puts (it) in my hand" KBo 17.3 i 15 (rit.), ed. StBoT 8:20f. w. n. 4 and 17; the dupl. KBo 17.1 i 20 (OS) has *ki-iš-ša-ri-iš-mi* "in their hand" (the context allows for either reading); *ū*⌈*k⸗wa*⌉ *a*[(*t-t*)]*i-m*[(*i*) *natt*]*a āššuš* "I am not liked by my father (or: dear to my father)" KBo 22.2 rev. 4-5 (Zalpa story), ed. StBoT 17:10f. ("bei meinem Vater nicht beliebt"), rest. from NS dupl. KBo 3.38 rev. 20, cf. Starke, StBoT 23.85; *katti⸗mi* "with me, to me": *kat-tim-mi* KBo 3.22:77 (Anitta, OS), ed. StBoT 18:14f. with var. *kat-te-mi* KUB 26.71 obv. 18 and KUB 36.98b rev. (5) (both NS); *kat*⌈*-tim*⌉*-mi* KBo 22.2 rev. 6 (Zalpa story, OS), ed. StBoT 17:10f., with dupl. *kat-te-mi* KBo 3.38 rev. 21 (NS); *kat-ti-mi* KBo 17.1 iv 6 (= KUB 34.121 iv 2), ed. StBoT 8:36f. □ cf. *nan ammel katta uwate* "bring him to me" KUB 33.5 ii 8-9 (Tel.Myth. 2nd vers., MS) and KUB 33.9 ii 6 (Tel.Myth. 3rd vers., NS), translit. Myth. pp. 40 and 45; and *nu waršulašteš ammel katta uwaru* KUB 36.44 iv 4 (OH/NS); Akkadogram *INA* KÁ.GAL-*YA* KBo 3.22:33 (Anitta, OS).

7′ abl./inst.: (no exx.).

8′-11′ pl.: (no exx.) [DUMU.MEŠ-*ma-aš-ša* in KBo 17.1 iii 10 and dupl. KBo 17.3 iii 10 should be translated (with Otten, StBoT 8:103f.) as "and their children" (*⸗šmaš⸗a*)].

b. In OH/MS — **1′** sg. nom. com. *-miš*: *ištanzaš⸗mi-iš tamatta pēdi zappiškizzi* KUB 30.10 rev. 15 (prayer of Kantuzzili), the NS dupl. KUB 36.79a iii 17 has ZI-⌈*YA*⌉; *annaš⸗mi-ša-mu* [*zi*]*k* KUB 30.10 rev. 25; Akkadogram: *numu ammel* DINGIR-*YA šallanuš* ibid. obv. 6, cf. obv. 7, 8, 9, 24, etc.; [DUM]U-*YA* KUB 17.10 i 22 (Tel.Myth, OH/MS).

2′ sg. voc. *-mi*: ᵈUTU-*i iš-ḫa-a-mi* KUB 30.10 rev. 10; possibly *ši-i-ú-ni-mi* "O my god!" KUB 30.10 rev. 11, for an interpretation as voc. or dat. see Güterbock, JNES 33:326 n. 15.

3′ sg. acc. com. *-man*: *nuza tu-ik-kam-ma-an* (< *tuekkan⸗man*) *natta papraḫḫun* "I did not defile my body" KUB 30.10 obv. 14, ed. Güterbock, JNES 33:325, tr. ANET 400, cf. *ša-a-a*[*k-l*]*i-ma-an* ibid. rev. 24 with NS var. *ša-ak-la-i-e-ma-an* KUB 31.127 iii 16.

4′ sg. nom.-acc. neut. *-mit*: [. . .] *iš-ḫe-eš-ša-mi-it-ta* KUB 30.10 obv. 7 with NS par. *la-ma-an-mi-it iš-ḫi-i*[*š-* . . .] FHG 1 (+ KUB 31.127) ii 17; *numu wa-aš-du-ul-mi-it teddu* "let him tell me my transgression" KUB 30.10 obv. 28, tr. ANET 400, cf. partly rest., ibid. 24-25, 26; *pé-e-da-mi-it* "my place" KUB 31.130 rev. 5 (prayer) with dupl. KUB 36.75 iii 20 (MS).

5′ sg. gen. **-maš*: Akkadogram *ŠA* DINGIR-*YA duddumar* KUB 30.10 obv. 10, 11.

6′ sg. dat.-loc. *-mi*: *ša-aš-ti-mi* "on my bed" KUB 30.10 rev. 18 with par. KUB 30.11 rev. 15 (MS) and *ša-aš-te-mi* KUB 31.127 iii 5 (NS); *lam-ni-mi šēr* "for my name" KUB 30.11 rev. 16 (omitted in par. KUB 30.10 rev. 19; KUB 31.127 iii 6 has *lamman⸗ma⸗mu*); *šiuni⸗mi piran* KUB 30.10 rev. 22; *ši-ú-ni-mi-ma-mu kuit šuppi adanna natta ara* "What, (being) sacred to my god, was not right for me to eat" KUB 30.10 obv. 13 (Kantuzzili prayer), ed. Güterbock, JNES 33:325, tr. ANET 400 □ note poss. *-mi* belonging to *šiuni*, beside personal pron. *-mu* depending on *natta ara*; for *šiuni⸗mi* ibid. rev. 11 see above sub voc.; *nat ši-i-ú-ni-mi* (var. *ši-ú-ni-mi*) *tuk mēmiškimi* "I shall tell it to you, (to) my god" KUB 30.10 rev. 17, tr. ANET 401, with NS par. KUB 36.79 iii 21 + KUB 31.127 iii 4; Akkadogram: *ANA* DINGIR-*YA* KUB 30.10 obv. 4, 12, rev. 11, (13).

7′ abl./inst.: (no exx.).

8′-11′ pl.: (no exx.).

c. In OH/NS — **1′** sg. nom. com. *-miš* — **a′** nom. as subj.: *ḫu-uḫ-ḫa-aš-mi-iš* "my grandfather" KUB 1.16 iii 41 (Ḫatt. I), ed. HAB 12f., KBo 12.18 obv. 8, KBo 12.14 obv. 11; *at-ta-aš-mi-iš* "my father" KBo 3.28:19 (= BoTU 10γ:18) (edict of Ḫatt. I); *ad-da-aš-mi-ša-aš-še* (= *addaš⸗miš⸗a⸗še*) "and my father to her" ibid. 22; DUMU-*mi-iš* "my son" KUB 1.16 ii 52, ed. HAB 8f.; DUMU-*mi-ša* "but my son" KBo 3.27 (= BoTU 10β) 14 (edict of Ḫatt. I); ÌR-*mi-iš lē* "let him not be my subject" ibid. 11; ᴸᵁ́KÚR-*aš-mi-iš uit* "my enemy came" KUB 40.5 ii? 7 (Syrian war of Ḫatt. I), ed. Kühne, ZA 62:244f. with dupl. KUB 40.4:2; [M]AŠKIM-

aš-mi-iš KUB 1.16 iii 39, ed. HAB 12f.; [*zig*]*a at-ta-aš-mi-iš ēš uga*! DUMU-*aš*⸗*tiš ēšlit* "[yo]u be my father, and let me be your son!" KUB 26.35:6; *at-ta-aš-mi-iš-ša-wa tarški*[*zzi*] "and my father keeps saying" KUB 33.24 i 40, dupls. *-mi-ša-* ("but"), translit. Myth. 55, tr. MAW 146; *UL* ⌈ANŠE⌉-*iš-mi-iš* "is it not my donkey?" KBo 13.78 obv. 11 (aetiological story), ed. Otten, ZA 55:158f. (without restoration ⌈ANŠE⌉-*iš*); LÚ.MEŠ(sic)-*aš*⸗*mi-iš* [*l*]*ē kišta gāinaš*⸗*mi-iš lē kišta* [*a-r*]*a-aš*⸗*mi-iš a-ra-a-aš-mi*<*-iš*> *ēš* "Do not become my man! Do not become my in-law! (But), O my friend, remain my friend!" KUB 29.1 i 11-13 (rit.), ed. Kellerman, Diss. 10f., 25, 35; cf. i 35, with Kellerman we accept Goetze's and Hoffner's emendation and understand the first *araš*⸗*miš* as nom. used as a direct address to the subject of the sentence and the second (emended) *arašmi*<*š*> as predicate; if unemended *arāšmi* were for **arā*⸗*mi*, a real vocative (so HW^{2} 222a), it would (like all true vocatives in *-e* or *-i*) stand alone in its own clause and not be imbedded in the *araš*⸗*miš* . . . *ēš* clause; with DN's: (While [the king] breaks (bread) for the gods of the [nether-wo]rld, [the scribe] calls out the name of each god) . . . "[The scribe ca]lls out ^{d}LAMMA-*aš-mi-iš* "My Protector God" KUB 20.24 iv 9 (fest.); cf. ^{d}*I*(*n*)*naras*⸗*miš* Otten, JCS 4:125 lines 26, 32, cf. Laroche, RLA 6:456; ^{d}IB-*aš-mi-eš* KBo 11.32:51 (NH); with GN: ^{URU}*A-ri-in-na-aš-mi-iš* KBo 3.55 rev. 8 (= BoTU 18 iii 7).

b′ nom. as voc.: cf. KUB 29.1 ii 11-13 in c 1′ a′.

2′ sg. voc. — **a′** *-mi*: ⌈^{d}⌉UTU-*e iš-ḫa-mi* (var. *iš-ḫa-a-mi*) "O Sungod, my lord" KUB 31.127 i 1 (Sun hymn), ed. Güterbock, JAOS 78:239 and AnSt 30:43, with dupl. KUB 31.128 i 1.

b′ *-met*: "Thus (spoke) Šarmaššu:" ⌈$^{d!}$⌉UTU-*me-et* "O My Sun (= O Your Majesty)! I have not yet gone . . ." KBo 3.34 i 22 (anecdotes); the photo shows a break running through the det.

3′ sg. acc. com. *-man*: ^{d}U-*an at-ta-ma-an* (<**attan*⸗*man*) "the Stormgod, my father" KUB 36.45:4; *ad-dam-ma-an* KBo 3.44(= BoTU 15) 9; [. . .] DUMU-*la-ma-an* (< DUMU-*lan*⸗*man*) *ḫalziḫḫun* "I called [him] my son" KUB 1.16 ii 4 (Ḫatt. I), ed. HAB 2f., cf. ibid. 57, 63; *iš-ta-an-za-na-ma-an* (< *ištanzanan*⸗*man*) ibid. iii 26; *a-ra-am-ma-an ḫalziḫḫ*[*un*] KUB 29.1 i 34; *ad-da-aš-ma-an* ^{d}U-*an* ibid. i 26; for *at-ta-ma-an* of the OS dupl. KUB 29.3:6 see a 3′.

4′ sg. nom.-acc. neut. *-met*/*-mit*: É-*er-me-et* "my house" KUB 1.16 iii 18, ed. HAB 12f.; É-*er-mi-it*, KBo 10.2 i 20 (annals Ḫatt. I), ed. Imparati, SCO 14:44f.; *ut-ni-mi-it* "my country" KUB 36.101 ii 13 (Ḫatt. I); KUR-*e-me-et-ta* KUB 1.16 iii 35, ed. HAB 12f.; *ut-ni-im-me-et* KBo 3.27 (= BoTU 10β) obv. 23; *ut-ne-me-et* É-*er-mi-it-ta* KUB 29.1 i 18 (rit.); *ke-er-mi-it* "my heart" KBo 12.18 i 11; *ḫa-at-ta-a-da-mi-it-ta* "and my wisdom" KUB 1.16 ii 56, ed. HAB 8f.; cf. ibid. iii 58; ŠU-*me-et* (= *keššar*⸗*met*) KBo 13.52 iii 16; *a-aš-šu-me-et* "my goods" KUB 31.64a:6; GIŠ.ḪUR-*mi-it-ta* "and my document" KUB 36.98b:10 (Ammuna inscr.) with dupl. KUB 26.71 i 23; ^{GIŠ}*el-zi-mi-it-wa* "my scales" KBo 6.13 i 8 (Law § 169); *i-ia-tar-mi-it* KUB 43.60 i 11 (myth. in rit.), ed. Güterbock, RHA XV/60:1.

5′ sg. gen. — **a′** *-maš*: *at-ta-aš-ma-aš ḫaršanī* "to my father's person" KBo 3.28:17 (BoTU 10γ:16); *nummu an-na-aš-ma-aš katta arnut* "bring me (for burial?) to my mother" KBo 3.40a + b (= BoTU 14α) rev.! 14; cf. *ú-wa-aš-ma-aš katta* ibid. (differently HW^{2} 80 a, cf. Hoffner, review of HW^{2} in BiOr, forthcoming); *an-na-aš-ma-aš* KUR-*e* "my mother's country" KUB 29.1 i 24 (rit.), ed. Kellerman, Diss. 11, 26; [*a*]*t-ta-aš-ma-aš annaš* (var. [*a*]*nnaš*⸗*ma*⸗*aš*) *ḫaššannaš* (var. *ḫaššandaš*⸗*ma-aš*) "my father's, (my) mother's, (my) family's (var. offspring's)" KUB 31.127 iv 38 (prayer), with dupl. KBo 14.74:6.

b′ *-man*: (cf. c 11′); *ḫu-uḫ-ḫa-ma-an* [. . . *ud*]*dār*⸗*šet* "the words (lit. his words) of my grandfather" KUB 1.16 iii 40-41 (Ḫatt. I), ed. HAB 12f., cf. ibid. 162; DUMU-*la-ma-aš-ša-an* (<DUMU-*lan*⸗*man*⸗*šan*) ibid. iii 62 (cf. HAB 186f.).

6′ sg. d.-l. and all. — **a′** d.-l. *-mi*, *-mit* — **1″** *-mi*: *ki-iš-ri-mi daīr* "they put in my hand" KBo 3.28:7 (= BoTU 10γ:6); ^{GIŠ}ŠÚ.A-*mi* "on my throne" ibid. 24, (23); *nuškan* [. . .] ⌈*ki*⌉-*iš-ša-ri-mi anda dai* "and put them [. . .] in my hand!" KBo 3.23 (= BoTU 9) rev. 5-6 (admonitions), cf. Archi, FsLaroche 41f., translating "leur mains" presupposing **kiššari*⸗<*š*>*mi*; DUMU-*mi Labarni* ⌈É-*er*⌉ *piḫḫun* "I gave a house to my son L." KUB 1.16 ii 31, ed. HAB 6f.; *šanašta at-ti-mi paknuer* "they denounced him to my father" KBo 3.34 ii

9-10 (anecdotes); cf. KBo 3.29 (= BoTU 11 α) 20, (21); KUB 26.35:3,4; *nat* DINGIR.MEŠ *at-ti-mi šanḫir* "the gods demanded it from my father" KUB 26.87:7 (anecdotes, similar to KBo 3.34 etc.).

2″ *-mit* (Houwink ten Cate, RHA XXIV/79: 123-25): *nu* URU*Ḫattuši* URU-*ri-mi-it* EGIR-*pa uwanun* "I returned to Ḫ., my city" KBo 10.2 i 44-45 (annals Ḫatt. I), ed. Imparati SCO 14:6f., cf. ibid. iii 9-10 (pp. 11f.); [*ti*]*ššumiuš*(?) *ki-iš-ši-ri-mi-i*[*t*] / [. . .] "cups in/into my hand . . ." (verb lost) KBo 3.29 (= BoTU 11 α) 5; *pal-ta-ni-mi-it* KBo 3.13 (= BoTU 3) rev. 15 (Naramsin "inscr."), ed. Güterbock, ZA 44:72f.; cf. ŠU-*mi-it* ibid. 14 below sub. sg. inst./abl.

b′ all. *-ma*: [*m*]*ānaš pár-nam-ma uizzi* "when she comes to my house" KUB 1.16 iii 18, ed. HAB 12f., cf. ibid. 144.

7′ sg. inst./abl.(?) *-mit*: ŠU-*mi-it ēppun* KBo 3.13 (= BoTU 3) rev. 14 (Naramsin "inscr."), ed. ZA 44:72f. □ read *keššaraz*⸗*mit* "with my hand" or *keššari*⸗*mit* "in my hand"? See loc./all. in *-mit*, above c 6′.

8′ pl. nom. com. *-miš*: [*nu ḫante*]*z-zi-ia-aš-mi-iš* ÌR.MEŠ-*YA šumeš* "You are my first servants" KUB 1.16 iii 33, ed. HAB 12f. □ note the unusual position of ⸗*miš* on the adj.; cf. ÌR.MEŠ-*YA* ibid. ii 41, iii 59, DUMU.MEŠ É.GAL-*YA* ii 73.

9′ pl. acc. com. *-muš*: LÚ.MEŠKÚR-*uš-mu-uš* "my enemies" KUB 1.16 ii 28, ed. HAB 4f.; GUD.ḪI.A-*uš-mu-uš* KUB 43.75 obv. 17 (myth or legend).

10′ pl. nom.-acc. neut. *-met*/*-mit*: *ud-da-a-ar-mi-it* KUB 1.16 ii 56 (Ḫatt. I), ed. HAB 8f., cf. ibid. iii 33; *ud-da-a-ar-me-et* ibid. iii 46, 56, 58, 71 (in bil. sec.); *ta* LUGAL-*wa*<*-aš*> *ud-da-a-ar-ra-me-et lē šarrattuma* "do not transgress my, the king's, words!" KBo 3.28 ii 20-21 (= BoTU 10γ ii 19-20); [*ud-d*]*a-a-ar-me-e*[*t*] KBo 3.27 (= BoTU 10β) obv. 24; *ša-a-ku-wa-me-et* "my eyes" KBo 3.28 ii 9 (= BoTU 10γ ii 8); IGI.ḪI.A-*mi-ta-wa* (*šakuwa*⸗*mit*⸗*a*⸗*wa*) *lē ēpši* "but do not seize my eyes!" VBoT 58 i 41 (myth.), translit. Myth. 24.

11′ pl. gen. *-man* (cf. c 5′ b′): [*šu*]*minzan*⸗*a* ÌR.MEŠ-*am-ma-an* UR.BAR.RA-*aš mān pang*[*ur*⸗*šmet*?] 1-*EN ēštu* "But let your clan, my subjects, be one like the wolf's" (lit. the clan of you, my subjects) KBo 3.27 (= BoTU 10β):15-16, (Ḫatt. I), cf. HAB 75; ÌR.MEŠ-*am-ma-an ištarna* ibid. 10.

d. in MH (MS and NS) — **1′** sg. nom. com. *-miš*: *attaš*⸗*mi-iš* KUB 23.21 obv. 26 (Arn. I, NS), ed. Madd. 156f.; KUB 23.14 ii 7 (Arn. I, NS); *addaš*⸗*mi-i*[*š*] KUB 23.16:2 (Tudḫ. III?, NS), ed. Carruba, SMEA 18:162f.; *ḫalugatal*<*l*>*aš*⸗*mi-iš* "my messenger" VBoT 1:23 (letter of Amenophis III), ed. Rost, MIO 4:335-336; contrast LÚ*ḫalugatallattin amella* LÚ*ḫalugatallan* "your messenger and my own messenger" ibid. 19-20; dUTU-*ŠI-iš* KBo 16.25 i 46, iv 62.

2′ sg. voc. — **a′** *-mi*: d⌈UTU⌉*-i iš-ḫa-a-mi* KUB 31.147 ii 17 (rit., NS?), cf. HT 88:7 (rit.); cf. EN-*mi* KBo 17.104 ii 3 (rit. of Ḫantidaššu, NS), par. KBo 11.14 ii 4 see sub d 2′ b′.

b′ *-mit*: dUTU-*ue* EN-*mi-it* "O Sungod, my lord!" KBo 11.14 ii 4 (rit. of Ḫantidaššu, NS), cf. *-mi*, above.

3′ sg. acc. com. — **a′** *-man*: *tu-uz-zi-ma-an* SUD-*nun* "I have moved my army" KUB KUB 23.11 ii 22 (ann. Tudḫ., MH/NS), ed. Carruba, SMEA 18:158f., with MS dupl. KUB 23.12 ii (16); AMAR-*un-ma-an* DUMU-*la-ma-an pāi* KBo 11.14 ii 5 (rit. of Ḫantidaššu, NS).

b′ *-min*: LÚ*ḫalugatallan*⸗*min* VBoT 1:12 (letter of Amenophis III), ed. Rost, MIO 4:334f.; (If someone . . .) [*nu*]*šmaš* dUTU-*ŠI-in piran* SIG5-*in memiškizzi* "[and] mentions His Majesty favorably in your presence, (listen to him!)" KBo 19.58 ii 12-14 (MS); *nu AŠŠUM BELIKUNU INA* EGIR.[UD-*MI*] dUTU-*ŠI-in-pát* [*šekten*] KUB 21.41 iv 8-9 (Šupp. I, late MS); cf. KBo 5.3 iv 29 (Šupp. treaty w. Ḫuqq.), ed. SV 2:134f.:45; ibid. i (15), ed. SV 2:108f.

4′ sg. nom./acc. neut. *-mit*: *idālu* ⌈*a*⌉*-i*!*-*!*iš-mi-it* "my evil mouth" KUB 43.68 obv.? 14 + KUB 36.91 obv. 9 (prayer, pre-NH/NS) □ the copy has TUR for *i*, followed by word space. [*pí-ra-an-mi-it* KBo 10.45 iv 46 is mistake for *pí-ra-aš-mi-it* (< *piran*⸗*šmit*) of the dupl. KUB 7.41 rev. 13, ed. Otten, ZA 54:140f.].

5′ sg. gen.: (no exx.).

6′ sg. dat.-loc. *-mi*: *nu*⸗*mu šumeš*⸗*pat* DINGIR.MEŠ LUGAL-*UT*[*-TAM ki-iš-š*]*a-ri-*

mi dāišten "You, O gods, put the kingship in my hand" KUB 36.91 obv. 5 + KUB 43.68 obv.? 11 (prayer, pre-NH/NS); *zi-ga-mu kat-ti-mi* KBo 5.3 ii 15 (Ḫuqq., NS), ed. SV 2:114f.; *nuwaratzakan ammel* A.ŠÀ-*ni*⸗*mi* [*an*]*da aniyami* KUB 31.84 iii 62-63 (Bel Madg., NS); *at-ti-mi kat*[*ta*(*n*?)] "with my father" KUB 23.21 obv. 12 (ann., Arn. I/NS); "If a fugitive goes from Ḫattuša to another country and from the other country goes to Kizzuwatna. [Šunaššura] will seize him" *nan* ^{d}UTU-*ŠI-mi*-x § KUB 8.81 + KBo 19.39 iii 9-12 (treaty w. Šunaššura, MH/NS □ the sign after *-mi* is unclear and probably erased; in the incomplete clause the verb "deliver" is to be understood, cf. *nan ANA* ^{d}UTU-*ŠI āppa pāu* ibid. ii 12-13, ed. Petschow, ZA 55:242f.; "We shall look at the daughter" ^{d}UTU-*mi kuin* DAM-*anni uwadanzi* "whom they will bring to My Majesty for marriage" VBoT 1:12-13 (Letter of Amenophis III), ed. Rost, MIO 4:334f.; in the greeting formula: *kat-ti-mi* SIG$_5$-*in* É.ḪI.A-*mi* DAM.MEŠ-*mi* DUMU.MEŠ-*mi* LÚ.MEŠ.GAL.GAL-*aš* ERÍN.MEŠ-*mi* ANŠE.KUR.RA.ḪI.A-*mi pí-ip-pí-it-mi* KUR.KUR.ḪI.A-*mi-kán anda ḫūman* SIG$_5$-*in* ibid. 3-6, *-mi* seems to be (mistakenly) used for the loc. regardless of number; cf. the immediately following paragraph with *-ti* "your"; cf. also the parallel Akk. formula in another letter of Amenophis III: *ana yāši šulmu ana* É-*ya ana* DAM.MEŠ-*ya ana* DUMU.MEŠ-*ya ana* LÚ.MEŠ.GAL.GAL.MEŠ-*ya* ANŠE.KUR.RA.MEŠ-*ya* ^{GIŠ}GIGIR.MEŠ-*ya* ERÍN.MEŠ-*ya ma-ad šulmu u* ŠÀ-*bi* KUR.KUR-*ya magal šulmu* EA 1:7-9; cf. *kat*[*-ti-mi*] SIG$_5$-*in* ABoT 65 obv. 3 (letter, MS).

7′-8′ pl. nom.: (no exx.).

9′ pl. acc. com. *-muš*: DINGIR.MEŠ *wa-aš-ta*⌈*-uš*⌉*-mu-uš ḫarnikten* "O gods, cancel/remove my sins!" KUB 43.68 obv.? 6 (prayer, pre-NH/NS).

10′-11′ pl. nom.-acc. neut. and pl. gen.: (no exx.).

e. In literary and traditional texts (all NS) — **1′** sg. nom. com. *-miš* — **a′** nom. as subj.: "For the nth time I shall describe my mother through a sign" *annaš*⸗*m*[*i-iš* . . .] "my mother (is) . . ." RS 25.421 iii 11 (Ugar. 5:444f.), ed. Laroche, Ugar. 5:773-76; *nu*⸗*mu annaš*⸗*mi-iš* . . . ibid. 32; *annaš*⸗*mi-ša* [. . .] ibid. 52, cf. ibid. 69; *šēnaš*⸗*me-iš* "my image" KBo 13.2 obv. 2 (Izi Bogh.?); *katkattimaš*⸗*me-iš* ibid. 6; *tešḫaš*⸗*me*-⌈*iš*⌉ ibid. 13; other exx. from this lex. text above under bil. section; *zaḫḫiya*⸗*ma* ERÍN.MEŠ[⸗*m*]*i-iš-ša* "But in battle my army, too, [will . . .]" KUB 8.34 ii 16 (omen apodosis) □ the text contains other first sg. forms, so that ⸗*miš*, not ⸗*šmiš* is in place; for ERÍN.MEŠ as sg. see Otten-Souček, StBoT 8:66; *tu-uz-z*[*i-iš*(?)]*-mi-iš* "my army" KBo 22.6 i 15 (Šar tamḫari), ed. Güterbock, MDOG 101:19, 22 □ "my" does not fit the context; one expects "his"; cf. ibid. p. 24; *numu at-ta-aš-mi-iš ammu*[*k*] IGI-*anda* TUKU.TUKU-*an arḫa peš*⸗*šiyaddu numu IŠTU ŠA ABIYA lē kuitki* ḪUL-*uešzi* "Let my father throw away the anger (he feels) against me, and let nothing from my father's side harm me!" KUB 31.66 iv 6-9 (prayer, NH) □ the text writes *A-BU-IA, A-BI-IA* throughout, except *attaš*⸗*miš* here and *attaštin* ii 25; cf. *at-ta-aš-mi-iš-ša* KBo 14.75 i 16 (sim. to plague prayers, NH); *at-ta-aš-m*[*i-iš*] KUB 29.39 i 12 (market protocol, pre-NH/NS).

b′ nom. for voc.: *ammel at-ta-aš*-⌈*mi*⌉*-eš* "O my father" KUB 36.35 i 15 (Ašertu myth), ed. Otten, MIO 1:126f.; cf. Myth. 140, tr. Hoffner, RHA XXIII/76:8.

2′ voc. — **a′** *-me*/*-mi*: *at-ti-me* (for expected **atta*⸗*mi*) "O my father" (you built a house for yourself . . .) KBo 12.70 rev.! 10b (wisdom), ed. Laroche, Ugar. 5:782; [ŠE]Š-*ni-mi* "O my brother" KUB 8.48 i 3 (Gilgameš), translit. Myth. 131, cf. Stefanini, JNES 28:41f.; EN-*mi* KUB 36.74 iii 8 (Atraḫasis), ed. Siegelová, ArOr 38:136; ^{d}U ŠEŠ-*mi* KBo 12.76 iv? 6 (kingship of ^{d}KAL), translit. Myth. 145 as var., with dupl. [. . . Š]EŠ-*ni-mi* KUB 33.114 i 2; ^{d}*Nāra* ŠEŠ⌈*-mi*⌉ KUB 36.2d iii 42 (same myth), ed. Otten, MGK 12, translit. Myth. 149, tr. MAW 163.

b′ *-mit*: (Ea said to Tašmišu:) *piran arḫa īt* DUMU-*mi-it lē*⸗*mu piran šarā artati* "Go ahead, my son! Do not stand before me!" KBo 26.65 iv 9-10 (Ullik. III A), ed. Güterbock JCS 6:28f. (still taking ⸗*mit* for inst.).

3′ sg. acc. com. — **a′** *-man*: (no exx.).

b′ *-min*: *nu apiyaya* ^{d}IM ^{URU}*Ḫatti attaš*⸗*mi-in ḫannišnit šarlāit* "And even then did the Stormgod of Ḫatti let my father prevail by (his) judgment" KUB 14.11 ii 21-23 (PP2, Murš. II), ed. Götze, KlF 1:210f., tr. ANET 395; the dupl. KUB 14.8 obv. 25 adds *BELĪYA* after the DN and writes *A-BA-I*[*A*], cf. bil. above.

4′ sg. nom.-acc. neut. *-met*/*-mit*: *e-eš-ri-me-et* "my figure" KBo 13.2 obv. 2 (Izi Bogh.?); *ḫa-aš-ša-tar-me-et* "my family" ibid. 12; *par-ga-tar-me-et* "my height" ibid. 15, cf. ibid. 19, 20 and passim on rev.; [L]Ú-*na-tar-mi-i*[*t*] "my manhood" KUB 31.1 ii 2 (Naramsin legend); LÚ-*natar⸗mi-it* KUB 33.120 i 29 (Kingship in Heaven); *me-m*[*i-ia*]*-an-mi-it* KUB 14.14 obv. 7 (PP2; Murš. II), ed. Götze, KlF 1:164f., with p. 178.

5′ sg. gen. *-maš*: *mān* DINGIR.MEŠ-*aš piran kuiški at-ta-aš-ma-aš an-na-aš-ma-aš waštaiš ēšzi* "If there is a sin of my father (or) my mother before the gods" KUB 21.19 + 1193/u iii 44-45 (prayer of Ḫatt. and Pud.); *šumešša at-ta-aš-ma-aš* [*uddār*] / *ḫannuan dāišt*[*en*] "You began to contest the [words] of my father" KUB 29.39 iv 7-8 (market protocol, pre-NH/NS).

6′ sg. d.-l. *-mi*: *nutta uddār kue tem*[*i na*]*t īt ANA* ᵈ*Nāra* ᵈ*Napšāra* ŠEŠ-*mi memi* "The words that I speak to you, go tell them to my brother N. N." KUB 36.2d iii 35-36 (Kingship of ᵈKAL), ed. Otten, MGK 12, translit. Myth. 149, tr. MAW 163; *ku-uš-ša-ni-mi* "for my wage" KBo 1.42 i 23 (see bil. above); (Whatever population there is now) *nu at*!*-ti⸗mi ḫu*[*ḫḫi⸗mi katta*]*n ēšta* "and was with my father and my grandfather" KBo 11.1 obv. 21 (prayer, Muw.), ed. Houwink ten Cate, RHA XXV/81:106, 115; *katti⸗mi* KBo 18.57a:6, KBo 18.69 obv. 7; *lappiyašwamukan genupi⸗mi*[(-). . .] KUB 17.8 iv 16 (pre-NH/NS) □ loc. *-mit* is not excluded.

7′ abl./instr.: (no exx.).

8′-9′ pl. nom. and acc. com. *-meš* and *-muš*: (no exx.).

10′ pl. nom.-acc. neut. *-mit*: [*ud-da-*]*a-ar-mi-it iš*[*tamaš*] KUB 33.112 iv 12 + KUB 33.114 iv 6 (Kingship of ᵈKAL), ed. Kum. *8, 11, translit. Myth. 149.

11′ pl. gen.: (no exx.).

12′ Mistaken usage: LUGAL-*ginaš* LÚ.MEŠUR.SAG-*liyaš ud-da-ni-mi-it t*[*ēt*] "Sargon spoke the word(! text: in my word?) to the heroes" KBo 22.6 i 10 (Šar tamḫari), ed. Güterbock, MDOG 101:19, 22; cf. ibid. pp. 24 and 26; URUDU*tapulliyammit* KBo 3.16 (BoTU 4a) ii 13 is apparently a mistake (acoustic) for URUDU*tapulliyannit*, as in line 7.

f. Non-literary NH — **1′** sg. nom. com. *-miš*: *tu-uz-zi-aš-mi-iš šaruwāit* "my army plundered" KBo 2.5 ii 13 (Murš. II), ed. AM 182f. □ cf. the same form as pl. acc.

2′ voc. *-mi* or *-mit*: (no exx.).

3′ sg. acc. com. — **a′** *-man*: no exx.; the passage ŠU-*an⸗ma-an ḫar*[*-ta?*/*zi?*] KUB 14.3 i 12 (Taw., Ḫatt. III), was interpreted by Sommer (AU 2f., 51f.) as "he holds/held my hand". But Sommer also admitted the interpretation as irrealis (*-man*), which fits the context much better: "He (sc. the *tartennu*) would have held (PN's) hand (but PN said 'no' to the *tartennu* and belittled him in the presence of the lands)". Without this passage there seems to be no example of the (older) *-man* form in NH.

b′ *-min*: (no exx.).

4′-5′ sg. nom.-acc. neut *-mit* and sg. gen. *-maš*: (no exx.).

6′ sg. d.-l. *-mi*: *ḫuḫḫi⸗mi* KUB 23.49:6 (hist., NH).

7′ sg. abl.-inst: (no exx.).

8′ pl. nom. com.: (no exx.).

9′ pl. acc. com. *-miš*: *tuzziuš⸗mi-iš ḫuit*[*ti-yanun*] "I moved my troops" KUB 19.37 iii 10 (Annals, Murš. II), ed. AM 172f.; *tuzziyaš⸗mi-iš ḫuittiyanun⸗pat* KBo 2.5 ii 3, ed. AM 182f; also ibid. iii 24-25, ed. AM 190 iii 49-50.

10′-11′ pl. nom.-acc. neut. and pl. gen.: (no exx.).

Hittite indicates the possessive relationship in several ways: with the enclitic possessive, with the genitive of the independent personal pronoun (*ammel*, etc.), and with the dative pronoun (*-mu*, etc.). Occasionally two of the methods are employed together, e.g., *annaš⸗miš⸗a⸗mu* [*zi*]*k* KUB 30.10 rev. 25, *nu⸗mu pittuliyai piran ištanzaš⸗miš tamatta pēdi zappiškizzi* ibid. rev. 14-15, *ammel* A.ŠÀ-*ni⸗mi* KUB 31.84 iii 62, *nu⸗war⸗an⸗naš⸗*(*š*)*an anzel* ZI-*ni piyawen*

KUB 13.4 iv 72-73 (instr. for temple officials, pre-NH/NS). On the other hand, use of both *-mi-* and *-YA* in the same phrase in [*ḫant*]*ezziyaš*⸗*miš* ÌR.MEŠ-*YA* above c 8′ can be explained by assuming that the Akk. *-YA* was only a graphic device.

The genitive forms of the independent personal pronoun (the *-el*/*-enzan* forms) are required in all periods of Hittite to express a predicate (". . . is/was mine", ". . . is/was yours"). But their use in attributive position in OH and MH expresses contrast ("mine [not yours or his]"), while the enclitic form (*-mi-*, *-ti-*, *-ši-*, etc.) serves as the non-contrasting attributive possessive.

Whereas the enclitic possessive pronoun has a wide use in OH and MH texts (including NS copies), its use in original NH compositions is restricted to text types with an OH or MH tradition (prayers, rituals, festivals, myths, treaties, vocabularies). Even in these traditional texts its use is sparing. In NH treaty texts only one example of *-mi-* (*kattimi*) occurs in the Šuppiluliuma I—Ḫukkana treaty and one *-ši-* (*pedišši*) in the Muršili II—Duppitešup treaty. Furthermore, in the NH occurrences there are differences in vocalization and inflection (see further below). In NH, examples of the non-contrasting attributive use of the *-el*/*-enzan* forms are fairly common, e.g., *maḫḫanmaza* ᵐ*Mūwatalliš apel* ŠEŠ-*ŠU* DINGIR-*LIM*-*iš kišat* "But when his brother Muwatalli became a god" KUB 21.27 i 38-39 (prayer of Pud.), *ītwa* ᵈ*Telepinun anzel* EN-*NI* DINGIR-*LAM ŠA* SAG.DU-*NI mugāi* "Go, invoke Telepinu, our lord, the god of our person(s)!" KUB 24.1 i 5-7 + 1122/v + 217/w (prayer of Murš. II), translit. Otten/Rüster, ZA 62:232. This shows that the NH *-el*/*-enzan* forms had assumed some functions of the OH and MH enclitic possessives. In the paradigm of possessives found in KBo 1.42 i 23-28 the three singular forms "my", "your" and "his/her" are expressed by the enclitic possessive, while the plural forms "your", "their" and "our" are expressed by the gen. of the independent personal pronoun (*šumenzan*, *apenzan*, *anzel*). Why did the scribe not use the enclitics throughout? It is possible that the phonetic or graphic differences between "your (*-šmi-*)", "their" (*-šmi-*) and "our" (*-šummi-*) were too slight for a proper differentiation. But it is equally possible that, when the scribe wrote, the enclitic forms for the plural had been replaced by the gen. of the independent personal pronoun, while the enclitic forms for the singular were still in use. It may be, therefore, that the use of *šumenzan*, *apenzan* and *anzel* in non-contrasting attributive situations began earlier than the non-contrasting use of *ammel*, *tuel* and *apel*.

That the dative occasionally expresses the possessive is well known (Friedrich, HE § 205). Götze (AM 310 sub *-ši* "D. an Stelle eines Poss.") once listed examples in the Muršili annals where the dat. pron. *-ši* expresses the poss. relationship. A replacement of poss. *-tiš* "your" in an OH prayer by *-ta* "to you" in NH can be seen by comparing *nu ḫannešnaš pēdi dariyašḫaš*⸗*tiš* NU.GÁL KUB 31.127 i 24-25 + KUB 36.79 (Sun hymn, OH/NS) with *nu*⸗*tta ḫannešnaš pedi tarriyašḫaš* NU.GÁL KUB 24.3 i 48 (prayer, Murš II), ed. Güterbock, AnSt 30:46, cf. idem, Frontiers 138. If the enclitic possessive continued in general use in NH, it is difficult to explain those NH texts in which its forms are so badly misused (e.g., KBo 22.6). Cf. also Starke, StBoT 23.189-91 on the misuse of *-šummi*. If it was no longer a part of the spoken language and was only used in making copies of older texts or in composing traditional texts in an archaic style, it is easy to understand that NH scribes would have found it difficult to use correctly. The situation is similar to the attempts to use OH *uk* in late NH.

The question of how the Akk. possessive suffixes were read in NH is a difficult one. There is no direct proof available. One can only draw tentative conclusions based upon indirect evidence. It would be circular reasoning to assume that the Akk. poss. suffixes were read either *ammel* or *-mi-* and then use that evidence to confirm a particular theory. Until the rules governing usage in the NH period are established based upon the unequivocal evidence of the syll. writings one may not make any assumptions about the reading of the Akkadographic examples. The remarks in the preceding paragraphs are based entirely on the syll. writings. NH texts show a significant decrease in examples of *-mi-* and the assumption of its functions by the *-el/-enzan* forms and the datives in NH. They do not show that the enclitic poss. was completely replaced, but rather that it was considerably restricted.

In some cases the Akk. poss. might still be read *-mi-*, if confusion would otherwise result. Thus in KBo 4.4 i 45 (AM 112) *ŠA ABI-YA* (= *attaš⸗maš*) *ammella lingauš* "The oaths of my father and me", if read *ammel attaš ammella lingauš*, might have caused confusion, since the two *ammel*'s function on different syntactic levels.

From this evidence we conclude that, while the question is still an open one, it is likely that the usual NH means of expressing non-contrasting possession was either with the *-el/-enzan* forms or with the dative. The enclitic possessive pronoun (*-mi-*, etc.) was used only in NS texts with an earlier tradition, in cases like KBo 4.4 i 45 (AM 112) where confusion might result from the use of the *-el/-enzan* form, and possibly in very common set expressions like *attaš⸗miš* "my father" (esp. in DŠ) and *pedišši*.

In MH a new vocalization of the sg. acc. com. (*-min*, etc.) replaced the older vocalization *-man*, *-šan*, etc. Beginning in NH, forms occur in which the case endings of the noun and the enclitic possessive do not agree (e.g., *attašmin* KUB 14.11 ii 22, *attaštin* KUB 31.66 ii 25). In KBo 12.70 the scribe writes the vocative *atti⸗me* (iii 10), the acc. sg. com. *attitten* (= *attin⸗ten*?, ii 6), and the gen. sg. *addaš⸗*⸢*daš*⸣ (ii 9).

meya-, miya- n.; (mng. unkn.); MH/NS.†

sg. nom. *mi-i-i-ia-aš* KUB 30.36 ii 11-12, *me-ia-aš* KUB 30.33 i 17, *mi-ia-aš* KBo 13.131 obv. 6 (all MH/NS).

waršīmaš⸗at apēlpat mi-i-ia-aš išḫāi ali⸗yanankan aliyanzinaš apēlpat mi-i-ia-aš kuenzi "The *waršīma-* (that is) its own *miya-* will bind it; the *aliyanzina-* (that is) its own *miya-* will strike the *a.*-sheep(?)" KUB 30.36 ii 11-12 (rit. for the purification of a town).

The two parallel passages KUB 30.33 i 16-17 and KBo 13.131 obv. 5-6 have replaced the hapax *waršīma-* with the more familiar GIŠ*waršama-* while KBo 13.131 obv. 5 omits *meyaš*; furthermore, both texts contain several other omissions and mistakes. Therefore, KUB 30.36 can be regarded as the version which better reflects the MH original.

miya- v. see *mai-*.

***mi(ya)ḫu(wa)nt-** **1.** (adj.) old (vs. young), elderly, aged (people and gods), **2.** (n.) old man or woman, elderly person, **3.** (pl.) elders (a body with political-military, judicial and religious functions); wr. (LÚ/SAL.)ŠU.GI; from OS.

nom. sg. com. LÚ.ŠU.GI-*an-za* KBo 1.42 iv 43, KUB 19.67 + 1513/u i 19, KUB 3.110:6 (all NH), ŠU.GI KBo 22.2 rev. 14 (OS), KUB 12.4 iv 2, KUB 10.93 iv 3 (both NH), LÚ.ŠU.GI KBo 11.1 obv. 42 (Muw.); **sg. acc.** LÚ.ŠU.GI KBo 11.1 obv. 23 (Muw.); **sg. dat.** (*ANA* DINGIR) ŠU.GI KUB 25.30 i 15; **pl. nom. com.** LÚ.ŠU. GI-*eš-š(a)* KBo 22.1 obv. 6 (OS), LÚ.MEŠ.ŠU.GI KBo 3.38 obv. 21 (OH/NS), KBo 4.4 iv 31 (Murš. II); **acc. com.** LÚ.MEŠ.ŠU.GI SAL.MEŠ.ŠU.GI(*-ya*) KBo 3.4 iii 14 (NH); **dat.** [LÚ].MEŠ.ŠU.GI-*aš* KBo 6.2 iii 62 (OS); **inst.?** *IŠTU* LÚ.MEŠ.ŠU.GI-*TIM* KUB 14.1 obv. 73. For KBo 3.67 (= BoTU 23C) ii 8 see **miyaḫuwantaḫḫ-*.

No syllabic writings are attested; *m.* is always written with the log. ŠU.GI, often accompanied by the det. LÚ or SAL. The reading **mi(ya)ḫu(wa)nt-* is based on the derived verb **miyaḫuwantaḫḫ-* q.v.

(Sum.) d[a-r]í = (Akk.) *la-bi-ru* "old (vs. new, recent, fresh)" = (Hitt.) *ú-iz-za!-pa-a-an* "old (vs. new) thing" (neut.)/(Sum.) [d]a-rí = (Akk.) *ši-e-bu* "old (vs. young) man" = (Hitt.) LÚ.ŠU.GI-*an-za* KBo 1.42 iv 42-43 (Izi Bogh. A), ed. MSL 13:141:269f.; cf. also KUB 3.110:6, where only the Hitt. col. is preserved; Goetze (Tunn. p. 59f.) attempted a free restoration of the Sum. and Akk.

1. (adj.) old (vs. young), elderly, aged (people and gods) — **a.** priest: *mān ANA* dZA.BA4.BA4 LÚSANGA ŠU.GI EZEN *zēnandaš IŠTU* É-*ŠU iyazi* "When the old priest celebrates the autumn festival for DN from his house" KUB 12.4 iv 2-3 (cult inv., NH); cf. KUB 10.93 iv 3-6 (fest.), cf. Mestieri 365 (without tr.); these passages may refer to an elderly priest (**miyaḫuwant-*) or a priest of long standing (*karuili-* or *annalla-*); they are treated here because they are written ŠU.GI "old, elderly (vs. young)" instead of

LIBIR.RA "old, previous (vs. new, recent)"; cf. LÚSANGA LIBIR.RA KUB 17.35 i 24, 26, 27, contrasted with LÚSANGA GIBIL "the new priest" ibid. i 25, 30; cf. Hoffner, EHGl 17f. n. 1.

b. king: "The (Hittite) king came (back) to Ḫattuša to worship the gods," *U* LUGAL ŠU.GI (var. *U* LÚ.MEŠ GAL) *apiya tāliš* "but the old king (var. the grandees) he left there (in Zalpa with the army)" KBo 22.2 rev. 14 (Zalpa tale, OS) w. dupl. KBo 3.38 rev. 30-31 (NS), ed. StBoT 17:12f., cf. KBo 3.38 obv. 20, ed. ibid. 8f., cf. comments by Otten, StBoT 17:55, who conceives the situation as a coregency; the NS scribe of KBo 3.38, failing to understand LUGAL ŠU.GI emended it to LÚ.MEŠ GAL "grandees".

c. god: *ANA* DINGIR ŠU.GI ᵈ*Ḫuwašš[an-naya* . . .] KUB 25.30 i 15 (fest.), cf. Laroche, Rech. 104 (ᵈŠU.GI); cf. DINGIR.MEŠ LIBIR.RA IBoT 2.119 iv 7, which according to Laroche, (FsGüterbock 179) = *karuileš šiuneš*.

2. (n.) old man or woman, elderly person (from OS) — **a.** as a special object of respect or pity: (When he heard that the Hittite king was approaching with troops, Manapa-ᵈU, king of the Šeḫa River Land, was terrified,) *našmu namma menaḫḫ[anda UL uit num]ukan* AMA-*ŠU* LÚ.MEŠ.ŠU.GI SAL.MEŠ.ŠU.GI-*ya* [*menaḫḫanda*] *parā naišta* "and as a result [did not come] against me, but sent his mother and old men and old women [to meet] me." (and they came and fell at my feet, and because the women fell at my feet, I relented and did not invade his land) KBo 3.4 iii 13-15 (ten-year annals of Murš. II), ed. AM 68-71, cf. HAB 103 n. 2 □ since "old women" are included with the men, it is probably better not to regard the LÚ.MEŠ.ŠU.GI as the political body of adult men called "elders" but simply elderly men and women as objects of respect and pity; in KBo 4.4 iv 31-32 (AM 138f.) and KBo 5.8 iv 11-12 (AM 160f.), however, the LÚ.MEŠ.ŠU.GI alone are an embassy of "elders" in the political sense (cf. mng. 3); so understood by Klengel, ZA 57:229f. and von Schuler, Kaškäer 72, but cf. HAB 103 n. 2; *numu* ᵐ*Arma*-ᵈU-*aš* [*ku*]*it išḫanaš antuḫšaš ēšta* [*na*]*mmaš* LÚ.ŠU.GI-*an-za ēšta* [*na*]*šmukan uwayattat* "Now because A. was a blood relative of mine, and furthermore he was an old man, I felt sorry for him," (and I let him off) KUB 19.67 + 1513/u i 17-20 (Apology of Ḫatt. III), ed. StBoT 5:185f., StBoT 24:18f.:25-26.

b. as a source of information about the past: (Keep [pl.] the word of my father! And if you [pl.] do not know what it was,) *kāni* LÚ.ŠU.GI-*eš-ša* NU.GÁL *nušmaš memai AWĀT ABĪYA* "are there not here also old men, one (of whom) may tell you (i.e., the LÚ.MEŠ GIŠTUKUL) the word of my father?" KBo 22.1 obv. 6 (instr., OS), ed. Archi, FsLaroche 45f., who reads *me-ma-i* as *pár-ku-i* and translates "Si vous ne (la) reconnaissez pas, voilà, l'âge de la vieillesse ne sera pas (pour vous)! Que la parole de mon père vous soit sacrée!' Archi followed Otten, StBoT 17:27 in interpreting LÚ.ŠU.GI-*eš-ša* as an abstract in *-ešša(r)*, cf. also Neu, FsNeumann 210f.; (I will inquire of the population which now exists which was contemporary with my father and my grandfather, and whatever I find from hieroglyphic records, I shall carry out . . .) *kuittaya šallin* LÚ.ŠU.GI *punuškimi nukan* [1-*an š*]*aklāin* EGIR-*and*[*a* GIM-*an*] *šekkanzi nat memanzi* "and whenever I consult a venerable (lit. great) old man, [as] they remember [one (certain)] rite and tell it," (I shall also carry it out) KBo 11.1 obv. 23-24 (prayer of Muw.), ed. Houwink ten Cate, RHA XXV/81:107, 115f.; [*UL-ma*]*tmu šalliš* LÚ.ŠU.GI *memai numu* DINGIR-*LIM kū*[*n*] *memian tešḫit parkunut* "[No] venerable old man tells it to me; may you, O god, make this matter clear to me in a dream" ibid. obv. 42, ed. RHA XXV/81: 108, 117.

c. in lists — **1′** in OH and MH land grant texts which list the members of households (É = *per*), the old people are listed last, after the adult males, the male children and infants, the adult females, and the female children and infants; e.g., in a MH text: ⌜É⌝ ᵐ*Pulliyanni* 2 LÚ ᵐ*Pulliyanniš* ᵐ*Ašša*[*rt*]*aš* 3 TUR.NITA ᵐ*Apar-kammiš* ᵐ*Iriyattīš* [ᵐ*Ḫ*]*apiluš* 4 SAL ᶠ*Tešmuš* ᶠ*Zidanduš* ᶠ*Šakkummilla* ᶠ*Ḫuliyāšuḫaniš* 3 TUR.SAL [ᶠ]*Kapaššanniš* ᶠ*Kapurtiš* ᶠ*Paškuwāš* 2 SAL.SU.GI ᶠ*Ārḫuwaššiš* ᶠ*Tuttuwaniš* [1]4 SAG.DU KBo 5.7 rev. 34-37 (land grant of Arn. I, MH/MS), ed. LS 1; 11 É.ḪI.A 26 LÚ 16 TUR.NITA 4 TUR.NITA.GAB 30 SAL 11 TUR.SAL 2 TUR.SAL.GAB 1 LÚ.ŠU.GI 1 SAL.ŠU.GI ŠU.NIGIN 91 SAG.DU ibid. rev. 12f.;